COMPETITIVE EQUILIBRIUM
Theory and Applications

BRYAN ELLICKSON
University of California, Los Angeles

W0010939

CAMBRIDGE
UNIVERSITY PRESS

PUBLISHED BY THE PRESS SYNDICATE OF THE UNIVERSITY OF CAMBRIDGE
The Pitt Building, Trumpington Street, Cambridge CB2 1RP, United Kingdom

CAMBRIDGE UNIVERSITY PRESS
The Edinburgh Building, Cambridge CB2 2RU, United Kingdom
40 West 20th Street, New York, NY 10011-4211, USA
10 Stamford Road, Oakleigh, Melbourne 3166, Australia

First published 1993
Reprinted 1997

Printed in the United States of America

Typeset in Times

A catalogue record for this book is available from the British Library

Library of Congress Cataloguing-in-Publication Data is available

ISBN 0-521-26660-2 hardback
ISBN 0-521-31988-9 paperback

Contents

Illustrations

For Phyllis, Paul
and
my parents

Preface

This book is the outgrowth of a course on general equilibrium theory I have taught to second year graduate students for the past dozen years or so. A few intend mathematical economics as their primary specialty, but most do not. This book is designed to meet the needs of both types of student. In my experience, it has been quite effective.

What specialist and nonspecialist alike need from a book like this is motivation: Where are we heading and why? The first three chapters provide that motivation, building the case that general equilibrium theory is indeed worth learning. What makes the approach work is a reliance on examples rather than theorems and proofs. Examples provide an excellent, and rather painless, opportunity to acquire facility with the abstract notation and concepts of general equilibrium theory. Applications are nontrivial and often unusual: overlapping generations, contingent commodities, indivisibility, local public goods, and hedonic theory. Exercises provide the opportunity to test and strengthen competence.

Although motivation is paramount, these first three chapters accomplish more than that. The reader finishing this introductory material is familiar with important facts about vector spaces and their duals, and sensitive to their geometry. She has learned how to translate the central concepts of general equilibrium theory into the formal language of mathematics, and the formality seems less abstract. And she has a stockpile of examples to draw upon to illustrate the theory building which follows.

The remaining five chapters build upon this foundation, making the transition from examples to rigorous theory. In most respects, the material covered here is quite conventional: for example, establishing existence and upperhemicontinuity of best response, proving existence of Walrasian equilibrium, and establishing core convergence and core equivalence. General equilibrium theorists using this as a text should find most of their favorite

topics covered using standard notation and standard proofs. What is different is the style of presentation and the emphasis:

- *Economic examples motivate the mathematics.* Although the main business of the second half of this book is learning to do proofs, motivating
  examples are not forgotten. Single-peaked preferences illustrate preference graphs; apples and bees the existence of equilibrium with externalities; and illicit drugs the seemingly bizarre possibility of equilibrium in
  the presence of nonordered preferences.

- *Nearly one hundred diagrams illuminate the text.* A well-chosen diagram
  can make the obscure seem obvious. This book uses diagrams of many
  types, none more important than the net trade diagram. Elegant but
  neglected, this device renders otherwise recondite proofs utterly transparent. Here the net trade diagram assumes its rightful place alongside its
  famous relative, the Edgeworth box.

- *General equilibrium theory is linked to game theory.* General equilibrium
  theory and game theory have much in common, a motivation increasingly important to many students. Although this is not a book on game
  theory, I emphasize the connections between these fields. Chapter 5 on
  "Best response," for example, applies equally well in either context. And
  Chapter 7, "Walras meets Nash," compares existence of competitive equilibrium in an economy with existence of Nash equilibrium in a game,
  stressing differences as well as similarities.

- *Finite dimensional analysis merges with infinite.* Some of the most exciting applications of modern general equilibrium theory — finance, macroeconomics, product differentiation — involve infinite dimensional commodity spaces. As befits an introductory text, this book restricts attention almost entirely to finite dimensions. However, I adopt a style which
  facilitates the transition from finite to infinite dimensions. The reader
  probably won't notice the difference until the end when, in Chapter 8, I
  describe briefly how that transition is made.

- *Exercises reinforce the text.* You can't learn a mathematical subject without working problems. Remarkably few texts on general equilibrium theory offer exercises. This book contains nearly two hundred. Work them
  if you really want to learn the material.

The above discussion conveys the essence of this text. The following is
more specific and probably meaningful only to someone already familiar
with the field.

Chapter 1 covers exchange, Chapter 2 production, and Chapter 3 Aumann's model. The first chapter presents the basics of vectors as com-

modities and linear functionals as prices, using these concepts to introduce Walrasian equilibrium, Pareto optimality, and the core. Throughout, the net trade diagram is used to highlight the separation involved in equilibrium as well as the logic behind the proofs of the First Fundamental Theorem of welfare economics and the Debreu-Scarf Core Equivalence Theorem. Chapter 2, which extends the analysis to production, includes applications to public goods and Marshallian joint supply. The chapter ends with a discrete version of Tom Muench's example of failure of core equivalence in the presence of public goods. Chapter 3 introduces Robert Aumann's model of an economy with a continuum of consumers. The first part of the chapter uses elementary calculus to illustrate the main ideas, including detailed examples (automobiles and houses) of economies with indivisibilities and nonconvexities. These examples in turn motivate a discussion of measure and integration theory. The chapter ends with an application of Andreu Mas-Colell's pioneering work on differentiated commodities to the hedonic theory of Sherwin Rosen and to Tiebout's theory of local public goods.

Chapter 4 marks a transition, a chapter of pure math separating the less formal discussion of the first part of the book from the more advanced theorem proving of the second. Topology is a roadblock for most economists coming to grips with mathematical economics. Though by no means a formal course in the subject, this chapter lets the reader in on the secret of what it is all about.

Chapter 5 begins the more rigorous half of the book. As the title suggests, this discussion of "Best Response" applies equally well to the players of a game or the consumers and firms of an economy. Beginning with an introduction to the vocabulary of choice (binary relations, orderings) and a discussion of the topological concepts needed for dealing with correspondences (lower- and upperhemicontinuity), the chapter culminates with a proof of the powerful Maximum Theorem.

Chapters 6 and 7 address the issue of existence of a competitive equilibrium from two different points of view. Chapter 6 adopts the more traditional perspective of market clearing, finding a price for which demand equals supply on each market. Focusing on pure exchange with singleton-valued demand, this chapter is able to exhibit clearly and simply the interconnections among the Brouwer Fixed Point Theorem, the KKM Theorem, and Scarf's algorithm. Playing each concept off of the others reinforces understanding of them all.

Chapter 7 shifts gears, adopting the perspective of noncooperative game theory. Although Walrasian equilibrium is not a game-theoretic concept, approaching competition from a game-theoretic perspective adds important insight into the Walrasian construction. The main tool used for proving existence in this chapter is the Kakutani Fixed Point Theorem. The exposition emphasizes novel applications: proving existence of equilibrium in the presence of externalities (with applications to James Meade's parable of apples and bees and to the voluntary provision of public goods), when preferences are intransitive or incomplete (with applications to the market for illicit drugs) and when firms or consumers face indivisibilities or other types of nonconvexity (via the Shapley-Folkman Theorem).

Chapter 8 concludes the book by asking "What is competition?" The core equivalence and core convergence results of Debreu and Scarf, Anderson, and Aumann occupy center stage. The chapter ends by examining briefly what happens when the analysis is expanded to allow for an infinite dimensional commodity space as well as a continuum of consumers. This is the arena in which the important applications lie, whether it be public goods, hedonic theory, financial markets, or macroeconomics. A proper treatment of infinite dimensional economics lies beyond the scope of this introductory text. Nevertheless, the approach I have adopted in discussing finite dimensional economics has been deliberately designed to facilitate the transition to the infinite.

As suggested by the length of the bibliography, this book builds on an extensive literature. The text is intentionally quite sparing with references. To provide background on the subjects covered here, in my courses I supplement this book with the review of fixed point theorems and related mathematics by Border (1985) and the survey articles in Volumes II and IV of the *Handbook of Mathematical Economics* by Debreu (1982), Hildenbrand (1982), Kehoe (1991), Mas-Colell and Zame (1991), Scarf (1982), and Shafer and Sonnenschein (1982).

Acknowledgments

I owe a large debt to many people. The students in my courses have been candid and helpful in letting me know what they thought about this book and making suggestions for its improvement. Four colleagues and friends must be singled out for special mention. Andreu Mas-Colell triggered my interest in mathematical economics when, early in his career and mine, he delivered a seminar on "A model of equilibrium with differentiated commodities." His work has been an inspiration ever since. In the years that Joe Ostroy and I have been friends and colleagues at UCLA, he has deeply influenced the way I think about general equilibrium theory. Lloyd Shapley taught me almost everything I know about game theory and provided much encouragement and support besides. Bill Zame has shared his insight, enthusiasm, and friendship.

I join the legions of mathematically oriented authors indebted to Donald Knuth for developing the typesetting program $T_{\!E}\!X$. This book might well not have been written without it. I would like to thank Colin Day at Cambridge University Press for suggesting this project and Scott Parris for his support in seeing it through to completion. I am grateful to the National Science Foundation and the UCLA Academic Senate for research support over the years.

Last but not least I want to thank my wife and son, Phyllis and Paul, for everything.

1

Exchange

Mathematics is a language. This sentiment, expressed by the physicist Willard Gibbs, seems rather apt, especially when it comes to learning mathematics. Gaining fluency in mathematics and mathematical economics has much in common with learning a foreign language. Worrying too much about vocabulary lists and good grammar is a good way to kill your interest in the subject. Taking the plunge, trying to speak the language despite the errors you make early on, is not only more effective but also more enjoyable. This book is aimed at the economist willing to accept such a strategy of total immersion. This does not mean that I avoid the careful statement of assumptions, the crafting of rigorous proofs, and the like. Learning to do those things is an important part of any course in mathematical economics. What makes the approach adopted here distinctive is less a matter of substance than of style. Emphasizing economic intuition, I concentrate first and foremost on helping you develop a good ear for what the language of mathematical general equilibrium theory is trying to say. Learning the vocabulary and the grammar is easy once you can follow the conversation. What this means for the moment is that you should not worry too much if I seem to move rather quickly. You can always come back later to focus on the details.

The main goal of this chapter is to learn how to translate the competitive model of a pure exchange economy into the formal language of sets, functions, vector spaces, and linear functionals. This sounds more intimidating than it is. By the end of the chapter you should be convinced that this part of mathematics provides a natural way to talk about economics, so natural that one might almost imagine it was invented with economics in mind. Section one provides a rapid tour of the mathematical tools — sets, functions, vector spaces, and linear functionals — that we need to get started. The second section introduces the competitive model of pure exchange, and translates this model into the geometry of the net trade diagram. Section three begins the exploration of some of the properties of competitive equilibrium: its efficiency properties and its connection to the cooperative game theory concept known as the core. Section four presents a numerical example. The fifth section concludes the chapter with some comments on the notion of a commodity and its price.

1.1 Mathematical prerequisites

To begin we need only a few fundamental notions from mathematics: sets and functions along with the special cases of linear sets (better known as vector spaces) and linear functionals. Much of this material may be quite familiar to you. For the rest, focus for now on getting the main ideas, not on the details.

1.1.1 Sets

Skirting over some delicate issues in set theory, we define a set S to be any collection of objects or "things." For example, $S = \{2, 4, 1, 2\}$ is a set with **elements** (or members) 1, 2, and 4. Note that repetition and order make no difference in describing a set, so the set S above is the same as the set $T = \{1, 2, 4\}$. The number of distinct elements in a set will be denoted $\#S$ provided that S has a finite number of elements. For the examples above, $\#S = \#T = 3$ because $\#$ counts only distinct elements of a set. To indicate that an element x is a member of a set S we write $x \in S$. If x does not belong to S, then we say $x \notin S$. Given two sets S and T we call S a **subset** of T, written $S \subset T$, if "$x \in S$ implies $x \in T$." Thus, $S = \{1, 2\}$ is a subset of $T = \{1, 2, 3\}$. $S \not\subset T$ means that S is not a subset of T. Two sets S and T are equal, $S = T$, iff[1] $S \subset T$ and $T \subset S$. Whenever we want to show that two sets are equal, we will show that the first is a subset of the second and that the second is a subset of the first. To indicate that a set S is a **proper** subset of T, so that $S \subset T$ but $S \neq T$, we will sometimes write $S \subset\subset T$. If S is a subset of T, then the **complement** of S in T is the set $T \backslash S := \{x \in T \mid x \notin S\}$.

Certain sets are used so frequently that they are given special symbols. $\mathbf{R}$ represents the set of real numbers, $\mathbf{Z}$ the set of integers (i.e., $\mathbf{Z} = \{0, \pm 1, \pm 2, \dots\}$). The set which has no members, the **empty set**, is denoted $\emptyset$. The empty set has the property that it is a subset of every other set. This statement, which seems surprising at first glance, follows by "vacuous

---

1 "iff" is a standard abbreviation for the phrase "if and only if."

implication": by definition, $\emptyset \subset S$ iff "$x \in \emptyset$ implies $x \in S$" and the latter statement is true because there is no x which belongs to $\emptyset$ and therefore no x for which the statement could be false!

Describing a set by listing all of its members, as we have done above, is usually not very convenient and may be impossible. It is usually more appropriate to define a set as follows: $S = \{\, x \in X \mid P(x)\,\}$ where X is a universe of possible candidates for membership in S, $\mid$ is read "such that," and $P(x)$ is a statement of the conditions that an element $x \in X$ must satisfy in order to belong to the set S. For example, $S = \{\, x \in \mathbf{R} \mid x/2 \in \mathbf{Z}\,\}$ describes the set of even integers $\{\, 0, \pm 2, \pm 4, \dots\,\}$.

We also need notation for the various ways in which sets can be combined to form new sets. For example, if S and T are subsets of some set X, then the **union** of S and T is the set

$$S \cup T = \{\, x \in X \mid x \in S \quad \text{or} \quad x \in T\,\}$$

where "or" is interpreted as "and/or." The **intersection** of S and T is the set

$$S \cap T = \{\, x \in X \mid x \in S \quad \text{and} \quad x \in T\,\}.$$

The **difference** operations,

$$S \backslash T = \{\, x \in X \mid x \in S \quad \text{and} \quad x \notin T\,\},$$

$$T \backslash S = \{\, x \in X \mid x \in T \quad \text{and} \quad x \notin S\,\},$$

and the **symmetric difference**,

$$S \triangle T = (S \backslash T) \cup (T \backslash S),$$

are also useful upon occasion.

The definitions of union and intersection extend readily to collections of more than two sets. Specifically, if $S_i \subset X$ for $i = 1, \dots, n$, then we define the union of the collection as

$$\bigcup_{i=1}^{n} S_i = \{\, x \in X \mid x \in S_i \quad \text{for some} \quad i \in \{\, 1, \dots, n\,\}\,\}$$

$$= \{\, x \in X \mid \exists\, i \in \{\, 1, \dots, n\,\} \ni x \in S_i\,\}$$

and the intersection as

$$\bigcap_{i=1}^{n} S_i = \{\, x \in X \mid x \in S_i \quad \text{for all} \quad i \in \{\, 1, \dots, n\,\}\,\}$$

$$= \{\, x \in X \mid x \in S_i \,\forall\, i \in \{\, 1, \dots, n\,\}\,\}$$

where $\forall$ is an abbreviation for "for all" or "for any," $\exists$ for "there exists" or "for some," and $\ni$ for "such that."

The set $I = \{1, \ldots, n\}$ used in the above definitions is an illustration of what is called an **index set**. This immediately suggests a way to define union and intersection for more general collections of sets. If A is any set that serves as an index set and $S_\alpha \subset X$ for all $\alpha \in A$, then the union of the collection is

$$\bigcup_{\alpha \in A} S_\alpha = \{\, x \in X \mid \exists\, \alpha \in A \ni x \in S_\alpha \,\}$$

and the intersection

$$\bigcap_{\alpha \in A} S_\alpha = \{\, x \in X \mid x \in S_\alpha\; \forall\, \alpha \in A \,\}.$$

For example, if $A = \mathbf{R}_+$ where $\mathbf{R}_+ := \{\, x \in \mathbf{R} \mid x \geq 0 \,\}$ and we consider the closed intervals $[-\alpha, \alpha] := \{\, x \in \mathbf{R} \mid -\alpha \leq x \leq \alpha \,\}$, then we can assert that $\bigcap_{\alpha \in \mathbf{R}_+} [-\alpha, \alpha] = \{\, 0 \,\}$. Incidentally, the preceding sentence employs a notational convention that we will use occasionally: $A := B$ means that A is defined as equal to B, and $A =: B$ that B is defined as equal to A. We do not use this notation every time that an equality holds by definition, but only when we want to emphasize that fact.

1.1.2 Functions

Given two sets X and Y, a function from X to Y, written $f \colon X \to Y$, is a rule that associates to each element $x \in X$ a *unique* element $f(x) \in Y$. When we want to indicate that the function carries a typical element $x \in X$ to $f(x) \in Y$, we will write this as $f \colon x \mapsto f(x)$. The set X is called the **domain** of the function and the set Y the **codomain**. For example, $f \colon \mathbf{R} \to \mathbf{R}_+$, $x \mapsto x^2$, describes the function which maps each real number to its square.

While a function can by definition never take a given point in its domain to more than one point in the codomain, it may map two or more points of its domain into the same point in its codomain: i.e., $f(x) = f(x')$ for some x and x' where $x \neq x'$. For example, the function described in the preceding paragraph maps both -2 and 2 to the image 4. If this situation never occurs, then the function is said to be **injective** (or one-to-one). Formally, $f \colon X \to Y$ is injective if $x \neq x'$ implies $f(x) \neq f(x')$ for all $x, x' \in X$. Often you will see this definition stated in the alternative, logically equivalent form given by the contrapositive: f is injective if $f(x) = f(x')$ implies $x = x'$ for all $x, x' \in X$.

As we let x vary over all elements in the domain X, it is quite possible that there are some points in Y that are not the image of anything in X. For a subset $S \subset X$, define the **image** of S to be the set

$$f(S) = \{\, f(x) \in Y \mid x \in S \,\}.$$

The image of X itself, i.e., $f(X)$, is called the **range** of f. If $f(X) = Y$, so that every point in Y is hit by some $x \in X$, then f is said to be **surjective** (or onto). The function defined above which associates each real number with its square is surjective, but it would not be if we changed the codomain from $\mathbf{R}_+$ to $\mathbf{R}$.

If $f: X \to Y$ is both injective and surjective, then f is **bijective**. The function taking real numbers to their squares, as defined above, is not bijective, but it would be bijective if the domain were changed from $\mathbf{R}$ to $\mathbf{R}_+$. Functions that are injective are called injections, those that are surjective are called surjections, and those that are bijective are called bijections.

If we are given two functions $f: X \to Y$ and $g: Y \to Z$, then the function $h: X \to Z$, $x \mapsto g(f(x)) =: h(x)$, is called the **composition** of f and g, and we write $h = g \circ f$.

For any set X, the map $\mathrm{id}_X: X \to X$ defined by $\mathrm{id}_X: x \mapsto x$ for all $x \in X$ is called the **identity map** for X. If $f: X \to Y$ is a bijection, then there exists a function $f^{-1}: Y \to X$ such that $f \circ f^{-1} = \mathrm{id}_Y$ and $f^{-1} \circ f = \mathrm{id}_X$. The function f^{-1} is called the **inverse** of f. Thus, the bijection $f: \mathbf{R}_+ \to \mathbf{R}_+$, $x \mapsto x^2$, has as its inverse the function which maps each nonnegative real number to its *positive* square root: $f^{-1}: \mathbf{R}_+ \to \mathbf{R}_+$, $x \mapsto |\sqrt{x}|$. It should be easy to convince yourself that either composition $f \circ f^{-1}$ or $f^{-1} \circ f$ is equivalent to the identity map $\mathrm{id}_{\mathbf{R}_+}: \mathbf{R}_+ \to \mathbf{R}_+$, $x \mapsto x$.

Paralleling our definition of the image $f(S)$, the set $f^{-1}(T) := \{\, x \in X \mid f(x) \in T \,\}$ is called the **inverse image** of $T \subset Y$. Note carefully that this is well defined even when f is not bijective (so that f^{-1} is not defined). While for that reason perhaps somewhat confusing, this notation is so convenient that it is often used in mathematics.

1.1.3 Vector spaces

A **vector space** (or linear space) is a set L along with two algebraic operations on the elements of L: addition and multiplication by a scalar. In this book "scalar" is synonymous with real number, in which case L is called a real vector space (or a vector space over $\mathbf{R}$). The elements of a vector space are conventionally referred to as **vectors**.

To qualify as a vector space, the operations of addition and multiplication by a scalar are required to satisfy a number of properties:

- For every pair of vectors x and y in L, the sum $x + y$ also belongs to L, and for this operation of vector addition it is always true that

$$x + y = y + x \quad \text{and} \quad x + (y + z) = (x + y) + z;$$

  L contains a unique vector 0 such that $x + 0 = x$ for every $x \in L$; and to each $x \in L$ there corresponds a unique vector $-x$ such that $x + (-x) = 0$.
- For any $\alpha \in \mathbf{R}$ and $x \in L$, the product αx belongs to L, and for this operation of scalar multiplication it is always true that

$$
\begin{aligned}
1x &= x \\
\alpha(x + y) &= \alpha x + \alpha y \\
(\alpha + \beta)x &= \alpha x + \beta x \, .
\end{aligned}
$$

The elements $\alpha, \beta \in \mathbf{R}$ are called scalars, and the unique vector 0 described above is referred to as the **zero vector** or **origin** of the vector space L. (If the scalar field $\mathbf{R}$ of real numbers is replaced by the field of complex numbers, then one obtains a complex vector space. In this book, we will deal only with real vector spaces.)

The definition of a vector space, while quite abstract, has a natural economic interpretation. Suppose that we interpret a vector as a **commodity bundle**, a description of everything which a consumer consumes. When viewed as a collection of commodity bundles, the requirements imposed on a vector space (or commodity space) L should seem intuitively rather obvious. Any two commodity bundles x and y can be added together to obtain a "sum" $x + y$. There is a unique commodity bundle 0, interpreted as the absence of all commodities, which contributes nothing when added to any other commodity bundle x. Any commodity bundle x can be scaled up or down by α to yield a new commodity bundle αx — so that, in particular, we can attach a meaning to doubling the bundle $(2x)$ or cutting it in half $(.5x)$. And so forth.

The vector space which is used most frequently in economics is, of course, $\mathbf{R^n}$, the set of all n-tuples of real numbers. If $x = (x_1, \ldots, x_n)$ and $y = (y_1, \ldots, y_n)$ are two vectors in $\mathbf{R^n}$, then the sum $x + y$ is obtained by "adding componentwise", $x + y = (x_1 + y_1, \ldots, x_n + y_n)$, and the result of multiplying x by the scalar α is simply $\alpha x = (\alpha x_1, \ldots, \alpha x_n)$. You should verify that, with this definition of vector addition and scalar multiplication, $\mathbf{R^n}$ satisfies the requirements of a real vector space.

Although $\mathbf{R^n}$ is very important, it is not the only example of a vector space that is useful in economics. By way of illustration, consider the set $\mathrm{Map}(T, \mathbf{R})$ of all mappings (i.e., functions) $f\colon T \to \mathbf{R}$ where T is an arbitrary set. For concreteness, suppose that $T = \mathbf{R}_+$ and that a function (vector) f represents the flow of consumption over time (so that $f(t)$ is the amount consumed at time t). Define the sum of two functions (vectors) $f\colon T \to \mathbf{R}$ and $g\colon T \to \mathbf{R}$ as the function $f + g\colon T \to \mathbf{R}$ which maps $t \mapsto f(t) + g(t)$ and the scalar multiple of the function f by $\alpha \in \mathbf{R}$ as the function $\alpha f\colon T \to \mathbf{R}$ mapping $t \mapsto \alpha f(t)$. With these definitions of vector addition and scalar multiplication, verify that $\mathrm{Map}(T, \mathbf{R})$ is a vector space.[2]

Leaving these illustrative examples, the abstract definition of a vector space L implies that if $\alpha, \beta \in \mathbf{R}$ and $x, y \in L$ then $\alpha x + \beta y \in L$. In fact, if $S = \{\, v^i \in L \mid i \in I \,\}$ is any collection of vectors indexed by the set I, then the **linear combination** $\sum_{i \in I} \alpha_i v^i \in L$ for $\alpha_i \in \mathbf{R}$ provided that only a finite number of the α_i are not equal to zero. (The proviso that there is not an infinite number of nonzero scalars α_i means that we do not have to worry whether an infinite sum of terms converges.)

Suppose that we start with a set S of vectors in a vector space, and consider the set of all possible linear combinations of vectors in S. The resulting set is called the **span** of S,

$$\mathrm{sp}\, S = \{\, x \in L \mid x = \textstyle\sum \alpha_i v^i, \alpha_i \in \mathbf{R}, v^i \in S \,\}$$

where the sums $\sum \alpha_i v^i$ are understood to be taken over index sets for which only a finite number of the scalars α_i are nonzero.[3]

To illustrate for the vector space $\mathbf{R}^2$, let $S = \{\, (1, 2), (2, 4) \,\}$. Then

$$\mathrm{sp}\, S = \{\, x \in \mathbf{R}^2 \mid x = \alpha(1, 2), \alpha \in \mathbf{R} \,\},$$

a line through the origin. If, in contrast, we let $S = \{\, (1, 2), (2, 1) \,\}$, then $\mathrm{sp}\, S = \mathbf{R}^2$ so that the span equals the whole vector space.

These simple examples in $\mathbf{R}^2$ have features which turn out to hold quite generally:

- If S is a nonempty subset of a vector space L, then $\mathrm{sp}\, S$ is a vector space, a **subspace** of L. If $\mathrm{sp}\, S$ does not coincide with L, as in the first example above, then it is called a **proper subspace** (a one-dimensional line through the origin in our example).

---

2 Note the analogy between the definitions of vector addition and scalar multiplication for $\mathrm{Map}(T, R)$ and the corresponding definitions for R^n. In both examples, vectors are added coordinate-by-coordinate and multiplication of a vector by a scalar α multiplies each coordinate of the vector by α. If you think of an n-tuple $x = (x_1, \ldots, x_n)$ as a function $x\colon T \to R$ where $T = \{\, 1, \ldots, n \,\}$, then the definitions coincide. Because of this analogy, mathematicians sometimes use R^T to denote the set $\mathrm{Map}(T, R)$.

3 In the interests of cleaner notation, I will often omit the index set from a summation sign when the index set is either arbitrary or obvious from the context and when the sum is over all of the elements of the index set.

- $\mathbf{R^n}$ can always be spanned by exactly n vectors (by two vectors in the case of $\mathbf{R}^2$ as the second example illustrates).

- A set $S \subset \mathbf{R^n}$ will fail to span the entire vector space $\mathbf{R^n}$ if there are fewer than n nonredundant vectors in S. (We call a vector in S redundant if it can be expressed as a linear combination of the other vectors in S.) In the first example, the two elements of S fail to span $\mathbf{R}^2$ because they are redundant: $(2, 4) = 2(1, 2)$ and $(1, 2) = .5(2, 4)$.

To generalize what we have learned about $\mathbf{R^n}$ to the case of an arbitrary vector space L, a collection of vectors $S \subset L$ is said to be **linearly indepen-dent** (what we called nonredundant above) if $v^i \notin \text{sp } S\backslash\{v^i\}$ for all $v^i \in S$. In other words, the members of S are linearly independent if no vector in S can be expressed as a linear combination of the remaining vectors in S.

As noted above, if S is a nonempty subset of the vector space L, then sp S may be a proper subspace of L: i.e., sp $S \subset L$, but sp $S \neq L$. However, if S does span all of L (i.e., sp $S = L$) and the elements of S are linearly independent, then S is called a **basis** for L. A fundamental theorem of vector space theory says that every vector space has a basis and every basis has the same cardinality.[4] Because every basis has the same cardinality, we can unambiguously define the **dimension** of a vector space as the cardinality of any basis for that vector space. When the basis S is finite, we set $\dim L = \#S$.

To find a basis for a vector space L, all that we need is to find any set S of linearly independent vectors in L which span L. For $\mathbf{R^n}$ this is especially easy. While $\mathbf{R^n}$ has an infinite variety of possible bases, one stands out as particularly easy to use: the **standard basis for $\mathbf{R^n}$**,

$$S = \{\, x \in \mathbf{R}^n \mid x = e^i,\ i \in \{\, 1, \ldots, n \,\} \,\}$$

where the vector $e^i = (0, 0, \ldots, 1, \ldots, 0)$ consists entirely of 0's except for a 1 in the ith position.

It is easy is check that the vectors in S are linearly independent. Any vector $x = (x_1, \ldots, x_n) \in \mathbf{R^n}$ can be written as a linear combination of the vectors in S, $x = \sum_{i=1}^{n} x_i e^i$, so we conclude that $L = \text{sp } S$. Therefore, S is a basis for $\mathbf{R^n}$ and, because there are n vectors in S, $\dim \mathbf{R^n} = n$, which is certainly the result we should have expected.

---

4 Mathematicians use the intimidating word cardinality to allow for sets with an infinite number of elements. When the basis is finite, which will be the case for most vector spaces appearing in this book, you may interpret cardinality as a synonym for the number of elements in the basis.

1.1.4 Linear functionals, hyperplanes, and halfspaces

A **linear functional** on a vector space L is a function $p: L \to \mathbf{R}$ which satisfies the conditions

- $p(x + x') = p(x) + p(x')$ for all $x, x' \in L$, and
- $p(\alpha x) = \alpha p(x)$ for all $x \in L$ and for all $\alpha \in \mathbf{R}$.

When writing the value of a linear functional p at a point x in its domain, we will usually write $p \cdot x$ rather than $p(x)$. The set L' of linear functionals on a vector space L is important enough to be given a special name: the **dual space** of L. As you can readily verify, the dual space L' is itself a vector space.[5]

In this book we will be concerned almost exclusively with linear functionals on finite dimensional vector spaces. Life is much simpler in that context because, as it turns out, the dual space of $\mathbf{R^n}$ is itself n-dimensional. This in turn justifies representing a linear functional as a **scalar product** with $p: \mathbf{R^n} \to \mathbf{R}$ mapping $p \mapsto p \cdot x := \sum_{i=1}^{n} p_i x_i$. You undoubtedly have seen this before. What you might not have realized is that, in writing a linear equation this way, you are tacitly exploiting the fact that every linear functional on $\mathbf{R^n}$ can be represented by a vector $p = (p_1, \dots, p_n) \in \mathbf{R^n}$, i.e., that $\mathbf{R^n}$ is its own dual space. Finding analogous ways to represent linear functionals on more general (infinite dimensional) vector spaces can be much more of a challenge.[6]

Returning to our general discussion, consider a linear functional with domain a vector space L. For the moment, suppose that L is $\mathbf{R^n}$, a restriction which will be removed shortly. We want now to examine the structure of the inverse image of 0, often called the **kernel** of the linear functional:

$$\ker p := p^{-1}\{0\} = \{\, x \in L \mid p \cdot x = 0 \,\}.$$

If the linear functional is identically zero, then, of course, $\ker p = L$ (the entire domain), which is not very interesting. However, provided that $p \neq 0$, the kernel is not equal to the entire domain but rather to a linear subspace with dimension one less than that of L.[7] This case is interesting, interesting enough in fact for the kernel to be called something different: a **hyperplane**.

---

5 Simply check that if f, g are linear functionals defined on a vector space L and α, β are scalars, then the linear combination $\alpha f + \beta g$ is also a linear functional on L.

6 Consider, for example, the vector space $\mathrm{Map}(T, R)$ discussed earlier. For concreteness, assume that T is the interval $[0, 1]$. If we restrict attention to the linear subspace of those functions $f \in \mathrm{Map}(T, R)$ which have a Riemann integral, the familiar integral of beginning calculus, then $p \cdot f := \int_T \pi(t) f(t) \, dt$ defines a linear functional $p: \mathrm{Map}(T, R) \to R$ mapping $f \in \mathrm{Map}(T, R)$ to $p \cdot f \in R$ where the function $\pi: T \to R$ is assumed Riemann integrable and $\int_T$ denotes integration over T.

7 I.e., if $L = R^n$, then the kernel is $n - 1$ dimensional.

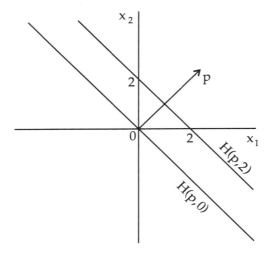

Fig. 1.1. Hyperplanes in $\mathbf{R}^2$.

If $\alpha \neq 0$, then the inverse image $p^{-1}\{\alpha\} = \{\, x \in \mathbf{R^n} \mid p \cdot x = \alpha \,\}$ is not a linear subspace (because it does not contain the 0 vector). However, as you can easily illustrate in $\mathbf{R}^2$ or $\mathbf{R}^3$, the inverse image $p^{-1}\{\alpha\}$ is a parallel translation of a linear subspace. Translated subspaces of this sort are called **affine subspaces**, and when, as is the case when $p \neq 0$, the subspace which has been translated is a hyperplane, the affine subspace is called an **affine hyperplane**. (In the sequel, we will often refer to affine hyperplanes as well as ordinary hyperplanes as simply hyperplanes, deleting the modifier affine.)

Because hyperplanes play a crucial role throughout this book, they are given a special notation:

$$H(p, \alpha) := p^{-1}\{\alpha\} = \{\, x \in \mathbf{R^n} \mid p \cdot x = \alpha \,\}.$$

Figure 1.1 illustrates the hyperplanes $H(p, 0)$ and $H(p, 2)$ in $\mathbf{R}^2$ for $p = (1, 1)$. Note in particular the convention of drawing the vector p as a vector normal (i.e., perpendicular) to the hyperplane.

Linear functionals and hyperplanes can seem rather exotic to the student of mathematics encountering them for the first time, but for the economist they should be natural and intuitive. It is no accident that we have denoted the typical linear functional by the letter p because, for us, the primary purpose of linear functionals will be to represent *prices*. Recalling our suggestion that vectors can be thought of as commodity bundles, a linear functional $p \colon L \to \mathbf{R}$ evaluated at $x \in L$ is interpreted as the value $p \cdot x$ of the bundle x

when prices are p. The linearity of p has a natural economic interpretation: if we multiply a commodity bundle by a scalar λ, the value of the bundle changes in the same proportion, $p(\lambda x) = \lambda p(x)$, and the value of the sum of two commodity bundles is the sum of their values, $p(x) + p(x') = p(x + x')$. The hyperplane $H(p, 0)$ represents the set of all commodity bundles with zero value while $H(p, \alpha)$ represents the set whose value equals α.

One of the most important properties of a hyperplane is that, no matter what the dimension of the vector space L, a hyperplane separates L into two parts called **halfspaces**, one halfspace lying on each side of the hyperplane. In our definitions, it will be convenient to distinguish two different types of halfspace, the **open halfspaces** which do not include the hyperplane and the **closed halfspaces** which do. Formally, we have the following:

Definition 1.1 *Corresponding to any hyperplane $H(p, \alpha)$, the* **open half-spaces** *are given by*

$$H_o^+(p, \alpha) = \{\, x \in L \mid p \cdot x > \alpha \,\} \quad and \quad H_o^-(p, \alpha) = \{\, x \in L \mid p \cdot x < \alpha \,\}$$

and the **closed halfspaces** *by*

$$H^+(p, \alpha) = \{\, x \in L \mid p \cdot x \geq \alpha \,\} \quad and \quad H^-(p, \alpha) = \{\, x \in L \mid p \cdot x \leq \alpha \,\}.$$

A few examples should help to fix these ideas. In $\mathbf{R}^1$ the hyperplane $H(p, 0)$ is the point 0, and the halfspaces $H_o^+(p, 0)$ and $H_o^-(p, 0)$ are the open intervals $(0, \infty)$ and $(-\infty, 0)$ respectively. In $\mathbf{R}^2$ the hyperplane $H(p, 0)$ is a straight line through the origin, and the halfspaces $H_o^+(p, 0)$ and $H_o^-(p, 0)$ are the sets of points lying "above" or "below" this line respectively. In $\mathbf{R}^3$ the hyperplane is an ordinary plane through the origin, described by the equation $p \cdot x = \sum_{i=1}^3 p_i x_i = 0$, and the halfspaces are the sets of points lying above or below this plane. Though pictures fail for dimensions greater than three, the geometric interpretation remains the same: hyperplanes separate vector spaces into two halfspaces, one lying above and the other below the hyperplane.

Again the economist has a decided advantage over the budding mathematician in interpreting these concepts. $H_o^+(p, 0)$ represents those commodity bundles whose value is greater than zero, $H_o^-(p, 0)$ those with value less than zero. For the economist, unlike the physicist for example, n (or even infinite) dimensions are as natural as two or three.[8]

---

8 It is worth noting that $H_o^+(p, 0)$ need not lie "above" (i.e., to the North) or $H_o^-(p, 0)$ "below" a hyperplane drawn in R^2 or R^3. The upper halfspace simply represents vectors with value greater than zero and the lower halfspace the vectors with value less than zero.

Although our focus is mainly on hyperplanes and halfspaces in finite dimensional vector spaces, these concepts apply in much the same way to infinite dimensional vector spaces. However, when you read the literature on infinite dimensional vector spaces, the definition of a hyperplane often looks quite different. Because infinite dimensional spaces are becoming increasingly important in general equilibrium theory, a brief indication why the alternative definitions are really equivalent seems worthwhile. You may skip to the next section if you wish.

We first introduce a procedure for representing a vector space as a direct sum of subspaces contained within it. If M_1 and M_2 are subspaces of a vector space L and $M_1 \cap M_2 = \{0\}$, then

$$M := \{\, x \in L \mid x = m_1 + m_2, \ m_1 \in M_1 \ \& \ m_2 \in M_2 \,\}$$

is called a **direct sum**, usually written as $M = M_1 \oplus M_2$. A major advantage of direct sums is that each $x \in M$ has a *unique* expression as $x = m_1 + m_2$ where $m_1 \in M_1$ and $m_2 \in M_2$. If the vector space itself can be expressed as the direct sum of two subspaces, say $L = M_1 \oplus M_2$, the subspaces M_1 and M_2 are called **complementary subspaces** and the dimension of M_1 (*resp.* M_2) is called the **codimension** of M_2 (*resp.* M_1); i.e., codim $M_2 = \dim M_1$ and codim $M_1 = \dim M_2$.

What is the point of decomposing vector spaces in this way? One primary motivation is to find a way to retain the intuitive, geometric notion that a hyperplane is a subspace one dimension less than the vector space in which it is contained when the ambient vector space is infinite dimensional, a characterization which seems absurd at first glance. Describing a hyperplane as a subspace of codimension one, the *definition* of a hyperplane encountered in most mathematics texts, does exactly that!

In this book we have defined hyperplanes not as subspaces of codimension one but rather as the kernel of some nontrivial linear functional (where nontrivial means that the linear functional is not identically zero). The two definitions are easily shown to be equivalent: linear subspaces of codimension one can always be represented as the kernel of a nontrivial linear functional and, conversely, the kernel of a linear functional $p \colon L \to \mathbf{R}$ always defines a subspace of codimension one provided that p is nontrivial (i.e., that $p \cdot z \neq 0$ for some $z \in L$).

1.2 Walrasian equilibrium

To keep matters simple, this chapter deals only with pure exchange: there is no production so that consumers, who begin with stocks of commodities, can improve their lot only through trade of their initial endowments. We assume that in equilibrium each commodity has associated with it an equilibrium price. Also by assumption, consumers act as though they have no ability to influence these prices; i.e., they are **price-takers**, not **price-makers**. All of this should seem quite familiar to you. How do we translate this standard description of the competitive model of exchange into the formal language of mathematics?

We begin by assuming that there are n consumers and m commodities in the economy indexed by the sets $I = \{1, \ldots, n\}$ and $J = \{1, \ldots, m\}$ respectively. Initial endowments and equilibrium allocations for each consumer are vectors in the **commodity space** $L = \mathbf{R}^m$. For each consumer $i \in I$, let the vector w_i denote the initial **endowment** and x_i the **allocation** of commodities received as the result of trade.

Describing the outcome of exchange as a vector x_i is not quite precise enough. Some of these vectors make no economic sense: e.g., the receipt of a negative amount of some commodity. If we want to rule such allocations out, we need to say so explicitly. The subset of the commodity space L to which an allocation for consumer i is restricted is called her **consumption set**, denoted X_i. Often we will assume simply that X_i coincides with the nonnegative orthant: $X_i = L_+ = \mathbf{R}_+^m$. But, as we will see later, in some applications the consumption set plays a much more active role in capturing important aspects of the economic environment: the fact that some commodities are available only in integer amounts, for example, or that a consumer can be physically located in only one place.

Considering all of the consumers at once, endowments can be viewed as a function $w: I \to L_+$, $i \mapsto w_i$, and allocations as another function $x: I \to L_+$, $i \mapsto x_i$, permitting us to refer to the endowment w and allocation x for the economy as a whole. Equilibrium prices are represented in a way which you have doubtless anticipated: as a linear functional p on the vector space L. In particular, $p \cdot w_i$ represents the value of the endowment and $p \cdot x_i$ the value of the final allocation for consumer i. For x to be an equilibrium allocation we require for each consumer $i \in I$ that

- the commodity bundle x_i be physically feasible, $x_i \in X_i$; and
- the value $p \cdot x_i$ not exceed the value of the consumer's endowment, $p \cdot x_i \leq p \cdot w_i$.

Putting both requirements together, we define the **budget set** of consumer i: $\beta_i(p) := \{x_i \in X_i \mid p \cdot x_i \leq p \cdot w_i\}$. An equilibrium allocation must assign to each consumer i a commodity bundle $x_i \in \beta_i(p)$.

The remaining ingredient which we need in order to model the equilibrium behavior of consumers is a specification of preferences, and to do so we consider commodity bundles a pair at a time. The set of all such **ordered pairs** is called the **Cartesian product** of the set X_i with itself, denoted $X_i \times X_i := \{ (x_i, y_i) \mid x_i \in X_i \ \& \ y_i \in X_i \}$. A **strict preference relation** $\succ_i$ defined on $X_i \times X_i$ is a rule which classifies the ordered pairs $(x_i, y_i) \in X_i \times X_i$ into one of two categories:

- ordered pairs for which y_i is **strictly preferred** to x_i, written $y_i \succ_i x_i$; and
- ordered pairs for which y_i is **not strictly preferred** to x_i, written $y_i \nsucc_i x_i$.

For the moment, the only assumption imposed on the strict preference relation is **irreflexivity**, $x_i \nsucc_i x_i$ for all $x_i \in X_i$, which rules out the absurdity of a commodity bundle strictly preferred to itself. The **strict preference map** for consumer i is the function[9]

$$P_i \colon X_i \to 2^{X_i}, \quad x_i \mapsto P_i(x_i) := \{ y_i \in X_i \mid y_i \succ_i x_i \}$$

where 2^{X_i} denotes the set of all subsets of X_i. Within the context of standard microeconomics textbooks, the **strict preference set** $P_i(x_i)$ corresponds to the set of commodity bundles lying strictly above the indifference contour passing through the point x_i.

The **demand set** for consumer i consists of those commodity bundles in the budget set for which there exist no strictly preferred commodity bundles that are affordable (i.e., which also lie in the budget set). Formally, $\phi_i(p) := \{ x_i \in \beta_i(p) \mid P_i(x_i) \cap \beta_i(p) = \emptyset \}$. Thus, a commodity bundle belongs to a consumer's demand set if and only if she can afford it and no better bundle is affordable.

Putting all of the pieces together, we can now formally define an **exchange economy**.

Definition 1.2 *An* **exchange economy** $\mathcal{E} := \{ X_i, P_i, w_i \mid i \in I \}$ *consists of a set of consumers* $I := \{ 1, \dots, n \}$ *and, for each* $i \in I$,

- *a consumption set* $X_i \subset L_+$;
- *a strict preference map* $P_i \colon X_i \to 2^{X_i}$, $x_i \mapsto P_i(x_i)$; *and*
- *an endowment* $w_i \in L_+$

where L *denotes the commodity space* $\mathbf{R}^m$.

---

9 We do not call this map a correspondence because, although the function is set valued, we have no reason to suppose as yet that the images $P_i(x_i)$ will be nonempty.

Prior to defining an equilibrium allocation for the exchange economy $\mathcal{E}$, all that remains is to capture "conservation of commodities," recognizing that commodities can be neither created nor destroyed during the process of exchange. Coupling this requirement with our earlier assumption that each individual's allocation must lie in that individual's consumption set, we introduce the following:

Definition 1.3 *An allocation $x: I \to L_+$ is* **feasible** *for the exchange economy $\mathcal{E}$ if*

- *for every consumer $i \in I$, the allocation x_i is physically possible, $x_i \in X_i$; and*
- *commodities are conserved (i.e., none are lost or gained in the process of exchange), $\sum_{i \in I} x_i = \sum_{i \in I} w_i$.*

The **set of feasible allocations for the economy $\mathcal{E}$** *is given by*

$$\mathrm{F}(\mathcal{E}, I) := \Big\{ x: I \to L \mid \sum_{i \in I} x_i = \sum_{i \in I} w_i \ \& \ x_i \in X_i \ \forall \ i \in I \Big\}.$$

With all of the preliminaries out of the way, the definition of an equilibrium for an exchange economy is remarkably succinct.

Definition 1.4 *A* **Walrasian equilibrium** *for an exchange economy $\mathcal{E}$ is an ordered pair (x, p) consisting of a feasible allocation $x \in \mathrm{F}(\mathcal{E}, I)$ and a price functional $p \in L' \setminus \{0\}$ such that $x_i \in \phi_i(p)$ for all $i \in I$.*

Of course, the brevity of this statement masks a lot of detail now hidden inside the definitions of concepts such as "feasible allocation" or "demand set." In particular, implicit in the definition of a Walrasian equilibrium are the two key requirements that one normally associates with competitive equilibrium:

- "Demand equals supply" (since $\sum_{i \in I} x_i = \sum_{i \in I} w_i$ is implied by feasibility); and
- "Each consumer is maximizing 'utility' subject to his or her budget constraint" (since x_i belongs to the demand set at prices p).

Because calling this equilibrium concept Walrasian rather than competitive seems less than felicitous, a comment seems in order. The point is that price-taking, general equilibrium is perfectly well-defined even in situations (such as the Edgeworth box!) where the behavior assumed makes little sense. Calling such equilibria competitive begs the question of what constitutes competition. For that reason, a fair number of mathematical economists refer to the concept as Walrasian equilibrium in honor of Leon Walras, the economist who first gave the notion a reasonably precise definition within a general equilibrium setting. I have adopted the practice because it seems a distinction worth making.

1.2.1 The geometry of exchange

Given the strong tradition of diagrammatic exposition in economics, our description of Walrasian equilibrium is notable for the absence of pictures. A complementary, geometric characterization is important not solely for pedagogic reasons but also because much of the mathematics employed in competitive equilibrium analysis is fundamentally geometric in nature.

We begin with a brief description of a geometric device that should seem familiar, the Edgeworth box. As we will see, however, the Edgeworth box is not sufficient for our purposes and, for that reason, we introduce another device — the net trade diagram — which better serves our needs.

The traditional Edgeworth box applies to the case of a pure exchange economy with two consumers, $I = \{1, 2\}$, and two commodities, $J = \{1, 2\}$. Consumption sets for both consumers coincide with the nonnegative orthant, $X_1 = X_2 = \mathbf{R}^2_+$.

Figure 1.2 presents the Edgeworth box diagram for an exchange economy of this type. The lower left hand corner of the diagram serves as the origin for consumer one's commodity space, and the upper right hand corner the origin for consumer two. Because the commodity space for consumer two has been rotated by 180 degrees, the box diagram cleverly embodies the conservation law for commodities: the breadth and height represent the total amounts of commodities one and two, respectively, available for distribution to consumers; and any point in the box represents a potential distribution of commodities to consumers adding up to the total available.

For concreteness, suppose that initial endowments are given by

$$w_i = \begin{cases} (1, 3) & \text{if } i = 1, \\ (3, 1) & \text{if } i = 2, \end{cases}$$

and the Walrasian equilibrium allocation by

$$x_i = \begin{cases} (2, 2) & \text{if } i = 1, \\ (2, 2) & \text{if } i = 2. \end{cases}$$

These functions are represented in the diagram by the single points labeled w and x respectively, and each side of the box has length equal to 4.

The straight line connecting w and x corresponds to the budget line for either consumer. Market prices determine the slope of the line, and, given

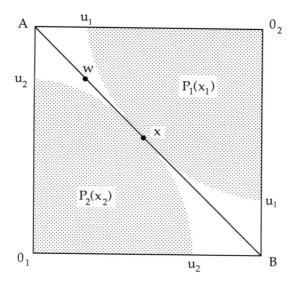

Fig. 1.2. The Edgeworth box.

prices, all points on the line have the same market value as the initial endowment. In this example, the two commodities clearly have equal prices which we can take, for example, to be $p_1 = p_2 = 1$. The budget set $\beta_1(p)$ for consumer one is then the lower triangular region $\Delta 0_1 AB$ and the budget set $\beta_2(p)$ the upper triangular region $\Delta 0_2 AB$.

The curved boundaries of the shaded areas, labeled $U_1 U_1$ and $U_2 U_2$, are the indifference curves for consumers one and two, respectively, which pass through the equilibrium allocation x. The strict preference set $P_1(x_1)$ is the shaded area lying above the indifference curve $U_1 U_1$ and the strict preference set $P_2(x_2)$ the shaded area lying below the indifference curve $U_2 U_2$. Thus, for either consumer the strict preference set does not intersect the corresponding budget set and so the equilibrium allocation x_1 lies in the demand set of consumer one and x_2 in the demand set of consumer two. Since the allocation x is feasible (by construction of the Edgeworth box) and $x_i \in \phi_i(p)$ for $i = 1, 2$ (as just shown), the ordered pair (x, p) is by definition a Walrasian equilibrium.

While the Edgeworth box is a wonderful expository device, generalizing the construction to more than two consumers or more than three commodities seems a hopeless task. Fortunately, the geometry can be generalized through the use of a complement to the Edgeworth box called the **net trade**

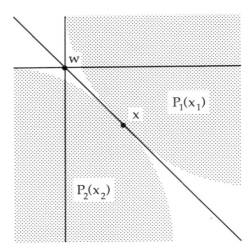

Fig. 1.3. The Edgeworth box with translated axes.

diagram. The net trade diagram is the main device we rely on throughout this book to give the modern, mathematical analysis of competition an intuitive, geometric interpretation.

The easiest way to understand the construction of a net trade diagram is to begin with the Edgeworth box. The key step in building the net trade diagram is a **change of coordinates**. Recall from our discussion of Figure 1.2 that in the Edgeworth box the coordinates of the commodity space for each consumer are chosen so that the vector $(0,0)$ is the origin. In the net trade diagram, the coordinates are translated to make the endowment point w_i the origin for each consumer $i \in I$. Figure 1.3 shows the Edgeworth box with the new set of coordinate axes imposed.

The next step in building the net trade diagram is to tear the Edgeworth box apart. We want to view the diagram from each consumer's point of view, so imagine that we now have two copies of Figure 1.3. Since consumer two is upside down, rotate the copy belonging to her by 180 degrees to make it right side up. Now paste the two diagrams together with the new origins (the endowment points) aligned. The result is the net trade diagram shown in Figure 1.4.

Because the coordinates have been translated, we need to have a consistent and easily remembered notation relating the various objects in the net trade diagram to the corresponding untranslated objects in the Edgeworth box. To indicate the translation, each object will be prefixed with a shift operator

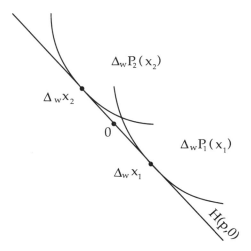

Fig. 1.4. The net trade diagram.

Δ_w and, in each case, we will distinguish the translated object verbally by prefixing the adjective net. In particular, we have for each consumer the **net consumption set** $\Delta_w X_i$; the **net strict preference set** $\Delta_w P_i(x_i)$; the **net budget set** $\Delta_w \beta_i(p)$; the **net demand set** $\Delta_w \phi_i(p)$; and the **net trade allocation** $\Delta_w x_i$. To avoid clutter, Figure 1.4 exhibits only the net trade allocations and the net strict preference sets.

Notice that, in pasting together the diagrams for the two consumers, the budget lines coincide. This reflects the assumption built into the Edgeworth box (and the definition of Walrasian equilibrium) that all consumers face the **same** market prices. Since the origin of the net trade diagram represents the endowment w_i for either consumer, the budget line passes through the origin of the net trade diagram. Using the terminology of Section 1.1, we have labeled this common budget line $H(p, 0)$ since it is a **hyperplane** passing through the origin of the vector space.

For either consumer the net budget *line*

$$\{\, \Delta_w x_i \in \Delta_w X_i \mid p \cdot \Delta_w x_i = p \cdot (x_i - w_i) = 0 \,\}$$

is a subset of the hyperplane $H(p, 0)$, and the net budget *set* by definition lies in the closed halfspace lying below the hyperplane: $\Delta_w \beta_i(p) \subset H^-(p, 0)$ for all $i \in I$. The definition of a Walrasian equilibrium requires $P_i(x_i) \cap \beta_i(p) = \emptyset$ for all $i \in I$, which, in net trade terms, translates to the requirement that $\Delta_w P_i(x_i) \subset H_o^+(p, 0)$ for all $i \in I$; i.e., since strict preference sets must lie above the budget line, net strict preference sets must lie in the **open** halfspace lying above the hyperplane $H(p, 0)$.

Finally, we examine what happens to the feasibility requirement for net trade allocations. A feasible allocation must be physically achievable for each consumer, which, in net trade terms, means that $\Delta_w x_i \in \Delta_w X_i$ for all $i \in I$. The more salient aspect of feasibility emerges, however, in translating the conservation of commodities requirement $\sum_{i \in I} x_i = \sum_{i \in I} w_i$. Since, by definition, $\Delta_w x_i := x_i - w_i$, the condition simply requires that net trades sum to zero: $\sum_{i \in I} \Delta_w x_i = \sum_{i \in I} (x_i - w_i) = 0$.

Thus, the geometric characterization of Walrasian equilibrium in terms of net trades is very straightforward:

Definition 1.5 *A net trade allocation* $\Delta_w x: I \to L$ *and a price functional* $p \neq 0$ *constitute a* **Walrasian equilibrium** *for the exchange economy* $\mathcal{E}$ *if*

- $\Delta_w x_i \in \Delta_w X_i$ *and* $\Delta_w P_i(x_i) \subset H_o^+(p, 0)$ *for all* $i \in I$*; and*
- $\sum_{i \in I} \Delta_w x_i = 0$.

To illustrate with the specific example provided by Figures 1.2 and 1.4, let us first agree to normalize prices to sum to one. (I will explain later why, within the current context, this is possible with no loss of generality. For now, accept it on faith.) In the example, equilibrium prices are uniquely determined and equal so that $p = (.5, .5)$. Untranslated, the (unique) Walrasian equilibrium allocation for this economy is the function

$$x_i = \begin{cases} (2, 2) & \text{for } i = 1, \\ (2, 2) & \text{for } i = 2. \end{cases}$$

The corresponding equilibrium net trade allocation is

$$\Delta_w x_i = x_i - w_i = \begin{cases} (1, -1) & \text{for } i = 1, \\ (-1, 1) & \text{for } i = 2. \end{cases}$$

Consumer one gives up one unit of the second commodity in exchange for one unit of the first commodity, and consumer two does the reverse. Feasibility requires that the net trades sum to zero: $\Delta_w x_1 + \Delta_w x_2 = (1, -1) + (-1, 1) = (0, 0)$.

Within the two-consumer, two-commodity context of the Edgeworth box, the net trade diagram seems as simple — and, in its own way, as elegant — as the traditional box diagram. However, its main advantage is that, in contrast to the Edgeworth box, it generalizes immediately to an arbitrary number of consumers and commodities.

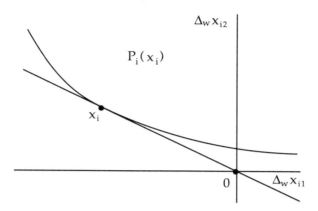

Fig. 1.5. Individual equilibrium (net trade).

1.2.2 Generalizing the net trade diagram

The key step in constructing the net trade diagram is choosing coordinates tailored to each consumer individually with origin anchored at the endowment w_i. There is nothing about this procedure specific to the Edgeworth box context of two consumers and two commodities.

Figure 1.5 exhibits the traditional picture of a consumer in equilibrium with the coordinate axes shifted to pass through the endowment point. (For the moment, we are still retaining the assumption that there are just two commodities.) No matter how many consumers in the economy, clearly we can paste these diagrams together into a net trade diagram just as before, and the resulting diagram will have essentially the same interpretation. In particular, if a net trade allocation represents an equilibrium, the net trades must sum to zero and the net strict preference sets must all lie in the open halfspace above the hyperplane.[10] Figure 1.6 illustrates an equilibrium allocation with many consumers.

Generalizing to more than two commodities is even more immediate, though of course we cannot actually draw a picture in more than three dimensions. The point is that the two-dimensional net trade diagram exhibits a geometrical structure which serves as an accurate metaphor for what happens in higher dimensions, a theme which will recur throughout

---

10 For completeness, we should also add that the net trade of each consumer must lie in that consumer's net consumption set. Usually we will suppress explicit mention of this "detail" since, while technically quite important, it plays a minor role in interpreting most results.

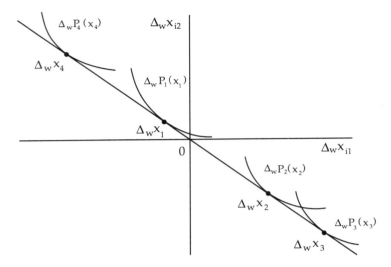

Fig. 1.6. Net trade diagram with many consumers.

this book. Because all consumers face the same prices (by hypothesis), the hyperplane $H(p, 0)$ serves as the budget plane common to every consumer. For any finite dimensional vector space,[11] the hyperplane divides the (translated) commodity space into two halfspaces. By construction, budget sets are always contained in the lower closed halfspace and, for an equilibrium allocation, net strict preference sets must be contained in the upper open halfspace. Finally, conservation of commodities requires that net trades sum to zero (i.e., to the origin of the net trade vector space). All of these conditions are accurately reflected within the two dimensions of Figure 1.6.

Although our geometrical exposition of the net trade operator is a useful metaphor, it is not mathematically precise. Fortunately, there is a way to turn our informal geometry into a formal, algebraic procedure while remaining entirely faithful to the geometry. The algebraic interpretation of the net trade operator uses a form of block notation popular in the mathematical literature on convex analysis. The essential idea is quite simple. Suppose that we are given a vector space L, arbitrary subsets $A, B \subset L$, an arbitrary vector $z \in L$, and an arbitrary scalar $\alpha \in \mathbf{R}$. We then define various **block operations** as follows:

$$A - z \;=\; \{\, x \in L \mid x = a - z,\, a \in A \,\},$$

---

11 And, under the right conditions, for infinite dimensions as well, although more subtle considerations of the topological as well as the algebraic properties of the vector space are involved.

$$\begin{aligned}
A + B &= \{\, x \in L \mid x = a + b,\, a \in A, b \in B \,\}, \\
A - B &= \{\, x \in L \mid x = a - b,\, a \in A,\, b \in B \,\}, \\
\alpha A &= \{\, x \in L \mid x = \alpha a, a \in A \,\}.
\end{aligned}$$

More generally, for any collection of scalars $\alpha_i \in \mathbf{R}$ and any collection of subsets $A_i \subset L$ indexed by a finite set I,

$$\sum_{i \in I} \alpha_i A_i = \Big\{ x \in L \mid x = \sum_{i \in I} \alpha_i x_i,\ x_i \in A_i\ \forall i \in I \Big\}.$$

Applying this notation to the special case of translation into net trades, we define:

$$\begin{aligned}
\Delta_w X_i &= X_i - w_i, \\
\Delta_w P_i(x_i) &= P_i(x_i) - w_i, \\
\Delta_w \beta_i(p) &= \beta_i(p) - w_i, \\
\Delta_w \phi_i(p) &= \phi_i(p) - w_i, \text{ and} \\
\Delta_w x_i &= x_i - w_i.
\end{aligned}$$

That is all that is required to turn our intuitively defined geometric procedure into a precisely defined mathematical operation regardless of the dimensionality of the vector space.

1.2.3 Walrasian equilibrium and net trades

We now have two alternative definitions of Walrasian equilibrium, one using net trades and the other which does not. Expanding the definition of feasibility for purposes of the present comparison, the original definition of Walrasian equilibrium given above reads as follows.

Definition 1.6 *The ordered pair* (x, p), $p \neq 0$, *is a* **Walrasian equilibrium** *for the exchange economy* $\mathcal{E}$ *if*

- $x_i \in X_i$ *and* $x_i \in \phi_i(p)$ *for all* $i \in I$, *and*
- $\sum_{i \in I} x_i = \sum_{i \in I} w_i$.

The net trade version has a parallel form.

Definition 1.7 *The ordered pair* $(\Delta_w x, p)$, $p \neq 0$, *is a* **Walrasian net trade equilibrium** *for the exchange economy* $\mathcal{E}$ *if*

- $\Delta_w x_i \in \Delta_w X_i$ *and* $\Delta_w x_i \in \Delta_w \phi_i(p)$ *for all* $i \in I$, *and*
- $\sum_{i \in I} \Delta_w x_i = 0$.

In the latter definition, the net trade allocation $\Delta_w x$ is simply the difference $x - w$ of the functions x and w defined in pointwise fashion: i.e., $\Delta_w x \colon I \to L$, $i \mapsto \Delta_w x_i := x_i - w_i$.

Let $\mathrm{WE}(\mathcal{E})$ and $\Delta_w \mathrm{WE}(\mathcal{E})$ denote the set of Walrasian equilibrium pairs (x, p) and $(\Delta_w x, p)$ respectively for an exchange economy $\mathcal{E}$. The following "theorem" demonstrating the equivalence of the two representations is really just a matter of notation.

Theorem 1.8 *For any exchange economy* $\mathcal{E}$,

$$(x, p) \in \mathrm{WE}(\mathcal{E}) \quad \textit{iff} \quad (\Delta_w x, p) \in \Delta_w \mathrm{WE}(\mathcal{E}).$$

Proof

$$x_i \in X_i \quad \text{iff} \quad x_i - w_i \in X_i - w_i \quad \text{iff} \quad \Delta_w x_i \in \Delta_w X_i;$$

$$x_i \in \phi_i(p) \quad \text{iff} \quad x_i - w_i \in \phi_i(p) - w_i \quad \text{iff} \quad \Delta_w x_i \in \Delta_w \phi_i(p);$$

$$\sum_{i \in I} x_i = \sum_{i \in I} w_i \quad \text{iff} \quad \sum_{i \in I}(x_i - w_i) = 0 \quad \text{iff} \quad \sum_{i \in I} \Delta_w x_i = 0.$$

$\square$

While block notation is clearly very useful, I end this discussion with a cautionary note. You should not jump to the conclusion that, just because we have attached a meaning to a "linear combination" of subsets $\sum_{i \in I} \alpha_i A_i$, block notation somehow converts the space of subsets 2^L of a vector space L into a vector space. For example, while $2A \subset A + A$ it is not true in general that $2A = A + A$.

1.3 Pareto optimality and the core

Once Walrasian equilibrium has been rigorously defined, we are in a position to ask questions about the nature of the model. Do solutions exist, and if so how do we find them? Does competition provide a "good" way for society to allocate resources? Is the price-taking hypothesis at all plausible, and if so under what circumstances?

Seeing how mathematical economists address issues such as these will occupy our attention throughout the rest of the book. In the present section, we will begin to address the latter two questions by exploring some aspects of the connection between Walrasian equilibrium and Pareto optimality (one answer to the question of whether Walrasian equilibrium is "good" from a social point of view) and the connection between Walrasian equilibrium and the game theoretic concept of the core (which touches on the issue of the plausibility of price-taking behavior).

This exploration of the connection between Walrasian equilibrium, Pareto optimality, and the core provides our first nontrivial exposure to the process of rigorous, mathematical proof. To avoid a possible source of confusion, it seems worthwhile to make a few comments on some matters of grammar.

Mathematical assertions — variously called lemmas, propositions, or theorems — typically involve an assertion that one body of statements (say "A") implies the truth of another body of statements (say "B"). In referring to such assertions, we say that "$A \Rightarrow B$," which can be read "A implies B" or "if A, then B." The assertion "$B \Rightarrow A$" (or, equivalently, "$A \Leftarrow B$") is called the **converse** of the proposition "$A \Rightarrow B$." If "$A \Rightarrow B$" and "$B \Rightarrow A$," then we write "$A \iff B$" and we read this as "A if and only if B" or, more concisely, "A iff B."

When "$A \Rightarrow B$," A is called a sufficient condition for B and B a necessary condition for A while "$A \iff B$" means that A is necessary and sufficient for B (and, by symmetry, B is necessary and sufficient for A). If, like me, you find it difficult to keep the meaning of necessary and sufficient straight, I recommend the use of the arrows $\Rightarrow$ and $\Leftarrow$.

It is extremely important to distinguish the converse of the proposition "$A \Rightarrow B$" from its **contrapositive**. While the converse simply involves reversing the direction of the arrow, the contrapositive also involves the negation of A and B. Thus, the contrapositive of "$A \Rightarrow B$" is the proposition "$\neg B \Rightarrow \neg A$," which is read "if B is not true, then A is not true" or, briefly, "not B implies not A." The important fact to realize is that a proposition and its contrapositive are simply different ways of saying the same thing: if one is true, so is the other, and if one is false the other is also. We will often find that, when trying to prove some proposition, it is easier to establish the validity of the contrapositive instead. The theorems presented in this section provide an illustration of that procedure.

1.3.1 Pareto optimality

The **First Fundamental Theorem** of welfare economics asserts that Walrasian equilibria are always Pareto optimal. While this is one of the most important results in economic theory, one should not read more into it than is there. The First Fundamental Theorem does not advance the Panglossian claim that the invisible hand produces the best of all possible worlds, but only that the resulting allocation is efficient in the sense that no other feasible allocation exists that could make everyone better off. Some might

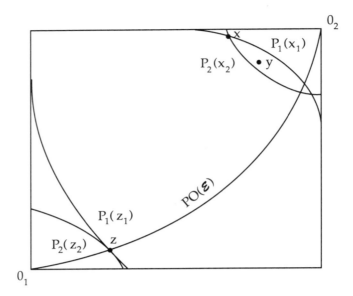

Fig. 1.7. Pareto domination and Pareto optimality.

be made better off, but only at the expense of others. Those who stand to
gain from some alternative allocation can presumably be counted upon to
argue that such a change would be an improvement from a societal point of
view. Those who stand to lose will undoubtedly disagree.

The Edgeworth box provides a good illustration of what Pareto optimality means. As shown in Figure 1.7, the **Pareto optimal allocations** are
identified by eliminating those which are **Pareto dominated**: i.e., those
allocations which can be improved upon because there is some other allocation in the box which both consumers would prefer. Thus, the allocation
x is Pareto dominated because the lens-shaped region — the intersection
$P_1(x_1) \cap P_2(x_2)$ of the strict preference sets corresponding to the allocation
x — is nonempty and, as a consequence, there exists an allocation y which
makes both consumers better off. On the other hand, no such dominating
allocation exists for the allocation z. The set of Pareto optimal allocations
consists of all allocations such as z, indicated in this example by the smooth
curve running from one corner of the box to the other, which cannot be
improved upon in the above sense.

Generalizing the definitions of Pareto domination and Pareto optimality
to the case of an arbitrary number of consumers and commodities is straightforward. Let us first agree to abbreviate the condition $y_i \succ_i x_i$ for all $i \in I$,

which asserts that all consumers prefer the allocation y over the allocation x, to $y \succ_I x$.

Definition 1.9 *In an exchange economy $\mathcal{E}$, a feasible allocation x is **Pareto dominated** if there exists another feasible allocation y which all consumers prefer to x. The set of all such allocations is denoted*

$$\mathrm{Dom}(\mathcal{E}, I) := \{\, x \in \mathrm{F}(\mathcal{E}, I) \mid \exists\, y \in \mathrm{F}(\mathcal{E}, I) \ni y \succ_I x \,\}.$$

*The **Pareto optimal allocations** are those feasible allocations left over after all dominated allocations have been eliminated:*

$$\mathrm{PO}(\mathcal{E}) := \mathrm{F}(\mathcal{E}, I) \backslash \mathrm{Dom}(\mathcal{E}, I).$$

The net trade diagram provides a geometric interpretation of Pareto domination and Pareto optimality, an interpretation which remains valid irrespective of the number of consumers and the number of commodities.

Lemma 1.10 *For an exchange economy $\mathcal{E}$,*

$$x \in \mathrm{Dom}(\mathcal{E}, I) \quad \textit{iff} \quad 0 \in \sum_{i \in I} \Delta_w P_i(x_i).$$

Proof $x \in \mathrm{Dom}(\mathcal{E}, I)$

$$\text{iff} \qquad \exists y \ni \sum_{i \in I} \Delta_w y_i = 0 \ \ \& \ \ \Delta_w y_i \in \Delta_w P_i(x_i) \ \ \forall i \in I$$

$$\text{iff} \qquad 0 \in \sum_{i \in I} \Delta_w P_i(x_i)$$

with the last step following from the definition of block notation. $\qquad\square$

Lemma 1.11 *For an exchange economy $\mathcal{E}$,*

$$x \in \mathrm{PO}(\mathcal{E}) \quad \textit{iff} \quad 0 \notin \sum_{i \in I} \Delta_w P_i(x_i).$$

Proof Recall that $\mathrm{PO}(\mathcal{E}) = \mathrm{F}(\mathcal{E}, I) \backslash \mathrm{Dom}(\mathcal{E}, I)$ and apply the preceding lemma. $\qquad\square$

Note that built into the definition of $P_i(x_i)$ is the guarantee that any $y_i \in P_i(y_i)$ belongs to the consumption set of consumer i. These two lemmas then say that a net trade allocation $\Delta_w y$ Pareto dominates a net trade allocation $\Delta_w x$ if (a) $\sum_{i \in I} \Delta_w y_i \in \sum_{i \in I} \Delta_w P_i(x_i)$ (so that all consumers prefer $\Delta_w y$ to $\Delta_w x$); and (b) $\sum_{i \in I} \Delta_w y_i = 0$ (so that $\Delta_w y$ is feasible). The net trade $\Delta_w x$ is Pareto optimal if $\Delta_w x$ cannot be dominated in this way.

I now digress briefly to address a question that might be bothering you: the contrast between the definition of Pareto optimality given above and the usual definition given in microeconomics textbooks (which I will refer to as **strong Pareto optimality**). If you were not bothered, you may skip the next few paragraphs!

Strong Pareto optimality involves a weaker criterion for domination than ours: x is weakly Pareto dominated if there exists a feasible allocation y which (i) all consumers regard as "at least as good" as x and (ii) at least one consumer regards as strictly better than x. Since the criterion for domination is weaker (i.e., it is easier to dominate), the criterion for strong Pareto optimality is indeed stronger than our criterion: i.e., the resulting set of strong Pareto optima will be a subset (possibly strict) of the set which we are calling optimal.

In some situations the alternative concepts can be quite distinct. For the applications considered in this book, however, the two definitions are equivalent. What is required for equivalence is the following: suppose that we have found an allocation y which weakly dominates x (e.g., $y_1 \succ_1 x_1$ while all other consumers are indifferent between y and x). To find another feasible allocation y^* which (strongly) dominates x, take a small amount away from consumer 1 (small enough to leave the consumer strictly better off than with x_1) and distribute the small amount to all of the other consumers (making them strictly better off).

For such a procedure to be successful (i) at least some commodities must be very finely divisible, (ii) it must be possible to take a small amount of such a commodity away from a consumer for whom $y_i \succ_i x_i$ while retaining strict preference, and (iii) the remaining consumers must have preferences sufficiently responsive to a small increment of the redistributed commodities to alter a situation of indifference to one of strict preference. In situations where most or all commodities are indivisible (i.e., available only in integer amounts) or consumers are satiated, this procedure may not be possible. Ordinarily economists assume sufficient divisibility and responsiveness of preferences to guarantee that it will work.

From now on I will ignore the traditional definition of Pareto optimality (strong Pareto optimality) in favor of Definition 1.9, the definition which has become quite standard in the mathematical analysis of general equilibrium.

We are now ready to prove our first result of economic substance, the assertion that every Walrasian equilibrium allocation is Pareto optimal. The Edgeworth box provides a quick proof for the case of two consumers and two commodities. Referring to Figure 1.2, if the point x is a Walrasian equilibrium allocation, then by definition the strict preference set $P_1(x_1)$

lies above the budget line and the strict preference set $P_2(x_2)$ lies below. Therefore, the two strict preference sets have an empty intersection, which means that x is Pareto optimal.

Turning to the general case, recall that $\mathrm{WE}(\mathcal{E})$ denotes the set of equilibrium pairs (x, p). In stating our theorem, it will be useful to break the ordered pairs into their constituent parts by defining the **set of Walrasian equilibrium allocations**

$$\mathrm{WE}^x(\mathcal{E}) := \{\, x \in \mathrm{F}(\mathcal{E}, I) \mid (x, p) \in \mathrm{WE}(\mathcal{E}) \,\}$$

and the **set of Walrasian equilibrium prices**

$$\mathrm{WE}^p(\mathcal{E}) := \{\, p \in L' \mid (x, p) \in \mathrm{WE}(\mathcal{E}) \,\}.$$

We will give two alternative proofs of the **First Fundamental Theorem** of welfare economics, one a proof by contradiction and the other a direct proof.

Theorem 1.12 *For any exchange economy $\mathcal{E}$, $\mathrm{WE}^x(\mathcal{E}) \subset \mathrm{PO}(\mathcal{E})$.*

Proof Suppose that $(x, p) \in \mathrm{WE}(\mathcal{E})$ but $x \notin \mathrm{PO}(\mathcal{E})$. By the definition of Pareto optimality, $x \in \mathrm{Dom}(\mathcal{E}, I)$ so there exists an allocation $y \in \mathrm{F}(\mathcal{E}, I)$ such that $y \succ_I x$. But then $\Delta_w y_i \in \Delta_w P_i(x_i)$ for all $i \in I$. By the definition of Walrasian equilibrium, this implies that $p \cdot \Delta_w y_i > 0$ (otherwise, since $y_i \in X_i$, y_i would lie in the budget set of consumer i). Therefore, using the fact that p is a linear functional,

$$p \cdot \sum_{i \in I} \Delta_w y_i = \sum_{i \in I} p \cdot \Delta_w y_i > 0.$$

However, this contradicts our initial hypothesis that $y \in \mathrm{F}(\mathcal{E}, I)$, which requires that $\sum_{i \in I} \Delta_w y_i = 0$. $\qquad\square$

Proof (Alternative.) If $(x, p) \in \mathrm{WE}(\mathcal{E})$, then every net strict preference set lies in the open halfspace above the hyperplane: $\Delta_w P_i(x_i) \subset H_o^+(p, 0)$ for all $i \in I$. Let z be any point belonging to $\sum_{i \in I} \Delta_w P_i(x_i)$. By definition of block notation, this means that $z = \sum_{i \in I} \Delta_w y_i$ where $\Delta_w y_i \in \Delta_w P_i(x_i)$ for all $i \in I$. Because $x \in \mathrm{WE}^x(\mathcal{E})$ and $\Delta_w y_i \in \Delta_w P_i(x_i)$ for all $i \in I$, $p \cdot \Delta_w y_i > 0$ for all $i \in I$. Therefore, $p \cdot z = \sum_{i \in I} p \cdot \Delta_w y_i > 0$ and, hence, $z \neq 0$. Since this argument applies to any point z chosen from $\sum_{i \in I} \Delta_w P_i(x_i)$, we conclude that $0 \notin \sum_{i \in I} \Delta_w P_i(x_i)$. By Lemma 1.11 this implies that $x \in \mathrm{PO}(\mathcal{E})$. $\qquad\square$

1.3.2 The core

In addition to the question of its efficiency, another issue worth raising about
Walrasian equilibrium is whether the hypothesis of price-taking behavior
is consistent with rational behavior: Under what circumstances will the
consumers in an exchange economy choose to act as price-takers as required
by the Walrasian model? This question can and has been addressed in
many different ways. One of the most fruitful involves the use of a concept
developed in game theory called the **core**.

The definition of the core of an economy, like Pareto optimality but unlike Walrasian equilibrium, makes no reference to prices. A priori there are
no restrictions imposed on the ability of consumers to exert their potential
monopoly power to the fullest. However, even in noncompetitive situations
this power is not unlimited: if a consumer tries to extract too much, the
other consumers may refuse to engage in trade. The core represents those allocations which remain after allocations which exceed the bounds of possible
monopoly power have been eliminated.

If an allocation x is to be regarded as a possible solution to the exchange
game, it clearly must be a feasible allocation: $x \in \mathrm{F}(\mathcal{E}, I)$. Consider now
an arbitrary nonempty subset S of the set of consumers I. What are the
limits which the members of S can impose on the ability of the consumers
not in S to exert monopoly power? An allocation $x \in \mathrm{F}(\mathcal{E}, I)$ which treats
the members of S so poorly that they could do better using only their own
resources does not seem to be a likely outcome of the exchange process.
The members of S would presumably refuse to engage in trade with the
consumers in $I \backslash S$, choosing instead to trade only among themselves.

To formalize this notion, we first define the set of allocations which are
feasible for the subset S using only its own resources:

$$\mathrm{F}(\mathcal{E}, S) = \Big\{ x : I \to L_+ \mid \sum_{i \in S} x_i = \sum_{i \in S} w_i \ \& \ x_i \in X_i \ \forall i \in S \Big\}.$$

Notice that the assertion $x \in \mathrm{F}(\mathcal{E}, S)$ says nothing about the x_i for consumers $i \in I \backslash S$. If trading among themselves, the members of S are unaf-
fected by what happens to consumers not in S.

If all consumers in S prefer an allocation y to an allocation x, $y_i \succ_i x_i$
for all $i \in S$, then we will write $y \succ_S x$. (The relation $\succ_S$ on the set of
allocations is called the **strict coalitional preference relation** of S.)

Definition 1.13 *An allocation $x \in \mathrm{F}(\mathcal{E}, I)$ is **dominated** by $S \neq \emptyset$ if there
exists an allocation $y \in \mathrm{F}(\mathcal{E}, S)$ which is preferred to x by all consumers in*

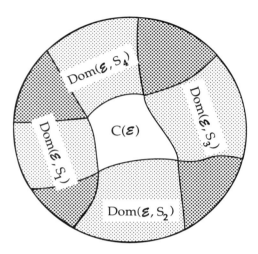

Fig. 1.8. The core.

S. The set of all such allocations is denoted

$$\mathrm{Dom}(\mathcal{E}, S) = \{\, x \in \mathrm{F}(\mathcal{E}, I) \mid \exists y \in \mathrm{F}(\mathcal{E}, S) \ni y \succ_S x \,\}.$$

(If $S = \emptyset$, then let $\mathrm{Dom}(\mathcal{E}, S) = \emptyset$.)

A nonempty subset $S \subset I$ is called a **coalition** in the literature on the core, a terminology which we will also adopt. However, it is worth noting that the word coalition is a little misleading. No implication is intended that the members of S constitute a power group, a union, a cartel, or any other explicit organization of consumers. A coalition is simply a subset of consumers.

Once these concepts have been introduced, the definition of the core is immediate. The core consists of those feasible allocations which are undominated, those which no coalition can improve upon using only its own resources. Figure 1.8 provides a graphic illustration of what is going on. The subsets $\mathrm{Dom}(\mathcal{E}, S)$ are eliminated from the set of feasible allocations for each coalition $S \subset I$. What remains (if anything), after all of these "bites from the apple," is the core.

Definition 1.14 *The **core of an exchange economy** $\mathcal{E}$ is the set*

$$\mathrm{C}(\mathcal{E}) = \mathrm{F}(\mathcal{E}, I) \backslash \bigcup_{S \subset I} \mathrm{Dom}(\mathcal{E}, S).$$

The definitions of $C(\mathcal{E})$ and $PO(\mathcal{E})$ are clearly very similar: each is defined as a residual obtained by eliminating from the set of feasible allocations those allocations which can be dominated by some coalition. In the case of the core, all possible subsets of I are considered; for Pareto optimality, only the set of all consumers (the "coalition of the whole"). Thus, simply as a matter of definition, we conclude that $C(\mathcal{E}) \subset PO(\mathcal{E})$.

In addition to Pareto optimality, core allocations must be **individually rational**: by definition, no single consumer could improve upon an allocation in the core using only his own resources. Letting

$$IR(\mathcal{E}) = F(\mathcal{E}, I) \backslash \bigcup_{i \in I} Dom(\mathcal{E}, \{i\})$$

denote the set of individually rational allocations, we conclude that $C(\mathcal{E}) \subset IR(\mathcal{E})$.

In the case of a two-consumer economy, the one-consumer coalitions $\{1\}$ and $\{2\}$ and the coalition of the whole, $I = \{1, 2\}$, exhaust the possibilities. Figure 1.9 illustrates the core for an Edgeworth box economy: the individually rational allocations are represented by the lens-shaped area bounded by the indifference curves for each consumer passing through the point of initial endowments; the Pareto optima are represented by the curved line; and the core is simply the intersection of these two sets, the segment of the curved line of Pareto optima lying within the lens-shaped area of individually rational allocations.

Figure 1.9 also illustrates a result which is true of any exchange economy: Walrasian allocations are always in the core. This is quite obvious in the Edgeworth box context. We already knew from the First Fundamental Theorem that Walrasian allocations are Pareto optimal, and individual rationality follows immediately from the fact that a consumer's initial endowment lies in his budget set.

Although the fact that Walrasian allocations are in the core is self-evident in the Edgeworth box, whether the assertion remains true when there are many consumers and many commodities is by no means obvious. As the number of consumers increases, the collection of domination sets $Dom(\mathcal{E}, S)$ to be considered increases very rapidly. It seems quite plausible that one or more of these sets could eliminate some or all of the Walrasian allocations from the core. The simplicity of the proof that this cannot happen is, therefore, all the more remarkable.

The analogs of Lemmas 1.10 and 1.11, proved in essentially the same way, provide a geometric interpretation of domination and the core in terms of the net trade diagram.

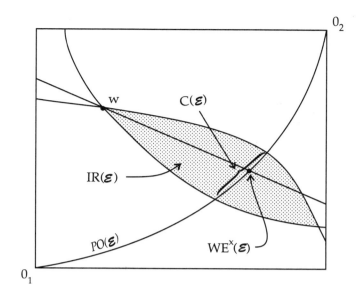

Fig. 1.9. The core in an Edgeworth box.

Lemma 1.15 *For an exchange economy $\mathcal{E}$ and a coalition $S \subset I$,*

$$x \in \mathrm{Dom}(\mathcal{E}, S) \quad \textit{iff} \quad 0 \in \sum_{i \in S} \Delta_w P_i(x_i).$$

Proof $x \in \mathrm{Dom}(\mathcal{E}, S)$

iff $\quad \exists y \ni \sum_{i \in S} \Delta_w y_i = 0 \quad \& \quad \Delta_w y_i \in \Delta_w P_i(x_i) \quad \forall i \in S$

iff $\quad 0 \in \sum_{i \in S} \Delta_w P_i(x_i)$

with the last step following from the definition of block notation. $\qquad\square$

Lemma 1.16 *For an exchange economy $\mathcal{E}$,*

$$x \in \mathrm{C}(\mathcal{E}) \quad \textit{iff} \quad 0 \notin \sum_{i \in S} \Delta_w P_i(x_i) \quad \textit{for all} \quad S \subset I.$$

Proof Recall that $\mathrm{C}(\mathcal{E}) = \mathrm{F}(\mathcal{E}, I) \backslash \bigcup_{S \subset I} \mathrm{Dom}(\mathcal{E}, S)$ and apply the preceding lemma. $\qquad\square$

The proof that Walrasian equilibria are always in the core, reported in Debreu and Scarf (1963), is credited to Lloyd Shapley.

Theorem 1.17 (Shapley) *For any exchange economy* $\mathcal{E}$,

$$\mathrm{WE}^x(\mathcal{E}) \subset \mathrm{C}(\mathcal{E}) \subset \mathrm{PO}(\mathcal{E}).$$

Proof As noted earlier, the inclusion $\mathrm{C}(\mathcal{E}) \subset \mathrm{PO}(\mathcal{E})$ is immediate from the definitions. To establish the first inclusion, suppose that $(x, p) \in \mathrm{WE}(\mathcal{E})$ but $x \notin \mathrm{C}(\mathcal{E})$. By the definition of the core, $x \in \mathrm{Dom}(\mathcal{E}, S)$ for some nonempty $S \subset I$ and so there exists an allocation $y \in \mathrm{F}(\mathcal{E}, S)$ such that $y \succ_S x$. But then $\Delta_w y_i \in \Delta_w P_i(x_i)$ for all $i \in S$. By the definition of Walrasian equilibrium, this implies that $p \cdot \Delta_w y_i > 0$. Therefore,

$$p \cdot \sum_{i \in S} \Delta_w y_i = \sum_{i \in S} p \cdot \Delta_w y_i > 0.$$

However, this contradicts our initial hypothesis that $y \in \mathrm{F}(\mathcal{E}, S)$, which requires that $\sum_{i \in S} \Delta_w y_i = 0$. $\square$

Note that Theorem 1.17 generalizes Theorem 1.12 since it immediately implies that $\mathrm{WE}^x(\mathcal{E}) \subset \mathrm{PO}(\mathcal{E})$ for any exchange economy $\mathcal{E}$.

1.4 A numerical example

Working through examples is critical to developing a genuine understanding of this material. This section presents a simple exchange economy in which consumers have Cobb-Douglas utility functions. This example also provides an opportunity to hint at developments which lie ahead.

1.4.1 *Walrasian equilibrium, Pareto optima, and the core*

The setting is the usual Edgeworth box economy with two consumers, $I = \{1, 2\}$, and two commodities, $J = \{1, 2\}$. Utility functions take the form

$$u_i(x_i) = \begin{cases} x_{i1}^{\alpha} x_{i2}^{1-\alpha} & \text{for } i = 1, \\ x_{i1}^{\beta} x_{i2}^{1-\beta} & \text{for } i = 2 \end{cases}$$

where $\alpha, \beta \in (0, 1)$. Endowments are given by $w_i = (a_i, b_i)$ for $i = 1, 2$ with $a_i > 0$ and $b_i > 0$. Consumer wealth is then

$$p \cdot w_i = \begin{cases} p_1 a_1 + p_2 b_1 & \text{for } i = 1, \\ p_1 a_2 + p_2 b_2 & \text{for } i = 2. \end{cases}$$

The Cobb-Douglas utility function is popular among economists because it yields demand functions which are moderately realistic and, more to the point, easy to compute. Demand sets are singleton-valued with

$$\phi_1(p) = \left(\frac{\alpha p \cdot w_1}{p_1}, \frac{(1-\alpha) p \cdot w_1}{p_2} \right) \quad \text{and}$$

$$\phi_2(p) = \left(\frac{\beta p \cdot w_2}{p_1}, \frac{(1-\beta) p \cdot w_2}{p_2} \right).$$

(So consumer 1 spends the fraction α of her wealth on the first commodity, $1 - \alpha$ on the second, while consumer 2 spends the fraction β of his wealth on the first commodity and $1 - \beta$ on the second.)

Clearing the market for the first commodity requires

$$\alpha \left(\frac{p_1 a_1 + p_2 b_1}{p_1} \right) + \beta \left(\frac{p_1 a_2 + p_2 b_2}{p_1} \right) = a_1 + a_2 \qquad (1.1)$$

while clearing the second requires

$$(1-\alpha) \left(\frac{p_1 a_1 + p_2 b_1}{p_2} \right) + (1-\beta) \left(\frac{p_1 a_2 + p_2 b_2}{p_2} \right) = b_1 + b_2. \qquad (1.2)$$

Since, with a little effort, you will find that these equations are equivalent, we have in effect only one equation to determine the two unknown prices p_1 and p_2.

This redundancy in the market clearing equations was one of the main discoveries of Leon Walras, who pioneered the mathematical analysis of competitive general equilibrium theory. He also recognized the implication that market clearing determines only relative rather than absolute price levels and hence that eliminating the indeterminacy requires an arbitrary normalization of prices. Walras chose to normalize by selecting one of the commodities as *numéraire*, setting its price equal to 1. In the modern literature, prices are usually normalized by setting their sum equal to 1, a practice that we follow here.

Substituting $p_2 = 1 - p_1$ into equation (1.1) and solving for p_1 yields the following expression for the equilibrium price of commodity one:

$$p_1 = \frac{\alpha b_1 + \beta b_2}{(1-\alpha)a_1 + \alpha b_1 + (1-\beta)a_2 + \beta b_2}.$$

The equilibrium price of the second commodity is then obtained from the normalization, $p_2 = 1 - p_1$.

Letting $\alpha = .75$, $\beta = .25$, $w_1 = (1,3)$, and $w_2 = (3,1)$ yields the Walrasian equilibrium price functional $p = (.5, .5)$ for the Walrasian equilibrium allocation

$$x_i = \begin{cases} (3,1) & \text{for } i = 1, \\ (1,3) & \text{for } i = 2. \end{cases}$$

and net trade allocation

$$\Delta_w x_i = \begin{cases} (2, -2) & \text{for } i = 1, \\ (-2, 2) & \text{for } i = 2. \end{cases}$$

Finding a general expression for the set of Pareto optima is somewhat more challenging. We begin by noting that the marginal rates of substitution (i.e., the absolute values of the slopes of the indifference curves) for the two consumers are given by the expressions

$$\text{MRS}_1(x_1) = \frac{\alpha}{1 - \alpha} \frac{x_{12}}{x_{11}} \quad \text{and} \quad \text{MRS}_2(x_2) = \frac{\beta}{1 - \beta} \frac{x_{22}}{x_{21}}$$

where x_{ij} denotes the amount of consumption of the jth commodity by the ith consumer. It will also be convenient to define the following expressions for the total endowment of each commodity:

$$a = a_1 + a_2 \quad \text{and} \quad b = b_1 + b_2.$$

With smooth indifference curves such as the Cobb-Douglas, Pareto optimality requires tangency of the indifference curves of the two consumers or, equivalently, equality of the marginal rates of substitution. Equating the MRS's, making the substitutions $x_{21} = a - x_{11}$ and $x_{22} = b - x_{12}$, defining

$$\gamma = \frac{\beta/(1 - \beta)}{\alpha/(1 - \alpha)}$$

and rearranging the resulting equation finally yields the following equation for the locus of Pareto optima:

$$\frac{x_{12}}{b} = \frac{\gamma(x_{11}/a)}{1 + (\gamma - 1)(x_{11}/a)}.$$

Using the specific numerical values assigned above, you should verify that the Walrasian allocation computed earlier is in fact Pareto optimal.

Since computations involving the core are more difficult, to illustrate core allocations we will simplify our example. Keeping endowment vectors the same, set $\alpha = \beta = .5$ so that $\gamma = 1$. The Walrasian equilibrium price functional is $p = (.5, .5)$ with corresponding Walrasian equilibrium allocation $x_i = (2, 2)$ for $i = 1, 2$. The equation describing the set of Pareto optima simplifies to $x_{12} = x_{11}$, a diagonal line connecting opposite corners of the Edgeworth box.

The endpoints of the set of core allocations are obtained by finding for each consumer the commodity bundle on the diagonal yielding the same utility as the consumer's initial endowment:

$$q = u_1(q, q) = u_1(a_1, b_1) = \sqrt{3} \quad \text{and} \quad q = u_2(q, q) = u_2(a_2, b_2) = \sqrt{3}.$$

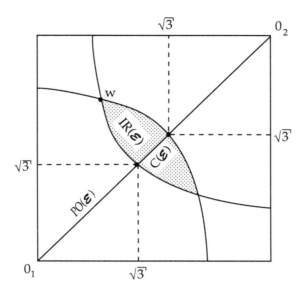

Fig. 1.10. Computing the core.

Thus, the set of core allocations is the line segment with endpoints $(\sqrt{3}, \sqrt{3})$ and $(4 - \sqrt{3}, 4 - \sqrt{3})$ as illustrated in Figure 1.10.

1.4.2 Core equivalence

The results we have obtained thus far regarding the relationship between Walrasian allocations and core allocations do not constitute a very convincing defense of the price-taking, competitive hypothesis. While Walrasian equilibria are always in the core, many other non-Walrasian allocations are in the core as well. This suggests that in a typical exchange economy there is wide scope for bargaining over terms of trade, no reason to single out Walrasian equilibria for special attention, and no **rational** reason why consumers should act as price-takers.

These conclusions should seem quite reasonable: an economy with only two consumers is an unlikely place to look for perfect competition. The usual defense of the competitive, price-taking hypothesis relies on **thick markets** with many consumers trading in the market for each commodity. The major accomplishment of studies of the relationship between the core and Walrasian equilibria over the past thirty years has been to give substance to the intuitive claim that in truly competitive environments price-taking is rational behavior.

While we postpone a general discussion of this topic until later, our Cobb-Douglas economy can be used to illustrate the nature of the results that can be obtained. Following the pioneering approach of Francis Edgeworth, we enhance the competitiveness of our original economy by replacing each of our two consumers with n_i consumers of the same type (i.e., with the same preferences and the same endowments). As Edgeworth observed, provided that we add the *same* number of consumers of each type (so that $n_1 = n_2$) and that preferences are sufficiently well-behaved (as are Cobb-Douglas preferences), Walrasian allocations and core allocations in the expanded economy will exhibit an **equal treatment property**: any Walrasian or core allocation will assign the same bundle to all of the consumers of the same type.

What this means is that we can represent the Walrasian and core allocations for the expanded economy in the same Edgeworth box diagram used for the two-person economy, interpreting the allocations to consumers 1 and 2 as the allocations to each consumer of type 1 and 2 respectively. Consider now the sequence of economies $\mathcal{E}^1, \mathcal{E}^2, \ldots, \mathcal{E}^r, \ldots$ formed as we add more and more consumers of each type where at the rth step we let $r = n_1 = n_2$ denote the number of consumers of each type. At each stage we exhibit the set of Walrasian allocations $\mathrm{WE}^x(\mathcal{E}^r)$ and the set of core allocations $\mathrm{C}(\mathcal{E}^r)$ in the Edgeworth box.

When we do this it is not too difficult to show[12] that the following will hold as we increase r.

- The set of Walrasian allocations remains the same:

$$\mathrm{WE}^x(\mathcal{E}^1) = \mathrm{WE}^x(\mathcal{E}^2) = \cdots = \mathrm{WE}^x(\mathcal{E}^r) = \cdots.$$

(Endowments and preferences are identical for consumers of the same type and so, for a given equilibrium price functional, budget sets — and hence demand sets — remain the same when the economy is replicated.)
- The Walrasian allocations always belong to the core:

$$\mathrm{WE}^x(\mathcal{E}^r) \subset \mathrm{C}(\mathcal{E}^r) \quad (r = 1, 2, \cdots).$$

(This follows immediately from Theorem 1.17.)
- The core can only shrink, not expand:

$$\mathrm{C}(\mathcal{E}^1) \supset \mathrm{C}(\mathcal{E}^2) \supset \cdots \supset \mathrm{C}(\mathcal{E}^r) \cdots.$$

(Any allocation which can be improved upon by a coalition at some stage

12 These claims will be proved in a more general setting in Chapter 8.

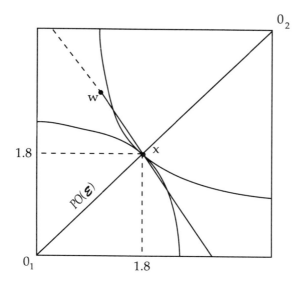

Fig. 1.11. A non-Walrasian core allocation.

in the sequence can be improved upon by a coalition with the same number of consumers of each type at a later stage in the sequence of replica economies.)

Edgeworth argued that, provided we add enough consumers of each type, eventually *every* non-Walrasian allocation will disappear from the core so that "in the limit" only Walrasian allocations remain. In this sense, price-taking behavior can be regarded as rational provided that the environment is sufficiently competitive.[13] To illustrate this part of the argument, consider an allocation in the core of our original Cobb-Douglas economy $\mathcal{E}^1$, say

$$x_i = \begin{cases} (1.8, 1.8) & \text{if } i = 1, \\ (2.2, 2.2) & \text{if } i = 2. \end{cases}$$

As shown in Figure 1.11, while the indifference curves of the two consumers are tangent to one another (since this allocation is Pareto optimal), they are *not* tangent to the straight line which passes through the endowment point and the point x. (If they were tangent to that line, x would be a Walrasian allocation with the line serving as a Walrasian hyperplane.) Figure 1.12

13 Of course, Edgeworth did not use the word core because game theory had not yet been invented. In fact, he didn't even use the Edgeworth box, which was also introduced later by others!

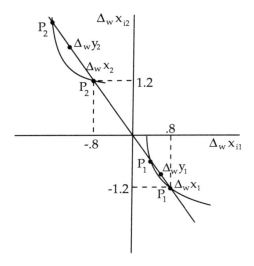

Fig. 1.12. Illustrating Edgeworth's result.

translates to the net trade diagram with net trade allocation

$$\Delta_w x_i = \begin{cases} (.8, -1.2) & \text{if } i = 1, \\ (-.8, 1.2) & \text{if } i = 2. \end{cases}$$

Suppose now that the economy has been replicated with r consumers of each type. Our goal is to find a coalition S in the replicated economy and a net trade allocation y feasible for that coalition for which $\Delta_w y_i \in \Delta_w P_i(x_i)$ for all $i \in S$. Figure 1.12 exhibits such an allocation where $\Delta_w y_1$ represents the net trade for *any* consumer of type 1, $\Delta_w y_2$ the net trade for *any* consumer of type 2, and the line segments $P_1 P_1$ and $P_2 P_2$ the preferred net trades for consumer types one and two respectively which lie along the hyperplane.

To form the coalition S, it suffices in this example to select r consumers of type 1 and $r - 1$ of type 2. For some $\epsilon > 0$, suppose that the net trade allocation takes the form

$$\Delta_w y_i = \begin{cases} (1 - \epsilon)(.8, -1.2) & \text{for consumers of type 1,} \\ (1 + \epsilon)(-.8, 1.2) & \text{for consumers of type 2.} \end{cases}$$

For example, if $\epsilon = .5$, then consumers of type 1 receive a net trade midway between the origin and $(.8, -1.2)$ while those of type 2 receive a net trade on the hyperplane 50% further from the origin than $(-.8, 1.2)$. Since these net trades are different distances from the origin, it looks as though the cancellation required for feasibility cannot be attained, a valid conclusion for coalitions with *equal* numbers of each consumer type. But the coalition S contains r members of type 1 and $r-1$ of type 2 so that feasibility requires

$$r(1 - \epsilon)(.8, -1.2) + (r - 1)(1 + \epsilon)(-.8, 1.2) = (0, 0).$$

Multiplying out each coordinate yields the two equations

$$r(1 - \epsilon)(.8) + (r - 1)(1 + \epsilon)(-.8) = 0$$
$$r(1 - \epsilon)(-1.2) + (r - 1)(1 + \epsilon)(1.2) = 0$$

which reduce to the same expression. Solving for ϵ as a function of r gives $\epsilon = 1/(2r - 1)$. If $r = 1$ then $\epsilon = 1$, which means that a coalition consisting of one consumer of type one and zero consumers of type two can only achieve the origin in this way (i.e., no trade, a conclusion which is obvious enough). However, as r increases, ϵ approaches 0. This implies that, given enough replication, we can find a net trade allocation $\Delta_w y$ of this form which lies in the preferred sets of each consumer no matter how minuscule the targets $P_1 P_1$ and $P_2 P_2$. Therefore, the allocation x can eventually be improved upon: it does not remain in the core for all r.

Largely ignored for over seventy-five years, Edgeworth's result (1881) was rediscovered by Shubik (1959), rigorously analyzed by Scarf (1962), and elegantly generalized to an arbitrary number of commodities and consumer types by Debreu and Scarf (1963). While the **Debreu-Scarf Core Equivalence Theorem** retains Edgeworth's assumption of exact replication with the replica economies required to have exactly the same number of consumers of each type, their result has itself inspired generalizations that go far beyond sequences of replica economies.

1.5 Commodities and prices

Of all the ways in which modern, mathematical general equilibrium theory has changed the way in which economists think about economics, perhaps none is more profound — or more elementary — than the way we view commodities. Handling an arbitrary number of commodities as easily as two, the modern perspective encourages a point of view in which any aspect of consumption or production which matters to consumers or firms is reflected in the definition of a commodity. What this means, in particular, is that each seemingly basic category (say, frozen orange juice) must be subdivided into distinct commodities according to location (Malibu, CA), date (when packaged or consumed), and state of the world (the weather in California and Florida).

Doing justice to the richness — and the limitations — of the competitive model applied to location, dynamics, risk, and uncertainty lies well beyond the scope of this book. The two brief illustrations which follow are intended only to whet your appetite, not to satisfy it.

1.5.1 *Contingent commodities*

Our first example treats risk. Suppose that there are two consumers and two types of commodity, rice (1) and wheat (2), available in two states of the world, s_1 or s_2. Each consumer plants both types of crop, rice (which prospers when it rains) and wheat (which benefits from lots of sun). When the rain comes, which it certainly will, it falls mostly on the plot of consumer 1 (state s_1) or on the plot of consumer 2 (state s_2).

Obeying the injunction to distinguish states of the world, we recognize that there are really four commodities, not two:

$1, s_1$: rice when the rain falls mostly on consumer 1;

$2, s_1$: wheat when the rain falls mostly on consumer 1;

$1, s_2$: rice when the rain falls mostly on consumer 2;

$2, s_2$: wheat when the rain falls mostly on consumer 2.

Let $w_{ij}(s)$ denote the endowment and $x_{ij}(s)$ the allocation of commodity j to consumer i in state of the world s. Assume that four units of rice and four units of wheat will be available in either state of the world, split between the two consumers as follows:

$$w_i := (w_{i1}(s_1), w_{i2}(s_1), w_{i1}(s_2), w_{i2}(s_2)) = \begin{cases} (3, 1, 1, 3) & \text{for } i = 1; \\ (1, 3, 3, 1) & \text{for } i = 2. \end{cases}$$

Figure 1.13 shows the Edgeworth box associated with each state of the world.

We will assume that each consumer is a von Neumann-Morgenstern utility maximizer.[14] Specifically, consumer i

- evaluates the allocation of rice and wheat received in state s via the state independent Cobb-Douglas utility function

$$u_i(x_i(s)) = .5 \log x_{i1}(s) + .5 \log x_{i2}(s); \quad \text{and}$$

- attaches subjective probability π_i to state s_1 and $1 - \pi_i$ to state s_2.

Therefore, under the expected utility hypothesis, consumer i evaluates the

---

14 I assume you are acquainted with the basic features of expected utility theory as presented, for example, in Kreps (1990), Chapter 3.

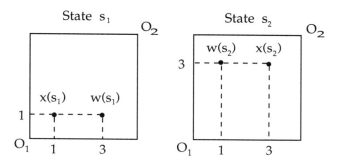

Fig. 1.13. Walrasian equilibrium under uncertainty.

entire four-component allocation according to the utility function

$$
\begin{aligned}
U_i(x_i) &= \pi_i u_i(x_i(s_1)) + (1 - \pi_i) u_i(x_i(s_2)) \\
&= \pi_i \left[.5 \log(x_{i1}(s_1)) + .5 \log(x_{i2}(s_1)) \right] \\
&\quad + (1 - \pi_i) \left[.5 \log(x_{i1}(s_2)) + .5 \log(x_{i2}(s_2)) \right].
\end{aligned}
$$

Finding the Walrasian equilibrium for this economy is now an easy application of what we have done before. Letting

$$
p = (p_1(s_1), p_2(s_1), p_1(s_2), p_2(s_2))
$$

denote the equilibrium prices associated with our four contingent commodities, the demand set of consumer i takes the usual Cobb-Douglas form

$$
\phi_i(p) = \left(\frac{.5\pi_i \, p \cdot w_i}{p_1(s_1)}, \ \frac{.5\pi_i \, p \cdot w_i}{p_2(s_1)}, \ \frac{.5(1 - \pi_i) \, p \cdot w_i}{p_1(s_2)}, \ \frac{.5(1 - \pi_i) \, p \cdot w_i}{p_2(s_2)} \right)
$$

with consumer wealth given by

$$
p \cdot w_i = \begin{cases} 3p_1(s_1) + p_2(s_1) + p_1(s_2) + 3p_2(s_2) & \text{for } i = 1; \\ p_1(s_1) + 3p_2(s_1) + 3p_1(s_2) + p_2(s_2) & \text{for } i = 2. \end{cases}
$$

We will normalize prices so that they sum to one.

Solving this system is then simply a matter of solving the (linear) clearing equations for any three of the markets plus the price normalization equation. We give the results for two special cases:

CASE 1: $\pi_1 = \pi_2 = \pi$. (The consumers agree on the probability of each state.) As you can easily verify, equilibrium prices are

$$p = \left(\frac{\pi}{2}, \frac{\pi}{2}, \frac{1-\pi}{2}, \frac{1-\pi}{2}\right).$$

Although equilibrium prices vary with π, consumer wealth and the equilibrium allocation do not: $p \cdot w_1 = p \cdot w_2 = 2$ and $x_i = (2, 2, 2, 2)$ for $i = 1, 2$ for any choice of π.

CASE 2: $\pi_1 = \pi$ and $\pi_2 = 1 - \pi$. (The two consumers attach diametrically opposed probabilities to the states.) From the symmetry of the problem, we conclude that $p = (1/4, 1/4, 1/4, 1/4)$ and so $p \cdot w_1 = p \cdot w_2 = 2$ for any choice of π. If $\pi = 1/2$, then each consumer receives the allocation $x_i = (2, 2, 2, 2)$ as before. However, if $\pi = 1/4$ then the equilibrium allocation becomes

$$x_i = \begin{cases} (1, 1, 3, 3) & \text{for } i = 1; \\ (3, 3, 1, 1) & \text{for } i = 2. \end{cases}$$

This allocation is illustrated in the Edgeworth boxes of Figure 1.13.

What interpretation do we give to trade in these commodities contingent on the state of the world? When translated into net trades, the allocation just considered becomes

$$\Delta_w x_i = \begin{cases} (-2, 0, 2, 0) & \text{for } i = 1; \\ (2, 0, -2, 0) & \text{for } i = 2. \end{cases}$$

Consumer one, relatively confident that the rain will fall mostly on her neighbor, offers to give up two units of rice in the event that the rain falls mostly on her in exchange for two units of rice in the event that the rain falls on her neighbor. Consumer two, equally confident that the odds run the opposite way, accepts this trade.

Viewing competitive markets in terms of contracts predicated on every possible contingency has had a major impact on the way we view insurance, stock markets, commodity futures, and the like. Equally important has been the realization that existing markets do not provide for every such contingency, clear evidence that the standard Walras-Arrow-Debreu model just illustrated is only part of the story.

1.5.2 Overlapping generations

To illustrate the treatment of time within the Walrasian model, we consider a simple but highly instructive version of an overlapping generations (OLG) model adapted from Geanakoplos (1987).

Consumers in the economy are indexed by the set

$$I = \{-T, -(T-1), \ldots, 0, \ldots, T-1, T\}$$

where T is a large, positive integer. In this model the set I does double duty, indexing time as well as consumers with $t = 0$ denoting the present, $-T$ the distant past, and T the distant future. There is a single perishable commodity available at each date $t \in I$.

A single consumer is born at each date $t \in I$, the sole representative of her generation, and lives for two periods. Consumer $t \in I$, the consumer born at time t, has endowment

$$w^t = (0, \ldots, e, 1-e, \ldots, 0) \in L_+ := \mathbf{R}_+^{2T+1}$$

defined by

$$w_s^t = \begin{cases} e & \text{if } s = t, \\ 1-e & \text{if } s = t+1, \\ 0 & \text{otherwise.} \end{cases}$$

Caring only about consumption during her lifetime, she has a Cobb-Douglas utility function $u^t(x^t) = (x_t^t)^a (x_{t+1}^t)^{1-a}$. Throughout we will assume that $e > a \geq 1/2$ and choose the time 0 commodity as *numéraire* (i.e., setting $p_0 = 1$). We will also find it convenient to introduce the ratios $q_t := p_{t+1}/p_t$ representing the price next period relative to the present.

Since the wealth of the consumer born at t is

$$p \cdot w^t = p_t e + p_{t+1}(1-e) = p_t[e + q_t(1-e)],$$

her demand for the commodity at time t becomes

$$\phi_t^t(p) = \frac{a\, p \cdot w^t}{p_t} = a[e + q_t(1-e)]$$

and her demand at time $t+1$

$$\phi_{t+1}^t(p) = \frac{(1-a)\, p \cdot w^t}{p_{t+1}} = \frac{(1-a)[e + q_t(1-e)]}{q_t}.$$

Solving for the unique Walrasian equilibrium in this model is easy provided that we work backward from the end of time. Since the consumer born at time $T-1$ will be the sole survivor in period T, she can do no better than to consume her endowment at that date: $x_T^{T-1} = 1-e$. But, because she has no hope of receiving anything more than her endowment in period T, there is nothing she can gain in exchange for relinquishing part of her endowment in period $T-1$. Thus, she consumes her endowment $x_{T-1}^{T-1} = e$ in period $T-1$. This in turn means that the old timer alive at date $T-1$,

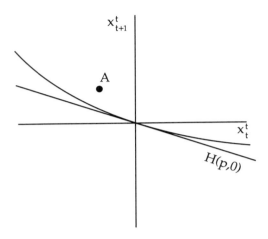

Fig. 1.14. Walrasian equilibrium in an OLG model.

the consumer born at $T - 2$, has no choice but to consume her endowment
at date $T - 1$: i.e., $x_{T-1}^{T-2} = 1 - e$. Continuing to work backward in this
fashion to the beginning of time leads to the dismal conclusion that the
only Walrasian allocation involves no trade: each consumer consumes her
own endowment. Figure 1.14 shows a two-dimensional slice of the net trade
diagram corresponding to the lifetime of the consumer born at time t along
with her net strict preference set and the unique hyperplane through 0 which
supports this no trade equilibrium. You should have no trouble verifying
that the equilibrium price functional takes the form

$$p = \left(\frac{1}{\bar{q}^T}, \frac{1}{\bar{q}^{T-1}}, \ldots, \frac{1}{\bar{q}}, 1, \bar{q}, \bar{q}^2, \ldots, \bar{q}^T \right)$$

with

$$q_t = \bar{q} = \left(\frac{1-a}{1-e} \right) \left(\frac{e}{a} \right).$$

The figure illustrates the case $e = 3/4$ and $a = 1/2$, which yields $\bar{q} = 3$.

Rather than assuming time begins and ends at a fixed date (which seems
rather artificial), suppose that we now allow time to extend from the indefinite past to the indefinite future. Thus, we replace the set I indexing
consumers and commodities by the entire set of integers,

$$\mathbf{Z} = \{ \ldots, -3, -2, -1, 0, 1, 2, 3, \ldots \}.$$

All other features of the model remain the same.

It is easy to see that no trade remains an equilibrium in this modified version of the model with $q_t = \bar{q}$ as before. However, now there is another equilibrium as well.[15] The market clearing equation at date t,

$$a[e + q_t(1 - e)] + \frac{(1 - a)[e + q_{t-1}(1 - e)]}{q_{t-1}} = 1,$$

has two solutions involving an unchanging value for q_{t-1}: the no trade solution with $q_t = \bar{q}$ and another with $q_t = 1$ for all t. The latter solution implies an equilibrium price functional

$$p = (\ldots, 1, 1, 1, \ldots) \in L'_+ := \mathbf{R}_+^{\mathbf{Z}}$$

with the consumer born at time t receiving the equilibrium commodity bundle

$$x^t = (\ldots, a, 1 - a, \ldots) \in L_+ := \mathbf{R}_+^{\mathbf{Z}}$$

defined by

$$x_s^t = \begin{cases} a & \text{if } s = t, \\ 1 - a & \text{if } s = t + 1, \\ 0 & \text{otherwise.} \end{cases}$$

Corresponding to this allocation is the net trade allocation $\Delta_w x^t \in L$ defined by

$$\Delta_w x_s^t = \begin{cases} a - e & \text{if } s = t, \\ e - a & \text{if } s = t + 1, \\ 0 & \text{otherwise,} \end{cases}$$

which is exhibited in Figure 1.14 as the point labeled A.[16]

Because the version of this model with finite time horizon falls within the scope of this chapter, that version's unique (no trade) Walrasian equilibrium is both Pareto optimal and in the core. However, in the infinite dimensional case (i.e., with $I = \mathbf{Z}$ and $L = \mathbf{R}^{\mathbf{Z}}$), our proofs of Theorems 1.12 and 1.17 no longer apply. And, in fact,

- the no trade Walrasian equilibrium with $q_t = \bar{q}$ for all t is not Pareto optimal; while
- the alternative stationary Walrasian equilibrium with $q_t = 1$ for all t is Pareto optimal but not in the core!

Verifying each of these assertions is quite easy:

15 In fact, there is a continuum of equilibria bracketed by the two stationary equilibria discussed here (see Geanakoplos (1987)).

16 With $e = 3/4$ and $a = 1/2$, the net trade allocation to consumer t becomes $(-1/4, 1/4)$.

- The function $x^a(1-x)^{1-a}$ is maximized at $x = a$ with $a^a(1-a)^{1-a} > e^a(1-e)^{1-a}$ so that the alternative stationary equilibrium is preferred to the no trade equilibrium by every consumer; and

- For any time $t_0 \in I$, the coalition $S = \{\, t \in I \mid t \geq t_0 \,\}$ can achieve its part of the alternative stationary equilibrium using only its own resources and improve upon it by giving to the young person at time t_0 the commodity bundle intended for the old. Thus, the alternative stationary equilibrium is not in the core.[17]

What do we learn from this shocking example? Primarily that we must be cautious in generalizing from finite to infinite dimensions. I have purposely adopted a coordinate-free notation in this book intended to make economies with infinite dimensional commodity spaces seem a natural extension of those in finite dimensions. But I do not want you to conclude that nothing changes. As we have just seen, the proofs of Theorems 1.12 and 1.17 — which seem so automatic in finite dimensions — fall apart in infinite dimensions.

1.6 Summary

The summary which ends each chapter of this book is intended not to recapitulate everything that has been said but rather to highlight what seems most important.

What is important in this chapter is the view of commodities as vectors, prices as linear functionals, and Walrasian equilibrium as separation by a hyperplane of what is preferred from what can be afforded. Geometry is a critical aid to intuition throughout the mathematical analysis of competition. The Edgeworth box excels at interpreting results, the net trade diagram in illuminating proofs. Both are valuable.

The proofs of the two main results of this chapter, that Walrasian equilibria are necessarily Pareto optimal and in the core, seem seductively simple. Do they only prove the obvious? As our discussion of the overlapping generations model indicates, in infinite dimensions both assertions can fail. The proofs in finite dimensions, while simple, are not vacuous.

Exercises

1.1   The most straightforward way to show that $S \subset T$ is to prove the

---

17 More precisely, it is not in the core defined using the weaker form of dominance. Can the alternative stationary equilibrium be strongly dominated by S?

following assertion:

$$\text{``if} \quad x \in S, \quad \text{then} \quad x \in T.\text{''} \qquad (*)$$

Any assertion of the form $A \Rightarrow B$ (read: "A implies B") can be transformed into the logically equivalent assertion given by the **contrapositive**: $\neg B \Rightarrow \neg A$ (read: "not B implies not A").

(a) Use the contrapositive of $(*)$ to obtain an equivalent assertion that can be used to show that $S \subset T$. Apply $(*)$ and its contrapositive to prove that $\mathbf{Z} \subset \mathbf{R}$.

(b) The **converse** of an assertion $A \Rightarrow B$ is the assertion $B \Rightarrow A$. Use assertion $(*)$ and its converse to illustrate that an assertion can be true but its converse false.

1.2 Prove that $\bigcap_{\alpha \in \mathbf{R}_+} [-\alpha, \alpha] = \{0\}$.

1.3 Which of the following functions $f \colon \mathbf{R} \to \mathbf{R}$ are injective? surjective? bijective?

(a) $f \colon x \mapsto 2 + 3x$
(b) $f \colon x \mapsto 2$
(c) $f \colon x \mapsto x^3 - x$
(d) $f \colon x \mapsto x/(1 + |x|)$.

For each function that fails to be bijective, find a restriction of the domain and/or range to a subset of $\mathbf{R}$ which will make the function bijective. For each bijective function $f \colon X \to Y$ obtained (where X and Y denote the subsets of $\mathbf{R}$ which you specified in order to make the function bijective), describe the inverse of the function and verify that $f \circ f^{-1} = \mathrm{id}_Y$ and $f^{-1} \circ f = \mathrm{id}_X$.

1.4 Describe the span of each of the following subsets of $\mathbf{R}^3$:

(a) $\{(0, 1, 1)\}$;
(b) $\{(0, 1, 1), (1, 0, 1)\}$;
(c) $\{(0, 1, 1), (1, 0, 1), (1, 1, 0)\}$.

1.5 Draw the hyperplanes and closed halfspaces in $\mathbf{R}^2$ corresponding to each of the following linear functionals represented by the vectors $p \in \mathbf{R}^2$:

(a) $p = (1, 2)$;
(b) $p = (1, -2)$;
(c) $p = (-1, -2)$.

1.6 Verify that the dual space of a vector space is itself a vector space.

1.7 Prove that if $M = M_1 \oplus M_2$ where M_1 and M_2 are subspaces of the vector space L, then each $x \in M$ can be uniquely expressed as a sum $x = m_1 + m_2$ where $m_1 \in M_1$ and $m_2 \in M_2$.

1.8 Suppose that M_1 is a subspace of codimension one of the vector space L. Let z be any nonzero vector that does not belong to the subspace M_1.

(a) For each $x \in L$, there is a *unique* scalar $p(x)$ and a *unique* vector $m_1(x) \in M_1$ such that $x = m_1(x) + p(x)z$. Why?

(b) Show that the mapping $p: L \to \mathbf{R}$ defined in part (a) is linear with kernel $H(p,0) = M_1$.

1.9 Conversely, suppose that we define a hyperplane to be the kernel of a linear functional $p: L \to \mathbf{R}$ where $p \cdot z \neq 0$ for some $z \in L$. Let $M_1 = \ker p$ and $M_2 = \{ x \in L \mid x = \lambda z, \lambda \in \mathbf{R} \}$. Prove that $L = M_1 \oplus M_2$, so that $M_1 = \ker p$ is a subspace of codimension one.

1.10 Describe the consumption set of a consumer in a two-commodity exchange economy in which:

(a) the first commodity is perfectly divisible while the second can be consumed only in integer amounts; and

(b) the quantities of both commodities are nonnegative.

1.11 Letting $A = \{ (1,1), (2,3) \}$ and $B = \{ (0,0), (-1,-2) \}$, describe the sets $A + B$, $2A$, and $2A + B$.

1.12 Give an example of a set $A \subset \mathbf{R}^2$ for which $2A \subset A + A$ but $2A \neq A + A$.

1.13 Develop an alternative proof of Theorem 1.17 along the lines of the alternative proof given for Theorem 1.12.

1.14 Consider a pure exchange economy with two consumers and two commodities. Each consumer has consumption set $X_i = \mathbf{R}_+^2$, and endowments are given by

$$w_i = \begin{cases} (1,3) & \text{for } i = 1, \\ (3,1) & \text{for } i = 2. \end{cases}$$

Utility functions are of "Leontief type" (i.e., indifference sets are L-shaped), described by utility functions of the form:

$$u_i(x_i) = \min\{ x_{i1}/\alpha_i, x_{i2}/\beta_i \}$$

where α_i and β_i are positive constants. For each of the following two cases, determine the set of Pareto optima, Walrasian, and core allocations for the economy. Illustrate each of the sets in an Edgeworth box and in a net trade diagram.

(a)
$$(\alpha_i, \beta_i) = \begin{cases} (2,1) & \text{if } i = 1, \\ (1,2) & \text{if } i = 2. \end{cases}$$

(b)
$$(\alpha_i, \beta_i) = (2,1) \quad \text{for} \quad i = 1, 2.$$

1.15 Repeat the preceding exercise for a two-person exchange economy in which endowments are given by

$$w_i = \begin{cases} (0,4) & \text{if } i = 1, \\ (4,0) & \text{if } i = 2 \end{cases}$$

and preferences are represented by the utility function

$$u_i(x_i) = x_{i1} + 2x_{i2} \quad \text{for} \quad i = 1, 2.$$

1.16 A pure exchange economy contains two consumers, both with preferences represented by a utility function of the form:

$$u_i(x_i) = x_{i1}(4 - x_{i2})$$

defined over the consumption set $[0,5] \times [0,3] \subset \mathbf{R}_+^2$. Thus, the first commodity is a "good" and the second a "bad." Endowments are given by

$$w_i = \begin{cases} (4,3) & \text{if } i = 1, \\ (1,0) & \text{if } i = 2. \end{cases}$$

(a) Show that consumer demand functions are given by

$$\phi_i(p) = \left(\frac{p \cdot w_i - 4p_2}{2p_1}, \frac{p \cdot w_i + 4p_2}{2p_2} \right).$$

(b) Show that a feasible allocation x is Pareto optimal iff $x_{11} + x_{12} = 4$ where $x_1 = (x_{11}, x_{12})$ is the commodity bundle allocated to consumer one.

(c) Determine the set of core allocations for this economy and illustrate in an Edgeworth box.

(d) Show that the Walrasian equilibrium price functional for this economy is $p = (1, -1)$ where prices have been normalized by choosing the first commodity as *numéraire*.

(e) Calculate the Walrasian equilibrium for this economy and indicate this allocation as a point in the Edgeworth box. (Hint: be careful to remember that $p_2 < 0$.)

(f) Sketch the relevant hyperplane, Walrasian allocation, and preferred net trade sets in the net trade diagram.

(g) What happens to the core and to the Walrasian equilibrium if the first consumer has the right to dump all of her endowment of the second commodity onto the second consumer (i.e., she is a polluter with the right to pollute without compensating the other consumer)?

(h) What happens to the core and to the Walrasian equilibrium if property rights regarding the second commodity are not assigned (i.e., whether the first consumer can dump her garbage onto the second consumer's lawn without compensating him depends on political or other considerations not specified by the model)?

1.17   Consider a two-person exchange economy in which endowments are given by

$$w_i = \begin{cases} (1,3) & \text{if } i = 1, \\ (3,1) & \text{if } i = 2 \end{cases}$$

and the preferences of both consumers by the **vector ordering preference relation**: i.e., for any two commodity bundles $x' = (\xi_1', \xi_2')$ and $x = (\xi_1, \xi_2)$, we have $x' \succ x$ iff $\xi_1' > \xi_1$ and $\xi_2' > \xi_2$. Illustrate in an Edgeworth box and in a net trade diagram the allocations which are Walrasian and those which are in the core.

1.18   The two consumers of an exchange economy have preferences represented by a utility function of the form

$$u_i(x_i) = \max\{\, \min\{\, x_{i1}, 2x_{i2} \,\}, \min\{\, 2x_{i1}, x_{i2} \,\} \,\},$$

which yield stair step indifference contours as illustrated below. Endowments are given by $w_1 = w_2 = (1.5, 1.5)$.

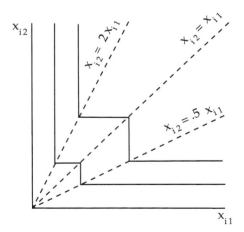

(a) Illustrate the budget set, demand set, and strict preference set

$P_i(x_i)$ for $x_i \in \phi_i(p)$ for either one of the consumers when $p = (.5, .5)$; when $p = (.25, .75)$.

(b) In an Edgeworth box, indicate the set of (i) individually rational, (ii) Pareto optimal, and (iii) core allocations for this economy.

(c) In this economy, there are two Walrasian allocations, say x and y. Determine the equilibrium price functional p (letting $p_1 + p_2 = 1$), and describe the allocations x and y. (Give the answer numerically.) Calculate the corresponding net trade allocations, and depict the Walrasian equilibria in a net trade diagram. In this sketch, show as well the strict preference sets corresponding to either allocation.

(d) Now suppose that there is a third consumer with the same consumption sets, preferences, and endowment as the other two. Using the net trade diagram, show that there is no Walrasian equilibrium for the economy.

(e) If we add a fourth consumer of the same type, do Walrasian equilibria exist for the economy?

(f) Combining your answers to parts (d) and (e), what is your conjecture about the existence or nonexistence of Walrasian equilibria if we continue to add consumers of the same type to this economy?

1.19 By writing down the analogs of equations (1.1) and (1.2) for a replica of the two-person Cobb-Douglas economy with r consumers of each type, verify that the Walrasian equilibrium prices and allocation do not change as r increases.

1.20 Following along the lines of the argument given in Section 1.4.2, show that in the sequence of Cobb-Douglas replica economies the allocation

$$x_i = \begin{cases} (2.2, 2.2) & \text{for } i = 1, \\ (1.8, 1.8) & \text{for } i = 2 \end{cases}$$

can eventually be improved upon by some coalition. (Hint: consider a coalition with $r - 1$ members of type 1 and r of type 2.)

1.21 Verify the assertions made for cases 1 and 2 in the contingent commodity model of Section 1.5.1.

1.22 It hardly seems possible that the points labeled x and w in Figure 1.13 lie on the hyperplane defined by $p = (1/4, 1/4, 1/4, 1/4)$, but they do. Explain.

1.23 Where do the proofs of Theorems 1.12 and 1.17 go wrong when applied to the infinite dimensional overlapping generations model?

2

Production

Pure exchange seems quintessentially academic, a storybook portrayal of economic interaction far removed from what we observe in all but the most primitive of societies. Production, and the organization of production by firms, must surely be regarded as the very essence of a modern, capitalistic economy. You might imagine, therefore, that allowing for production would lead to a drastic modification of the theory of general equilibrium. But you would be wrong because, at least as the theory is currently formulated, adding production changes very little.

Of course, the fact that not much changes is a signal that the general equilibrium theory of production does not amount to much. The passive, price-taking firm in Walrasian equilibrium provides little scope for entrepreneurial skill or managerial know-how. But, having acknowledged these shortcomings, it is equally important to give the general equilibrium treatment of production its due. Viewed on its own terms, it is an intellectual *tour de force* — the first (some would say the only!) successful attempt to build a model in which consumers and firms interact in a logically consistent fashion.

The goal of this chapter is neither to disparage the general equilibrium theory of production nor to claim more than the theory can deliver. Rather I emphasize what is perhaps the most attractive feature of this theoretical point of view, the clear parallel which it draws between economies of pure exchange and those with production, a parallel emphasized both through choice of notation and through the use of an (appropriately modified) net trade diagram.

The chapter begins with a discussion of the mathematics of convexity. The second section develops the basic features of Walrasian equilibrium with production operating under constant returns to scale. The third section briefly surveys two leading alternatives to the constant returns formulation, the Arrow-Debreu economy (which allows for diminishing returns) and the coalition production economy (which emphasizes the core).

Because this chapter stresses the similarities between pure exchange and production, you might well wonder whether introducing production is worth the bother. I end the chapter with a discussion of a lively dispute concerning the relationship between joint production and public goods which should ease those doubts.

2.1 Geometry of vector spaces

We begin by taking a closer look at some of the geometric aspects of vector spaces.

2.1.1 Convexity

Recall that a linear combination of elements in a vector space L is an expression of the form $\alpha x + \beta y$ where $x, y \in L$ and $\alpha, \beta \in \mathbf{R}$. Two specific types of linear combination merit special attention: affine combination and convex combination. Moving from linear, to affine, to convex combination involves the placing of additional restrictions on the scalars used in forming the combination. Linear combination requires only that the scalars be real numbers. Affine combination adds the restriction that the scalars sum to one. Convex combination further demands that each scalar be nonnegative (and so, since they must add to one, each must lie between 0 and 1).

A set S in a vector space is called a **linear subspace** if it is closed with respect to linear combination: forming a linear combination of elements in S yields a vector that also belongs to S. Similarly, S is an **affine subspace** if it is closed with respect to affine combination and a **convex set** if it is closed with respect to convex combination. Formally,

Definition 2.1 *A subset S of a vector space L is*

- *a **linear subspace** if $\alpha x + \beta y \in S$ for all $x, y \in S$ and for all $\alpha, \beta \in \mathbf{R}$;*
- *an **affine subspace** if $\alpha x + (1 - \alpha)y \in S$ for all $x, y \in S$ and for all $\alpha \in \mathbf{R}$;*
- *a **convex set** if $\alpha x + (1 - \alpha)y \in S$ for all $x, y \in S$ and for all $\alpha \in [0, 1]$.*

In addition to using linear, affine, or convex combination to test whether a set is linear, affine, or convex we can build sets with those properties. Specifically,

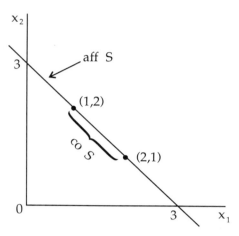

Fig. 2.1. aff S and co S.

Definition 2.2 *Let S be an arbitrary collection of vectors in the vector space L.*

- *The set of all possible linear combinations of vectors in S is called the **span** of S, denoted sp S. Equivalently, sp S is the smallest linear subspace which contains S.*

- *The set of all possible affine combinations of vectors in S is called the **affine hull** of S, denoted aff S. Equivalently, aff S is the smallest affine subspace which contains S.*

- *The set of all possible convex combinations of vectors in S is called the **convex hull** of S, denoted co S. Equivalently, co S is the smallest convex set which contains S.*

Turning full circle, we conclude that a set S contained in a vector space L is a linear subspace if $S = $ sp S, an affine subspace if $S = $ aff S, and a convex set if $S = $ co S. There is nothing new in this, of course, but the rephrasing provides useful insight nevertheless.

Where is the geometry in all of this? Just as in the case of the hyperplanes and halfspaces of Chapter 1, examples in two or three dimensions provide an accurate metaphor for what happens in vector spaces of arbitrary dimension.

Consider, for example, the vector space $L = \mathbf{R}^2$ and the set

$$S = \{\,(2,1),(1,2)\,\}.$$

In the first chapter, we found that $\text{sp}\, S = \mathbf{R}^2$ because S is a basis for L. However,

$$\text{aff}\, S = \{\, x \in \mathbf{R}^2 \mid x = \alpha(2,1) + (1-\alpha)(1,2),\ \alpha \in \mathbf{R} \,\}$$

is not equal to $\mathbf{R}^2$. Evaluating this affine combination yields

$$\alpha(2,1) + (1-\alpha)(1,2) = (1+\alpha, 2-\alpha).$$

As α varies from $-\infty$ to $+\infty$, the point $(1+\alpha, 2-\alpha)$ traces out a *line* passing through $(2,1)$ and $(1,2)$ as illustrated by the line labeled aff S in Figure 2.1. If we further restrict α to lie between 0 and 1, then as α varies from 0 to 1 we obtain only the *line segment* with endpoints $(2,1)$ and $(1,2)$ as shown by the line segment labeled co S in Figure 2.1.

Note that aff S looks very much like a vector subspace: it is a one-dimensional line extending indefinitely in both directions. It is *not* a vector subspace because it does not pass through the point $(0,0)$ and every vector subspace must contain the 0 vector. However, we can express the set $A = \text{aff}\, S$ as a *translation* of a linear subspace

$$M = \{\, x \in \mathbf{R}^2 \mid x = \alpha(1,-1),\ \alpha \in \mathbf{R} \,\}.$$

Specifically, $A = c + M$ where[1] $c = (1,2)$. For any $a \in A$, we have

$$a = c + m = (1,2) + \alpha(1,-1) = (1+\alpha, 2-\alpha),$$

precisely the expression we obtained above for a typical element of A. As this example suggests, an alternative definition of what it means for a subset S of a vector space L to be an **affine subspace**, equivalent to the definition given earlier, is that S can be expressed in the form $S = c + M$ where M is a linear subspace.

Suppose that we add a third vector $(2,2)$ to the set $S = \{\, v^1, v^2 \,\} = \{\, (2,1), (1,2) \,\}$ to obtain $S' = \{\, v^1, v^2, v^3 \,\} = \{\, (2,1), (1,2), (2,2) \,\}$. Since $\text{sp}\, S = \mathbf{R}^2$, the set S' cannot be linearly independent. v^3 is redundant, and adding it to S does not increase the span: $\text{sp}\, S = \text{sp}\, S' = \mathbf{R}^2$. However, adding v^3 to S does change the affine hull and the convex hull: aff $S' = \mathbf{R}^2$, and

$$\text{co}\, S' = \{\, x \in L \mid x = \alpha_1 v^1 + \alpha_2 v^2 + \alpha_3 v^3;\, a_1, a_2, a_3 \in [0,1];\, \textstyle\sum \alpha_i = 1 \,\}.$$

The affine hull of S' now equals all of $\mathbf{R}^2$, and the convex hull is the triangle shown in Figure 2.2.

Although not used in this chapter, the following two theorems provide

---

1 The choice of $c = (1,2)$ is not uniquely determined. Any $c' \in$ aff S will lead to the result $A = c' + M$.

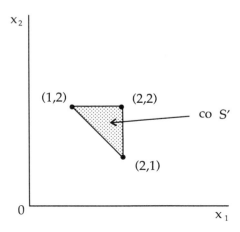

Fig. 2.2. co S'.

a good opportunity to observe how visualizing in two dimensions helps in understanding abstract proofs about vector spaces. Before presenting the theorems we need to clear up one piece of unfinished business regarding operations on sets. Up to this point, we have used the concept of a Cartesian product rather informally: $S_1 \times S_2$ is the set of ordered pairs of the form (x_1, x_2) where $x_1 \in S_1$ and $x_2 \in S_2$ or, more generally, $\prod_{i \in I} S_i$ for $I = \{1, \ldots, n\}$ is the set of ordered n-tuples of the form $(x_1, \ldots, x_n)$ where $x_i \in S_i$ for all $i \in I$.

What meaning if any can we attach to a product $\prod_{i \in I} S_i$ for an arbitrary index set which might have an uncountable number of elements, say, $I = [0, 1]$? The key is to view the n-tuple $(x_1, \ldots, x_n)$ from a different perspective, as a function $x \colon I \to \bigcup_{i \in I} S_i$, $i \mapsto x_i \in S_i$. Viewed this way, a general definition of Cartesian product is easy to establish: $\prod_{i \in I} S_i = \{x \colon I \to \bigcup_{i \in I} S_i \mid i \mapsto x_i \in S_i\}$. An element of the Cartesian product is simply a function which selects a representative element from each of the sets in the product.

Theorem 2.3 *Let $\{S_i \subset L_i \mid i \in I\}$ be a collection of nonempty sets indexed by a set I where each L_i is a vector space. The cartesian product $L := \prod_{i \in I} L_i$ is then a vector space. If each S_i is a linear subspace (resp. affine subspace, convex subset) of L_i, then $\prod_{i \in I} S_i$ is a linear subspace (resp. affine subspace, convex subset) of L.*

Proof Verifying that L is a vector space is immediate. If $x, x' \in S$, $\alpha, \beta \in \mathbf{R}$, and each S_i is a linear subspace, then $\alpha x + \beta x'$ is a function mapping $i \mapsto \alpha x_i + \beta x'_i \in S_i$. Therefore, by definition $\alpha x + \beta x' \in \prod_{i \in I} S_i$. Modifying the proof to cover affine subspaces or convex sets is easy!   □

The next result shows that the operations of intersection and linear combination are similarly well-behaved.

Theorem 2.4 *Let $\{\, S_i \subset L \mid i \in I \,\}$ be a collection of nonempty subsets of a vector space L and $\{\, \alpha_i \mid i \in I \,\}$ a collection of scalars where I is an index set and at most a finite number of the scalars α_i are nonzero. If each S_i is a linear subspace (resp. affine subspace, convex subset) of L, then $\bigcap_{i \in I} S_i$ and $\sum_{i \in I} \alpha_i S_i$ are linear subspaces (resp. affine subspaces, convex subsets) of L.*

Proof We will prove that the linear combination of convex sets is convex, leaving the rest of the proof as Exercise 2.7.

Let $S = \sum_{i \in I} \alpha_i S_i$ and consider an arbitrary pair of vectors $x, x' \in S$. By definition we can write $x = \sum_{i \in I} \alpha_i x_i$ and $x' = \sum_{i \in I} \alpha_i x'_i$ where $x_i, x'_i \in S_i$ for all $i \in I$. For any $\lambda \in [0, 1]$,

$$
\begin{aligned}
\lambda x + (1 - \lambda) x' &= \lambda \left[\sum_{i \in I} \alpha_i x_i \right] + (1 - \lambda) \left[\sum_{i \in I} \alpha_i x'_i \right] \\
&= \sum_{i \in I} \alpha_i \left[\lambda x_i + (1 - \lambda) x'_i \right] \\
&\in S
\end{aligned}
$$

since $\lambda x_i + (1 - \lambda) x'_i \in S_i$ for all $i \in I$ because each set S_i is convex.   □

Note that the corresponding assertions for $\cup_{i \in I} S_i$ need not be valid: unions of linear subspaces (*resp.* affine subspaces, convex subsets) of a vector space L can easily fail to be linear subspaces (*resp.* affine subspaces, convex sets) of L.

2.1.2 *Linear and affine transformations*

This section explores yet another facet of the remarkable geometric properties of vector spaces: linear subspaces, affine subspaces, and convex sets retain their characteristic property when subjected to linear or affine transformation. Without this fact, the net trade diagram introduced in Chapter 1 would have little value.

We begin by defining these two classes of function, linear and affine. The definition of a linear transformation mirrors that of a linear functional except that now we replace the codomain $\mathbf{R}$ with an arbitrary vector space Y.

Definition 2.5 *If X and Y are vector spaces, then a function $A\colon X \to Y$ is called a* **linear transformation** *if*

- $A(x + x') = Ax + Ax'$ *for all $x, x' \in X$, and*
- $A(\alpha x) = \alpha Ax$ *for all $x \in X$ and for all $\alpha \in \mathbf{R}$.*

Notice that we follow the convention of deleting parentheses when the argument of the linear function consists of a single letter: i.e., $A(x)$ and $A(x')$ are written as Ax and Ax' respectively.

In elementary algebra courses, an equation of the form $y = c + bx$ is often described as linear even though the constant term is not equal to zero. However, according to standard mathematical usage this is improper since, by definition, a linear function always maps the 0 vector in its domain to the 0 vector of its codomain. From this perspective, a function expressed as the sum of a linear function plus a constant term is more properly called an affine function.

Definition 2.6 *If X and Y are vector spaces, then a function $B\colon X \to Y$ is called an* **affine transformation** *if there exists a linear transformation $A\colon X \to Y$ and a vector $c \in Y$ such that $Bx = Ax + c$ for all $x \in X$.*

The defining properties of a linear transformation imply an exact correspondence between linear operations in X and linear operations in Y. If $x, x' \in X$ are combined to yield the vector $\alpha x + \beta x' \in X$, then the same linear combination of the images $A(x)$ and $A(x')$ in Y yields the image of $\alpha x + \beta x'$ in Y: $\alpha A(x) + \beta A(x') = A(\alpha x + \beta x')$. This is the sense in which linear transformations are said to preserve linear structure. As a consequence, linear transformations transform linear or affine subspaces and convex sets into sets of the same type as indicated by the following theorem.

Theorem 2.7 *Let $A\colon X \to Y$ be a linear transformation from the vector space X to the vector space Y and consider the subsets $S \subset X$ and $T \subset Y$.*

(a) *If S is a linear subspace (resp. affine subspace, convex subset) of X, then AS is a linear subspace (resp. affine subspace, convex subset) of Y;*

(b) *If T is a linear subspace (resp. affine subspace, convex subset) of Y, then $A^{-1}T$ is a linear subspace (resp. affine subspace, convex subset) of X.*

Proof We will prove the assertions involving convex subsets, leaving the corresponding claims involving linear or affine subspaces as Exercise 2.8.

(a) Let $y, y' \in AS$ and $\alpha \in [0,1]$. We want to show that $\alpha y + (1 - \alpha)y' \in AS$. By definition, $y = Ax$ and $y' = Ax'$ for some $x, x' \in S$. Therefore,

$$\alpha y + (1 - \alpha)y' = \alpha Ax + (1 - \alpha)Ax' = A(\alpha x + (1 - \alpha)x') \in AS$$

since $\alpha x + (1 - \alpha)x' \in S$.

(b) For any $x, x' \in A^{-1}T$ and $\alpha \in [0,1]$, we have $y := Ax \in T$ and $y' := Ax' \in T$. Because T is convex, $\alpha y + (1 - \alpha)y' \in T$ and so

$$\alpha Ax + (1 - \alpha)Ax' = A(\alpha x + (1 - \alpha)x') \in T.$$

Therefore, $\alpha x + (1 - \alpha)x' \in A^{-1}T$.

□

Since affine transformations are just translations of linear transformations, the conclusions of the preceding theorem extend in the obvious way to that case as well.

Theorem 2.8 *Let $B: X \to Y$ be an affine transformation from the vector space X to the vector space Y and consider the subsets $S \subset X$ and $T \subset Y$.*

(a) *If S is an affine subspace (resp. convex subset) of X, then BS is an affine subspace (resp. convex subset) of Y;*

(b) *If T is an affine subspace (resp. convex subset) of Y, then $B^{-1}T$ is an affine subspace (resp. convex subset) of X.*

Proof Exercise 2.10.   □

The most important application we make of Theorem 2.8 is to the translations involved in constructing the net trade diagram, maps of the form $B: L \to L$, $x \mapsto Bx = Ix - c = x - c$ where $I: L \to L$ is the identity map and c is a vector which is to serve as the new origin of the vector space. In the case of the net trade operator Δ_w, for example, the affine transformation is $\Delta_w: L \to L$, $x_i \mapsto x_i - w_i$. According to Theorem 2.8, the image of any convex set under the net trade operator (for example, a strict preference set or a budget set) remains convex.

In fact, we can claim even more. If a linear transformation $A: X \to Y$ is bijective, then the connection between the domain and codomain is particularly tight: X and Y are essentially identical as vector spaces apart from a change of coordinates. The net trade transformation is only an affine and not a linear transformation, but, because I is bijective, Δ_w will be bijective. As a result, the effect of Δ_w is much the same as that of a bijective, linear translation: the resulting image is a copy of the original with a shift of origin. All of this should, of course, seem rather obvious in $\mathbf{R}^2$, but the point is that the same "obvious" conclusions hold regardless of the dimension of the vector space.

2.1.3 Cones

A cone is a subset of a vector space closed with respect to multiplication by positive scalars.

Definition 2.9 *A subset S of a vector space L is a **cone** if $x \in S \,\&\, \lambda > 0 \Rightarrow \lambda x \in S$. (Note that, because we have written $\lambda > 0$ rather than $\lambda \geq 0$, 0 may or may not be contained in S.) A cone S is a **proper cone** if $S \cap (-S) = \{0\}$ or $\emptyset$ and a **convex cone** if S is convex. Finally, a proper cone S is a **pointed cone** if $0 \in S$.*

A few examples should help to clarify this concept:

- a hyperplane or a closed halfspace and the vector space L itself are convex cones which are not proper;
- the origin 0 of the vector space is a proper, pointed, convex cone;
- a set $S \subset L$ closed under multiplication by nonnegative scalars is a proper, pointed cone if it is contained in an open halfspace.

In reading the literature, you should be aware that the terminology for describing cones has not been standardized. Some authors define a cone to be a set closed under multiplication by nonnegative (rather than positive) scalars; others define a cone to be what we call a convex cone; and so forth. The terminology adopted here follows Choquet (1969), Volume I, 275.

The positive and negative orthant in $\mathbf{R}^2$ provide important examples of proper, convex, pointed cones. To define the corresponding concepts for $\mathbf{R}^n$, we first introduce the following notation for inequalities between vectors.

Definition 2.10 *For vectors $x, y \in \mathbf{R}^n$ and $I = \{1, \ldots, n\}$, we write*

- $x \geq y$ *if $x_i \geq y_i$ for all $i \in I$;*
- $x > y$ *if $x_i \geq y_i$ for all $i \in I$ and $x \neq y$;*
- $x \gg y$ *if $x_i > y_i$ for all i.*

If $n > 1$, then the binary relation $\geq$ is not complete since, for example, neither $(1, 2) \geq (2, 1)$ nor $(2, 1) \geq (1, 2)$. However, $\geq$ does partially order $\mathbf{R^n}$ in the following sense.

Definition 2.11 *A binary relation $\geq$ on a set X is called a* **partial ordering** *if it is*

- *reflexive: $x \geq x$ for all $x \in X$;*
- *transitive: $x \geq y$ and $y \geq z$ implies $x \geq z$ for all $x, y, z \in X$; and*
- *antisymmetric: $x \geq y$ and $y \geq x$ iff $x = y$ for all $x, y \in X$.*

You can easily check that the vector ordering $\geq$ does partially order $\mathbf{R^n}$. In fact, it turns $\mathbf{R^n}$ into what is called an ordered vector space.

Definition 2.12 *A vector space L equipped with a partial ordering $\geq$ is an* **ordered vector space** *if for any $x, y \in L$ such that $y \geq x$*

- *$y + z \geq x + z$ for all $z \in L$; and*
- *$\alpha y \geq \alpha x$ for all $\alpha \in \mathbf{R_+}$.*

Again it is easy to check that the vector ordering $\geq$ on $\mathbf{R^m}$ satisfies the two additional requirements.

Generalizing the positive and negative orthant to an arbitrary ordered vector space is immediate.

Definition 2.13 *If L is an ordered vector space with partial ordering $\geq$, then*

- *the* **positive cone** *of L is the set $L_+ = \{\, x \in L \mid x \geq 0 \,\}$; and*
- *the* **negative cone** *of L is the set $L_- = \{\, x \in L \mid x \leq 0 \,\}$.*

Verification that L_+ and L_- are proper, convex, pointed cones is left as an exercise.

2.1.4 Recession cones

In this section we confine our attention to the vector space $L = \mathbf{R^n}$. If C is a nonempty, convex subset of L, then the **recession cone** $\mathrm{rc}\, C$ captures all of the directions (if any) in which the set C is unbounded, the directions in which it recedes to infinity.

Definition 2.14 *If C is a nonempty, convex subset of the vector space L, then the* **recession cone** *of C is defined by the relationship $y \in \mathrm{rc}\, C$ iff $x + \lambda y \in C$ for all $\lambda \geq 0$ and for all $x \in C$. Equivalently, $\mathrm{rc}\, C = \{\, y \in L \mid C + y \subset C \,\}$.*

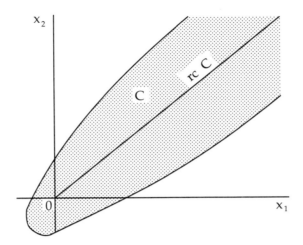

Fig. 2.3. A recession cone.

Thus, C recedes in the **direction** y if C contains a closed **halfline**

$$\{\, z \in L \mid z = x + \lambda y, \; \lambda \geq 0 \,\},$$

and the recession cone of C consists of all the directions y in which C recedes.

You should be able to verify without much difficulty that the recession cone of a nonempty convex set is, in fact, a cone: more precisely, a convex cone containing the 0 vector. In particular, the recession cone of a vector space L is L itself, $\mathrm{rc}\, L = L$; the recession cone of a halfspace corresponding to a hyperplane passing through the origin is the halfspace itself, $\mathrm{rc}\, H^{+}(p, 0) = H^{+}(p, 0)$ and $\mathrm{rc}\, H_{o}^{+}(p, 0) = H_{o}^{+}(p, 0)$; and the recession cone of the positive or negative orthant is the orthant itself $\mathrm{rc}\, L_{+} = L_{+}$ and $\mathrm{rc}\, L_{-} = L_{-}$. Less trivially, Figure 2.3 illustrates what happens with a convex set C which is not a cone: in this example, $\mathrm{rc}\, C$ is a halfline with vertex 0 pointing in the direction $(1, 1)$, the 45° line in the diagram.

The last example illustrates a remarkable phenomenon that is true quite generally for convex sets in $\mathbf{R^{n}}$: the collection of closed halflines in C which recede to infinity in some direction y is independent of the choice of vertex x. Since the set contains the 45° line with endpoint $(0, 0)$, a closed halfline of the form $\{\, z \in L \mid z = x + \lambda(1, 1), \; \lambda \geq 0 \,\}$ is also contained in C for *any* choice of vertex $x \in C$.

Actually, the assertion in the preceding paragraph is not quite correct, but before looking at the correct answer you should try to find a counterexample on your own. The following example shows what can go wrong. Consider the set $C = \mathbf{R}_{++}^2 \cup \{0\}$, where $\mathbf{R}_{++} := \{\, x \in \mathbf{R} \mid x > 0 \,\}$. Although C is a cone, the recession cone $\operatorname{rc} C$ does not equal C. While the halfline with vertex $(1,1)$ running parallel to one of the axes, say,

$$\{\, z \in \mathbf{R}^2 \mid z = (1,1) + \lambda(0,1),\ \lambda \geq 0 \,\},$$

is contained in C, the closed halfline in the same direction with vertex $(0,0)$ is not contained in C! Therefore, the recession cone of C excludes the directions parallel to the axes, and we have $\operatorname{rc} C = \mathbf{R}_{++}^2$.

The difficulty arises because the convex set C in this example does not contain its boundary points. If C does contain its boundary points (more precisely, if it is a closed set — a concept which will be defined precisely in Chapter 4), then the problems disappear. The following theorem summarizes some useful properties of recession cones under the assumption that the convex set we are dealing with is closed.

Theorem 2.15 *Let C be a nonempty, closed convex subset of the vector space $L = \mathbf{R}^\mathbf{n}$.*

- *If C contains a closed halfline with direction y and vertex $x_o \in C$, then C contains every halfline pointing in the direction y which has a vertex $x \in C$.*
- *The recession cone $\operatorname{rc} C$ is a closed, convex cone containing 0.*
- *C is bounded[2] if and only if $\operatorname{rc} C = \{0\}$.*

Proof See Rockafellar (1970), 60–64. □

2.1.5 Polar cones

Suppose that, given a closed, convex cone K in the vector space $L = \mathbf{R}^\mathbf{n}$, we want to compute the value of elements in K using a price functional $p \in L'$, the dual space of L. If we can find any $x \in K$ for which the value $p \cdot x > 0$, then the value is unbounded on K: since K is a cone, $\lambda x \in K$ for all $\lambda > 0$ so that by increasing λ we can make the value $p(\lambda x) = \lambda\, p \cdot x$ as large as we like. Therefore, if we want to guarantee that the value is always bounded we must restrict attention to those price functionals p for which $p \cdot x \leq 0$ for *all* $x \in K$. The set of such p is called the **polar cone** of K.

---

2 Formally, a set C is bounded if the maximum distance from the origin to any point in C is finite where "distance" is measured according to the Euclidean metric. Metrics are discussed in Chapter 4.

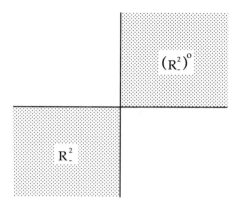

Fig. 2.4. The cone $\mathbf{R}^2_-$ and its polar.

Definition 2.16 *If K is a nonempty, closed, convex cone in $L = \mathbf{R}^n$, then the **polar cone** is the set $K^o := \{\, p \in L' \mid p \cdot x \le 0 \;\forall x \in K \,\}$.*

It is easy to verify that K^o is also a nonempty, closed, convex cone [See Rockafellar (1970), 121].

As noted in Chapter 1, the dual space of $\mathbf{R}^n$ can be represented by $\mathbf{R}^n$ itself: i.e., since a linear functional on $L = \mathbf{R}^n$ can be written in the form $p\colon L \to \mathbf{R}$, $x \mapsto p \cdot x := \sum_{i=1}^{n} p_i x_i$, we can regard p as a vector in $\mathbf{R}^n$. This means that a cone and its polar can both be represented in the same diagram.

As illustrated in Figure 2.4, the cone $K = L_-$ has polar cone $K^o = L_+$: if prices for all commodities are all nonnegative, then the value of every commodity bundle in the negative orthant will be nonpositive; however, if the price of any commodity is negative, then there exist commodity bundles in K with arbitrary large positive value. Experiment until you convince yourself that this is true.

2.2 CRS production

The introduction of production improves the descriptive power of competitive theory, but at a price: it is easy to lose sight of the forest for the trees. To avoid getting lost in details, our presentation focuses on production subject to constant returns to scale — a case which, though special, is general enough to illustrate the main principles involved.

2.2.1 Activity vectors

The central concept used to describe production is the **activity vector**, a vector $y = (y_1, \ldots, y_m) \in L$ representing a production process. Negative components of an activity vector are interpreted as inputs and positive components as outputs of the process. A few examples for an economy with five commodities ($L = \mathbf{R}^5$) should make this idea seem less abstract:

- **Simple production.** Three units of commodity one and two units of commodity two are used to produce five units of commodity three, $y = (-3, -2, 5, 0, 0)$.
- **Disposal.** The same inputs are used to destroy five units of commodity three (garbage collection), $y = (-3, -2, -5, 0, 0)$.
- **Joint production.** The same inputs are used to produce two units each of commodities four and five, $y = (-3, -2, 0, 2, 2)$.
- **Integrated production.** If $y^1 = (-3, -2, 1, 0, 0)$ produces a machine (commodity three) by using three units of unskilled and two units of skilled labor and if $y^2 = (-5, 0, -1, 0, 100)$ uses the machine and five units of unskilled labor to produce 100 units of some final product (commodity five), then the activity $y = y^1 + y^2 = (-8, -2, 0, 0, 100)$ gives the net effect of the combined process, hiding the role of the machine as intermediate product.

2.2.2 Technology sets

The set of all possible production activities available to a particular economy is denoted by Y, the **aggregate technology set**. Saying that $y \in Y$ does *not* imply that the economy has the resources required to undertake the activity y, but only that y is technically possible — a part of the current state of the art.

The key simplifying assumptions which we make about Y are as follows:

- Y is a proper, closed, pointed, convex cone; and
- $Y \cap L_+ = \{0\}$.

I want to emphasize that we are adopting these assumptions only to improve the clarity of the exposition which follows, not because they are particularly realistic.

In some respects these assumptions are quite acceptable:

- Assuming that Y is closed is an innocuous technical requirement, at least in finite dimensions. Loosely speaking, it means that Y contains its boundary points.

- Requiring that $Y \cap L_+ \subset \{0\}$ is also reasonable. No outputs can be produced without some input. When Y is a cone, this requirement is clearly necessary for a sensible model: otherwise an activity vector $y > 0$ consisting only of outputs could be scaled upward indefinitely since availability of inputs imposes no bound.
- Strengthening the condition to one of equality, $Y \cap L_+ = \{0\}$, is appropriate for a long-run analysis since it implies that production can be shut down entirely $(0 \in Y)$.
- Insisting that the cone Y be proper imposes the plausible requirement that production is irreversible: if $y \in Y$ and $y \neq 0$, then $-y \notin Y$.

However, other aspects of these assumptions are far more restrictive from an economic point of view:

- The fact that Y is a cone means that all production activities in the economy exhibit **constant returns to scale**: if y is a possible activity for the economy $(y \in Y)$, then so is any positive scalar multiple of y. In particular, (a) production can be scaled down to arbitrarily small size $(\lambda y \in Y$ for any $\lambda \in [0, 1))$, and (b) production can be scaled up to arbitrarily large size $(\lambda y \in Y$ for any $\lambda \in (1, \infty))$. Implication (a) rules out economies of scale and implication (b) diseconomies of scale.
- Assuming that Y is a *convex* cone implies that production processes are **additive**: $y^1, y^2 \in Y$ implies $y^1 + y^2 \in Y$. This means, in particular, that there are no external diseconomies in production (see Exercise 2.17).

Clearly, weakening these assumptions is a worthwhile endeavor, and in the following section I will comment on some of the ways in which this can be done. The main virtue of the simplified model we are considering is that it is simple, but not overly so. Assuming constant returns allows us to move quickly and cleanly through the process of generalizing the concepts of Walrasian equilibrium, Pareto optimality, and the core to economies with production. Once you have a good grasp of the basic principles involved, comprehending the more elaborate models appearing in the literature is an easy task.

2.2.3 Sup and inf

Before continuing with our story, we need to digress briefly to introduce a pair of mathematical concepts which may not be familiar to you. In the next subsection, we will consider a set of real numbers representing levels of profit associated with the various production activities available to the economy, and we would like to refer to the maximum such profit. But that raises a problem: what if there is no such maximum?

Suppose, for example, the set takes the form $S = [-2, 10)$ or $S' = [3, \infty)$. Neither S nor S' has a maximum since S does not contain the point 10 and S' is unbounded. A similar issue arises in the case of the search for a minimum as illustrated by the sets $T = (-2, 10]$ and $T' = (-\infty, 3]$.

To finesse the issue we introduce the notion of a least upper bound (*supremum*) and a greatest lower bound (*infimum*) defined in an obvious way:

- To find the supremum of a set of real numbers, consider all upper bounds (numbers greater than or equal to the elements in the set) and let the supremum equal the smallest (least) such upper bound.
- Similarly, to find the infimum, consider all lower bounds (numbers less than or equal to the elements in the set) and let the infimum equal the largest (greatest) such lower bound.

The reason that the finesse works is that every subset of real numbers ordered by $\geq$ has an infimum and a supremum provided that we agree to take $-\infty$ as the infimum of sets which have no lower bound and $+\infty$ as the supremum of sets which have no upper bound. In the case of S and T defined above, $\sup S = 10$ and $\inf T = -2$ while for the unbounded sets S' and T' $\sup S' = \infty$ and $\inf T' = -\infty$.

To summarize, sup and inf are what you use in place of max and min when the existence of the latter is in doubt. If a maximum exists for a set S, then $\max S = \sup S$. Similarly, $\min S = \inf S$ if the minimum exists. Using the examples given above to illustrate, $\min S = \inf S = -2$ and $\max T = \sup T = 10$.

2.2.4 *Prices and profit*

One of the most important simplifications which our assumption of constant returns allows is that we can treat profit maximization in the aggregate without having to bother about who does the producing: firms are pushed into the background.

If market prices are represented by the linear functional $p \in L' \backslash \{0\}$, then the aggregate **profit** derived from activity y is simply $p \cdot y$. For example, with the simple production activity described at the beginning of this section, $p \cdot y = 5p_3 - 3p_1 - 2p_2$, while the joint production process yields $p \cdot y = 2p_4 + 2p_5 - 3p_1 - 2p_2$ so that in either case the amount of profit equals the difference between revenue and cost.

While general equilibrium theorists like to define inputs as negative, most

economists tend to think of inputs as positive. Since both points of view
have merit, the following notation is useful in making the translation. If for
any activity vector y we define

$$y^+ := (\max\{\, y_1, 0\,\}, \dots, \max\{\, y_m, 0\,\})$$

and

$$y^- := (\max\{\, -y_1, 0\,\}, \dots, \max\{\, -y_m, 0\,\}),$$

then $y = y^+ - y^-$ decomposes y into a vector of outputs (y^+) and a vector
of inputs (y^-) while $p \cdot y = p \cdot y^+ - p \cdot y^-$ splits profit into the difference
between revenue and cost. To illustrate, for the joint production process
described above $y^+ = (0,0,0,2,2)$ and $y^- = (3,2,0,0,0)$ yielding $p \cdot y^+ = 2p_4 + 2p_5$ and $p \cdot y^- = 3p_1 + 2p_2$.

The producers in the economy are assumed to maximize profit and, since
this is a Walrasian model, they take prices as given. For a given price
functional $p \in L'$, let $p \cdot Y := \{\, p \cdot y \mid y \in Y\,\}$ denote the set of possible
profit levels as y ranges over Y. (The notation $p \cdot Y$ is another form of block
notation frequently encountered in the literature.)

In modeling the profit-maximizing behavior of producers, we are looking
for an activity vector y yielding the maximum profit in the set $p \cdot Y$. At
this stage, we have no guarantee that such a maximum exists and so, to
finesse the issue for a while, define as the aggregate **profit function** for the
economy the function $\pi(p) := \sup p \cdot Y$ where $\sup p \cdot Y$ is the supremum of
the set of numbers $p \cdot Y$.

Definition 2.17 *The* **supply set** *for a production economy with aggregate
technology set Y consists of those production activities in Y which maximize
profit at prices p:*

$$
\begin{aligned}
\eta(p) &= \{\, y \in Y \mid \{\, y' \in Y \mid p \cdot y' > p \cdot y\,\} \cap Y = \emptyset\,\} \\
&= \{\, y \in Y \mid H_o^+(p, p \cdot y) \cap Y = \emptyset\,\} \\
&= \{\, y \in Y \mid p \cdot y = \pi(p)\,\}
\end{aligned}
$$

The middle line of this definition is meant to emphasize the strong parallel
between the supply set for producers and the demand set for a consumer.
The set Y plays the role of the budget set and $H_o^+(p, p \cdot y)$ the role of the
strict preference set. An activity vector y belongs to $\eta(p)$ if it belongs to Y
and if there is no other activity belonging to Y which producers prefer to y.

A Walrasian equilibrium will exist at prices $p \in L' \backslash \{0\}$ only if the supply
set is nonempty which imposes restrictions on the possible candidates for
an equilibrium price functional. Since Y is a cone, an equilibrium price

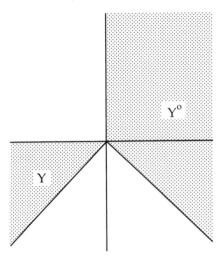

Fig. 2.5. Y and Y^o with costly disposal.

functional must lie in the polar cone Y^o of Y. This restriction has a very natural economic interpretation best demonstrated by example:

- *Pure exchange.* In a pure exchange economy, $Y = \{0\}$: i.e., no production activity is allowed. The polar cone equals L so that no restrictions are imposed on equilibrium price functionals (of course, we must insist that $p \neq 0$ to obtain a hyperplane).

- *Free disposal.* If $Y = L_-$, then noxious commodities can be made to disappear costlessly. The polar cone is L_+, implying that equilibrium prices must be nonnegative.

- *Costly disposal.* If the cone Y is a proper subset of L_-, then the equilibrium price of a noxious commodity might be negative. However, such a price will be bounded below by the marginal (= average) cost of disposal. In Figure 2.5 the second commodity can be eliminated by using an equal amount of the first commodity as input. Disposal of the first commodity is costless. Equilibrium prices are then restricted to the polar cone Y^o consisting of all price functionals (p_1, p_2) for which $p_1 \geq 0$ and $p_2 \geq -p_1$.

- *The standard case.* The technology economists most often have in mind incorporates both free disposal ($L_- \subset Y$) and costly production of some of the commodities. Figure 2.6 illustrates for the case of two commodities where commodity 2 can be produced using equal amounts of commodity

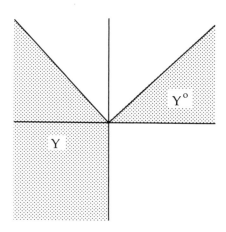

Fig. 2.6. Y and Y^o: the standard case.

1 as an input. Equilibrium prices are restricted to the polar cone Y^o consisting of all price functionals (p_1, p_2) for which $p_1 \geq 0$ and $p_2 \geq p_1$.

The assumptions which we have imposed on Y impose a severe restriction on the level of profit generated in equilibrium. Since $0 \in Y$, the maximum profit $\pi(p)$ must be greater than or equal to zero. Because Y is a cone, any activity y yielding a strictly positive profit cannot be an equilibrium activity: any multiple λy, $\lambda > 0$, would yield a higher level of profit. We conclude, therefore, that the only possible value for maximum profit is zero: $\pi(p) = 0$. It is this implication of constant returns which is most responsible for the simplicity of the exposition which follows. More elaborate versions of the model must allow for positive profit and, consequently, must address the issue of how this profit is distributed.

2.2.5 Consumption sets

Introducing production into the Walrasian model requires a modification in the treatment of consumption sets for the consumers in the economy. In Chapter 1 we argued for the restriction $X_i \subset L_+$ since, in a model of pure exchange, negative consumption makes no sense. However, models with production typically involve labor inputs, and the flow of labor input from consumer i is best viewed as a negative component of the allocation x_i. Therefore, we no longer require $X_i \subset L_+$. Of course, there are physical limits to the quantity of labor services that a consumer can supply so that X_i is bounded below by some vector $b_i \in L$. However, this is a matter that will concern us only in later chapters when establishing existence and other properties of Walrasian equilibrium.

For the moment we are only concerned with the interpretation of negative components of an allocation x_i to consumer i. Suppose there are three commodities in the economy, the first representing labor and the rest produced commodities. Assume that the consumer has an endowment vector $w_i = (0, 2, 0)$ and that, in equilibrium, she supplies 10 units of labor services. Formally, our definition of the budget set is the same as in Chapter 1: $\beta_i(p) = \{ x_i \in X_i \mid p \cdot x_i \le p \cdot w_i \}$. Writing out the constraint, we have

$$p_1(-10) + p_2 x_{i2} + p_3 x_{i3} \le p_2(2)$$

so that the wealth $2p_2$ does not include income derived from the sale of labor services. However, if we transfer the first term to the right hand side of the inequality, the budget constraint takes the form

$$p_2 x_{i2} + p_3 x_{i3} \le 10 p_1 + 2 p_2.$$

Conditional on the decision to supply 10 units of labor services, the consumer has a source of income $10p_1$ from the sale of labor services in addition to the value of the endowment, $2p_2$.

The convention of treating labor services as negative components of the consumption vector, rather than as components of the endowment vector, correctly emphasizes the endogenous aspect of the decision of how much labor to supply. However, as illustrated above, this point of view is easily translated into a form which interprets wages as a part of consumer income.

2.2.6 Walrasian equilibrium

Extending the concepts and results of Chapter 1 to an economy with production is quite straightforward.

Definition 2.18 *A CRS production economy* $\mathcal{E} := (\{ X_i, P_i, w_i \mid i \in I \}, Y)$ *consists of a set of consumers* $I := \{ 1, \ldots, n \}$,

- *a technology set* $Y \subset L$ *which is a proper, closed, pointed, convex cone satisfying the condition* $Y \cap L_+ = \{0\}$,

and, for each $i \in I$,

- *a consumption set* $X_i \subset L$,
- *a strict preference map* $P_i \colon X_i \to 2^{X_i}$, $x_i \mapsto P_i(x_i)$, *and*

- *an endowment* $w_i \in L$

where L *denotes the commodity space* $\mathbf{R^m}$.

In a pure exchange economy commodities cannot be created or destroyed. An allocation x must satisfy the conservation law: $\sum_{i \in I} x_i = \sum_{i \in I} w_i$ or, equivalently, $\sum_{i \in I} \Delta_w x_i = 0$. Production allows this conservation law to be broken, replacing conservation of commodities with the requirement that the aggregate net trade vector is producible.

Definition 2.19 *An allocation* $x \colon I \to L$ *for* $\mathcal{E} = (\{\, X_i, P_i, w_i \mid i \in I \,\}, Y)$ *is* **feasible** *if*

- *for every consumer* $i \in I$ *the allocation* x_i *is physically possible,* $x_i \in X_i$, *and*
- *the aggregate net trade vector is producible,* $\sum_{i \in I} \Delta_w x_i \in Y$.

The **set of feasible allocations for the economy** $\mathcal{E}$ *is given by*

$$\mathrm{F}(\mathcal{E}, I) := \Big\{ x \colon I \to L \mid \sum_{i \in I} \Delta_w x_i \in Y \ \& \ x_i \in X_i \ \forall i \in I \Big\}.$$

Since there is no profit to distribute under constant returns, consumer budget and demand sets are defined exactly as in Chapter 1. The definition of equilibrium follows directly.

Definition 2.20 *A* **Walrasian equilibrium for a production economy** $\mathcal{E}$ *is an ordered pair* (x, p) *consisting of a feasible allocation* $x \in \mathrm{F}(\mathcal{E}, I)$ *and a price functional* $p \in L' \backslash \{0\}$ *such that*

- $x_i \in \phi_i(p)$ *for all* $i \in I$;
- $\sum_{i \in I} \Delta_w x_i = y \in \eta(p)$.

2.2.7 The net trade diagram

The net trade diagram generalizes immediately to a production economy. Consumers are treated just as before with coordinate axes translated to pass through the endowment w_i for each consumer $i \in I$. The aggregate technology set requires no translation.

Figure 2.7 illustrates a two-commodity production economy in which the first commodity is used to produce the second. Assume that there are two consumers with consumption sets $X_i = [-4, 0] \times \mathbf{R}_+$ and preferences represented by the utility functions

$$u_i(x_{i1}, x_{i2}) = \begin{cases} (x_{i1} + 4)^{.25} x_{i2}^{.75} & \text{for } i = 1, \\ (x_{i1} + 4)^{.75} x_{i2}^{.25} & \text{for } i = 2. \end{cases}$$

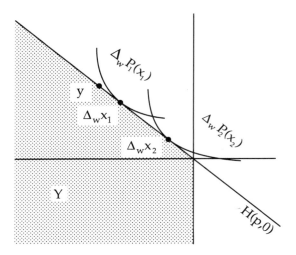

Fig. 2.7. Net trade diagram.

Assume also that neither consumer owns either commodity prior to trade: $w_i = (0,0)$ for $i = 1, 2$. The aggregate technology set is identical to that portrayed in Figure 2.6 with

$$Y = \{\, (y_1, y_2) \in \mathbf{R}^2 \mid y_1 \leq 0,\ y_2 \leq -y_1 \,\},$$

and demand sets take the form

$$\phi_i(p) = \begin{cases} (-3, 3p_1/p_2) & \text{for } i = 1, \\ (-1, p_1/p_2) & \text{for } i = 2. \end{cases}$$

Since clearly a positive amount of commodity two will be produced in equilibrium, the equilibrium hyperplane coincides with the diagonal boundary of the aggregate technology set. Therefore, with prices normalized to sum to one, the equilibrium price functional $p = (.5, .5)$. Since consumer endowments equal $(0,0)$, the equilibrium allocation and equilibrium net trade allocation are the same:

$$x_i = \Delta_w x_i = \begin{cases} (-3, 3) & \text{for } i = 1, \\ (-1, 1) & \text{for } i = 2. \end{cases}$$

This example motivates the following geometric characterization of Walrasian equilibrium, equivalent to the formal definition given above.

Definition 2.21 *A net trade allocation* $\Delta_w x \colon I \to L$ *and a price functional*

$p \neq 0$ *constitute a* **Walrasian equilibrium for a production economy**
$\mathcal{E}$ *if and only if*

- $\Delta_w x_i \in \Delta_w X_i$ *and* $\Delta_w P_i(x_i) \subset H_o^+(p, 0)$ *for all* $i \in I$;
- $Y \subset H^-(p, 0)$; *and*
- $\sum_{i \in I} \Delta_w x_i = y \in Y$.

Once again the two-dimensional illustration of the net trade diagram gives
an accurate picture of what happens in arbitrary dimensions. The hyperplane passes through zero (since equilibrium profit is zero), and equilibrium
net trades as well as the aggregate production activity vector lie on the hyperplane. Perhaps even more clearly than in the case of pure exchange, the
net trade diagram highlights the crucial role of the hyperplane in providing
separation: the hyperplane separates what is possible (the set Y) from what
consumers strictly prefer (the sets $\Delta_w P_i(x_i)$). The main feature distinguish-
ing the net trade diagram with production from that for pure exchange is
that now net trades sum to the aggregate activity vector y rather than to
the zero vector.

2.2.8 Pareto optimality

Because we have already incorporated production into the definition of feasibility, the key concepts used to identify Pareto optimal allocations are
identical in form to those for a pure exchange economy.

Definition 2.22 *In a production economy* $\mathcal{E}$, *a feasible allocation* x *is* **Pareto dominated** *if there exists another feasible allocation* x' *which all consumers prefer to* x. *The set of all such allocations is denoted*

$$\mathrm{Dom}(\mathcal{E}, I) := \{\, x \in \mathrm{F}(\mathcal{E}, I) \mid \exists x' \in \mathrm{F}(\mathcal{E}, I) \ni x' \succ_I x \,\}.$$

The **Pareto optimal allocations** *are those feasible allocations left over
after all dominated allocations have been eliminated:*

$$\mathrm{PO}(\mathcal{E}) := \mathrm{F}(\mathcal{E}, I) \backslash \mathrm{Dom}(\mathcal{E}, I).$$

The proof of the First Fundamental Theorem of welfare economics for
a production economy follows closely along the lines of the proof for pure
exchange.

Theorem 2.23 *For any production economy* $\mathcal{E}$, $\mathrm{WE}^x(\mathcal{E}) \subset \mathrm{PO}(\mathcal{E})$.

Proof Suppose that $(x, p) \in \mathrm{WE}(\mathcal{E})$, but $x \notin \mathrm{PO}(\mathcal{E})$. By the definition of
Pareto optimality, $x \in \mathrm{Dom}(\mathcal{E}, I)$ so there exists an allocation $x' \in \mathrm{F}(\mathcal{E}, I)$

such that $x' \succ_I x$. But then $\Delta_w x'_i \in \Delta_w P_i(x_i)$ for all $i \in I$. By the definition of Walrasian equilibrium, this implies that $p \cdot \Delta_w x'_i > 0$ and hence

$$p \cdot \sum_{i \in I} \Delta_w x'_i =: p \cdot y' > 0. \qquad (*)$$

However, our initial hypothesis that $x' \in F(\mathcal{E}, I)$ requires that

$$y' := \sum_{i \in I} \Delta_w x'_i \in Y.$$

But any such $y' \in Y$ yields a nonpositive profit at prices p by definition of Walrasian equilibrium. Hence, $p \cdot y' \leq 0$ in contradiction to $(*)$. $\qquad \square$

Lemmas 1.10 and 1.11 extend readily to the production context, providing a geometric interpretation of domination and Pareto optimality, and the analog of Lemma 1.11 can be used to give an alternative proof of the First Fundamental Theorem as in Chapter 1.

Lemma 2.24 *For a production economy $\mathcal{E}$,*

$$x \in \text{Dom}(\mathcal{E}, I) \quad \text{iff} \quad Y \cap \sum_{i \in I} \Delta_w P_i(x_i) \neq \emptyset.$$

Proof Exercise 2.19. $\qquad \square$

Lemma 2.25 *For a production economy $\mathcal{E}$,*

$$x \in \text{PO}(\mathcal{E}) \quad \text{iff} \quad Y \cap \sum_{i \in I} \Delta_w P_i(x_i) = \emptyset.$$

Proof Exercise 2.19. $\qquad \square$

2.2.9 The core

Extending the results on the core to an economy with production is a little more complicated because we need to decide what activity vectors are available to a coalition which chooses to go it alone. Let Y_S denote the aggregate technology set available to coalition S using only its own resources. We adopt the plausible assumption that activity vectors available to coalition S are also available to the coalition of the whole: $Y_S \subset Y$ for all $S \subset I$. No additional restrictions on Y_S are needed in this chapter.[3]

---

3 In the literature on the core, often you will see Y denoted Y_I. We continue to assume that Y_I is a closed, convex, proper, pointed cone with $Y_I \cap L_+ = \{0\}$. However, no such assumptions are needed at this juncture on the sets Y_S for $S \subset\subset I$ except for the requirement that $Y_S \subset Y_I$.

The definitions of Chapter 1 now generalize immediately to an economy with production.

Definition 2.26

- *The set of allocations* **feasible for the coalition** S *using only its own resources is given by*

$$\mathrm{F}(\mathcal{E}, S) = \Big\{ x \colon I \to L \mid \sum_{i \in S} \Delta_w x_i \in Y_S \,\&\, x_i \in X_i \,\forall i \in S \Big\}.$$

- *An allocation* $x \in \mathrm{F}(\mathcal{E}, I)$ *is* **dominated by the coalition** $S \neq \emptyset$ *if there exists an allocation* $x' \in \mathrm{F}(\mathcal{E}, S)$ *which is preferred to* x *by all consumers in* S. *The set of all such allocations is denoted*

$$\mathrm{Dom}(\mathcal{E}, S) = \{\, x \in \mathrm{F}(\mathcal{E}, I) \mid \exists x' \in \mathrm{F}(\mathcal{E}, S) \ni x' \succ_S x \,\}.$$

(If $S = \emptyset$, let $\mathrm{Dom}(\mathcal{E}, S) = \emptyset$.)

- *The* **core of a production economy** $\mathcal{E}$ *is the set*

$$\mathrm{C}(\mathcal{E}) = \mathrm{F}(\mathcal{E}, I) \backslash \bigcup_{S \subset I} \mathrm{Dom}(\mathcal{E}, S).$$

Generalizing Lemmas 1.15 and 1.16 is left as an easy exercise.

Lemma 2.27 *For a production economy $\mathcal{E}$ and a coalition $S \subset I$,*

$$x \in \mathrm{Dom}(\mathcal{E}, S) \quad \textit{iff} \quad Y_S \cap \sum_{i \in S} \Delta_w P_i(x_i) \neq \emptyset.$$

Proof Exercise 2.20. □

Lemma 2.28 *For a production economy $\mathcal{E}$,*

$$x \in \mathrm{C}(\mathcal{E}) \quad \textit{iff} \quad Y_S \cap \sum_{i \in S} \Delta_w P_i(x_i) = \emptyset \quad \textit{for all} \quad S \subset I.$$

Proof Exercise 2.20. □

We prove that Walrasian allocations are in the core following along the lines of the alternative proof of Theorem 1.17 (left as an exercise in Chapter 1).

Theorem 2.29 *For any production economy $\mathcal{E}$,*

$$\mathrm{WE}^x(\mathcal{E}) \subset \mathrm{C}(\mathcal{E}) \subset \mathrm{PO}(\mathcal{E}).$$

Proof The inclusion $C(\mathcal{E}) \subset PO(\mathcal{E})$ is immediate from the definitions. To establish the first inclusion, note first that if $(x, p) \in WE(\mathcal{E})$ then every net strict preference set lies in the open halfspace above the hyperplane: $\Delta_w P_i(x_i) \subset H_o^+(p, 0)$ for all $i \in I$. Choose any coalition $S \subset I$ and let z be any point belonging to $\sum_{i \in S} \Delta_w P_i(x_i)$. By definition of block notation, this means that $z = \sum_{i \in S} \Delta_w y_i$ where $\Delta_w y_i \in \Delta_w P_i(x_i)$ for all $i \in S$. Because $(x, p) \in WE(\mathcal{E})$ and $\Delta_w y_i \in \Delta_w P_i(x_i)$ for all $i \in S$, $p \cdot \Delta_w y_i > 0$ for all $i \in S$. Therefore, $p \cdot z = \sum_{i \in S} p \cdot \Delta_w y_i > 0$. Since $Y \subset H^-(p, 0)$, we conclude that $z \notin Y$ and hence, because z was chosen arbitrarily from $\sum_{i \in S} \Delta_w P_i(x_i)$,

$$Y \cap \sum_{i \in S} \Delta_w P_i(x_i) = \emptyset.$$

But $Y_S \subset Y$ so that

$$Y_S \cap \sum_{i \in S} \Delta_w P_i(x_i) = \emptyset.$$

Since the choice of coalition S was arbitrary, we conclude that

$$Y_S \cap \sum_{i \in S} \Delta_w P_i(x_i) = \emptyset \quad \text{for all} \quad S \subset I.$$

By Lemma 2.28 this implies that $x \in C(\mathcal{E})$. $\qquad\qquad\square$

2.3 Alternative models of production

Although production with constant returns serves the purposes of this book quite well, there are occasions when more elaborate models of production are called for. In this section we will briefly consider two of the more common variations encountered in the literature: the **Arrow-Debreu economy** and the **coalition production economy**.

2.3.1 *The Arrow-Debreu economy*

The general equilibrium framework developed by Arrow and Debreu (1954) begins with a list of all of the firms which could conceivably be formed, represented by a finite index set K. Each firm $k \in K$ is characterized by its **technology set** Y_k. The aggregate technology set derives from the firm technology sets through summation, $Y = \sum_{k \in K} Y_k$, and aggregate production vectors are linked to individual firm activity vectors in the same way: $y = \sum_{k \in K} y_k$ where $y_k \in Y_k$ for all $k \in K$.

The maximum profits which firms can earn are given by the **firm profit functions** $\pi_k(p) := \sup p \cdot Y_k$ for each $k \in K$ and the supply responses by the **firm supply sets** $\eta_k(p) := \{\, y_k \in Y_k \mid p \cdot y_k = \pi_k(p)\,\}$ for each $k \in K$. It is not hard to establish the connection between these functions and the corresponding aggregate constructs we introduced earlier:

$$\pi(p) = \sum_{k \in K} \pi_k(p) \quad \text{and} \quad \eta(p) = \sum_{k \in K} \eta_k(p).$$

Arrow and Debreu assume that the technology sets Y_k are convex but not necessarily cones so that profits or losses may occur in equilibrium. To simplify the discussion, we assume that $0 \in Y_k$ for all $k \in K$ so that equilibrium profits are nonnegative. If $y_k = 0$ in equilibrium, then the kth firm chooses not to produce or, said differently, this *potential* firm does not form into an *actual* firm.

If the Y_k are not cones, then there typically will be profits to be distributed to the consumers in the economy. Let θ_{ik} be the fixed share claimed by consumer i to the profit of firm k where

- each share is a fraction lying between 0 and 1 ($0 \le \theta_{ik} \le 1$ for all $i \in I$ and for all $k \in K$); and
- the shares in any firm sum to 1 ($\sum_{i \in I} \theta_{ik} = 1$ for all $k \in K$).

Modify the budget sets of each consumer to include shares in profits, $\beta_i(p) := \{\, x_i \in X_i \mid p \cdot x_i \le p \cdot w_i + \sum_{k \in K} \theta_{ik} \pi_k(p)\,\}$, and define consumer demand sets just as before,

$$\phi_i(p) := \{\, x_i \in \beta_i(p) \mid P_i(x_i) \cap \beta_i(p) = \emptyset \,\}.$$

The definition of a Walrasian equilibrium for an Arrow-Debreu economy is identical to that given before:

Definition 2.30 *A* **Walrasian equilibrium** *for an Arrow-Debreu production economy* $\mathcal{E}$ *is an ordered pair* (x, p) *consisting of a feasible allocation* $x \in \mathrm{F}(\mathcal{E}, I)$ *and a price functional* $p \in L'\backslash\{0\}$ *such that*

- $x_i \in \phi_i(p)$ *for all* $i \in I$; *and*
- $\sum_{i \in I} \Delta_w x_i = y \in \eta(p)$.

All that is changed is the interpretation:

- In equilibrium, part of consumer wealth is derived from a share in equilibrium profits.
- The aggregate activity vector decomposes into the sum of activity vectors by firms, $y = \sum_{k \in K} y_k$ where $y_k \in \eta_k(p)$ for all $k \in K$.
- Aggregate equilibrium profit decomposes into the sum of profits earned by each firm, $\pi(k) = \sum_{k \in K} \pi_k(p)$.

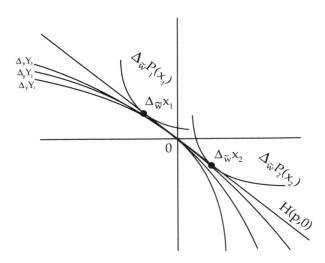

Fig. 2.8. Net trade diagram (Arrow-Debreu).

Thus, generalizing the simple CRS production model to the Arrow-Debreu economy involves little more than accounting for the distribution of profits.

Generalizing the net trade diagram to the Arrow-Debreu economy is complicated to some extent by the existence of profits: if consumers earn positive income from profits, then net trades no longer lie on the hyperplane passing through the endowment points. We can construct a modified version of the net trade diagram which accurately represents the separating role of the hyperplane in this new framework. However, the coordinate transformations required now depend on the specific equilibrium that we want to represent.

Consider a given Walrasian equilibrium with price functional p and firm activity vectors $\{\, y_k \mid k \in K \,\}$.

- Define for each consumer an extended endowment vector $\widetilde{w}_i = w_i + \sum_{k \in K} \theta_{ik} y_k$, and use this extended endowment vector to translate consumer preferred sets, budget sets, and the like: e.g., $\Delta_{\widetilde{w}} P_i(x_i) = P_i(x_i) - \widetilde{w}_i$ for all $i \in I$.
- Translate each firm's technology set by y_k, $\Delta_y Y_k := Y_k - y_k$ for all $k \in K$.

A typical net trade diagram for an Arrow-Debreu economy is illustrated in Figure 2.8 for the case of two commodities, two firms, and two consumers where commodity one (say, labor) is used to produce commodity two by each of the firms. Thanks to this rather elaborate change of coordinates, the separating role of the equilibrium hyperplane emerges once again:

- strict preference sets for each consumer lie in the open halfspace above the hyperplane, $\Delta_{\tilde{w}} P_i(x_i) \subset H_o^+(p, 0)$;
- firm technology sets lie in the closed halfspace below the hyperplane, $\Delta_y Y_k \subset H^-(p, 0)$;
- the equilibrium net activity vector of each firm equals zero, $\Delta_y y_k := y_k - y_k = 0$; and
- consumer net trades sum to zero, $\sum_{i \in I} \Delta_{\tilde{w}} x_i = 0$.

In Exercise 2.22 you are asked to illustrate this construction by modifying the example given in Section 2.2.7. Since the First Fundamental Theorem of welfare economics is an immediate consequence of the existence of a separating hyperplane, the theorem should generalize to the Arrow-Debreu economy. Exercise 2.23 asks you to provide the simple proof.

2.3.2 Coalition production economies

One aspect of competitive analysis that does not generalize easily to the Arrow-Debreu model is the concept of the core. When considering what a coalition $S \subset I$ can produce using only its own resources, what are we to assume if the members of S collectively own part, but not all, of a firm $k \in K$ (i.e., $\sum_{i \in S} \theta_{ik} < 1$)? One possible resolution is to abandon the notion of a firm and to associate technology sets with coalitions instead.

In a model of a **coalition production economy** the primitive information on production is captured by specifying a technology set $Y_S \subset \mathbf{R^m}$ for each coalition $S \subset I$. Let $Y := Y_I$ denote the aggregate technology set and $\pi(p) := \sup p \cdot Y$ the profit function for the economy as a whole. Assume that $0 \in Y$ so that equilibrium profit is necessarily nonnegative.

If equilibrium profit is strictly positive, then it must be distributed to consumers in some fashion. The Arrow-Debreu specification resolves this issue by specifying the fixed shares θ_{ik} of consumers in firm profits. The formulation of a coalition production economy introduces the notion of a **stable profit distribution**.

Definition 2.31 *For some $p \in L' \backslash \{0\}$, let $\{\, \widehat{\pi}_i(p) \mid i \in I \,\}$ denote a distribution of profit to consumers where $\sum_{i \in I} \widehat{\pi}_i(p) = \pi(p)$. The profit distribution $\{\, \widehat{\pi}_i(p) \mid i \in I \,\}$ is a **stable profit distribution** if $\sum_{i \in S} \widehat{\pi}_i(p) \geq \sup p \cdot Y_S$ for all $S \subset I$.*

Just as for the Arrow-Debreu economy, we modify the budget sets of each consumer to include shares in profit

$$\beta_i(p) := \{\, x_i \in X_i \mid p \cdot x_i \leq p \cdot w_i + \widehat{\pi}_i(p) \,\}$$

and define consumer demand sets just as before,

$$\phi_i(p) := \{\, x_i \in \beta_i(p) \mid P_i(x_i) \cap \beta_i(p) = \emptyset \,\}.$$

Definition 2.32 *A* **Walrasian equilibrium** *for a coalition production economy $\mathcal{E}$ is an ordered pair (x, p) consisting of a feasible allocation $x \in F(\mathcal{E}, I)$ and a price functional $p \in L' \backslash \{0\}$ such that*

- $x_i \in \phi_i(p)$ *for all* $i \in I$;
- $\sum_{i \in I} \Delta_w x_i = y \in \eta(p)$;
- $\{\, \widehat{\pi}_i(p) \mid i \in I \,\}$ *is a stable profit distribution.*

Clearly the definition of a coalition production economy and a stable profit distribution is set up to guarantee that the analog of Theorem 2.29 will be valid. In Exercise 2.24 you are asked to supply the proof.

2.4 Public goods and joint supply

The formal model of competitive equilibrium with production is obviously very general. But does it offer anything new? What, if anything, does this type of mathematical abstraction contribute to economics? We end this chapter by considering from this formal perspective a rather lively topic which has generated considerable controversy over the years: the connection between Marshallian joint supply and the "competitive" provision of public goods. This example is but one of many which could be used to demonstrate the value of allowing for production within general equilibrium theory.

2.4.1 Marshallian joint supply

To illustrate Alfred Marshall's model of joint supply, we consider a very specific example. We are given an economy with two consumers and three commodities: mutton, hides, and sheep. Each consumer is endowed initially with some sheep which she both enjoys as pets and slaughters to provide mutton and hides. When slaughtered, a sheep provides "one sheep's worth" of mutton and "one sheep's worth" of hides. It is the jointness of this production process that is the source of the puzzle that Marshall sought to resolve. There is no meaningful notion of marginal cost for mutton or hides because they are jointly produced. How then can we determine equilibrium prices as the "Marshallian cross" of demand and supply?

We will now translate this verbal story into a mathematical model. The commodity space is $\mathbf{R}^3$ with coordinates representing (1) mutton, (2) hides, and (3) sheep. Both consumers have a positive initial endowment of sheep

and own no mutton or hides: $w_i = (0, 0, a_i)$ with $a_i > 0$ for $i = 1, 2$.
Preferences, defined over the consumption set R_+^3, are described by Cobb-Douglas utility functions with consumer one caring only for mutton and sheep, $u_1(x_1) = x_{11}x_{13}$, and consumer two only for hides and sheep $u_2(x_2) = x_{22}x_{23}$. Choose the third commodity (sheep) as *numéraire* so that $p_3 = 1$. Hence consumer wealth is given by $p \cdot w_1 = a_1$ and $p \cdot w_2 = a_2$ and demand functions by

$$\phi_1(p) = (a_1/2p_1, 0, a_1/2) \quad \text{and} \quad \phi_2(p) = (0, a_2/2p_2, a_2/2)$$

where $p = (p_1, p_2, p_3)$ represents prices. To describe technology we assume (a) one sheep produces one unit of mutton and one unit of hides and (b) constant returns to scale. Therefore, the aggregate technology set is given by the cone $Y = \{ \lambda(1, 1, -1) \mid \lambda \geq 0 \}$.

Since sheep serve as *numéraire*, the marginal cost of obtaining the *joint* product of one sheep's worth of mutton and one sheep's worth of hides is unity. However, as noted earlier, there is no meaningful notion of marginal cost for mutton and hides considered separately. Nevertheless, Marshall was able to capture this model within the classical context of supply and demand through the following ingenious trick.

- Given the demand functions $x_{11} = a_1/2p_1$ and $x_{22} = a_2/2p_2$, solve for the inverse demand functions $p_1 = a_1/2x_{11}$ and $p_2 = a_2/2x_{22}$.
- Plot both of the inverse demand functions in a conventional Marshallian supply and demand diagram with prices on the vertical axis and quantities on the horizontal axis (see Figure 2.9).
- Sum the inverse demand functions vertically. The equilibrium number of sheep slaughtered occurs where the graph of the summed demand function crosses the horizontal supply function (price = marginal cost).
- The equilibrium price of a sheep equals one and the equilibrium prices of mutton and hides are given by the heights of the inverse demand functions for mutton (from consumer 1) and hides (from consumer 2). Note also that, by construction, the price of mutton plus the price of hides equals the price of a sheep: $p_1 + p_2 = p_3 = 1$. Thus, even though the marginal cost of mutton and hides is indeterminate, the equilibrium prices of both commodities can nevertheless be determined.

Formally, equating the sum of the inverse demand functions to the price of a sheep gives

$$p_1 + p_2 = \frac{a_1}{2x_{11}} + \frac{a_2}{2x_{22}} = 1.$$

Joint production plus the fact that consumer one desires only mutton and

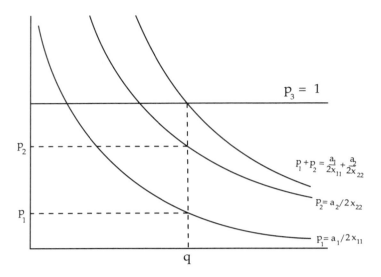

Fig. 2.9. Marshallian joint supply.

consumer two only hides implies that $x_{11} = x_{22} = y_3^- := q$. Combining these equations, we conclude that $q = (a_1 + a_2)/2$ is the equilibrium quantity of sheep which will be slaughtered with equilibrium prices for mutton and hides given by

$$p_1 = \frac{a_1}{2q} = \frac{a_1}{a_1 + a_2} \quad \text{and} \quad p_2 = \frac{a_2}{2q} = \frac{a_2}{a_1 + a_2}.$$

This construction is exceedingly clever, Alfred Marshall at his best. In some respects, however, the argument seems too clever: plotting both the inverse demand functions in a single diagram requires the right choice of units ("one sheep's worth") and the assumption that each of the consumers desires only one of the two joint products. How can we be certain that the conclusions generalize to more complicated instances of joint supply?

We have already taken some liberties with the Marshallian style in presenting Marshall's argument in a form consistent with the general equilibrium framework developed earlier in this book. The advantage of the general equilibrium formulation is that joint supply involves nothing special: the specifications of endowments, preferences, and technology all fit within the general framework. In particular, the existence proofs to be given later cover this case, and the results we have proved already show that the Walrasian equilibria are Pareto optimal and in the core.

From a purely theoretical point of view, this is perhaps all that needs to be said. Marshallian joint supply is just another garden variety Walrasian equilibrium. However, much of the interest and charm of Marshall's model stems from the intuitive result that $p_1 + p_2 = p_3$: the market value of a joint product is the sum of the values of its constituent products. As we now show, even this conclusion — which seems so intimately connected with Marshall's graphical device of vertically summing inverse demand functions — emerges naturally from the general equilibrium formulation.

Since technology exhibits constant returns to scale, if production takes place at all we know that equilibrium profit will equal zero: $p \cdot y = 0$. From the specification of the technology set Y we know that, provided production occurs, a typical activity vector takes the form $\lambda(1, 1, -1)$ where $\lambda > 0$. We conclude, therefore, that

$$0 = p \cdot y = (p_1, p_2, p_3) \cdot (\lambda(1, 1, -1))$$

which upon simplification yields $p_1 + p_2 - p_3 = 0$ or $p_1 + p_2 = p_3$. Thus, we reach Marshall's conclusion immediately without mention of marginal cost!

2.4.2 Public goods

Pure public goods seem at first glance quite different from Marshallian joint supply. Consider an economy with two consumers and two commodities, one public and the other private. Denote the consumption vector of consumer i by $x_i := (y_i, z_i)$ where y_i represents consumption of the public good and z_i consumption of the private good. Let (y, z) denote the aggregate consumption in this economy where $y = y_1 = y_2$ and $z = z_1 + z_2$. Thus, for the private good aggregate consumption is obtained by *summing* individual consumption (this is what we mean by a private good) while for the public good individual consumption *equals* the aggregate consumption. More generally, in an economy with n consumers indexed by $I = \{1, \ldots, n\}$ we have $\sum_{i \in I} z_i = z$ for a pure private good and $y_1 = \cdots = y_n = y$ for a pure public good. A typical example of a pure public good is national defense. (If country B is the enemy of A, then consumers in B might regard the collective defense commodity provided by country A as a "bad," not a "good," so "public commodity" would be a more accurate phraseology.)

Altering the representation of the commodity space converts this problem into one which appears formally identical to Marshallian joint supply. Specifically, for our two-consumer, two-commodity world we expand the commodity space from $\mathbf{R}^2$ to $\mathbf{R}^3$, denoting the typical commodity bundle for consumer i by $(y_1, y_2, z_i) \in \mathbf{R}^3_+$ to which consumer i associates the utility $u_i(y_1, y_2, z_i)$.

In keeping with the interpretation of the first paragraph, the utility of consumer one depends on y_1 and z_1, but not on y_2, and that of consumer two on y_2 and z_2 but not on y_1.[4] This corresponds exactly to the simplifying assumption about preferences employed in our model of Marshallian joint supply: consumer one desires only mutton (commodity one) and consumer two only hides (commodity two).

Thus, the computation of Walrasian equilibrium in the preceding section carries over immediately to this new context with only a trivial change in notation. Assume that both consumers have a positive initial endowment of the private good but own none of the public good: $w_i = (0, 0, a_i)$ with $a_i > 0$ for $i = 1, 2$. Preferences, just as before, are Cobb-Douglas: $u_1(x_1) = y_1 z_1$ and $u_2(x_2) = y_2 z_2$. Assume that one unit of the private good can produce one unit of the public good subject to constant returns to scale, implying once again a technology set of the form $Y = \{ \lambda(1, 1, -1) \mid \lambda \geq 0 \}$.

Equilibrium prices can be computed by vertically summing inverse demand functions exactly as with Marshallian joint supply, a construction employed in the public goods context by Erik Lindahl. Denoting the equilibrium price functional by $p = (p_y^1, p_y^2, p_z)$, we can immediately apply the formulas of the preceding section to conclude that the equilibrium amount of public good production is $q = (a_1 + a_2)/2$ and equilibrium prices are

$$p_y^1 = \frac{a_1}{a_1 + a_2} \quad \text{and} \quad p_y^2 = \frac{a_2}{a_1 + a_2}$$

where the third commodity once again serves as *numéraire* with $p_z = 1$.

In the public goods literature, the **personalized prices** p_y^i for the consumers $i \in I$ are called **Lindahl prices** and the corresponding Walrasian equilibrium a **Lindahl equilibrium**. Just as for joint supply, we conclude that $p_y^1 + p_y^2 = p_z$ so that the sum of the Lindahl public good prices to each consumer equals the price of the joint (collective) good.

2.4.3 What is competition?

The analogy between Marshallian joint supply and pure public goods is illuminating but controversial. When Lindahl proposed what is now called Lindahl equilibrium, he defended the notion as a model of what legislators might do in choosing an optimal amount of the public good. (Since the First Fundamental Theorem applies to this model of joint supply/public goods, we know that Lindahl equilibrium will be Pareto optimal. Theorem 2.29 implies that it will also be in the core.) Paul Samuelson, originator of the

---

4 With n consumers, the commodity space is expanded to R^{n+1}. A typical commodity bundle for consumer i would be $(y_1, y_2, \ldots, y_n, z_i)$ with associated utility $u_i(y_1, y_2, \ldots, y_n, z_i)$ where the utility of consumer i depends only on y_i and z_i and not on y_j for $j \neq i$.

modern treatment of pure public goods, has been quite unsympathetic with
the Lindahl construction: he characterizes the demand functions for public
goods as "pseudo-demand functions" and Lindahl prices as

pseudo-tax-prices ... at which the referee *pretends* the [consumer] can buy as much
or as little of the public goods as he pleases. (What kinds of exclusion devices
would be needed to make this pretense less bizarre, I shall not go into ....)

(Samuelson (1969b), 103)

And just in case his point might be missed, he adds

Hence, as Wicksell sensed when he threw the problem out of the market-place and
into the legislature, it pays no one to behave according to the voluntary-exchange
theory. So they will not. All of Lindahl's prattling about 'equality of bargaining
power' as leading to his solution, with the implication that unbalanced power situations will spread around his solution the way errors spread around a mean value,
is gratuitous assertion. Who believes it? Why should anyone?

(Samuelson (1969b), 115)

Samuelson's reaction to efforts by authors such as Buchanan (1967) to
identify public goods production with the Marshallian model of joint supply
and perhaps even to suggest that competitive, private production of public
goods might be possible [Demsetz (1970)] is, if anything, more severe:

The theory of public goods is sometimes confused with the theory of joint production. This is in the nature of a pun, or a play on words: for, as I have insisted
elsewhere, as we increase the number of persons on both sides of the market in the
case of mutton and [hides], we converge in the usual fashion to the conditions of
perfect competition. But when we increase the number of persons in the case of a
typical public good, we make the problem *more indeterminate* rather than less.

(Samuelson (1969a), 26)

The justification which Samuelson gives for his claim is not rigorous.
What, after all, is meant by the assertion that the public good problem
becomes "more indeterminate rather than less"? As our examples illustrate, both Marshallian joint supply and Lindahl equilibrium are determi-
nate models in the sense that, under the standard assumptions regarding
preferences and technology, equilibria exist. The analogy between Marshallian joint supply and Lindahl equilibrium is both accurate and general (see
Foley (1970) for a general presentation along the lines given above).

Thus, Lindahl equilibrium for pure public goods must be regarded as just
another garden variety Walrasian equilibrium, just like Marshallian joint

supply. What Samuelson is driving at goes beyond the mechanics of Walrasian equilibrium to the issue of whether price-taking behavior is a reasonable hypothesis. His point is that with public goods, in contrast to joint supply, markets can *never* become thick no matter how many consumers are present in the economy and therefore that the Walrasian, price-taking hypothesis is inappropriate in this context. Turning this intuition into a theoretically rigorous proposition provides an illuminating illustration of how the concept of the core can contribute to economic theory.

Marshallian joint supply fits within the framework of the core equivalence theorem which we alluded to in Chapter 1. If we replicate the model of joint supply presented above, then it is not hard to show that the core of the replicated economy "converges" to the Walrasian equilibrium just as for the example given at the end of Chapter 1. In the model of Lindahl equilibrium, on the other hand, the core does not converge.

To simplify discussion of this example, we will describe core allocations in terms of utility rather than physical quantities of commodities. Suppose that we increase the number of consumers in our economy to n with $I = \{1, \ldots, n\}$ indexing the set of consumers. Assume as before that utility functions take the form $u_i(y, z_i) = yz_i$ where y is the quantity of the pure public good and z_i the consumption of the private good by consumer i. To simplify matters, assume that all consumers have the same endowment of the private good: $w_i = (0, a)$ where $a > 0$ for all $i \in I$. Continue to assume that public goods are produced subject to constant returns to scale with one unit of the private good required to produce one unit of the public good.

Proceeding just as before, you should have no difficulty demonstrating that the Lindahl allocation assigns $(y, z_i) = (na/2, a/2)$ to each consumer $i \in I$ with Lindahl prices $(p_y^i, p_z) = (1/n, 1)$ where we again set $p_z = 1$ as *numéraire*. At the Lindahl equilibrium each consumer achieves a utility level $u_i = (na/2)(a/2) = na^2/4$.

In the Lindahl equilibrium, all consumers receive the same allocation and hence achieve the same level of utility. However, in contrast to what happens when replicating private goods economies, core allocations in a replicated public goods economy will typically not exhibit the "equal treatment property."

Just how unequal can the allocation for this economy be and still remain in the core? To answer this question, we proceed along classical Samuelsonian lines. Consider a coalition S with $n(S)$ members. Assuming that this coalition has access to the same production technology available to the economy as a whole, the production possibility frontier (to use Samuelson's terminology) takes the form

$$F(y, z) := y + z - n(S)a = 0$$

where y is the quantity of public good produced and $z(:= \sum_{i \in S} z_i)$ the *aggregate* amount of the private good produced. Samuelson's condition for Pareto optimality equates the sum of marginal rates of substitution to the marginal rate of transformation, $\sum_{i \in S} \text{MRS}_i = \text{MRT}$, which in our case becomes $\sum_{i \in S} z_i/y = 1$ or, equivalently, $y = \sum_{i \in S} z_i = z$. Substituting this expression into the equation for the production possibility frontier, we conclude that the Pareto optimal quantity of public good production for the coalition S using only its own resources is given uniquely by $y = n(S)a/2$. As a consequence, the utility frontier (again using Samuelson's terminology) for this coalition is

$$V(S) := \max\Big\{\sum_{i \in S} u_i(y, z_i) \mid F(y, z) = 0\Big\} = \frac{[n(S)]^2 a^2}{4}.$$

Because all of the consumers in this economy are identical, it is easy to determine utility allocations which are in the core: A utility allocation $u := (u_1, \ldots, u_n)$ is in the core if and only if $\sum_{i \in S} u_i \geq V(S)$ for all $S \subset I$. (If the sum of utilities assigned to a coalition S were less than $V(S)$, then the coalition could improve upon the allocation since it can achieve the sum $V(S)$ using only its own resources.)

Following along the lines of Muench (1972), we can compare the Lindahl and core allocations for this economy in a Lorentz-type diagram (see Figure 2.10). The way this diagram is constructed is as follows:

- For any utility allocation $u := (u_1, \ldots, u_n)$, order the consumers from the worst to the best treated.
- For a given utility allocation u, define a distribution function F such that $F(S) = (\sum_{i=1}^{s} u_i)/(\sum_{i=1}^{n} u_i)$ for each $S = \{1, \ldots, s\} \subset I$. (Remember that the set I is reordered from worst to best treated!)
- Plot F with the fraction of consumers $\mu(S) := n(S)/n = s/n$ on the horizontal axis and the fraction $F(S)$ of total utility achieved by S on the vertical axis.

The Lindahl allocation assigns equal utility to all consumers, corresponding to the stair step graph moving along the 45° diagonal with distribution function

$$F^1(S) = \frac{\sum_{i=1}^{s} u_i}{\sum_{i=1}^{n} u_i} = \frac{n(S)na^2/4}{n^2 a^2/4} = \mu(S).$$

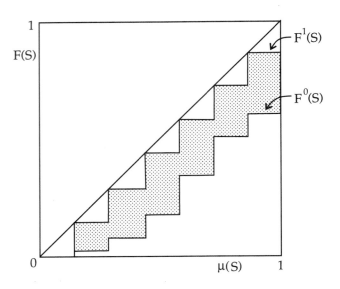

Fig. 2.10. Lorentz diagram (finite).

The least equal core allocation possible will assign to each coalition $S = \{1, \ldots, s\} \subset I$ a utility allocation summing to $V(S)$ with corresponding distribution function

$$F^0(S) = \frac{\sum_{i=1}^{s} u_i}{\sum_{i=1}^{n} u_i} = \frac{[n(S)]^2 a^2/4}{n^2 a^2/4} = [\mu(S)]^2.$$

Any allocation with corresponding distribution function lying somewhere between these two graphs is a core utility allocation.

As illustrated in Figure 2.10, the Walrasian (Lindahl) allocation is in the core, but the core contains other allocations as well. This is no surprise since, with a finite number of consumers in the economy, we expect some room for the exercise of market power. However, what happens in the limit as the number of consumers goes to infinity?

What we have constructed here is a finite version of an example formulated by Muench (1972) for an economy with a continuum of consumers. Much more will be said about such models in the next chapter. But for now we simply suppose that we can replace the index set $I = \{1, \ldots, n\}$ with the interval $I = [0, 1]$ where each point $i \in I$ represents a different consumer. As shown by Aumann, private goods economies with a continuum of consumers typically exhibit *core equivalence*: Walrasian and core allocations coincide.

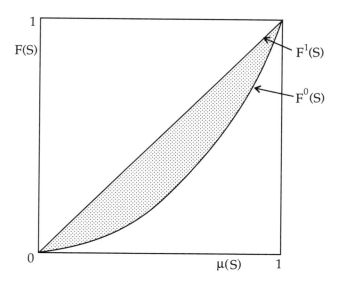

Fig. 2.11. Lorentz diagram (continuum).

In particular, this will be true for the Marshallian model of joint supply that we constructed above when extended to the continuum setting.

But what about the public goods economy? In the limiting continuum economy (as constructed by Muench), the formulas we have derived generalize in an immediate and obvious way:

- Once again in constructing the Lorentz diagram we order the consumers in I from worst to best treated.
- The Lindahl allocation continues to give equal treatment to all consumers with distribution function $F^1(S) = \mu(S)$ where $\mu(S)$ is the fraction of consumers in $S = [0, s]$. This now corresponds *exactly* to the 45° line in Figure 2.11.
- The most unequal core allocation also continues to correspond to the distribution function $F^0(S) = [\mu(S)]^2$ for $S = [0, s]$ which now corresponds to the smooth curve graphed in Figure 2.11.

Every allocation in the shaded area is a core allocation for this economy with the Lindahl (Walrasian) allocation representing but one of many. Thus, the core has not converged to the Lindahl equilibrium in the limit.

How then are we to assess the contribution of mathematical economics to this debate? Certainly the results on the core give support to Samuelson's conclusion that Walrasian equilibrium for a public goods economy is fundamentally different from that for joint supply. However, few debates this intense are likely to be settled by mathematics alone. In the present instance the argument over whether public goods and joint supply are the same in fact masks a deeper conflict regarding the proper roles of governmental versus private production. What the mathematical treatment contributes is clarification of the issues. If a case for private provision of public goods is to be made, it must be supported not by arguing that private suppliers of public goods will act as perfect competitors but rather that they will do a better job — in some sense which needs to be specified — than the government. The core analysis presented here does not begin to address that question.

2.5 Summary

The standard general equilibrium view of production has grievous faults and outstanding virtues. This chapter emphasizes the virtues, the smooth transition which it provides from pure exchange to a world with production. Once again the net trade diagram captures the geometry precisely. Exploring the connections between joint supply and public goods demonstrates the power of a mathematical approach to general equilibrium theory, cutting effectively through the obscurities of Marshall and providing a more precise expression of the sense in which Marshallian joint supply can truly be said to be competitive while public goods cannot.

Exercises

2.1   Find $\operatorname{sp} S$, $\operatorname{aff} S$, and $\operatorname{co} S$ for each of the following subsets of $\mathbf{R}^2$. Illustrate your answers with a diagram.

(a) $S = \{(1,1)\}$
(b) $S = \{(1,1),(2,2)\}$
(c) $S = \{(1,1),(2,3)\}$
(d) $S = \{(1,1),(2,3),(0,-1)\}$
(e) $S = \{(1,1),(2,3),(-1,0)\}$.

2.2   Properly speaking, the equivalent definitions of the span, affine hull, and convex hull given in the text should be proved to be equivalent. To see how this is done, take as a definition that the convex hull of S is the set of all convex combinations of the vectors in S. If S is any subset of a vector space L, prove that $\operatorname{co} S$ is the smallest convex set containing S by justifying each step in the following proof:

Let $\mathcal{C}$ be the collection of all convex sets which contain S and define $B = \bigcap_{C \in \mathcal{C}} C$. B is convex, and it is the smallest convex set which contains S. For any sets $E \subset F \subset L$, it is always true that $\mathrm{co}\, E \subset \mathrm{co}\, F$. Therefore, $\mathrm{co}\, S \subset B$. But $B \subset \mathrm{co}\, S$. Hence, $\mathrm{co}\, S = B$, which proves the theorem.

2.3   Show that a subset S of a vector space is convex iff $\alpha S + (1-\alpha)S \subset S$ for all $\alpha \in [0,1]$.

2.4   To illustrate the operation of taking linear combinations of convex sets, let

$$
\begin{aligned}
C_1 &= \{\, x \in \mathbf{R}^2 \mid x = (x_1, 0),\ x_1 \in [0,1]\,\} \\
C_2 &= \{\, x \in \mathbf{R}^2 \mid x = (0, x_2),\ x_2 \in [0,1]\,\}.
\end{aligned}
$$

Let $C = \alpha C_1 + (1-\alpha)C_2$. Illustrate the set C for α equal to 1, .75, .5, .25, and 0.

2.5   Let $S = \mathbf{R}_+^n$. Prove that $S - S = \mathbf{R}^n$.

2.6   Let $(2^L)_o^C$ denote the set of all nonempty convex subsets of a vector space L. Because linear combinations of elements in this set also belong to the set, it is tempting to conclude that $(2^L)_o^C$ is a vector space. Why is this conclusion false?

2.7   Complete the proofs of Theorems 2.3 and 2.4.

2.8   Prove the parts of Theorem 2.7 involving linear or affine subspaces.

2.9   Illustrate Theorem 2.7 for a map $A \colon \mathbf{R}^2 \to \mathbf{R}^2$.

2.10   Prove Theorem 2.8.

2.11   Prove that $L_+ = \mathbf{R}_+^n$ and $L_- = \mathbf{R}_-^n$ are proper, convex, pointed cones.

2.12   For $L = \mathbf{R}^n$, define $L_{++} = \{\, x \in L \mid x \gg 0\,\}$ and $L_{--} = \{\, x \in L \mid x \ll 0\,\}$. Prove that these sets are proper, convex cones. Are they pointed?

2.13   Verify that the set of all subsets of a set X is partially ordered by $\supset$: i.e., the definition $S \geq T$ iff $S \supset T$ yields a partial ordering $\geq$ on 2^X. Give a simple example illustrating that this partial ordering need not be complete (usually it is not).

2.14   Show that the binary relation $\geq$ on $\mathbf{R}^n$ given by Definition 2.10 is a partial ordering and that $\mathbf{R}^n$ equipped with that partial ordering is an ordered vector space.

2.15   Verify that the function space $\mathrm{Map}(T, \mathbf{R})$ described in Chapter 1 is partially ordered by the relation $\geq$ if we define $g \geq f$ iff $g(t) \geq f(t)$ for all $t \in T$. Verify that with this partial ordering $L := \mathrm{Map}(T, \mathbf{R})$ is an ordered vector space. Describe the positive and negative cones L_+ and L_- for this case.

2.16   Find the polar cone of the following cones and illustrate both the cone and its polar in a diagram.

(a) $K = \mathbf{R}_+^2$;
(b) $K = \{ x \in \mathbf{R}^2 \mid x_1 \leq 0 \,\&\, x_2 \leq x_1 \}$.

2.17   Consider a production economy with four commodities: (1) labor, (2) widgets, (3) clean shirts, and (4) soot. Activity vectors come in two varieties:

(a) A factory uses labor to produce widgets and soot using a positive scalar multiple of the activity vector $y^1 = (-1, 1, 0, 1)$.
(b) A laundry uses labor to produce clean shirts, but the labor required depends on how much soot is present. Letting s denote the amount of soot, activity vectors available to the laundry conditional on the amount of soot are positive scalar multiples of $y^2 = (-(s+1), 0, 1, 0)$.

Show by example that the aggregate technology set fails to be additive.

2.18   Modify the example of a two-commodity production economy given in Section 2.2.7 to allow the first consumer to have endowment $w_1 = (0, 1)$.

2.19   (a) Prove Lemmas 2.24 and 2.25.
(b) Interpret the conclusions of both lemmas in terms of the net trade diagram.
(c) Show that Lemmas 2.24 and 2.25 reduce to Lemmas 1.10 and 1.11 when $Y = \{0\}$ (i.e., for pure exchange).
(d) Use Lemma 2.25 to provide an alternative proof of Theorem 2.23.

2.20   (a) Prove Lemmas 2.27 and 2.28.
(b) Show that these lemmas reduce to Lemmas 1.15 and 1.16 of Chapter 1 when $Y = \{0\}$.

2.21   Prove Theorem 2.29 by mimicking the proof of Theorem 1.17.

2.22   Modify the economy described in Section 2.2.7 by assuming:

(a) the set of firms is $K = \{1, 2\}$ with technology sets

$$Y_1 = Y_2 = \{ (y_1, y_2) \in \mathbf{R}^2 \mid y_1 \leq 0, y_2 \leq \sqrt{-y_1} \};$$

(b) the shares of consumers in profits of the firms are given by $\theta_{11} = .25$, $\theta_{12} = .75$, $\theta_{21} = .75$, and $\theta_{22} = .25$.

Solve for the Walrasian equilibrium and display the result in a net trade diagram.

2.23   Prove the First Fundamental Theorem of welfare economics for an Arrow-Debreu economy.

2.24   Prove that a Walrasian equilibrium for a coalition production economy is Pareto optimal and in the core. Illustrate the conclusion using an appropriately modified net trade diagram.

2.25   Illustrate in a diagram the solution to the model of Marshallian joint supply described in Section 2.4.1 when $a_1 = 4$ and $a_2 = 6$.

2.26   Modify the model of Marshallian joint supply to handle the more general case in which one sheep produces b_1 units of mutton and b_2 units of hides.

2.27   Joint supply applies quite naturally to the production of contingent commodities. Consider an economy with a single consumer (Eve) and three types of commodity. Labor (commodity 3) is used to produce two contingent commodities, (1) fish when the fishing is good and (2) fish when the fish are not biting, according to the constant returns technology $Y = \{ y \in \mathbf{R}^3 \mid y = \lambda(3, 1, -1), \ \lambda \geq 0 \}$. Eve is capable of supplying at most one unit of labor during the day. She maximizes the expected utility function

$$U(x) = \pi \log(x_1) + (1 - \pi) \log(x_2)$$

where π is the probability that fishing is good on the day in question. Eve's endowment is $w = (0, 0, 0)$. Normalize prices so that $p_3 = 1$.

(a) Find the Walrasian equilibrium allocation and prices for this economy.

Now suppose that Eve has two activity vectors to choose from, $y^1 = (3, 1, -1)$ and $y^2 = (1, 2, -1)$, which can be interpreted as fishing at either of two sites. Assuming that she can split her time between the two locations, the technology set becomes

$$Y = \{ y \in \mathbf{R}^3 \mid y = \lambda_1 y^1 + \lambda_2 y^2; \ \lambda_1, \lambda_2 \geq 0 \}.$$

(b) Find the Walrasian equilibrium allocation and prices for this economy. Show in a graph how the equilibrium values for p_1, p_2, x_1, and x_2 depend on π. (Hint: consider separately Case A: $\lambda_1 > 0, \lambda_2 = 0$; Case B: $\lambda_1 = 0, \lambda_2 > 0$; and Case C: $\lambda_1 > 0, \lambda_2 > 0$.)

2.28   Using the parameter values of Exercise 2.25, construct a **Lindahl diagram** analogous to the Marshallian joint supply diagram (Figure 2.9) for the two-consumer public goods model developed in Section 2.4.2.

3

Aumann's model

In most models with a finite number of consumers the core is larger than the set of Walrasian equilibria. What is this telling us? Perhaps that the core is a flabby concept, Walrasian equilibrium precise. But, more likely, this discrepancy signals a problem with the Walrasian hypothesis of price-taking behavior. In most situations where the Walrasian model has been applied, consumers can influence price. The core recognizes the associated opportunities to haggle and bargain. Walrasian equilibrium assumes them away.

Of course, economists have an answer to this criticism. We are not that naive! Although we illustrate the competitive model with an Edgeworth box, the typical applications we have in mind involve not two consumers but many, so many that each consumer has a negligible influence on price. In 1964 the game theorist Robert Aumann made a bold suggestion: if economists intend their models of competition to apply in situations where consumers have negligible influence on price, why not reformulate the model to be consistent with this tacit assumption? The opening two paragraphs of his paper state the case with great force and clarity:

The notion of *perfect competition* is fundamental in the treatment of economic equilibrium. The essential idea of this notion is that the economy under consideration has a "very large" number of participants, and that the influence of each participant is "negligible." Of course, in real life no competition is perfect; but, in economics, as in the physical sciences, the study of the ideal state has proved very fruitful, though in practice it is, at best, only approximately achieved.

Though writers on economic equilibrium have traditionally assumed perfect competition, they have, paradoxically, adopted a mathematical model that does not fit this assumption. Thus a *mathematical model appropriate to the intuitive notion of perfect competition must contain infinitely many participants.* We submit that the most natural model for this purpose contains a *continuum* of participants, similar to the continuum of points on a line or the continuum of particles in a fluid.

Very succinctly, the reason for this is that one can integrate over a continuum, and changing the integrand at a single point does not affect the value of the integral, that is, the actions of a single individual are negligible.

(Aumann (1964), 39 [Italics in original.])

I am introducing Aumann's model early in this book in the belief that the perspective it offers is too important to be put off until later. Because this discussion does appear at an early stage, I will defer a proof of Aumann's equivalence theorem — the equality of core and Walrasian allocations in economies with a continuum of consumers — to a later chapter. However, many aspects of this appealing formulation of competitive theory can be appreciated without much formal mathematics. The first two sections of this chapter explore some concrete applications of Aumann's model presented with a minimum of mathematical fuss. Section one covers the basics while the second illustrates the striking implications of Aumann's approach in situations involving nonconvexity. With these applications serving as motivation, the third section offers a brief tour of some of the basic features of measure and integration theory which underlie his approach. Section four concludes with a discussion of product differentiation and the market for local public goods intended to demonstrate the fundamental way in which Aumann's model should change the way we think about economics.

3.1 Applying Aumann's model

3.1.1 A simple illustration

The surface features of Aumann's program are easily grasped. We begin, in a model of pure exchange, by replacing the finite index set of consumers $I = \{1, \ldots, n\}$ by $I = [0, 1]$, the closed interval of real numbers lying between 0 and 1.[1] For each consumer $i \in I$, we define all of the relevant economic concepts (e.g., consumption sets, budget sets, strict preference sets, and demand sets) just as before. An allocation is a function $x: I \to L_+$, $i \mapsto x_i$, and an endowment a function $w: I \to L_+$, $i \mapsto w_i$. Sums are replaced by integrals, so that feasibility of an allocation requires[2] $\int_0^1 x_i \, di = \int_0^1 w_i \, di$, which we abbreviate to $\int_I x = \int_I w$ where $\int_I$ means "integrate over the set I." The set of feasible allocations becomes

$$\mathrm{F}(\mathcal{E}, I) = \left\{ x: I \to L_+ \mid \int_I x = \int_I w \ \& \ x_i \in X_i \ a.e. \ i \in I \right\}$$

---

1 It might help to think of $i \in I$ as the consumer's "social security number," but where we now require all consumers — except for a lucky few — to memorize an infinite string of digits!

2 In models with a continuum of consumers, you will often see x_i written $x(i)$ and w_i written $w(i)$, giving the integral the more familiar appearance $\int_0^1 x(i) \, di = \int_0^1 w(i) \, di$.

where X_i denotes the consumption set of consumer i and "a.e.," an abbreviation for "almost every," replaces the requirement "for all" used in the finite case.[3] A Walrasian equilibrium is a pair (x, p) with $x \in F(\mathcal{E}, I)$ and $p \in L' \backslash \{0\}$ such that $x_i \in \phi_i(p)$ (a.e. $i \in I$).

This brief overview of the Aumann model is superficial, glossing over the technical refinements necessary for a rigorous model. In particular, we really do not know at this point what constitutes an "integral." The Riemann integral encountered in beginning calculus courses is appropriate if the function x or w is a continuous function of i, but why should allocations or endowments vary continuously with one's social security number? However, let's continue playing fast and loose for the moment by considering a simple example of how Aumann's model is applied when Riemann integration is the right thing to do.

Suppose that we have a pure exchange economy with a continuum of consumers ($I = [0, 1]$) and two commodities ($L = \mathbf{R}^2$). Assume that all consumers have the same endowment, $w_i = (2, 2)$ for all $i \in I$. However, consumers have varying tastes: those with low social security numbers have a relatively weak preference for the first commodity and those with high social security numbers a relatively strong preference. More precisely, we assume that consumer $i \in I$ has Cobb-Douglas preferences represented by the utility function $u_i(x_i) = x_{i1}^{\alpha_i} x_{i2}^{1-\alpha_i}$ where $\alpha: I \to [0, 1]$ is a *continuous* function which for specificity we take to be $\alpha: i \mapsto \alpha_i = i$.

Normalizing prices to sum to one, we conclude that consumer i has wealth $p \cdot w_i = 2$ and hence demand

$$\phi_i(p) = \left(\alpha_i \frac{p \cdot w_i}{p_1}, (1 - \alpha_i) \frac{p \cdot w_i}{p_2} \right) = \left(\frac{2i}{p_1}, \frac{2 - 2i}{p_2} \right).$$

Since the endowment function w is a constant (and, hence, trivially continuous in i) and since ϕ_i is singleton-valued and, for fixed price functional p, a continuous function of i, the Riemann integrals we require are well-defined. Solving for a Walrasian equilibrium amounts to finding a price functional $p \in L'$ and an allocation $x_i \in \phi_i(p)$ (a.e. $i \in I$) such that $\int_I x = \int_I w$ or, market by market, $\int_I x_1 = \int_I w_1$ and $\int_I x_2 = \int_I w_2$. Evaluating the left hand side of each of these market clearing equations yields $\int_I x_1 = \int_0^1 2i/p_1 di = 1/p_1$ and $\int_I x_2 = \int_0^1 (2 - 2i)/p_2 \, di = 1/p_2$. Evaluating the right hand sides yields $\int_I w_1 = \int_0^1 2 \, di = 2$ and $\int_I w_2 = \int_0^1 2 \, di = 2$. Therefore, the market clearing condition reduces to $(1/p_1, 1/p_2) = (2, 2)$ or $p = (.5, .5)$.

Using this equilibrium price functional, we find that the equilibrium allo-

---

3 For the moment, interpret "a.e." as "for all." The meaning of "almost every" will be clarified shortly.

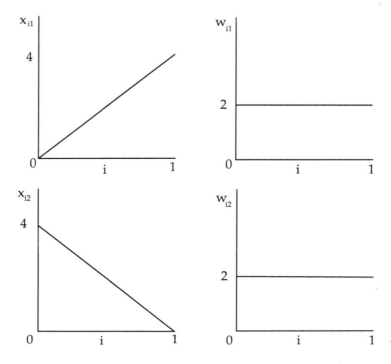

Fig. 3.1. Equilibrium: example 1.

cation assigns to consumer i the commodity bundle

$$x_i = \left(\frac{2i}{p_1}, \frac{2-2i}{p_2}\right) = (4i, 4-4i).$$

Figure 3.1 displays the equilibrium allocation as well as the initial endowment for each of the markets. Notice in particular the geometric interpretation of the integrals: $\int_I x_1 = \int_I w_1$ translates to the assertion that the area under the function x_1 equals that under the function w_1, and the same holds for commodity two.

The Walrasian equilibrium allocation implies a net trade allocation $\Delta_w x = x - w$ which assigns $\Delta_w x_i = (4i, 4-4i) - (2, 2) = (4i-2, 2-4i)$ to consumer i. As we should expect, the net trades "sum" (i.e., integrate) to zero: $\int_I \Delta_w x = (\int_I (4i - 2) \; di, \int_I (2 - 4i) \; di) = (0, 0)$. The corresponding net trade diagram is exhibited in Figure 3.2 with a few of the consumer strict preference sets. Although of course we cannot illustrate them all, net trades are in fact uniformly distributed along the hyperplane from $(-2, 2)$ to $(2, -2)$.

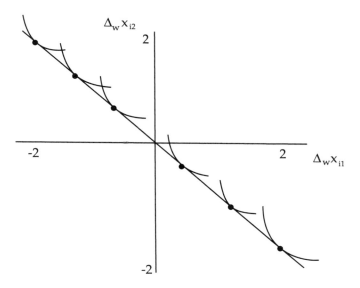

Fig. 3.2. Net trade diagram: example 1.

Production economies with a continuum of players can be handled with equal ease. Consider a two-commodity economy in which the first commodity is used to produce the second with a constant returns technology described by the technology set

$$Y = \{\, y \in \mathbf{R}^2 \mid y = \lambda(-\beta, 1), \ \lambda \geq 0 \,\}$$

where β is a positive constant. Assume that all consumers have the same endowment, $w_i = (2,0)$, and hence, under the normalization $p_1 = 1$, wealth $p \cdot w_i = 2$. Let utility functions take the form $u_i(x_i) = x_{i1}^{\alpha_i} x_{i2}^{1-\alpha_i}$ where again we assume that $\alpha_i = i$ for purposes of illustration.

If the second commodity is produced at all, then, because of constant returns, profit must equal zero. Thus, $0 = p \cdot y = p \cdot [\lambda(-\beta, 1)]$ for all $\lambda > 0$ implies $-\beta p_1 + p_2 = 0$ or $p_2 = \beta p_1 = \beta$ where in the last step we use the normalization $p_1 = 1$. Since utility functions are Cobb-Douglas, the demand set of consumer i is $\phi_i(p) = (i\, p \cdot w_i / p_1, (1-i)\, p \cdot w_i / p_2) = (2i/p_1, (2-2i)/p_2)$. Taking $\beta = 1$ results in an equilibrium price functional $p = (1,1)$, demand sets $\phi_i(p) = (2i, 2-2i)$, and net trade demand sets $\Delta_w \phi_i(p) = (2i, 2-2i) - (2,0) = (2i-2, 2-2i)$.

The most natural way to interpret this equilibrium at the aggregate level is in per capita terms. Thus, the allocation x assigning $x_i = (2i, 2-2i)$ to each consumer $i \in I$ yields per capita allocations $\int_I x_1 = \int_0^1 2i \, di = 1$ and $\int_I x_2 = \int_0^1 (2 - 2i) \, di = 1$. The feasibility condition $\int_I x - \int_I w = y$ translates to $(1, 1) - (2, 0) = (-1, 1)$ with the activity vector y also viewed in per capita terms: one unit of the first commodity per capita is used to produce one unit of the second commodity per capita.

When portrayed in the net trade diagram, net trades are uniformly distributed along the hyperplane from $(-2, 2)$ (for consumer $i = 0$) to $(0, 0)$ (for consumer $i = 1$) with an average value equal to the per capita activity vector $(-1, 1)$.

3.1.2 A type economy

Assuming that allocations, endowments, and demand functions are continuous functions of "social security numbers" is clearly not very natural. As we will see later, **type economies** of the sort we are about to consider point the way toward a more satisfactory interpretation of the Aumann model.

Once again we take as our starting point a continuum of consumers represented by the interval $I = [0, 1]$. However, we now assume that the index set I can be partitioned into a *finite* number of disjoint subsets

$$I = S_1 \cup S_2 \cup \ldots \cup S_r \quad \text{where} \quad S_i \cap S_j = \emptyset \quad \text{for all} \quad i \neq j,$$

and that all consumers belonging to a given subset have identical preferences and endowments. Consumers belonging to the same subset S_t ($t \in \{1, \ldots, r\} =: T$) are said to have the same **type**.

Assume, for simplicity, that there are just two types of consumer, so that $I = S_1 \cup S_2$ with $S_1 \cap S_2 = \emptyset$, and that the commodity space is $\mathbf{R}^2$. All consumers of a given type t have identical Cobb-Douglas preferences, $u_i(x_i) = x_{i1}^{\alpha_t} x_{i2}^{1-\alpha_t}$, identical endowments, $w_i = (a_t, b_t)$, and therefore identical demand functions,

$$\phi_i(p) = \left(\alpha_t \frac{p_1 a_t + p_2 b_t}{p_1}, (1 - \alpha_t) \frac{p_1 a_t + p_2 b_t}{p_2} \right).$$

Let $\lambda(S_1)$ and $\lambda(S_2)$ denote the fraction of consumers of type one and type two respectively, where $\lambda(S_1) + \lambda(S_2) = 1$. As we noted a moment ago, the integrals we have been computing can be interpreted not only as areas under various curves but also as the *average* demand and *average* endowment of consumers in the economy. This suggests the appropriate definition of the corresponding integrals in the current context. The average endowment of commodity one is $\int_I w_1 := a_1 \lambda(S_1) + a_2 \lambda(S_2)$ and the average endowment of commodity two $\int_I w_2 := b_1 \lambda(S_1) + b_2 \lambda(S_2)$. Similarly, an allocation $x_i \in \phi_i(p)$ (a.e. $i \in I$) yields an average allocation

$$\int_I x_1 = \frac{\alpha_1(p_1 a_1 + p_2 b_1)}{p_1} \lambda(S_1) + \frac{\alpha_2(p_1 a_2 + p_2 b_2)}{p_1} \lambda(S_2)$$

for commodity one and

$$\int_I x_2 = \frac{(1 - \alpha_1)(p_1 a_1 + p_2 b_1)}{p_2} \lambda(S_1) + \frac{(1 - \alpha_2)(p_1 a_2 + p_2 b_2)}{p_2} \lambda(S_2)$$

for commodity two.

Since the two market clearing equations are redundant, we can normalize prices $(p_1 + p_2 = 1)$ and clear only one of the markets (say, the first). Thus, $\int_I x_1 = \int_I w_1$ implies

$$\frac{\alpha_1(p_1 a_1 + p_2 b_1)}{p_1} \lambda(S_1) + \frac{\alpha_2(p_1 a_2 + p_2 b_2)}{p_1} \lambda(S_2) = a_1 \lambda(S_1) + a_2 \lambda(S_2)$$

which, after simplification, yields

$$p_1 = \frac{\alpha_1 b_1 \lambda(S_1) + \alpha_2 b_2 \lambda(S_2)}{[(1 - \alpha_1)a_1 + \alpha_1 b_1]\lambda(S_1) + [(1 - \alpha_1)a_2 + \alpha_2 b_2]\lambda(S_2)} \tag{3.1}$$

as the equilibrium price of the first commodity and $p_2 = 1 - p_1$ as the equilibrium price of the second.

Suppose, for example, that $\alpha_1 = .5$, $\alpha_2 = .5$, $(a_1, b_1) = (1, 3)$, and $(a_2, b_2) = (3, 1)$. Equation (3.1) reduces to

$$p_1 = \frac{3\lambda(S_1) + 1 - \lambda(S_1)}{4\lambda(S_1) + 4(1 - \lambda(S_1))} = .25 + .5\lambda(S_1).$$

If $\lambda(S_1) = .5$, so that there are equal numbers of each consumer type, the equilibrium price of the first commodity is $p_1 = .5$, precisely the result we obtained in the two-consumer case (with the same choice of preferences and endowments for each type) in Chapter 1. However, now we have the ability to vary the proportion of each type. Since consumers of type one are endowed with three units of the second commodity but only one unit of the first while consumers of type two have the reverse, if we increase the proportion of consumers of type one the first commodity will be in increasingly short supply. The equation derived above yields the plausible conclusion that, as the proportion of type one increases, the equilibrium price of the commodity which is becoming relatively scarce (commodity one) will increase.

Figure 3.3 portrays the net trade diagram for this economy when $\lambda(S_1) = .25$ and $p = (3/8, 5/8)$. A simple computation yields the net trade allocation $(2, -6/5)$ for consumers of type one and $(-2/3, 2/5)$ for consumers of type

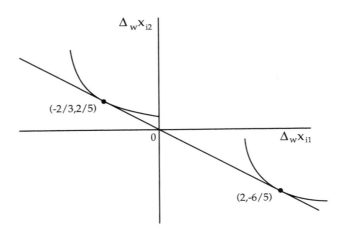

Fig. 3.3. Net trade diagram: example 2.

two. In contrast to Chapter 1, the net trades no longer cancel to 0 because it is no longer the case that there are equal numbers of consumers of each type. Instead it is the weighted net trade vector, $\int_I \Delta_w x = (2, -6/5)(.25) + (-2/3, 2/5)(.75)$, which sums to zero.

3.2 Dealing with nonconvexity

Although Aumann's original focus was on core equivalence, his reformulation of the competitive model has another consequence at least as profound. Convexity, like price-taking behavior, is a mainstay of the standard Walrasian model, a feature which economists had come to believe they could not do without. Such a development would surely have horrified our intellectual forebear, Adam Smith: specialization was central to his vision of the workings of the competitive market, but convexity is the enemy of specialization.

What Aumann found was that his reformulation of the Walrasian model eliminated much of the need for convexity hypotheses at the level of the individual consumer or firm. Just as with the discrepancy between Walrasian and core allocations, economists' reliance on convexity hypotheses turned out to be largely an artifact of an inconsistently formulated model, a model in which individuals were posited to have negligible influence when in fact they did not. Remove the inconsistency and you eliminate the artifact. Although we will defer a rigorous examination of the "convexifying effect of thick markets" for now, demonstrating how readily Aumann's model accommodates nonconvexity requires no fancy mathematics.

3.2.1 Nonconvex preferences

The economy explored in Exercise 1.18 (indifference curves look like stair steps) illustrates the typical difficulties which nonconvexity poses for competitive equilibrium theory: Walrasian equilibria may exist, or they may fail to exist, depending on the circumstances (the number of consumers in this case). With a continuum of consumers, the existence problem disappears since it is always possible to give half of the consumers the net trade $(-1, 1)$ and the other half the net trade $(1, -1)$ implying $\Delta_w x_i \in \phi_i(p)$ for all $i \in I$ and $\int_I \Delta_w x = (-1, 1)(.5) + (1, -1)(.5) = 0$.

A related example illustrates even more vividly the beneficial effects of large numbers in dealing with nonconvexity. Suppose that consumers are represented by the interval $[0, 1]$ with endowments $w_i = (1, 2)$ and utility functions $u_i(x_i) = \sqrt{x_{i1}^2 + (i x_{i2})^2}$ for each $i \in I$. It is easy to see that the upper contour sets for these preferences are nonconvex: e.g., for $i = 1$ the indifference curve corresponding to utility level 1 is a quarter circle with origin $(0, 0)$ and radius 1. For $i < 1$ these circles stretch out in the direction of increasing x_1, but the upper contour sets remain nonconvex.

Since both commodities are "goods," not "bads," equilibrium prices (if they exist) will necessarily be positive. When faced with positive prices for each commodity, a consumer clearly maximizes utility by choosing one of the corner solutions where indifference curves touch either the x_1 or the x_2 axis. Apart from the special case where the two corner solutions yield equal utility, the consumer will spend all of her wealth on one of the commodities or the other. Normalizing $p_1 = 1$, I claim that the demand set for consumer i takes the form

$$\phi_i(p) = \begin{cases} (p \cdot w_i, 0) & \text{if } i \in [0, p_2), \\ (0, p \cdot w_i / p_2) & \text{if } i \in (p_2, 1], \\ (p \cdot w_i, 0) \cup (0, p \cdot w_i / p_2) & \text{if } i = p_2. \end{cases}$$

To validate this conclusion, compare the utilities at each of the corner solutions: $u_i(p \cdot w_i, 0) = p \cdot w_i$ and $u_i(0, p \cdot w_i / p_2) = i p \cdot w_i / p_2$. Thus, $u_i(p \cdot w_i, 0) > u_i(0, p \cdot w_i / p_2)$ iff $i < p_2$; $u_i(p \cdot w_i, 0) < u_i(0, p \cdot w_i / p_2)$ iff $i > p_2$; and $u_i(p \cdot w_i, 0) = u_i(0, p \cdot w_i / p_2)$ iff $i = p_2$. When $i = p_2$, the consumer is indifferent between the two corner solutions. Since a single point on the continuum has negligible influence, which bundle we assign to this consumer is irrelevant. We arbitrarily choose the assignment which sets $x_i = (0, p \cdot w_i / p_2)$ if $i = p_2$.

By Walras' Law it suffices to clear one of the two markets, say, the first. If $x_i \in \phi_i(p)$ for a.e. $i \in I$, then the per capita allocation of the first commodity is $\int_I x_1 = \int_0^{p_2} p \cdot w_i \ di = p_2 + 2p_2^2$ and the per capita endowment $\int_I w_1 = \int_0^1 1 \ di = 1$. Equating $\int_I x_1 = \int_I w_1$ yields the quadratic equation $2(p_2)^2 + p_2 - 1 = 0$, which has as its solution $p_2 = (-1 \pm \sqrt{1 + 8})/4 = \{-1, .5\}$. Since both commodities are "goods," we can eliminate the negative solution. Therefore, the Walrasian equilibrium price functional is $p = (1, .5)$ and the Walrasian equilibrium allocation

$$x_i = \begin{cases} (2, 0) & \text{for all } i \in [0, .5), \\ (0, 4) & \text{for all } i \in [.5, 1]. \end{cases}$$

If you plot the allocations and endowments as functions of i, once again you will find that in equilibrium the area under x_1 equals the area under w_1 and the area under x_2 equals the area under w_2.

3.2.2 A market for automobiles

Consumer durables such as cars are clearly indivisible. Indivisibility is another source of nonconvexity which Aumann's approach handles with ease. To illustrate we now construct two models of the market for automobiles, one a pure exchange economy and the other with production.

Assume that there are only two commodities in the economy, a perfectly divisible "composite commodity" (commodity one) and automobiles (commodity two). Let the consumption set for consumer $i \in I$ be $X_i = \mathbf{R}_+ \times \{0, 1, 2\}$ where for simplicity we assume that at most two cars can be consumed. Suppose consumers have identical utility functions, $u_i(x_i) = x_{i1}(1 + 2x_{i2})$, and endowments

$$w_i = \begin{cases} (10i, 0) & \text{for } i \in S_1 := [0, .9), \\ (10i, 10) & \text{for } i \in S_2 := [.9, 1]. \end{cases}$$

Thus, consumers in S_2 are the car dealers who begin with an initial endowment of 10 cars per capita. Normalize prices so that $p_1 = 1$.

As usual in problems involving nonconvexity, demand functions involve case statements. I claim that for consumer $i \in S_1$,

$$\phi_i(p) = \begin{cases} (p \cdot w_i, 0) & \text{if } i \in [0, .15p_2), \\ (p \cdot w_i - p_2, 1) & \text{if } i \in [.15p_2, .35p_2), \\ (p \cdot w_i - 2p_2, 2) & \text{if } i \in [.35p_2, .9), \end{cases}$$

corresponding to the case where the consumer purchases 0, 1, or 2 cars respectively.[4]

To derive the first part of this statement, note that consumer i prefers to purchase no car if

$$u_i(p \cdot w_i, 0) > u_i(p \cdot w_i - p_2, 1),$$

which, upon substitution of the explicit equations for the utility function and endowment, becomes $p \cdot w_i > 3(p \cdot w_i - p_2)$ and finally $i < .15p_2$. Similarly, purchasing a single car is more attractive than purchasing two if

$$u_i(p \cdot w_i - p_2, 1) > u_i(p \cdot w_i - 2p_2, 2),$$

which reduces to $3(p \cdot w_i - p_2) > 5(p \cdot w_i - 2p_2)$ and finally $i < .35p_2$.

The demand function for the consumers in set S_2 is derived in exactly the same way. However, to reduce the computational burden, I have rigged the numbers so that all car dealers will end up consuming two cars (they are rich!), so we have no need to derive their demand function explicitly: we "know" that in equilibrium $\phi_i(p) = (p \cdot w_i - 2p_2, 2)$ for all $i \in [.9, 1]$.

Once again we need only clear one of the markets (the other then clears automatically thanks to Walras' Law). We will clear the market for automobiles. If $x_i \in \phi_i(p)$ for all $i \in I$, then

$$\int_I x_2 = \int_{.15p_2}^{.35p_2} 1 \, di + \int_{.35p_2}^1 2 \, di = 2 - .5p_2.$$

Per capita endowment of automobiles in the economy is $\int_I w_2 = \int_{.9}^1 10 \, di = 1$. Equating $\int_I x_2 = \int_I w_2$ yields $p = (1, 2)$ as the Walrasian equilibrium price functional, implying an equilibrium wealth distribution

$$p \cdot w_i = \begin{cases} 10i & \text{for } i \in S_1, \\ 10i + 20 & \text{for } i \in S_2. \end{cases}$$

and a Walrasian equilibrium allocation

$$x_i = \begin{cases} (10i, 0) & \text{for } i \in [0, .3), \\ (10i - 2, 1) & \text{for } i \in [.3, .7), \\ (10i - 4, 2) & \text{for } i \in [.7, .9), \\ (10i + 16, 2) & \text{for } i \in [.9, 1]. \end{cases}$$

As a check on our computations, we can verify that the market for the

---

4 The knife-edge cases where $i = .15p_2$ (consumer i is indifferent between purchasing zero cars and purchasing a single car) and $i = .35p_2$ (consumer i is indifferent between purchasing a single car and purchasing two cars) have been arbitrarily assigned.

first commodity also clears:

$$\int_I x_1 = \int_0^{.3} 10i\, di + \int_{.3}^{.7} (10i - 2)\, di + \int_{.7}^{.9} (10i - 4)\, di + \int_{.9}^1 (10i + 16)\, di$$
$$= 5$$

and $\int_I w_1 = \int_0^1 10i\, di = 5$.

Now suppose that we modify the description of our economy to allow for the production of automobiles. Assume that preferences are as before and that endowments are given by $w_i = (10i, 0)$ with no cars owned initially. However, the divisible commodity can be used as an input to produce automobiles subject to constant returns:[5]

$$Y = \{\, y \in \mathbf{R}^2 \mid y = \lambda(-\beta, 1), \lambda \geq 0 \,\}$$

where β is a positive constant.

If cars are produced at all, then profits will equal zero in equilibrium, implying that $-\beta p_1 + p_2 = 0$ or $p_2 = \beta p_1 = \beta$ where in the last step we normalize prices by setting $p_1 = 1$. Consumer demand takes exactly the same form as that given above in the pure exchange case for the non-car dealers (no one in this production economy owns cars initially). Therefore,

$$\phi_i(p) = \begin{cases} (10i, 0) & \text{if } i \in [0, .15\beta), \\ (10i - \beta, 1) & \text{if } i \in [.15\beta, .35\beta), \\ (10i - 2\beta, 2) & \text{if } i \in [.35\beta, 1]. \end{cases}$$

From the first line of this case statement, we conclude that no cars will be produced if $.15\beta > 1$ or, equivalently, $\beta > 20/3$. From the second line or the third, we conclude that no consumer will purchase two cars instead of one if $.35\beta > 1$ or, equivalently, $\beta > 20/7$. Suppose we choose a value for the input parameter β small enough to permit the wealthiest consumers to afford two cars, say, $\beta = 2$. We conclude immediately that the Walrasian allocation will be

$$x_i = \begin{cases} (10i, 0) & \text{if } i \in [0, .3), \\ (10i - 2, 1) & \text{if } i \in [.3, .7), \\ (10i - 4, 2) & \text{if } i \in [.7, 1]. \end{cases}$$

Notice how naturally some consumers become "priced out" of the market for cars. This is a phenomenon which is very hard to capture in a model without indivisibility, but — as many students can attest — quite characteristic of the "real world."

---

5 This example highlights why the elements of Y ought to be interpreted in per capita terms: the fact that $(-\beta/2, .5) \in Y$ means that $\beta/2$ units of input per capita is capable of producing .5 cars per capita and not that producers are somehow able to build half a car.

To compute the number of cars produced per capita, we simply integrate the allocation x_2 to obtain

$$\int_I x_2 = \int_{.3}^{.7} 1 \, di + \int_{.7}^1 2 \, di = 1.$$

The per capita input of the divisible commodity needed to produce this output is just as easy to determine:

$$\beta \int_I x_2 = \beta \left(\int_{.3}^{.7} 1 \, di + \int_{.7}^1 2 \, di \right) = \beta = 2.$$

Therefore, the per capita aggregate activity vector for this economy in equilibrium is $y = (-2, 1)$.

To compute the per capita consumption of the divisible commodity, we integrate the allocation x_1

$$\begin{aligned} \int_I x_1 &= \int_0^{.3} (10i) \, di + \int_{.3}^{.7} (10i - \beta) \, di + \int_{.7}^1 (10i - 2\beta) \, di \\ &= 3. \end{aligned}$$

If we have stayed on track, our solution should satisfy the feasibility requirement $\int_I x - \int_I w = y$, and it does: from the computations above, $\int_I x = (3, 1)$, $\int_I w = (5, 0)$, and $y = (-2, 1)$.

3.2.3 A market for houses

The market for houses provides yet another illustration of how Aumann's model permits a natural modeling of indivisibility. We imagine now an economy with three commodities: a low quality house, a high quality house, and a perfectly divisible commodity. We assume that a consumer will consume at most one house so that consumption sets take the form

$$X_i = (\{0\} \times \{0\} \times \mathbf{R}_+) \cup (\{1\} \times \{0\} \times \mathbf{R}_+) \cup (\{0\} \times \{1\} \times \mathbf{R}_+).$$

All consumers $i \in I$ have identical utility functions given by $u_i(x_i) = (1 + x_{i1} + 3x_{i2})x_{i3}$ and endowments

$$w_i = \begin{cases} (0, 0, 100i) & \text{for } i \in S_1 := [0, .9), \\ (6, 3, 100i) & \text{for } i \in S_2 := [.9, .1]. \end{cases}$$

Thus, consumers belonging to the set S_2, the *landlords*, own all of the houses initially. We adopt the price normalization $p_3 = 1$.

As in the case of automobiles, the demand function for a consumer $i \in S_1$

is given by a case statement:[6]

$$\phi_i(p) = \begin{cases} (0,0,p \cdot w_i) & \text{if } i \in [0, .02p_1), \\ (1,0,p \cdot w_i - p_1) & \text{if } i \in [.02p_1, .02p_2 - .01p_1), \\ (0,1,p \cdot w_i - p_2) & \text{if } i \in [.02p_2 - .01p_1, .9). \end{cases}$$

This assertion is proved in much the same way as with automobiles. A consumer chooses no house over a low quality house if

$$u_i(0,0,p \cdot w_i) > u_i(1,0,p \cdot w_i - p_1),$$

which reduces to $p \cdot w_i > 2(p \cdot w_i - p_1)$ and finally $i < .02p_1$. Similarly, a consumer chooses a low quality house over a high quality house if

$$u_i(1,0,p \cdot w_i - p_1) > u_i(0,1,p \cdot w_i - p_2),$$

which reduces to $2(p \cdot w_i - p_1) > 4(p \cdot w_i - p_2)$ and finally $i < .02p_2 - .01p_1$.

The demand function for consumers in set S_2 is derived in essentially the same way, but again the numbers have been rigged so that the landlords (who are rich) always get good houses. Thus, we "know" that $\phi_i(p) = (0,1,p \cdot w_i - p_2)$ for all $i \in S_2$.

We now have three markets to clear rather than two, but it suffices to clear all but one. We will clear the two housing markets. Choosing the divisible commodity as *numéraire*, $p_3 = 1$, the consumer wealth functions become

$$w_i = \begin{cases} 100i & \text{if } i \in S_1, \\ 6p_1 + 3p_2 + 100i & \text{if } i \in S_2. \end{cases}$$

If $x_i \in \phi_i(p)$ for all $i \in I$, then

$$\int_I x_1 = \int_{.02p_1}^{.02p_2 - .01p_1} (1) \, di = .02p_2 - .03p_1,$$

$$\int_I x_2 = \int_{.02p_2 - .01p_1}^{1} (1) \, di = 1 - .02p_2 + .01p_1,$$

$$\int_I w_1 = \int_{.9}^{1} 6 \, di = .6,$$

$$\int_I w_2 = \int_{.9}^{1} 3 \, di = .3.$$

Equating $\int_I x_1 = \int_I w_1$ and $\int_I x_2 = \int_I w_2$ gives $2p_2 - 3p_1 = 60$ and $2p_2 - p_1 = 70$, which yields as the Walrasian equilibrium price functional $p = (5, 37.5, 1)$. The boundary points separating consumers making the three

---

6 Once again the knife-edge consumers must be given an arbitrary assignment.

different types of choice are $.02p_1 = .1$ and $.02p_2 - .01p_1 = .7$, so the equilibrium allocation is

$$x_i = \begin{cases} (0,0,100i) & \text{for } i \in [0,.1), \\ (1,0,100i-5) & \text{for } i \in [.1,.7), \\ (0,1,100i-37.5) & \text{for } i \in [.7,.9), \\ (0,1,100i+105) & \text{for } i \in [.9,1]. \end{cases}$$

Note once again how indivisibility allows for consumers to be priced out of the market: the consumers $i \in [0,.1]$ are homeless. Integrating the equilibrium allocation yields the per capita consumption $\int_I x = (.6,.3,50)$, which, of course, equals the per capita initial endowment $\int_I w = (.6,.3,50)$.

This model is easily modified to allow for production. Assume that both low and high quality houses are produced subject to constant returns with technology sets

$$\begin{aligned} Y_1 &= \{\, y \in \mathbf{R}^3 \mid y = \lambda(1,0,-\beta_1), \lambda \geq 0) \,\} \\ Y_2 &= \{\, y \in \mathbf{R}^3 \mid y = \lambda(0,1,-\beta_2), \lambda \geq 0) \,\} \end{aligned}$$

(where $\beta_2 > \beta_1 > 0$) and aggregate production technology set $Y = Y_1 + Y_2$. We will assume that consumer endowments are given by $w_i = (0,0,100i)$ so that no houses are owned initially.

If both types of house are produced in equilibrium, then the zero profit condition implies that $p_1 = \beta_1 p_3$ and $p_2 = \beta_2 p_3$ or, with the normalization $p_3 = 1$, $p_1 = \beta_1$ and $p_2 = \beta_2$. Demand functions have exactly the form derived for the consumers in S_1 for the pure exchange economy:

$$\phi_i(p) = \begin{cases} (0,0,100i) & \text{for } i \in [0,.02\beta_1), \\ (1,0,100i-\beta_1) & \text{for } i \in [.02\beta_1,.02\beta_2-.01\beta_1), \\ (0,1,100i-\beta_2) & \text{for } i \in [.02\beta_2-.01\beta_1,1]. \end{cases}$$

Since high quality houses presumably take more inputs to produce than low, we assume that $\beta_2 > \beta_1$. We conclude immediately that houses will be produced only if $.02\beta_1 < 1$ or, equivalently, $\beta_1 < 50$, and high quality houses will be produced only if $.02\beta_2 - .01\beta_1 < 1$ or, equivalently, $\beta_2 < (100+\beta_1)/2$.

Suppose we choose $\beta_1 = 20$ and $\beta_2 = 50$. The boundaries between the consumers choosing the three different options become $.02\beta_1 = .4$ and $.02\beta_2 - .01\beta_1 = .8$, and the equilibrium Walrasian allocation is

$$x_i = \begin{cases} (0,0,100i) & \text{for } i \in [0,.4), \\ (1,0,100i-20) & \text{for } i \in [.4,8), \\ (0,1,100i-50) & \text{for } i \in [.8,1]. \end{cases}$$

Since, as you can easily verify, $\int_I x = (.4,.2,32)$, $\int_I w = (0,0,50)$, and

$y = (.4, .2, -18)$, the feasibility condition is satisfied: $\int_I x - \int_I w = y$ becomes $(.4, .2, 32) - (0, 0, 50) = (.4, .2, -18)$.

3.3 Measure and integration

This informal presentation of Aumann's model has, I hope, stimulated your curiosity about what it takes to make the theory rigorous. In this short space I clearly cannot duplicate a course in real analysis, nor should I. If you reach the conclusion that learning more mathematics is worth the investment, the proper place to learn is in the mathematics department. This rapid tour of measure and integration theory is simply an introduction, intended to dispel some of the aura of mystery which you might otherwise associate with the subject and to provide some of the economic motivation and interpretation which mathematicians are unlikely to supply.

We begin by reviewing the definition of the integral used in beginning calculus courses, known as the Riemann integral.

3.3.1 The Riemann integral

For concreteness, consider the interval $I = [0, 1]$ and suppose that I has been partitioned into a finite collection of disjoint subintervals $\{ I_t \mid t \in T \}$ which collectively cover I. Specifically, let $\{ s_0, s_1 \ldots, s_r \}$ be a collection of elements of the interval $[0, 1]$ with

$$0 = s_0 < s_1 < \cdots < s_r = 1$$

and define $I_t = [s_{t-1}, s_t)$ for $t = 1, \ldots, r - 1$ and $I_r = [s_{r-1}, s_r]$.

We define a **step function** on I to be a function $\psi \colon I \to \mathbf{R}_+$ which is constant over each of the subintervals I_t in some partition of I such as the one defined above: i.e., $\psi(i) = a_t \in \mathbf{R}_+$ for all $i \in I_t$ and $t \in T$. The reason for beginning with step functions is that everyone agrees how to define the integral of such a function: it is simply the sum of the areas of all the rectangles which lie below the graph of the function. Thus,

$$\int_I \psi := \int_I \psi(i) di = \sum_{t \in T} a_t \ell(I_t)$$

where $\ell(I_t)$ is the length of the subinterval I_t.

Given any bounded function $f \colon I \to \mathbf{R}_+$, the idea behind the Riemann integral is to try to approximate the function as closely as possible by the type of functions which we know how to integrate, the step functions. In approximating f, we can try to approximate either "from below" or "from above."

If we consider step functions lying everywhere on or above f, written $\psi \geq f$, then to approximate the area under f we want to find a step function ψ such that the integral $\int_I \psi$ is as small as possible. The best we can hope for is to find a step function whose integral equals the greatest lower bound (infimum) of such integrals, $\inf_{\psi \geq f} \int_I \psi$. Thus, we define the **upper Riemann integral**

$$R^u \int_I f = \inf_{\psi \geq f} \int_I \psi.$$

If, on the other hand, we try to approximate from below, then the best we can hope for is to find a step function $\psi \leq f$ whose integral equals the least upper bound (supremum) of such integrals, $\sup_{\psi \leq f} \int_I \psi$. Thus, we define the **lower Riemann integral**

$$R_l \int_I f = \sup_{\psi \leq f} \int_I \psi.$$

Provided that f is bounded, the upper and lower Riemann integrals will exist and be finite, and it is obvious that

$$R_l \int_I f \leq R^u \int_I f.$$

If these two integrals agree, then we say that f is Riemann integrable and define the Riemann integral to be their common value, which we denote as $R \int_I f$.

The key fact that makes beginning calculus a going concern (at least the integration part) is that *every continuous function is Riemann integrable.* In other words, under such circumstances we have a reasonable notion of the integral of f (interpreted as the area under the graph of the function), and, since lots of useful functions are continuous, there is no difficulty coming up with enough material to fill a year's course in introductory calculus.

3.3.2 The Lebesgue integral

However, not every bounded function on the interval $[0,1]$ is Riemann integrable. A standard counterexample is the following. Let $f: I \to \mathbf{R}_+$ be the function defined by

$$f(i) = \begin{cases} 0 & \text{if } i \text{ is irrational,} \\ 1 & \text{if } i \text{ is rational.} \end{cases}$$

Because every interval contains an irrational number, the only step function $\psi \le f$ is the function which equals 0 everywhere. Because every interval contains a rational number, any step function $\psi \ge f$ must everywhere on $[0, 1]$ take on values at least equal to 1. Therefore, the lower Riemann integral of f equals 0 and the upper integral equals 1, and so f is not Riemann integrable.[7]

The type economies considered in Section 3.1.2 provide a hint of how one can generalize the notion of integration to cover functions such as the one given above. Let S_1 denote the set of rational numbers and S_2 the set of irrational numbers in the interval $[0, 1]$. Suppose that, somehow, we could measure the fraction of points lying in each of these sets, say $\lambda(S_1)$ and $\lambda(S_2)$ where $0 \le \lambda(S_1) \le 1$ and $0 \le \lambda(S_2) \le 1$. To make much sense as fractions, we want the fractions to add to one, $\lambda(S_1) + \lambda(S_2) = 1$, since S_1 and S_2 are disjoint and their union equals the entire set I. Just as with a type economy, the integral of f should simply be the average: i.e.,

$$\int_I f = (1)\lambda(S_1) + (0)\lambda(S_2) = \lambda(S_1).$$

Thus, the problem of defining a reasonable notion of the integral of f reduces to the problem of measuring the "size" of S_1 and S_2.

The subset S_1, the set of rational numbers in the interval $[0, 1]$, is countably infinite and, as we will see shortly, countably infinite subsets of the interval $[0, 1]$ have (Lebesgue) measure zero. Therefore, $\lambda(S_1) = 0$, $\lambda(S_2) = 1$, and $\int_I f = 0$.

Perhaps the most natural interpretation of this result is in probabilistic terms. If we imagine drawing a number randomly from the interval $[0, 1]$ where all numbers are equally likely to be drawn (the uniform distribution on $[0, 1]$), then we are claiming that the probability of drawing a rational number is zero while the probability of drawing an irrational number is one. The following consideration may make this assertion seem more plausible. The decimal expansion of any rational number eventually begins to repeat itself: e.g.,

$$\frac{1}{4} = .25000000\ldots$$

$$\frac{1}{3} = .33333333\ldots$$

$$\frac{1}{11} = .09090909\ldots$$

---

7 Note that f is not continuous on $[0, 1]$. In fact, it is not even continuous almost everywhere. Therefore, f is not necessarily Riemann integrable, and we have just shown that it is not.

Decimal expansions of irrational numbers, on the other hand, never get locked into such repetition: patterns may persist for a while, but the repetition always breaks down. If we imagine generating these infinite sequences of digits by repeated independent trials where in each trial we randomly select an integer between 0 and 9, then it seems plausible that any pattern will almost certainly be broken eventually: i.e., the probability of obtaining an irrational number is one. The assertion that $\int_I f = 0$ has, therefore, a simple interpretation. It says that if we draw numbers randomly from the interval $[0, 1]$ and register a zero when we get an irrational and a one when we get a rational, then "on average" we will register a zero. Or, stated differently, the expected value of f is 0.

The trick which allowed us to integrate the function f given above was to shift our attention from step functions to simple functions. Recall that in defining a **step function** we began with a partition of the set I into subintervals, and a step function was a function which was constant on each subset in the partition. To define a **simple function** we simply relax the requirement that the subsets of the partition be intervals, allowing them to be arbitrary subsets subject only to the requirement that we can measure their size (i.e., determine the measure $\lambda(S_t)$ for each subset S_t in the partition). Given a partition $\{\, S_t \mid t \in T \,\}$ of I into disjoint measurable subsets, where T is a finite index set, a simple function $\psi\colon I \to \mathbf{R}_+$ relative to this partition is constant over each of the subsets I_t: i.e., $\psi(i) = a_t \in \mathbf{R}_+$ for all $i \in S_t$ and $t \in T$.

As in the case of step functions, the reason for focusing on simple functions is that everyone agrees on how to define the integral of such a function: if $\psi(i) = a_t$ for $i \in S_t$, then

$$\int_I \psi = \sum_{t \in T} a_t \lambda(S_t);$$

i.e., $\int_I \psi$ is the weighted average value of f over I, where the measures $\lambda(S_t)$ are the weights. And, of course, this is exactly what we did in computing equilibrium solutions for our type economies.

To define a (Lebesgue) integral for bounded functions $f\colon I \to \mathbf{R}_+$ more general than simple functions, we proceed just as for the Riemann integral by using the simple functions to define the Lebesgue upper and lower integral of f. The **upper Lebesgue integral**, which approximates the integral of f from above, is defined as

$$L^u \int_I f = \inf_{\psi \geq f} \int_I \psi$$

where the infimum is taken over all simple functions lying on or above f. Similarly, the **lower Lebesgue integral**, which approximates the integral of f from below, is defined as

$$L_l \int_I f = \sup_{\psi \le f} \int_I \psi$$

where the supremum is taken over all simple functions which lie on or below f. Just as with the Riemann integral, the function f is said to be **Lebesgue integrable** if the upper and lower Lebesgue integrals coincide. The fact which makes the Lebesgue integral a useful concept is that a function f may be Lebesgue integrable even though it is not Riemann integrable.

Definition 3.1 *A function* $f: I \to \mathbf{R}_+$ *is* **Lebesgue measurable** *if the strict upper contour sets,* $\{\, i \in I \mid f(i) > a \,\}$, *are measurable for all* $a \in \mathbf{R}_+$.

It is then not difficult to prove the following:

Theorem 3.2 *For any bounded function* $f: I \to \mathbf{R}_+$,

$$L^u \int_I f = L_l \int_I f \quad \text{iff } f \text{ is Lebesgue measurable.}$$

Proof See Royden (1968), 77 (Proposition 3).   □

When the upper and lower integrals coincide, we write $\int_I f$ rather than $L \int_I f$ for the Lebesgue integral of f.

   The function f which is zero on the irrationals and one on the rationals is Lebesgue measurable, and as we have seen, it has Lebesgue integral equal to 0. If f is continuous or continuous a.e. on I, then f is Lebesgue measurable, but, as this example illustrates, the converse is false.[8] The connection between the Riemann and Lebesgue integral is nicely summarized by the following result:

Theorem 3.3 *For any bounded function* $f: I \to \mathbf{R}_+$,

$$R_l \int_I f \le L_l \int_I f \le L^u \int_I f \le R^u \int_I f.$$

Proof This follows directly from the fact that every step function is a simple function.   □

---

8 However, in a certain sense measurable functions are nearly continuous — see Royden (1968), 68 (Proposition 2).

As an immediate consequence of this theorem, we see that if f is Riemann integrable then equality holds throughout and so $R \int_I f = \int_I f$; i.e., the Riemann and Lebesgue integrals of f coincide. It is this fact which permitted us to use introductory calculus in computing the Walrasian equilibrium for the model presented in Section 3.1, and also what justifies writing Riemann integrals in the form $\int_I f$ rather than in the awkward notation $R \int_I f$.

Although for many, if not most, economic applications the functions $f: I \to \mathbf{R}_+$ to be integrated are bounded, sometimes they are not. Since attempting to approximate an unbounded function from above leads to obvious difficulties, the standard procedure is to define the Lebesgue integral solely in terms of approximation from below:

Definition 3.4 *If $f: I \to \mathbf{R}_+$ is Lebesgue measurable, then its integral is given by*

$$\int_I f = \sup_{\psi \le f} \left\{ \int_I \psi \mid \psi \text{ is a simple function on } I \right\}.$$

Of course, when f is unbounded the integral may be infinite, a situation we always avoid in our applications.

Definition 3.5 *If $f: I \to \mathbf{R}_+$ is Lebesgue measurable and $\int_I f < \infty$, then f is said to be* **Lebesgue integrable**.

Another complication which also needs to be addressed is what to do if the function to be integrated takes on negative values. Up to this point we have defined the Riemann or Lebesgue integral only for functions taking on nonnegative values, functions of the form $f: I \to \mathbf{R}_+$. However, for some purposes (for example, integrating excess demand) we want to be able to integrate functions which assume negative as well as positive values at various points in their domain. There is a standard trick for reducing this problem to the preceding case. Given a function $f: I \to \mathbf{R}$, define the nonnegative part $f^+: I \to \mathbf{R}_+$ by letting $f^+(i) = \max\{f(i), 0\}$ for all $i \in I$ and the nonpositive part $f^-: I \to \mathbf{R}_+$ by letting $f^-(i) = \max\{-f(i), 0\}$ for all $i \in I$. We then define $\int_I f := \int_I f^+ - \int_I f^-$. Since the two integrals on the right are well-defined (because the functions being integrated are nonnegative), this procedure yields a valid definition for the integral on the left.

Our discussion of this trick ignores one possible source of difficulty: if both integrals on the right equal $+\infty$, then the definition translates to the expression $\int_I f = \infty - \infty$, which is meaningless. To avoid this difficulty, we require that $\int_I f^+ < \infty$ and $\int_I f^- < \infty$ or, equivalently, that

$\int_I |f| := \int_I (f^+ + f^-) < \infty$. As a natural extension of our earlier terminology, measurable functions which satisfy this requirement are also said to be **Lebesgue integrable**.

3.3.3 Lebesgue measure

It seems all that is involved in constructing a theory of integration appropriate to the Aumann model is to imitate the procedures of introductory calculus with step functions replaced by simple functions. However, we have left unanswered a major question: how are we to measure the size of the subsets — coalitions — used to define the simple functions? One of the features that makes Riemann integration seem so easy is that this problem does not arise. Step functions are defined on intervals, and the size of an interval is "obviously" just its length.

Suppose that we tentatively let $\mathcal{C}$ denote the set of all coalitions in our economy — the set of all subsets of the interval $[0, 1]$. Let $\mathcal{C}^*$ denote the collection of all intervals in I. We seek a measure for each of the coalitions in $\mathcal{C}$, a function which assigns to each $S \in \mathcal{C}$ a "size" $\lambda(S)$. We know how to measure the size of coalitions $S \in \mathcal{C}^*$. The measure of an interval is simply its length: $\lambda(S) = \ell(S)$ for all $S \in \mathcal{C}^*$ where by definition $\ell(S) = b - a$ for any interval S of the form $[a, b]$, $[a, b)$, $(a, b]$, or (a, b) where we have $0 \le a \le b \le 1$. If we assume that λ is **countably additive** on $\mathcal{C}^*$, we can also measure any set expressible as a countable disjoint union of intervals by assigning $\lambda(\bigcup_{t \in T} S_t) = \sum_{t \in T} \lambda(S_t)$ where each S_t is an interval and T is a countable index set. Proceeding along these lines we might hope to assign a measure to every set $S \subset I$.

Unfortunately this turns out to be impossible, and as a consequence the Lebesgue theory of measure and integration is forced to lower its sights a little. Rather than attempt to extend the measure λ defined on $\mathcal{C}^*$ to 2^I, it is extended to the set $\mathcal{C}$ of subsets which can be obtained by taking complements, countable unions, or countable intersections of the intervals in I. The intuitive idea is that this class of **Borel sets**, though not equal to 2^I, is nevertheless "very large": large enough to be regarded as the class of all coalitions in I "for all practical purposes."

Once we agree to restrict attention to the family of Borel sets, then it is possible to extend the measure λ from the collection of intervals $\mathcal{C}^*$ to the collection of Borel sets and to do so in a way which preserves **countable additivity**: $\lambda(\bigcup_{t \in T} S_t) = \sum_{t \in T} \lambda(S_t)$ where now $\{ S_t \mid t \in T \}$ is any countable collection of disjoint coalitions in $\mathcal{C}$ (rather than just $\mathcal{C}^*$).

The details of how this is done need not concern us. The point is that we can assign a measure to "practically all" coalitions in the interval $[0, 1]$, and this measure adds up just like the fractions in our simple (type) economies.

3.3.4 Abstract measure and integration

Mathematicians love to generalize, and the Lebesgue theory invites generalization. Much the same procedure developed by Lebesgue can be applied to integration over an arbitrary set Ω provided that we can attach a measure to an appropriate collection of subsets of Ω. The result is called the theory of abstract measure and integration. Since you will often encounter this terminology when reading the literature on Aumann-type models, restating the basic definitions in this more abstract language seems worthwhile.

The key feature of the collection $\mathcal{C}$ which we have been using to represent coalitions is that $\mathcal{C}$ is a sigma algebra.

Definition 3.6 *A collection $\mathcal{C} \subset 2^\Omega$ is a **sigma algebra** (abbreviated as σ-algebra) provided that*

(a) $\emptyset \in \mathcal{C}$ and $\Omega \in \mathcal{C}$;
(b) if $S \in \mathcal{C}$, then $\Omega \backslash S \in \mathcal{C}$;
(c) if $\{ S_t \mid t \in T \}$ is a countable collection of subsets in $\mathcal{C}$, then
   $\bigcup_{t \in T} S_t \in \mathcal{C}$ *and* $\bigcap_{t \in T} S_t \in \mathcal{C}$.

*Any pairing $(\Omega, \mathcal{C})$ of a set Ω with a σ-algebra $\mathcal{C}$ of subsets of Ω is called a **measurable space**, and the subsets belonging to $\mathcal{C}$ are said to be $\mathcal{C}$-measurable.*

Identifying the measurable subsets with coalitions,

(a) says that the size of the empty coalition and the set of all consumers can be measured,
(b) that the size of a coalition can be measured if the size of its complement can be measured, and
(c) that countable unions and countable intersections of measurable coalitions can be measured.

Definition 3.7 *A nonnegative function $\mu \colon \mathcal{C} \to \mathbf{R}_+ \cup \{\infty\}$ defined on a σ-algebra $\mathcal{C}$ of a measurable space $(\Omega, \mathcal{C})$ is called a **measure** if it is countably additive: i.e., $\mu\left(\bigcup_{t \in T} S_t\right) = \sum_{t \in T} \mu(S_t)$ for every collection $\{ S_t \in \mathcal{C} \mid t \in T \}$ of disjoint, measurable subsets indexed by a countable set T. The triple $(\Omega, \mathcal{C}, \mu)$ is then called a **measure space**. If $\mu(\Omega) < \infty$, then μ is a **finite measure** and $(\Omega, \mathcal{C}, \mu)$ a **finite measure space**. If $\mu(\Omega) = 1$, then μ is called a **probability measure** and $(\Omega, \mathcal{C}, \mu)$ a **probability space**.*

Sigma-algebras are clearly just technical devices which mathematicians use to get the math to work. Since σ-algebras usually do not arise naturally in applications, the standard procedure is to start with some collection of subsets (coalitions) $\mathcal{S}$ whose size we care about and to *define* $\mathcal{C}$ to be the smallest σ-algebra which includes all of the sets in $\mathcal{S}$.

Theorem 3.8 *If $\mathcal{S}$ is any collection of subsets of a set Ω, then there exists a smallest σ-algebra $\sigma(\mathcal{S})$ containing $\mathcal{S}$, called the σ-**algebra generated by** $\mathcal{S}$.*

Proof See Rudin (1974), Theorem 1.10.   □

In practice the most important case arises when $(\Omega, \mathcal{S})$ is a **topological space**, a concept discussed in considerable detail in the next chapter. Ignoring for now what all of this means, accept the fact that associated with any topological space is a collection $\mathcal{S}$ of subsets which define the topology where each subset $S \in \mathcal{S}$ is called an **open set**. Then, as just indicated, we can use this collection of subsets — however defined — to generate a σ-algebra on Ω.

Definition 3.9 *If $(\Omega, \mathcal{S})$ is a topological space, then $\mathcal{B}(\Omega) := \sigma(\mathcal{S})$ is called the **Borel σ-algebra** generated by $\mathcal{S}$.*

Using this abstract language we can summarize Aumann's setup as follows. Consumers are represented by a measure space $(I, \mathcal{B}(I), \lambda)$ where

- $I = [0, 1]$ is the set of consumers,
- $\mathcal{B}(I)$ is the σ-algebra of Borel subsets generated by the open sets of I (where "open" means in the standard Euclidean topology of $\mathbf{R}$ restricted to the interval I, discussed fully in the next chapter), and
- λ is Lebesgue measure (by definition the unique measure on the measurable space $(I, \mathcal{B}(I))$ which assigns to each interval of I its length).

One unfinished piece of business which remains is to define the phrase "almost everywhere" scattered throughout the beginning of this chapter. The definition should by now seem rather obvious!

Definition 3.10 *If $(\Omega, \mathcal{C}, \mu)$ is a measure space, then a property $P(\omega)$ is said to hold **almost everywhere** if it holds for all ω in some set $S \in \mathcal{C}$ for which either*

- *$\mu(S) = \mu(\Omega)$ (i.e., S is in this sense "as large as" Ω); or equivalently,*

- *if the set $\Omega \backslash S$ has measure zero (i.e., the set $N := \Omega \backslash S$ where $P(\omega)$ does not hold is of "negligible" size).*

If the underlying measure is not clear from the context, it may be referenced in parentheses.

For example, two measurable real-valued functions f and g defined on a measure space $(\Omega, \mathcal{C}, \mu)$ are said to be equal a.e. (or, more specifically, a.e. (μ)) if $\mu(\{\, \omega \in \Omega \mid f \neq g \,\}) = 0$. As Aumann indicates in the quotation which opens this chapter, an important consequence of equality almost everywhere between functions is that two functions f, g equal a.e. have the same integral, $\int_\Omega f = \int_\Omega g$. In particular, altering the value of the integrand on any set of measure zero (for example, at a finite or countably infinite number of points) will not change the value of the integral. We exploited this property repeatedly in assigning arbitrary allocations to the "knife-edge" consumers of Section 3.2.

Of course, to make sense of the preceding paragraph we should extend our definition of "measurable function" to this abstract setting, and so on for all of the remaining concepts of the Lebesgue theory we want to generalize. However, you have seen enough to understand the main idea — Lebesgue integration is a special case of abstract integration — and enough to apply Aumann's model with a fair degree of confidence.

3.3.5 Nonatomic measure spaces

Before ending this discussion of the mathematical foundations for Aumann's model we have one more matter to discuss: why did he single out the measure space $(I, \mathcal{B}(I), \lambda)$ as particularly appropriate for a competitive economy? The critical ingredient is that this measure space is nonatomic. Nonatomicity, for Aumann, is the essence of competition.

You might find this assertion puzzling at first. In some other branches of the economics literature, perfect competition is called "atomic" — reflecting, presumably, the notion that the competitors are quite tiny. But tiny is not the same as infinitesimal, and Aumann apparently knows his Greek. Atoms are particles (things of substance) incapable of further subdivision.

Definition 3.11 *Let $(\Omega, \mathcal{C}, \mu)$ be a measure space. A subset $A \subset \Omega$ is an* **atom** *if*

- *$\mu(A) > 0$ (the subset has "substance"); and*
- *any subset $S \subset A$ with measure $\mu(S) > 0$ has measure $\mu(S) = \mu(A)$ (the atom is indivisible).*

If $(\Omega, \mathcal{C}, \mu)$ has no atoms, then it is said to be **atomless**.

A probability measure defined on a finite (or even countably infinite) set of consumers can never be nonatomic. But the set $I = [0,1]$ is uncountable and, as you doubtless have realized by now, the measure space $(I, \mathcal{B}(I), \lambda)$ nonatomic. Every coalition $S \subset I$ of strictly positive size can be broken into pieces, each subcoalition strictly smaller than the original but strictly larger than zero. As we will see later, it is this nonatomicity — this ability to break up every coalition of nonnegligible size into more than one nonnegligible piece — which is responsible both for core equivalence and for the convexifying effect of large numbers in the Aumann economy.

3.3.6 Formalizing Aumann's model

In the first part of this chapter we learned to appreciate the simplicity — and the significance — of Aumann's model without worrying much about technicalities. Having acquired some background in measure and integration, we are now in a position to understand more fully the mathematics which lies behind this revolutionary approach to competitive theory.

Perhaps the most obvious difference between economies with a finite and those with an infinite set of consumers lies in the treatment of the functions x and w. Summing the individual vectors x_i or w_i over I no longer makes sense. Instead we integrate and, for this to be possible, we require not just that x and w be functions, i.e., that $x, w \in \mathrm{Map}(I, L_+)$, but also that they be integrable, $x, w \in \mathcal{L}(I, \mathcal{B}(I), \lambda, L_+)$, where $L_+ = \mathbf{R}_+^{\mathbf{m}}$ and $\mathcal{L}(I, \mathcal{B}(I), \lambda, L_+)$ denotes the set of functions $f: I \to L_+$, $i \mapsto (f_{i1}, \ldots, f_{im})$ with each component $f_j: i \mapsto f_{ij}$ Lebesgue integrable on $(I, \mathcal{B}(I), \lambda)$.

The definitions introduced in Chapter 1 for the finite case generalize in a straightforward manner. To maintain compatibility with the beginning of this chapter, we take as our set of consumers the measure space $(I, \mathcal{B}(I), \lambda)$ with $I = [0,1]$, $\mathcal{B}(I)$ the σ-algebra of Borel sets, and λ Lebesgue measure. You may substitute an arbitrary nonatomic probability space $(\Omega, \mathcal{C}, \mu)$ if you prefer. To save space, we abbreviate the set $\mathcal{L}(I, \mathcal{B}(I), \lambda, L_+)$ to $\mathcal{L}(I)$.

Definition 3.12 *An* **exchange economy** $\mathcal{E} = \{\, X_i, P_i, w_i \mid i \in I \,\}$ *consists of a measure space of consumers* $(I, \mathcal{B}(I), \lambda)$ *and for each* $i \in I$

- *a consumption set* $X_i \subset L_+$,
- *a strict preference map* $P_i: X_i \to 2^{X_i}$, $x_i \mapsto P_i(x_i)$, *and*
- *an endowment* $w_i \in L_+$

where $w \in \mathcal{L}(I)$ *for the function defined by* $i \mapsto w_i$.

Just as for endowments, feasible allocations must be integrable.

Definition 3.13 *The* **set of feasible allocations** *for the economy $\mathcal{E}$ is*

$$\mathrm{F}(\mathcal{E}, I) := \{\, x \in \mathcal{L}(I) \mid \int_I x = \int_I w \ \& \ x_i \in X_i \ a.e. \ i \in I \,\}.$$

The main feature to note about the next definition is that only coalitions of nonnegligible size influence the core.

Definition 3.14 *If $\mathcal{E}$ is an exchange economy and $S \in \mathcal{B}(I)$ a coalition with $\lambda(S) > 0$, then we define*

- *the* **set of allocations feasible for** S,

$$\mathrm{F}(\mathcal{E}, S) := \Big\{ x \in \mathrm{F}(\mathcal{E}, I) \mid \int_S x = \int_S w \ \& \ x_i \in X_i \ a.e. \ i \in S \Big\};$$

- *the* **set of allocations dominated by** S,

$$\mathrm{Dom}(\mathcal{E}, S) := \{\, x \in \mathrm{F}(\mathcal{E}, I) \mid \exists \, y \in \mathrm{F}(\mathcal{E}, S) \ni y_i \succ_i x_i \ a.e. \ i \in S \,\};$$

- *the* **set of Pareto optimal allocations** *for $\mathcal{E}$,*

$$\mathrm{PO}(\mathcal{E}) := \mathrm{F}(\mathcal{E}, I) \backslash \mathrm{Dom}(\mathcal{E}, I);$$

- **the core of the economy** $\mathcal{E}$,

$$\mathrm{C}(\mathcal{E}) := \mathrm{F}(\mathcal{E}, I) \backslash \bigcup_{\substack{S \in \mathcal{B}(I) \\ \lambda(S) > 0}} \mathrm{Dom}(\mathcal{E}, S).$$

Apart from the qualification "almost every," the definition of a Walrasian equilibrium looks the same.

Definition 3.15 *A* **Walrasian equilibrium** *for an exchange economy $\mathcal{E}$ is an ordered pair (x, p) consisting of a feasible allocation $x \in \mathrm{F}(\mathcal{E}, I)$ and a price functional $p \in L' \backslash \{0\}$ such that $x_i \in \phi_i(p)$ for almost every $i \in I$.*

As before, we let $\mathrm{WE}^x(\mathcal{E})$ denote the set of Walrasian equilibrium allocations for the economy $\mathcal{E}$.

The analog of Theorem 1.17 is proved in almost the same way.

Theorem 3.16 *For any exchange economy $\mathcal{E}$, $\mathrm{WE}^x(\mathcal{E}) \subset \mathrm{C}(\mathcal{E}) \subset \mathrm{PO}(\mathcal{E})$.*

Proof The inclusion $\mathrm{C}(\mathcal{E}) \subset \mathrm{PO}(\mathcal{E})$ is immediate from the definitions. To show that $\mathrm{WE}^x(\mathcal{E}) \subset \mathrm{C}(\mathcal{E})$, suppose not: there exists an allocation $x \in \mathrm{WE}^x(\mathcal{E})$ but $x \notin \mathrm{C}(\mathcal{E})$. Because x is not in the core, some coalition of nonnegligible size can improve upon it: i.e., there exists a coalition $S \in \mathcal{B}(I)$ with measure $\lambda(S) > 0$ and an allocation $y \in \mathrm{F}(\mathcal{E}, S)$ such that $y_i \succ_i x_i$ for a.e. $i \in S$. But then $p \cdot y_i > p \cdot w_i$ (a.e. $i \in S$) and so[9] $\int_S p \cdot y > \int_S p \cdot w$ or $\int_S p \cdot (y - w) = p \cdot \int_S (y - w) > 0$, contradicting the hypothesis that y is feasible for S and hence that $\int_S (y - w) = 0$.   □

We can allow for production subject to constant returns to scale in the obvious way. To each coalition $S \in \mathcal{B}(I)$ associate a technology set $Y(S)$, and modify accordingly the definition of feasible allocations for the economy,[10]

$$\mathrm{F}(\mathcal{E}, I) := \left\{ x \in \mathcal{L}(I) \mid \int_I (x - w) \in Y(I) \ \& \ x_i \in X_i \ a.e. \ i \in I \right\},$$

and the definition of feasible allocations for coalitions of nonnegligible size,

$$\mathrm{F}(\mathcal{E}, S) := \left\{ x \in \mathrm{F}(\mathcal{E}, I) \mid \int_S (x - w) \in Y(S) \ \& \ x_i \in X_i \ a.e. \ i \in S \right\}.$$

The remaining parts of Definition 3.14 require no change. If, as in Chapter 2, we assume that $Y(I)$ is a proper, closed, pointed, convex cone satisfying the condition $Y(I) \cap L_+ = \{0\}$, then there will be no profits to distribute in equilibrium and the definition of Walrasian equilibrium is much simplified. The aggregate supply set is defined just as in Chapter 2.

Definition 3.17 *The* **supply set** *at prices $p \in L' \backslash \{0\}$ for a production economy with aggregate technology set $Y(I)$ is given by*

$$\eta(p) := \{ y \in Y(I) \mid p \cdot y = \sup p \cdot Y(I) \}.$$

And, apart from the usual fuss about "a.e.," the definition of Walrasian equilibrium also looks the same.

Definition 3.18 *A* **Walrasian equilibrium** *for a production economy $\mathcal{E}$ is an ordered pair (x, p) consisting of a feasible allocation $x \in \mathrm{F}(\mathcal{E}, I)$ and a price functional $p \in L' \backslash \{0\}$ such that*

- *$x_i \in \phi_i(p)$ for almost every $i \in I$; and*
- *$\int_I (x - w) = y \in \eta(p)$.*

If we add the rather innocuous hypothesis that $Y(S) \subset Y(I)$ for all coalitions $S \in \mathcal{B}(I)$, then Theorem 3.16 generalizes to the production context. The statement and proof of this generalization is left as an exercise.

Theorem 3.16 (as well as its generalization to production economies) is

---

9 This is where the fact that $\lambda(S) > 0$ is used!

10 Because in the production context we allow allocations to take on negative values, $\mathcal{L}(I)$ is now an abbreviation for $\mathcal{L}(I, \mathcal{B}(I), \lambda, L)$ rather than $\mathcal{L}(I, \mathcal{B}(I), \lambda, L_+)$.

unsurprising, a "technical" extension of the finite result to the continuum of consumers setting. What makes Aumann's model special is the much stronger **Core Equivalence Theorem**: under quite general conditions the core and the set of Walrasian allocations of an exchange economy coincide, $C(\mathcal{E}) = WE^x(\mathcal{E})$. Core equivalence also obtains in the constant returns to scale production economy provided that all coalitions have access to the same technology ($Y(S) = Y(I)$ for all $S \in \mathcal{B}(I)$) or, more generally, if the production correspondence mapping each coalition S to $Y(S)$ is "additive." However, for now we drop this topic, returning to core equivalence in Chapter 8 after we have learned a little more mathematics.

3.3.7 Economies in distribution form

Treating the consumers in Aumann's model as points in the interval $[0, 1]$ is an innocent but artificial device. We might ask: If consumers have negligible influence, should an individual's identity really matter? Presumably not. All that should matter is what a consumer is like — her endowment, preferences, consumption set — and not her name. This macroscopic perspective is the more statistical view of the large economy advanced by Werner Hildenbrand in his influential reformulation of Aumann's model.

In this section I will try to give you an appreciation for Hildenbrand's approach without getting too abstract. This is not an easy task! To simplify a little, suppose that all consumers have the same consumption set,[11] which we will call $\mathcal{X}$. In contrast to this conformity in consumption sets, we allow each consumer i her own distinctive strict preference relation $\succ_i$ on $\mathcal{X}$ and her own endowment w_i. We call this pair $t_i := (\succ_i, w_i)$ the **characteristics** of consumer i. What Hildenbrand has shown is that for many purposes we can ignore the label i attached to a particular consumer. What matters is just the consumer **type** $t = (\succ, w)$ and not her name $i \in I$.

To translate Aumann's model into **distribution form**, a form in which only characteristics, not names, matter, Hildenbrand interprets an economy $\mathcal{E}$ as a function associating to every consumer her relevant characteristics or type: $\mathcal{E}: I \to \mathcal{T} := \mathcal{P} \times \mathcal{W}$, $i \mapsto t_i := (\succ_i, w_i)$, where $\mathcal{T}$ denotes the set of possible consumer types, the Cartesian product of the set $\mathcal{P}$ of possible strict preference relations and the set $\mathcal{W}$ of possible endowment vectors.

---

11 Although Hildenbrand (1974) allows consumption sets to vary as well, our simplified version looks the same as his. Hildenbrand cleverly incorporates consumption sets as part of the definition of preference, identifying the strict preference relation of consumer i with the set $\{(x, y) \in X_i \times X_i \mid y \succ_i x\}$. Thus, even in Hildenbrand's more general formulation, knowing preference and endowment suffices to characterize everything of economic relevance about a consumer.

In Hildenbrand's view, names — the labels $i \in I$ attached to each consumer — really should be irrelevant. This suggests that, rather than focusing on the function $\mathcal{E}$, we should describe our economy by a probability measure τ on the measure space[12] $(\mathcal{T}, \mathcal{B}(\mathcal{T}))$. Constructing this **image measure** is easy, and the procedure works whether I is a continuum or finite.

In the case of finite I, we simply assign to every subset $T \subset \mathcal{T}$ the fraction of consumers whose characteristics t lie in T.

Definition 3.19 *If the economy $\mathcal{E}$ has a finite number of consumers $I = \{1, \ldots, n\}$, then the **image measure** is the normalized counting measure τ on $(\mathcal{T}, 2^{\mathcal{T}})$ defined by $\tau(T) = \#\mathcal{E}^{-1}(T)/\#I$ for each $T \in 2^{\mathcal{T}}$.*

$\mathcal{E}^{-1}(T)$ represents the set of consumers whose characteristics lie in the set T, and $\#\mathcal{E}^{-1}(T)$ counts the number of such consumers. Dividing by the total number $\#I$ of consumers in the economy gives the normalized measure, the fraction of consumers whose characteristics lie in T.

Economies with a continuum of consumers are handled similarly apart from the need to restrict attention to subsets of consumer characteristics which are measurable.

Definition 3.20 *For an economy $\mathcal{E}$ with a nonatomic measure space of consumers $(I, \mathcal{B}(I), \lambda)$, where $I = [0, 1]$, the **image measure** is the measure τ on $(\mathcal{T}, \mathcal{B}(\mathcal{T}))$ defined by $\tau(T) = \lambda(\mathcal{E}^{-1}(T))/\lambda(I) = \lambda(\mathcal{E}^{-1}(T))$ for each $T \in \mathcal{B}(\mathcal{T})$.*

$\lambda(\mathcal{E}^{-1}(T))$ measures the proportion of consumers with characteristics lying in T, a measure already normalized since I has length (Lebesgue measure) one.

With the economy described in distribution form, the next step is to purge any mention of names from the constructions we use to characterize consumer choice.

Definition 3.21 *To a consumer with characteristics $(\succ, w)$ we associate the **strict preference set** $P(x, \succ) := \{y \in \mathcal{X} \mid y \succ x\}$, the **budget set** $\beta(p, w) := \{x \in \mathcal{X} \mid p \cdot x \leq p \cdot w\}$, and the **demand set***

$$\phi(p, \succ, w) := \{x \in \beta(p, w) \mid P(x, \succ) \cap \beta(p, w) = \emptyset\}.$$

Each of these constructions has a ready interpretation.

---

12 Here we are getting in slightly over our heads. By the end of Chapter 5, you will understand how we can impose a topology on the set $\mathcal{T}$ and, consequently, generate the sigma-algebra $\mathcal{B}(\mathcal{T})$ of Borel sets. For now, take it on faith.

- $P(x, \succ)$ represents the set of bundles which any consumer with preference relation $\succ$ prefers to x;
- $\beta(p, w)$ gives the budget set for any consumer with endowment w facing prices p; and
- $\phi(p, \succ, w)$ stands for the demand set which a consumer with characteristics $(\succ, w)$ associates with prices p.

Thus, all differences in strict preference sets, budget sets, and demand sets among consumers are captured by the "variables" $\succ$ and w.

Expressed in distribution form, Walrasian equilibrium avoids any mention of names, viewing equilibrium instead as a probability distribution on the triples $(x, \succ, w) \in \mathcal{X} \times \mathcal{P} \times \mathcal{W} =: \Omega$ where

- $\mathcal{X}$ is the consumption set common to all consumers,
- $\mathcal{P}$ denotes the set of conceivable preference relations, and
- $\mathcal{W}$ represents the set of conceivable endowment vectors.[13]

Definition 3.22 *Given an exchange economy τ on $(\mathcal{T}, \mathcal{B}(\mathcal{T}))$, a* **Walrasian equilibrium distribution** *is a measure μ on $(\Omega, \mathcal{B}(\Omega))$ such that*

(a) $\mu \circ \mathrm{proj}_{\mathcal{T}}^{-1} = \tau$

(b) $\int_\Omega \mathrm{proj}_{\mathcal{X}} \, d\mu = \int_\Omega \mathrm{proj}_{\mathcal{W}} \, d\mu$

(c) there exists a price functional $p \in L' \backslash 0$ such that

$$\mu\{\, (x, \succ, w) \in \Omega \mid x \in \phi(p, \succ, w) \,\} = 1.$$

Despite my earlier promise, this definition is admittedly rather abstract! Fortunately, it is quite easily interpreted.

(a) The first condition says that the distribution of consumer characteristics implicit in the equilibrium distribution is consistent with the initial data describing the economy. The symbol $\mathrm{proj}_{\mathcal{T}}$ stands for "projection onto $\mathcal{T}$," the function $\mathrm{proj}_{\mathcal{T}} \colon \Omega \to \mathcal{T}$, $(x, \succ, w) \mapsto (\succ, w)$ which extracts from the triple $(x, \succ, w)$ the part $(\succ, w)$ which describes the consumer type. To say that $\mu \circ \mathrm{proj}_{\mathcal{T}}^{-1} = \tau$ means that

$$\mu \circ \mathrm{proj}_{\mathcal{T}}^{-1}(T) = \tau(T) \quad \text{for every} \quad T \in \mathcal{B}(\mathcal{T}).$$

Thus, we are requiring that the measures $\mu_{\mathcal{T}} := \mu \circ \mathrm{proj}_{\mathcal{T}}^{-1}$ and τ assign the same measure to every measurable set T of consumer characteristics, precisely what it means to say that the measures are equal. Using the language of a statistician, the marginal distribution $\mu_{\mathcal{T}}$ of μ on $\mathcal{T}$ agrees with the initial distribution τ.

13 To make this discussion more concrete, you may if you wish take $\mathcal{W} = \mathcal{X} = L_+$.

(b) The second condition corresponds to our familiar requirement of feasibility: the per capita allocation must agree with the per capita endowment available for distribution. The functions $\text{proj}_{\mathcal{W}}$ and $\text{proj}_{\mathcal{X}}$ project Ω onto $\mathcal{W}$ and $\mathcal{X}$ respectively in the sense that $\text{proj}_{\mathcal{W}}\colon \Omega \to \mathcal{W}$ maps $(x, \succ, w) \mapsto w$ and $\text{proj}_{\mathcal{X}}\colon \Omega \to \mathcal{X}$ maps $(x, \succ, w) \mapsto x$. Using the language of probability theory the condition

$$\int_{\Omega} \text{proj}_{\mathcal{X}} \; d\mu = \int_{\Omega} \text{proj}_{\mathcal{W}} \; d\mu$$

is nothing more than the requirement $Ex = Ew$ equating the expected value of the final allocation x with the expected value of the initial endowment w.

(c) The third condition translates into distribution form the requirement that a Walrasian allocation assign to almost every consumer a commodity bundle in her demand set: almost every triple $(x, \succ, w)$ observed in equilibrium matches a bundle x with a consumer type $(\succ, w)$ containing x in its demand set at prices p.

Hildenbrand's construction is much simpler and more intuitive than this abstract presentation seems to suggest. To illustrate, consider a slightly more elaborate version of the example with which we began this chapter. Consumers have preferences represented by a Cobb-Douglas utility function $u(x) = x_1^{\alpha} x_2^{1-\alpha}$ where α is uniformly distributed on $[0, 1]$ with probability measure $\tau_{\mathcal{P}}$. Consumer endowments take the form $w = (\beta, \beta)$ where β is uniformly distributed on $[0, 4]$ with probability measure $\tau_{\mathcal{W}}$. Assuming as well that α and β are independently distributed, their joint distribution τ assigns to each measurable subset $P \times W \in \mathcal{P} \times \mathcal{W}$ the probability $\tau(P \times W) = \tau_{\mathcal{P}}(P)\tau_{\mathcal{W}}(W)$.

Normalizing prices to sum to one, a consumer with characteristics $t = (\alpha, \beta)$ will have demand set[14] $\phi(p, \alpha, \beta) := (\alpha\beta/p_1, (1 - \alpha)\beta/p_2)$. Applied to the market for commodity one, condition (b) of the definition of Walrasian equilibrium translates to[15]

$$\int_0^1 \int_0^4 \frac{\alpha\beta}{4p_1} \; d\alpha d\beta = \int_0^4 \frac{\beta}{4} \; d\beta.$$

Evaluating the integrals and simplifying yields $p = (.5, .5)$ as the equilibrium price functional. The equilibrium distribution μ assigns to almost every

---

14 In the formal definition, the demand set takes the form $\phi(p, \succ, w)$. Here I have substituted the parameters (α, β) for $(\succ, w)$ and, in what follows, replaced integration over the spaces $\mathcal{P}$ and $\mathcal{W}$ with integration over the intervals $[0, 1]$ and $[0, 4]$ within which the parameters α and β lie.

15 The factor $1/4$ appearing in the integrands represents the density of the uniform distribution on $[0, 4]$.

consumer with characteristics (α, β) the commodity bundle $(2\alpha\beta, 2(1-\alpha)\beta)$ in her demand set, consistent with requirement (c). Requirement (a) is clearly satisfied as well.

The type economy we constructed early in this chapter provides another illuminating illustration of Hildenbrand's construction. Recall that in this example consumers belong to one of a finite number of types, characterized by the endowment vector (a, b) and the preference parameter α in the Cobb-Douglas utility function $u(x) = x_1^\alpha x_2^{1-\alpha}$. Thus, a consumer type can be characterized by $t = (\succ, w) := (\alpha, (a, b))$.

Intuitively, the measure τ on $(\mathcal{T}, \mathcal{B}(\mathcal{T}))$ describing this economy should depend only on the fractions of consumers of each type. To capture this idea formally, we define a measure on $(\mathcal{T}, \mathcal{B}(\mathcal{T}))$ such that

$$\delta_t: \mathcal{B}(\mathcal{T}) \to \{0, 1\}, \quad T \mapsto \delta_t(T) := \begin{cases} 1 & \text{if } t \in T \\ 0 & \text{otherwise,} \end{cases}$$

the **point mass** which concentrates all of the measure on the single type t, assigning that type measure (probability) one.[16] Using these point masses as building blocks, the measure τ describing the economy can be written $\tau = \sum_{t \in \mathcal{T}} \lambda_t \delta_t$ where λ_t represents the fraction of consumers of type t. Applied to any subset $T \in \mathcal{B}(\mathcal{T})$, we conclude that $\tau(T) = \sum_{t \in T} \lambda_t$ just as it should be: $\tau(T)$ gives the fraction of consumers whose characteristics lie in T, the sum of the fractions corresponding to each individual consumer type.

Point masses also provide the building blocks we need for representing the equilibrium measure μ for this economy. Let $\delta_{(x,t)}$ denote the probability measure concentrating all of its mass at the point (x, t). Provided that only a finite number of such pairings (x, t) are observed in equilibrium, the equilibrium measure μ takes the form of a finite linear combination of point masses, say

$$\mu = \sum_{(x,t) \in \mathcal{X} \times \mathcal{T}} \gamma_{(x,t)} \delta_{(x,t)}$$

where $\gamma_{(x,t)}$ represents the fraction of consumers who are of type t and receive the commodity bundle x in equilibrium. Solving explicitly for the equilibrium allocation, as we did earlier in this chapter, amounts to determining the actual pairings (x, t) observed in equilibrium and the fractions $\gamma_{(x,t)}$ associated with each such pairing. Characterizing the distributions τ

---

16 Since $\mathcal{T}$ is finite and hence $\mathcal{B}(\mathcal{T}) = 2^{\mathcal{T}}$, we could define these point masses more simply. However, the definition given here — which works equally well for infinite $\mathcal{T}$ — provides a more natural transition to the next section. What this definition says is that every measurable subset containing the point t has measure one while every subset which does not contain t has measure zero, a roundabout way of saying that all of the mass is concentrated on the point t.

and μ for the simple two-type economy presented earlier in this chapter is left as (easy) Exercise 3.17.

Interpreting the formal Definition 3.22 of a Walrasian equilibrium distribution is quite straightforward in this example. Whether with two types or many, every consumer of a given type in this economy receives the same equilibrium allocation: say x_t for consumers of type t. Consequently, we can write the equilibrium distribution as a sum over $\mathcal{T}$ alone,

$$\mu = \sum_{t \in \mathcal{T}} \widehat{\gamma}_t \delta_{(x_t, t)}$$

where $\widehat{\gamma}_t := \gamma_{(x_t, t)}$ for each $t \in \mathcal{T}$. Since consumers of a given type exhibit no variation in consumption, the marginal distribution $\mu_{\mathcal{T}}$ is simply: $\mu_{\mathcal{T}} = \sum_{t \in \mathcal{T}} \widehat{\gamma}_t \delta_t$. Equating this marginal distribution to the initial distribution τ, requirement (a) of Walrasian equilibrium, gives $\sum_{t \in \mathcal{T}} \widehat{\gamma}_t \delta_t = \sum_{t \in \mathcal{T}} \lambda_t \delta_t$ and that in turn requires $\widehat{\gamma}_t = \lambda_t$ for all $t \in \mathcal{T}$. Requirement (b) becomes $\sum_{t \in \mathcal{T}} \lambda_t x_t = \sum_{t \in \mathcal{T}} \lambda_t w_t$ and requirement (c) $x_t \in \phi_t(p, t)$ for all $t \in \mathcal{T}$. Just as in Exercise 3.6, we find the Walrasian equilibrium by plugging the explicit Cobb-Douglas equations for $x_t \in \phi(p, t)$ into the market clearing equations of requirement (b) and solving for the equilibrium price functional p.

3.4 Hedonic theory and local public goods

Aumann's model is much more than an excuse for doing fancy mathematics, and there is no better illustration of the practical relevance of Aumann's approach than the remarkable theory of product differentiation advanced by Andreu Mas-Colell (1975). In discussing Mas-Colell's model I will emphasize in particular its application to the hedonic theory of Sherwin Rosen (1974) and the local public goods theory of Charles Tiebout (1956), theories which have attracted the widespread attention of applied economists.

3.4.1 Commodity bundles as measures

In coming to grips with Mas-Colell's model, we can take advantage of the abstract approach to vector spaces advanced in the first two chapters. As I have emphasized, to a mathematician vector spaces are abstractions, nothing more than sets satisfying a particular collection of axioms.[17] Thinking of vectors as lists of numbers, say $x = (x_1, x_2, x_3, \ldots)$, is often convenient, but it is not essential. And sometimes, particularly in infinite dimensional contexts, this familiar way of representing vectors can be quite inappropriate.

17 There is no need to repeat the formal definition given in Chapter 1.

So it is in Mas-Colell's approach to product differentiation, an approach in which vectors are represented not as lists but as measures.

To keep on familiar ground for as long as possible, we begin in finite dimensions. As usual, let $J := \{1, \ldots, m\}$ index commodities with $j \in J$ identifying the commodity of type j. Letting $\mathcal{B}(J) = 2^J$, we define for each $j \in J$ the **point mass**

$$\delta_j: \mathcal{B}(J) \to \{0, 1\}, \quad B \mapsto \delta_j(B) := \begin{cases} 1 & \text{if } j \in B, \\ 0 & \text{otherwise,} \end{cases}$$

a probability measure on the measure space $(J, \mathcal{B}(J))$ which concentrates all of its mass at the point j. The interpretation is straightforward: A consumer choosing commodity bundle $x = \delta_j$ receives one unit of commodity j and nothing else.[18] Arbitrary commodity bundles take the form of linear combinations of these building blocks, $x = \sum_{j \in J} x_j \delta_j$, $x_j \in \mathbf{R}$, with x_j representing the quantity consumed of commodity j. Defining vector addition and scalar multiplication in the obvious way

- if $x = \sum_{j \in J} x_j \delta_j$ and $y = \sum_{j \in J} y_j \delta_j$, then $x + y := \sum_{j \in J} (x_j + y_j) \delta_j$, and
- if $x = \sum_{j \in J} x_j \delta_j$ and $\alpha \in \mathbf{R}$, then $\alpha x := \sum_{j \in J} \alpha x_j \delta_j$,

you should have no trouble verifying that this commodity space of measures, denoted $M(J)$, satisfies the formal axioms for a vector space.

Describing commodity bundles as measures is only part of the story. For the economist as for the mathematician, vector spaces are of limited use without a supply of linear functionals. In Mas-Colell's framework, prices p play a dual role, as a function[19]

$$p: J \to \mathbf{R}, \quad j \mapsto p_j$$

on J and as a linear functional

$$p: M(J) \to \mathbf{R}, \quad x \mapsto p \cdot x$$

on $M(J)$.

Viewing the price system p as a function on J seems quite natural: p_j is simply the price of one unit of commodity j. Using p to construct a linear functional on the space of measures $M(J)$, on the other hand, is considerably less obvious. We begin by specifying what p does to the delta functions δ_j, requiring that[20] $p \cdot \delta_j = p_j$ for all $j \in J$, so that the value of "one unit"

---

18 In the conventional representation of vectors as lists, this corresponds to setting $x = e_j$, where e_j is the jth unit vector.

19 Viewed as a function on J, there is no reason to suppose that p is linear. Why should it be linear when nothing we have said implies that J is even a vector space?

20 In the formal mathematical literature, the property we are describing is often taken to be the defining characteristic of the delta function.

of commodity j is simply p_j. (What could be more natural?) Remarkably, this is all that is needed since linearity takes care of the rest. An arbitrary element $x = \sum_{j \in J} x_j \delta_j \in M(J)$ has value

$$p \cdot x = \sum_{j \in J} p \cdot (x_j \delta_j) = \sum_{j \in J} x_j (p \cdot \delta_j) = \sum_{j \in J} p_j x_j,$$

a result which seems obvious in hindsight!

Having mastered this novel way of viewing commodity bundles and price functionals, the rest is easy: we simply adapt our earlier definitions to this new setting. Consider, for example, the notion of a consumption set X_i. In a pure exchange context consumption bundles are typically confined to the "nonnegative orthant,"

$$M_+(J) := \left\{ x \in M(J) \mid x = \sum_{j \in J} x_j \delta_j, \ x_j \geq 0 \right\}$$

in our new notation. Other restrictions can be added with equal ease. To illustrate we will now translate one of the models of indivisibility treated earlier in this chapter into the Mas-Colell framework.

In our market for automobiles presented in Section 3.2.2, commodities were of two types: a car (which we now label k) or a composite commodity (which we label c), summarized by the index set $J = \{ c, k \}$. The production activity vector $y = (-\beta, 1) \in \mathbf{R}^2$ of Section 3.2.2 now becomes $y = -\beta \delta_c + \delta_k \in M(J)$ in our new notation, and hence the technology set translates to $Y = \{ y \in M(J) \mid y = \lambda(-\beta \delta_c + \delta_k), \lambda \geq 0 \}$. Applying the equilibrium price functional p to the equilibrium activity vector $y = \lambda(-\beta \delta_c + \delta_k)$ yields the zero profit condition

$$p \cdot y = \lambda(-\beta p \cdot \delta_c + p \cdot \delta_k) = \lambda(-\beta p_c + p_k) = 0,$$

which implies, just as before, that $p_k = \beta p_c$ if cars are produced at all.

Letting $\beta = 2$ and choosing $p_c = 1$ as *numéraire*, we concluded in Section 3.2.2, after some computational effort, that the Walrasian equilibrium assigned to consumer $i \in I$ the allocation

$$x_i = \begin{cases} (10i, 0) & \text{if } i \in [0, .3) \\ (10i - 2, 1) & \text{if } i \in [.3, .7) \\ (10i - 4, 2) & \text{if } i \in [.7, 1] \end{cases}$$

with the commodity vectors represented in the conventional way. Translated to the vector space $M(J)$, this becomes

$$
x_i = \begin{cases} 10i\delta_c & \text{if } i \in [0, .3) \\ (10i - 2)\delta_c + \delta_k & \text{if } i \in [.3, .7) \\ (10i - 4)\delta_c + 2\delta_k & \text{if } i \in [.7, 1]. \end{cases}
$$

Finally, suppose that we translate this into distribution form. Letting ω ($= 10i$ for consumer $i \in I$) denote consumer wealth, we conclude that

$$
x = \begin{cases} \omega\delta_c & \text{if } \omega \in [0, 3) \\ (\omega - 2)\delta_c + \delta_k & \text{if } \omega \in [3, 7) \\ (\omega - 4)\delta_c + 2\delta_k & \text{if } \omega \in [7, 10]. \end{cases}
$$

3.4.2 Hedonic theory

Within a finite-dimensional setting, Mas-Colell's approach amounts to little more than window dressing: using measures rather than "ordinary" vectors adds nothing of substance. In infinite dimensions, on the other hand, the generalization he offers is profound. While a full-blown exposition is beyond the scope of this book, we can gain considerable insight into Mas-Colell's model by exploiting the analogy with the finite case.

Suppose we replace our finite index set by a union of disjoint sets $J :=$ $\{1, \ldots, m\} \cup K$ where $\{1, \ldots, m\}$ indexes conventional, perfectly divisible commodities (still assumed finite in number) while K, assumed to be a compact metric space,[21] characterizes the indivisible, differentiated commodities.

Since arguably all commodities are indivisible (How can one buy less than a penny's worth?), why do we bother including the class of perfectly divisible commodities? Only for technical reasons: in order to prove existence of a Walrasian equilibrium, there must be at least one such commodity. Following Mas-Colell, we will assume for simplicity that there is exactly one which we label c so that the index set becomes $J := \{c\} \cup K$.

The set K should be viewed as capturing all of the relevant characteristics of every commodity[22] which a consumer buys: cars, houses, appliances, clothing, food, and the like. We might imagine, for example, that K decomposes into a disjoint union $K = \bigcup_{s \in S} K_s$ with each K_s a closed and bounded subset of a finite dimensional vector space. In such a specification, K_1 could refer to automobiles, K_2 to houses, K_3 to washing machines and the like with the characteristics $(k_{s1}, k_{s2}, \ldots) = k_s \in K_s$ capturing attributes

---

21 The terms "compact" and "metric space" will be explained in the next chapter. For now, take K to be any closed and bounded subset of R^n.

22 Apart from the perfectly divisible commodity c.

such as floor space, horsepower, power consumption, or anything else which comes to mind.

Returning to the general setting, we define our collection of delta functions just as before: δ_j is the measure

$$\delta_j : \mathcal{B}(J) \to \{0, 1\}, \quad B \mapsto \delta_j(B) := \begin{cases} 1 & \text{if } j \in B, \\ 0 & \text{otherwise,} \end{cases}$$

where $\mathcal{B}(J)$ represents the collection of all Borel measurable subsets of J. Commodity bundles take the form $x = x_c \delta_c + \sum_{k \in K} x_k \delta_k$ where $x_c \in \mathbf{R}_+$, $x_k \in \mathbf{Z}_+$, and at most a finite number of the coefficients x_k are not equal to zero.

Rather than continue at this level of generality, we will now specialize to the main case treated in Rosen's (1974) development of hedonic theory. Assume that, in addition to the perfectly divisible commodity, consumers consume at most one unit of one type of indivisible commodity: i.e., $x_k \in \{0, 1\}$ for all $k \in K$ with at most one of the x_k not equal to zero. Suppose further that commodity differentiation is one-dimensional, say $K = [0, \bar{k}]$ where $\bar{k} > 0$.

Within this simple context, commodity bundles take the form $x = x_c \delta_c + x_k \delta_k$ where $x_c \in \mathbf{R}_+$ and $x_k \in \{0, 1\}$. Suppose that all consumers have identical tastes, described by the utility function $u(x) = x_c(1 + \alpha k)$ $(\alpha > 0)$, and initial endowments $w = \omega \delta_c$ parameterized by $\omega > 0$. Setting the price of the divisible commodity equal to one as *numéraire*, consumer wealth also equals ω. The indivisible commodities, none of which are owned initially, are produced using the divisible commodity as input. Assume that this production exhibits constant returns to scale at marginal cost βk with $\beta > 0$, described by the technology sets

$$Y_k = \{y \in M(J) \mid y = \lambda(-\beta k \delta_c + \delta_k), \lambda \geq 0\}$$

for each commodity type $k \in K$.

Solving for a Walrasian equilibrium proceeds much as with the finite-dimensional models of indivisibility presented earlier in the chapter. A consumer choosing to consume one unit of the divisible commodity of type k while spending the rest of her wealth on the divisible commodity will attain a level of utility $V^k = (\omega - \beta k)(1 + \alpha k)$. Provided that $\omega \geq \beta/\alpha$ and $\bar{k}$ is large enough, this expression is maximized at $k = (\alpha\omega - \beta)/2\alpha\beta$, yielding a maximum level of utility

$$V^* = \begin{cases} \frac{(\alpha\omega + \beta)^2}{4\alpha\beta} & \text{if } \omega \geq \beta/\alpha, \\ \omega & \text{otherwise.} \end{cases}$$

Suppose, for example, that $\alpha = 1$, $\beta = 2$, $\bar{k} \geq 3$, and ω is uniformly distributed over the interval $[6, 14]$. Since the optimizing choice of indivisible commodity depends affinely on wealth, the equilibrium distribution of k is also uniform with support $[1, 3] \subset K$.

Rosen's (1974) approach to solving this "hedonic" model seems quite different on the surface, characterizing consumer choice through "bid prices." If, as in our simple example, consumers have identical preferences, **bid price** $\widetilde{p}(k, \omega, u)$ is the price associated with an indivisible good of type k which would allow a consumer with wealth ω to attain a utility level u. Within the context of our example, bid price is defined implicitly as the solution to $(\omega - \widetilde{p}(k, \omega, u))(1 + \alpha k) = u$, yielding

$$\widetilde{p}(k, \omega, u) = \omega - \frac{u}{1 + \alpha k}.$$

Although it may seem roundabout, viewing consumer choice in terms of bid price confers one major advantage: the easily interpreted **Rosen diagram** exhibited in Figure 3.4. The curve labeled p represents the **hedonic price function**, the locus of equilibrium prices of the indivisible commodities viewed as a function of the characteristic k. Bid prices curves $\widetilde{p}$ are analogous to indifference contours, one for each level of utility u, with lower curves corresponding to higher levels of utility. As suggested in the diagram, the optimal choice of k occurs at a point of tangency of a bid price curve and the locus of hedonic prices.

For our specific example and writing $p(k)$ instead of p_k, the Rosen tangency condition

$$\frac{d\widetilde{p}}{dk}(k, \omega, u) = \frac{dp}{dk}(k)$$

becomes $u\alpha/(1 + \alpha k)^2 = \beta$. Substituting the equilibrium utility level $u = V^* := (\alpha\omega + \beta)^2/4\alpha\beta$ and simplifying yields $k = (\alpha\omega - \beta)/2\alpha\beta$, just as before.

What makes the Rosen diagram so useful is its clear illustration of why markets such as this tend to stratify, producing a strong association between the type of household and the type of product chosen. In the example just described, consumers with higher wealth have more steeply sloped bid price curves, reflecting their greater willingness to pay for "higher quality." Hence, they select a product with a higher quality k. In more complex specifications, consumers might also stratify by age, family size, or other household attributes.

What is missing from the Rosen diagram, and from his paper, is an account of how markets clear. Mas-Colell provides that missing ingredient, in

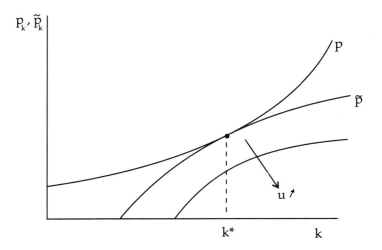

Fig. 3.4. The Rosen hedonic diagram.

essence adding a third "quantity" dimension to the Rosen diagram in which demand and supply are equated in the market for each indivisible commodity. Filling in this dimension turns Rosen's theory into a fully articulated general equilibrium model of product differentiation ripe for application. The fact that essentially no such applications have been forthcoming in the nearly two decades since the publication of Mas-Colell's paper is a sad tribute to the gulf that separates high theory from applied economics.

3.4.3 Tiebout equilibrium

Applying Mas-Colell's theory to Rosen's hedonic model is scarcely controversial. Not so with the topic we are about to discuss, Tiebout equilibrium with local public goods. I hope to convince you that Mas-Colell provides the obvious way to think about Tiebout, supplanting a literature which is at best misleading or confusing and often just plain wrong.

Tiebout's (1956) argument was simple and devoid of technicality. Reacting to the publication of Samuelson's theory of public goods, Tiebout offered a critique not of the theory but rather its empirical relevance. Most public goods, he argued, are only partially, not purely, public, provided to proper subsets of the population through the agency of local government. Serving their clients much as do firms, local governments are forced to compete for the households who, "voting with their feet," pick and choose among them.

For Tiebout the case seemed clear: the market for local public goods is a market just like any other.

Despite its apparent simplicity, Tiebout's vision has proved remarkably resistant to formalization. As Truman Bewley observed in his trenchant review of the literature, "... Tiebout's notion of equilibrium does not have the nice properties of general competitive equilibrium, except under very restrictive assumptions." [Bewley (1981), 713.] While an accurate assessment of the literature spawned by Tiebout, Bewley's judgment about Tiebout is too harsh. My main claim is that Tiebout makes perfectly good sense provided we view the problem in the right way: from the perspective of Mas-Colell's model of product differentiation.

To provide context for this discussion, we begin by reviewing some approaches which fail. Assume for concreteness that our economy has only two types of commodity, one private and the other public. Only the public good can be produced, using the private good as input. Consumers are finite in number, indexed by the set $I = \{1, \ldots, n\}$. Recall from Chapter 2 the approach pioneered by Foley (1970): if the public good is purely public, then public good production can be regarded as a form of joint production in which "the" public good is replaced by n individualized public goods, one for each consumer. A typical activity vector takes the form $y := (y_1, \ldots, y_n, -z) = \lambda(1, \ldots, 1, -\beta)$ where $\lambda\beta$ units of private good input are used to provide λ units of public good output to each of the consumers in the economy. As illustrated in Chapter 2 and rigorously demonstrated by Foley, with production subject to constant returns to scale and standard conditions on preferences, a Lindahl equilibrium will exist for this economy with price functional $(p_y^1, \ldots, p_y^n, p_z)$. The zero profit condition implies that equilibrium prices satisfy[23] $\sum_{i \in I} p_y^i = \beta p_z$, paralleling the Samuelson condition for Pareto optimality $\sum_{i \in I} \mathrm{MRS}_i = \mathrm{MRT}$.

Adapting Foley's idea to an economy with local public goods seems quite straightforward. Suppose that the set I is partitioned into subsets, say $I = \bigcup_{s \in S} J_s$ where $J_s \cap J_{s'} = \emptyset$ for all $s \neq s'$ with each subset J_s representing a distinct political jurisdiction and S indexing the entire collection of jurisdictions. For example we might have $I = \{1, 2, 3, 4, 5\}$ partitioned into the two local jurisdictions $J_1 = \{1, 3, 5\}$ and $J_2 = \{2, 4\}$ with consumers 1, 3, and 5 belonging to one jurisdiction and consumers 2 and 4 to another. Each jurisdiction supplies the local public good to its "residents" exactly as in Foley, but, in contrast to the case of pure public goods, only residents enjoy the benefits. Using our five-consumer, two-jurisdiction economy to

---

23 In Chapter 2 I chose units such that $\beta = 1$, yielding the more familiar condition $\sum_{i \in I} p_y^i = p_z$.

illustrate, jurisdiction 1 might have technology set

$$Y_1 = \{\, y \in \mathbf{R}^6 \mid \lambda(1,0,1,0,1,-\beta_1) \quad \lambda \geq 0 \,\}$$

and jurisdiction 2 technology set

$$Y_2 = \{\, y \in \mathbf{R}^6 \mid \lambda(0,1,0,1,0,-\beta_2) \quad \lambda \geq 0 \,\}.$$

Provided that the assignment of consumers to jurisdictions is fixed, Foley's proof extends immediately to this new context. In particular, there exists a natural generalization of Lindahl equilibrium to economies with local public goods and, once again assuming that the assignment of consumers to jurisdictions is fixed, these equilibria will be Pareto optimal and in the core. Applying the zero profit condition to production in each jurisdiction J_s implies that equilibrium prices will satisfy $\sum_{i \in J_s} p_y^i = \beta_s p_z$, paralleling the generalized Samuelson condition for Pareto optimality $\sum_{i \in J_s} \mathrm{MRS}_i = \mathrm{MRT}^s$ frequently encountered in the literature on this subject. In retrospect these results hardly seem surprising. What they say, in effect, is that from the point of view of a region's residents public goods regionally supplied act just like pure public goods provided that the residents do not have the option to leave. Since many, if not most, illustrations of pure public goods involve benefits confined to national boundaries (national defense?), perhaps most are really regional public goods in the sense described above.[24]

Fixing the assignment of consumers to jurisdictions leads, therefore, to a mildly useful generalization of Samuelson's theory of public goods. It is not, however, an acceptable restriction within the context of Tiebout's model, a model in which "voting with one's feet" is of the essence. What happens when the assignment of consumers to jurisdictions is allowed to be endogenous? Bluntly put, the model falls apart. Existence becomes a delicate issue. Allocations which are Lindahl equilibria for some particular assignment can be Pareto dominated by allocations achievable with a different assignment of consumers to jurisdictions. And the core may be empty, casting even more doubt on the chances of finding a suitable notion of Tiebout equilibrium. Some positive results are possible but only under very restrictive hypotheses, typically implying "perfect homogeneity" of the populations within each jurisdiction. As Bewley concludes of such efforts,

Perhaps the reader finds this model satisfactory. I find a model with homogeneous communities and profit maximizing governments startling and strikingly in conflict with my everyday experience. Tiebout seems to imply that this narrow model is

---

24 For a more extended discussion and proofs of the assertions in this paragraph and the next, see Ellickson (1973, 1983a, 1983b).

only meant to illustrate an idea with wider application. It seems that no wider model exists.

(Bewley (1981), 735)

Why is the Tiebout model such a dismal failure? The fault lies in forcing Tiebout into an inappropriate mold, the Procrustean bed of conventional public goods theory. From Samuelson on, orthodox theory has regarded a public good as a commodity piling up on consumers' shelves like loaves of bread.[25] Even in the pure public goods context, thinking of public goods this way seems rather unnatural. After all, Samuelson himself objected strenuously to the conceit that consumers might be charged for public goods loaf by loaf.[26] However, while there may be reasons to maintain this fiction in the world of pure public goods, for understanding Tiebout it is a disaster. In Tiebout, consumers mainly choose where to live and only indirectly the kind of public services that choice entails. Making sense of Tiebout requires a framework in which discrete choice among jurisdictions is paramount and choice of services secondary.

Reduced to an aphorism, this new view of Tiebout replaces quantity with quality. Rather than a quantity shared, the offering of each local political jurisdiction becomes a characteristic k defining what matters to consumers. In mechanical translations of the older literature on Tiebout, k can be viewed as the common level of output shared by the residents of a jurisdiction. However, once liberated from the confines of that older literature, we have much more flexibility in interpreting k as we wish. In applications, k would typically be a list $(k_1, \ldots, k_r)$ of attributes whose elements are either quantitative measures of quality (e.g., average student performance on standardized exams) or qualitative characterizations of performance (progressive or conservative curricula). However interpreted, we assume that the characteristic $k \in K$, where K is a compact metric space, completely captures all of the utility-relevant aspects of choosing to live in a particular political jurisdiction.[27]

To illustrate the application of Mas-Colell to Tiebout, we can save computational effort by borrowing from our earlier illustration of Rosen. There

---

25 I realize that loaves are themselves indivisible, but concrete examples of perfectly divisible commodities are hard to come by!

26 "[charging] *pseudo*-tax-prices $(P_{n+1}^i, \ldots, P_{n+m}^i)$ at which the referee *pretends* the man can buy as much or as little of the public goods as he pleases." [Samuelson (1969b), 497. Italics in original.]

27 More precisely, what is being described here is a "theory of clubs" in the Buchanan (1965) sense in which all that matters is the collective benefit derived from membership in the club. Choosing where to live involves more, of course, including the kind of house one lives in. There are no particular difficulties in expanding the discussion to include such considerations. The resulting model is more complex computationally, not conceptually.

are two classes of commodity in the economy, one private and the other locally public, with the class of local public goods characterized by the quality
$k \in K := [0, \bar{k}]$, $\bar{k} > 0$. Consumers choose a quantity of private good and
a jurisdiction, consuming a commodity bundle $x = x_c \delta_c + \delta_k$ consisting of
$x_c \in \mathbf{R}_+$ units of the private good and a public good of type k. (Note that we
are forcing consumers to live somewhere.) Preferences are represented by the
utility function $u(x) = x_c(1 + \alpha k)$ (with $\alpha > 0$), and initial endowments take
the form $w = \omega \delta_c$ for some $\omega > 0$. For the moment, assume that each local
public good of type k is produced subject to constant returns to scale as in-
dicated by the technology set $Y_k = \{ y \in M(J) \mid y = \lambda(-\beta k \delta_c + \delta_k), \lambda \geq 0 \}$
where $J = \{c\} \cup K$. Set $p_c = 1$ as *numéraire*. Suppose, as in our illus-
tration of Rosen's model, that wealth ω is uniformly distributed on $[6, 14]$.
Assuming that $\bar{k} \geq 3$, we conclude just as before that an equilibrium exists
with optimal choices of public good quality k uniformly distributed over the
interval $[1, 3]$.

While perhaps capturing Tiebout's main idea, this outcome hardly seems
realistic: jurisdictional populations are infinitesimal with each consumer in
effect constituting his or her own locality! The missing element inducing
consumers with heterogeneous preferences to share collective consumption
is, of course, increasing returns in public goods production.

Figure 3.5(a) portrays a technology set Y_k with initial increasing returns
to scale. Here, as elsewhere in this chapter, an element $y_k = \alpha_k \delta_k - \beta_k \delta_c \in Y_k$
should be interpreted in per capita terms: β_k units of the private good per
capita yield α_k units per capita of the public good of type k. An output
$\alpha_k = 1$, with the public good supplied to everyone in the economy, is the
obvious upper bound. In this figure, production exhibits constant returns to
scale for jurisdictions above some minimum size, say $\alpha_k = .25$, but increasing
returns for jurisdictions serving a smaller fraction of the population.

Nonconvex technology sets generally preclude existence of a Walrasian
equilibrium. We can gain some insight into situations such as this by "convexifying the economy," replacing each nonconvex technology set Y_k by its
convex hull co Y_k (see Figure 3.5(b)). As discussed more fully in Chapter 7,
equilibrium for this convexified economy will typically exist. Whether the
resulting equilibrium is also an equilibrium for the original economy will
depend on whether the equilibrium activity vectors y_k^* lie in Y_k as well as
co Y_k. Assuming that increasing returns are nonnegligible, this condition
fails in the example described earlier: "each" consumer forms her own jurisdiction in the convexified economy, implying a pattern of production which
is not feasible for the original economy. However, suppose that instead of
a uniform distribution of wealth over the interval $[6, 14]$, we have an econ-

a: Nonconvex technology set.

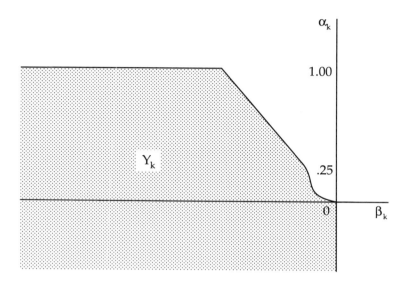

b: Convexified technology set.

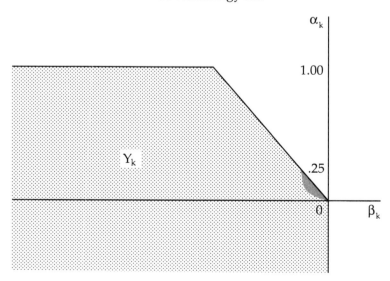

Fig. 3.5. Production with increasing returns.

omy with just two levels of wealth, say $\omega = 8$ and $\omega = 12$, with half the consumers of each type. Then, provided that scale economies are exhausted for jurisdictions serving half the population or more, an equilibrium for the convexified economy will be an equilibrium for the original economy.

As you are asked to illustrate in Exercise 3.21, the same idea can be exploited in any economy with a finite number of consumer types. And so we have uncovered the basis for the "homogeneous community" condition alluded to in the quotation from Bewley. From our new vantage point, this feature of the Tiebout literature should seem much less mysterious, a natural consequence of allowing for increasing returns with an infinite variety of product types. Since jurisdictions are in reality never perfectly homogeneous, does this provide grounds for dismissing Tiebout's contribution as narrow and contrived? I think not.

Contrasting the Rosen and Tiebout models helps to put matters in perspective. Suppose we viewed a typical application of the Rosen model with the skepticism which Bewley reserves for Tiebout. Items of clothing provide an appropriate example. If economies to scale were negligible, we might all prefer clothing tailored to the individual. Since scale does matter, it seems we must require perfect homogeneity of consumers choosing a particular item of clothing if competitive equilibrium is to exist. With private goods, of course, we are well trained to resist such impulses. Instead we realize that the competitive model is an abstraction and, with that in mind, either impose an assumption of constant returns or aggregate the infinite variety of goods that could be produced into a finite number of "homogeneous commodities."[28]

Tiebout offers a similar abstraction which should be dealt with in a similar way. In the area where I live, cities one-tenth of 1% the size of the City of Los Angeles offer a full complement of public services. Splitting Los Angeles into a thousand communities the size of Beverly Hills or Culver City would probably produce a market for public goods that looked much more competitive! I am not arguing that such extreme decentralization makes sense as public policy. It probably does not. But thought experiments such as this are valuable and indicative of the fresh perspective which Tiebout brings to the study of local public goods. Thanks to the model of product differentiation developed by Mas-Colell, we can now make sense of what Tiebout was trying to say.

---

28 The latter alternative is pursued in Ellickson (1979). Because that article does not employ a continuum of consumers, the resulting Tiebout equilibrium is approximate.

3.5 Summary

Aumann, by forcing economists to take the assumptions underlying perfect competition more seriously, has profoundly altered the way we think about economics. Although relying on rather sophisticated mathematics, his model is surprisingly intuitive and easily applied. This chapter stresses such applications. While Aumann's approach is even able to breathe new life into the staid Edgeworth box, the more exciting applications treat aspects of indivisibility and nonconvexity largely ignored by economists since the dawn of the neoclassical revolution. Pursued throughout this chapter, this theme reaches its ultimate expression in Mas-Colell's theory of competitive product differentiation, a theory with numerous potential applications.

Exercises

3.1 Assume a continuum of consumers indexed by the set $I = [0, 1]$. All consumers have identical preferences described by the Cobb-Douglas utility function $u_i(x_i) = x_{i1}x_{i2}$ with consumption set $\mathbf{R}_+^2$ and demand function $\phi_i(p) = (p \cdot w_i /2p_1, p \cdot w_i /2p_2)$. Endowments are specified by the functions $w_{i1} = 2 + 20i$ and $w_{i2} = 10 - 8i$. Find the Walrasian equilibrium for this economy.

3.2 Consider an exchange economy with two commodities and a continuum of consumers indexed by the set $I = [0, 1]$. Consumer $i \in I$ has consumption set $\mathbf{R}_+^2$, endowment $w_{i1} = w_{i2} = 4i(1-i)$, and demand function $\phi_i(p) = (i^2 p \cdot w_i /p_1, (1-i^2) p \cdot w_i /p_2)$. Find the Walrasian equilibrium for this economy.

3.3 Consider an exchange economy with a continuum of consumers, $I = [0, 1]$. All consumers have identical utility functions $u_i(x_i) = x_{i1}x_{i2}x_{i3}^2$, consumption sets $\mathbf{R}_+^3$, and demand functions $\phi_i(p) = (p \cdot w_i /4p_1, p \cdot w_i /4p_2, p \cdot w_i /2p_3)$. Endowments are given by $w_{ij} = 4i - 4i^2$ for $j = 1, 2, 3$. Find the Walrasian equilibrium for this economy.

3.4 Consider a production economy with three commodities and a continuum of consumers indexed by the set $I = [0, 1]$. Demand functions are given by $\phi_i(p) = (p \cdot w_i /3p_1, p \cdot w_i /3p_2, p \cdot w_i /3p_3)$, consumption sets by $\mathbf{R}_+^3$, and endowments by $w_i = (ki, ki, 0)$ for all $i \in I$ where k is a positive constant. Commodity 3 is produced using commodity 1 as an input: one unit of commodity 3 can be obtained by using .5 units of commodity 1. Production exhibits constant returns to scale with free disposal of all commodities. Using the normalization $p_1 + p_2 = 1$, find the Walrasian equilibrium for this economy.

3.5   Consider an exchange economy with a continuum of consumers, $I =$
       $[0, 1]$, and two commodities. The consumption set of each consumer
       equals $\mathbf{R}_+^2$. For each consumer $i \in I$, endowment is given by $w_i =$
       (k_i, k_i) and demand by $\phi_i(p) = (\alpha_i\, p \cdot w_i\, /p_1, (1-\alpha_i)\, p \cdot w_i\, /p_2)$ where
       $k: i \ \mapsto \ k_i \ \in \ \mathbf{R}_+$ and $\alpha: i \ \mapsto \ \alpha_i \ \in \ (0, 1)$ are Riemann integrable
       functions of i. Find the Walrasian equilibrium for this economy.

3.6   Generalize equation (3.1) to an economy with r types of consumer.

3.7   Verify that the preferences introduced at the start of Section 3.2.1
       are nonconvex. (*Hint:* Compare the utility derived from the com-
       modity bundles $(1, 0)$, $(0, 1/i)$ with that derived from the convex
       combination $.5(1, 0) + .5(0, 1/i)$.)

3.8   Repeat the computations in Section 3.2.2 using the price normaliza-
       tion $p_1 + p_2 = 1$.

3.9   This problem modifies the model of the automobile market presented
       in Section 3.2.2 to allow for production as well as an initial en-
       dowment of cars. There are three commodities: (1) used cars, (2)
       newly produced cars, and (3) a perfectly divisible composite com-
       modity. Assume a continuum of consumers indexed by $I = [0, 1]$.
       All consumers have preferences represented by the utility function
       $u_i(x_i) = (1 + x_{i1} + 2x_{i2})x_{i3}$. Cars are indivisible so that x_{i1} and
       x_{i2} must be either 0 or 1. Assume (for simplicity) that consumers
       can consume either no car, a used car, or a new car but not both a
       used car and a new car. Initially no new cars are owned, and initial
       endowments are given by

$$w_i = \begin{cases} (0, 0, 12i) & \text{for } i \in [0, .5), \\ (1, 0, 12i) & \text{for } i \in [.5, 1]. \end{cases}$$

New car production is described by the technology set

$$Y = \{\, y \in \mathbf{R}^3 \mid y = \lambda(0, 1, -4), \lambda \geq 0 \,\}.$$

Normalize prices by setting $p_3 = 1$.

   In equilibrium some of the wealthier consumers who currently own
(used) cars will choose to purchase a new car and, as a consequence,
some of the used cars will become available to the less wealthy consumers. The final allocation of cars divides the interval I into three
subintervals: $[0, k_1)$ where no cars are consumed; $[k_1, k_2)$ where used
cars are consumed; and $[k_2, 1]$ where new cars are consumed. (The
allocation to consumers $i = k_1$ and $i = k_2$ is arbitrary.)

(a) What is the equilibrium price of a new car?

(b) Prove that $k_1 = p_1/6$ and $k_2 = (p_2 - p_1)/4$. (You may assume that $0 < k_1 < .5$ and $.5 < k_2 < 1$.)

(c) Derive the equilibrium price for used cars by clearing the used car market.

(d) What fraction of the population end up with no car? With a used car? With a new car?

3.10   Construct a model of a housing market which combines the features of the model of pure exchange and that of production: consumers begin with initial stocks of houses, and new houses can be produced.

3.11   This exercise represents a blend of the model for houses and the model for automobiles. Assume pure exchange with three commodities and a continuum of consumers indexed by the set $I = [0, 1]$. The third commodity is perfectly divisible while the first and second are indivisible. For concreteness, imagine that the two indivisible commodities represent two alternative brands of automobile, say Honda's and Porsche's. Any consumer may choose to consume either a Honda or a Porsche, or both. The endowment distribution takes the form:

$$w_i = \begin{cases} (0, 0, 10i) & \text{if } i \in [0, .9), \\ (4, 5, 10i) & \text{if } i \in [.9, 1]. \end{cases}$$

Utility functions are given by $u_i(x_i) = (1+x_{i1})(1+2x_{i2})x_{i3}$. Normalize prices by selecting the third commodity as *numéraire* ($p_3 = 1$).

   To simplify computation, this problem has been set up so that the equilibrium allocation can be described in terms of four subsets of I: $S_1 = [0, k_1)$ where $x_{i1} = 0$ and $x_{i2} = 0$; $S_2 = [k_1, k_2)$ where $x_{i1} = 1$ and $x_{i2} = 0$; $S_3 = [k_2, k_3)$ where $x_{i1} = 0$ and $x_{i2} = 1$; and $S_4 = [k_3, 1]$ where $x_{i1} = 1$ and $x_{i2} = 1$. Intuitively, you would expect that $0 < k_1 < k_2 < k_3 < 1$ so that as i (and hence wealth) increases consumers progress from purchasing no car ($i \in S_1$), to a Honda ($i \in S_2$), a Porsche ($i \in S_3$), and finally both a Honda and a Porsche ($i \in S_4$). As usual, the allocation to consumers on the boundary points is arbitrary: for example, $i = k_1$ represents a consumer indifferent between buying no car and buying a Honda; hence, k_1 could be included either in set S_1 or in set S_2, and we have arbitrarily assigned it to S_2.

(a) Give a formal description of the consumption set of consumer i.

(b) Show that the boundary points are $k_1 = .2p_1$, $k_2 = .3p_2 - .2p_1$, and $k_3 = .2p_1 + .1p_2$. (*Hint:* You may assume that $k_3 < .9$ so that $k_1, k_2, k_3 \in [0, .9)$.)

(c) By clearing the two markets for automobiles, find the Walrasian equilibrium price functional.

(d) Verify that the market for the divisible commodity also clears at these equilibrium prices.

3.12 This problem extends the Marshallian joint supply model of Chapter 2 to a continuum of consumers, $I = [0, 1]$. Commodities one and two represent mutton and hides, produced using commodity three (sheep) as an input. Endowments are given by $w_i = (0, 0, k_i)$ where k is a Riemann integrable function of i with $k_i > 0$ denoting the positive quantity of sheep owned initially by consumer i. Production of mutton and hides is described by the technology set

$$Y = \{ (y \in \mathbf{R}^3 \mid y = \lambda(1, 1, -\beta), \lambda \geq 0 \}$$

where β is a positive constant. The preferences of consumer $i \in I$ are represented by the utility function $u_i(x_i) = x_{i1}^{\alpha_{i1}} x_{i2}^{\alpha_{i2}} x_{i3}^{\alpha_{i3}}$ where the functions $\alpha_j (j = 1, 2, 3)$ are Riemann integrable functions of i satisfying $0 \leq \alpha_{ij} \leq 1$ for $j = 1, 2, 3$ and $\alpha_{i1} + \alpha_{i2} + \alpha_{i3} = 1$ for all $i \in I$. Normalize prices by setting $p_3 = 1$.

(a) Prove that if mutton and hides are supplied in strictly positive amount, then the Walrasian equilibrium prices must satisfy the condition $p_1 + p_2 = \beta$.

(b) Derive an expression for the per capita amount of mutton and the per capita amount of hides produced in equilibrium as well as the equilibrium price of each.

(c) Now specialize the model derived above by assuming that $w_i = (0, 0, 2)$ for all $i \in I$, that $\beta = 1$, and that

$$(\alpha_{i1}, \alpha_{i2}, \alpha_{i3}) = \begin{cases} (.5, 0, .5) & \text{for } i \in S_1, \\ (0, .5, .5) & \text{for } i \in S_2, \end{cases}$$

where S_1 and S_2 are disjoint subsets of I with $S_1 \cup S_2 = I$ and measure $\lambda(S_1)$ and $\lambda(S_2)$ respectively with $\lambda(S_1) + \lambda(S_2) = 1$. Solve for the Walrasian equilibrium price functional, the equilibrium quantity of mutton and hides per capita produced in equilibrium, and the equilibrium Walrasian allocation.

3.13 Let S_1 be the set of rational numbers and S_2 the set of irrational numbers in the interval $I = [0, 1]$ and let λ be Lebesgue measure. Justify each of the following assertions:

(a) $\lambda(I) = 1$;

(b) $\lambda(\{x\}) = 0$ for any singleton set $\{x\} \subset I$;

(c) $\lambda(S_1) = 0$;

(d) $\lambda(S_2) = 1$.

3.14 Verify that the function $f: [0, 1] \to \mathbf{R}_+$ defined by

$$f(i) = \begin{cases} 0 & \text{if } i \text{ is irrational,} \\ 1 & \text{if } i \text{ is rational.} \end{cases}$$

is Lebesgue measurable.

3.15 **Counting measure** on a finite set $I = \{1, \ldots, n\}$ is defined by setting $\mu(S) = \#S$ for all $S \subset I$ and **normalized counting measure** by setting $\mu(S) = \#S/\#I$ for all $S \subset I$. Verify that each of these "measures" is in fact a measure in the sense of Definition 3.7. Is either a probability measure? A nonatomic measure?

3.16 State and prove a generalization of Theorem 3.16 appropriate to an economy with a continuum of consumers and production subject to constant returns to scale.

3.17 In Section 3.1.2 we solved explicitly for the equilibrium of a type economy with two types of consumer in which consumer characteristics took the form

$$(\alpha, (a, b)) = \begin{cases} (.5, (1, 3)) & \text{for consumers of type 1,} \\ (.5, (3, 1)) & \text{for consumers of type 2,} \end{cases}$$

with a fraction .25 consumers of type 1 and .75 of type 2. Characterize the initial distribution τ and the equilibrium distribution μ for that economy.

3.18 Characterize the initial distribution τ and the equilibrium μ for the type economy with stair step preferences discussed at the beginning of Section 3.2.1.

3.19 Using the measure x described at the end of Section 3.4.1, compute $x(B)$ for each of the sets $\emptyset$, $\{k\}$, $\{c\}$, and $\{k, c\}$. (Compute the results separately for $\omega \in [0, 3)$, $\omega \in [3, 7)$, and $\omega \in [7, 10]$.) Verify that, provided J is finite, $\{\delta_j \mid j = k, c\}$ is a basis for $M(J)$.

3.20 In the example worked out in Section 3.4.2, the hedonic price p_k is linear in k. However, as Rosen emphasizes, there is no reason why the hedonic price should be linear in characteristics ("... two 6-foot cars are not equivalent to one 12 feet in length, since they cannot be driven simultaneously ..." [Rosen (1974), 38]). Retaining the other assumptions in our example, suppose that the utility associated with commodity bundle $x = x_c \delta_c + \delta_k$ is given by $u(x) = x_c(1 + \alpha k^2)$ and that indivisible goods of type k are produced subject to constant returns at marginal cost βk^2.

(a) Assuming that $\omega > \beta/\alpha$, solve for the optimizing value of k. Letting $\alpha = 1$ and $\beta = 2$, illustrate the optimal choice for a consumer with wealth $\omega = 10$ in a Rosen diagram.

(b) If ω is uniformly distributed on $[6,14]$, find the support of the equilibrium distribution of consumption of the indivisible commodity in K. Will this equilibrium distribution be uniform?

3.21   Consider the Tiebout economy described in Section 3.4.3 but with a type economy in which wealth can take on the values 6, 8, 10, 12, or 14 with equal measure. Assume that any local political jurisdiction enjoys constant returns to scale provided that it serves at least 10% of the population. Illustrate the Tiebout equilibrium for the convexified economy in a Rosen diagram. Will this equilibrium be an equilibrium for the original economy? How do your answers change if jurisdictions serving less than one-fourth of the population are subject to increasing returns?

4

Topology

Much of the mathematics discussed thus far has probably seemed both familiar and useful. Topology is quite different. Most economists pass their lives quite innocent of its existence. And those who happen to make contact with this branch of mathematics will, likely as not, conclude that it is useless: a web of closely interwoven, almost circular definitions that don't seem to "do" anything. In fact topology is crucial to the development of a rigorous theory of competition. Without it we could not move past the definitions, notation, and examples of the preceding chapters to the theorems and proofs of the chapters which follow. For now you have to accept that on faith.

How then are we to come to grips with this subject? You need a better understanding of topology than a simple summary of the "main facts" would provide. On the other hand, attempting to compress a course in topology into the confines of a single chapter is clearly impossible, and probably worthless as well. What I have chosen to do instead is to "tell a story" about topology, to paint a mental picture of what it tries to accomplish and how.[1] Don't try to absorb all of the details at once because that is scarcely possible and totally unnecessary. Try instead to grasp the main ideas, the broad outline of what topology is about. As we progress through the book and you see how topology is applied the subject will come to seem more and more natural.

This chapter is divided into two parts, the first concerned with general topology and the second with the more specialized topologies of vector

---

1 This chapter makes no attempt at formal derivation, substituting informal explanation for rigorous proof. If you become a convert to mathematical economics, you eventually will want to supplement the account given here by reading one of the many good textbooks on general topology. Kelley (1955) or Munkres (1975) is particularly recommended.

Table 4.1. *Unions and intersections.*

	Finite		Arbitrary	
	$\cup$	$\cap$	$\cup$	$\cap$
Open sets	open	open	open	
Closed sets	closed	closed		closed

spaces. Although the latter topic is the most useful for economists, beginning with the basics makes everything easier.

4.1 Introduction to topology

4.1.1 Topological spaces

If you are encountering the definition of topology for the first time, your reaction is likely to be: How can anything so bland — so unspecific — possibly lead to something useful? What turns a set X into a topological space? Subject to a few restrictions, simply declare a collection of subsets τ of X to be open! The coupling of a set X with a topology τ, often represented as an ordered pair (X, τ), is called a **topological space** and the collection τ a **topology**.

Definition 4.1 (X, τ) *is a* **topological space** *(and, therefore, τ a* **topology** *on X) provided that:*

- $\emptyset \in \tau$ *and* $X \in \tau$;
- *any[2] union of sets in τ belongs to τ;*
- *any finite intersection of sets in τ belongs to τ.*

The members of τ are called **open sets**. *The complement of an open set is called a* **closed set**.

Since a closed set is, by definition, the complement of an open set, these restrictions on open sets immediately imply some parallel restrictions on closed sets:

- $\emptyset$ and X are closed sets;
- any finite union of closed sets is closed;
- any intersection of closed sets is closed.

---

2 No matter whether a finite, countably, or even uncountably infinite collection of sets is involved.

For convenience, these rules are summarized in Table 4.1. The main point to remember is that unions or intersections of open sets are open and unions or intersections of closed sets are closed with the following exception: to guarantee that the intersection of open sets is open or the union of closed sets is closed, the index set must be finite; with arbitrary index sets, the result is unpredictable.[3]

It is clearly quite easy to turn any set into a topological space. Simply specify a collection τ satisfying the above requirements for open sets, and we have a topology.[4] For example, every subset of X can be declared open, yielding what is called the **discrete topology**. Or, to go to the opposite extreme, we could declare that only $\emptyset$ and X are open, obtaining the **indiscrete (or trivial) topology**. These examples highlight the flexibility we have in creating a topology, but neither of these topologies is very useful. In general, the most useful topologies have fewer open sets than the discrete topology but more than the indiscrete topology.

Since a set can have more than one topology, it is natural to seek ways to compare alternative topologies τ and τ' on a set X. One way is by set inclusion. If $\tau \subset \tau'$, so that every open set under the topology τ is an open set under τ', then τ is said to be **coarser** than τ' (or, equivalently, τ' is **finer** than τ). If $\tau \subset \tau'$ and $\tau' \subset \tau$, then $\tau = \tau'$ and the two topologies are identical (i.e., have the same open sets). Often you will see the term **weak** used as a synonym for coarse and the term **strong** for fine.

The rationale for this terminology is that the fineness of a topology affects its ability to discriminate between points in the set. Given two points $x, y \in X$, if we can find two disjoint open sets G_x and G_y with $x \in G_x$ and $y \in G_y$, then the points must not be arbitrarily close to one another: we can "see" a gap between them. Fine topologies, like a high powered microscope, offer high resolution while coarse topologies make the gaps between nearby points disappear. The discrete topology is clearly the finest possible topology on a set, and the trivial topology the coarsest.

Because the ability of a topology to discriminate between objects in a set is an important property, it is useful to have ways of characterizing this ability other than comparison by set inclusion. In the first place, comparing two topologies by set inclusion is an imperfect classification because the relation of set inclusion is often incomplete: i.e., given two topologies τ and τ', it

---

3 You may encounter the notation G_δ and F_σ to classify the result of taking the intersection of a countable collection of open sets and the union of a countable collection of closed sets respectively. While G_δ (*resp.* F_σ) sets need not be open (*resp.* closed), they do have useful properties: e.g., they are Borel sets.

4 The requirements imposed on closed sets do not have to be checked: they follow automatically from the requirements on the open sets.

is possible (in fact, rather likely) that neither $\tau \subset \tau'$ nor $\tau' \subset \tau$. Secondly, we often need to have more explicit information on how well the topology discriminates between various types of objects (not necessarily just pairs of points). For these reasons some or all of the following **separation axioms** are often imposed on a topology.

Definition 4.2 (Separation Axioms) *If (X, τ) is a topological space, then X is:*

- *T_1 if for any $x, y \in X$ such that $x \neq y$ there is an open set G_x with $x \in G_x$ and $y \notin G_x$;*
- *T_2 (**Hausdorff**) if for any $x, y \in X$ such that $x \neq y$ there exist disjoint open sets G_x and G_y with $x \in G_x$ and $y \in G_y$;*
- *T_3 (**regular**) if X is T_1 and for any point $x \in X$ and closed set $F \subset X$ not containing x there exist disjoint open sets G_x and G_F such that $x \in G_x$ and $F \subset G_F$;*
- *T_4 (**normal**) if X is T_1 and for each pair of disjoint closed subsets $F, F' \subset X$ there exist disjoint open sets G_F and $G_{F'}$ such that $F \subset G_F$ and $F' \subset G_{F'}$.*

T_1 is equivalent to the assumption that every subset of X consisting of a single point is closed. Figure 4.1 illustrates the basic idea behind each of the separation axioms.

The statement of these separation axioms contains a construction which is used repeatedly in topology and, therefore, merits a special name: if G_x or G_S is an open set containing the point x or subset S respectively, then G_x (*resp.* G_S) is called an **open neighborhood** of x (*resp. S*).

4.1.2 The Euclidean topology

The discussion so far has been quite abstract with no example of a topology which is truly useful. This section describes a natural topology, in a sense the only natural topology, for the real line.

Much of the initial motivation for topology came from studying the role that open intervals on the real line play in calculus. While open intervals are clearly natural candidates for the open sets of a topology on **R**, open intervals by themselves do not constitute a topology: the union of disjoint open intervals is not itself an open interval. To overcome this defect, we use the open intervals to generate a larger collection of open sets which does meet the requirements for a topology.

The technique described here illustrates a general procedure for using a

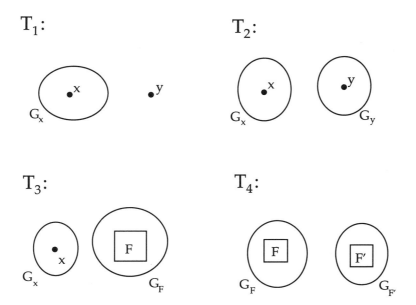

Fig. 4.1. The separation axioms.

basis of sets to generate a topology, in loose analogy to the way a set of basis vectors can be used to generate a linear subspace.

Definition 4.3 *A collection $\beta \subset 2^X$ is a **basis** for a topology on X if*

- *each $x \in X$ is contained in some basis element $B \in \beta$; and*
- *for any pair of basis elements $B_1, B_2 \in \beta$ and for any $x \in B_1 \cap B_2$ there exists another basis element $B_3 \in \beta$ such that $x \in B_3 \subset B_1 \cap B_2$.*

The open sets in the topology τ generated by the basis β are the subsets $G \subset X$ such that:

- *every element $x \in G$ belongs to a basis element which in turn is contained in G; or, equivalently,*
- *G can be expressed as the union of basis elements.*

It is easy to verify that the collection of open intervals in **R** of the form (a, b), where $a < b$, is a basis for a topology on **R**, called the standard (or Euclidean) topology for **R**.

What do the open sets generated from a basis look like? Clearly, the basis elements themselves are open sets in the topology which they generate so, in the case of the standard Euclidean topology on **R**, the open intervals are open. More generally,

- a set $G \subset \mathbf{R}$ is open if for any $x \in G$ there exists an open interval containing x and contained in G; or, equivalently,

- any open set is equal to a union of open intervals.

Thus, the open sets generated in this way provide a natural generalization of what one intuitively would mean in referring to an *interval* (a, b) as "open" and clearly justifies calling the resulting topology *standard*.

The Euclidean topology on **R** also provides a nice illustration of a concept closely related to a basis which is often quite useful.

Definition 4.4 *A collection γ of subsets of X is a* **subbasis** *for a topology if finite intersections of the elements of γ yield a basis for a topology.*

The intervals of the form $(-\infty, b)$ and (a, ∞) in **R** are clearly a subbasis since, if $a < b$, then $(a, b) = (-\infty, b) \cap (a, \infty)$.

Bases provide another way to classify topologies, the cardinality of the bases used to define them. A set is said to be (i) **finite**, (ii) **countably infinite**, or (iii) **uncountable** if its elements can be put into one-to-one correspondence with (i) the set $\{1, \ldots, n\}$, (ii) the set of nonnegative integers, or (iii) the points of the real line respectively. A set which is finite or countably infinite is termed **countable**.

Definition 4.5 (Countability axioms) *Suppose that a topological space (X, τ) has basis β.*

- *A topological space is* **first countable** *if for any $x \in X$ the set of basis elements containing x is countable.*

- *A topological space is* **second countable** *if the entire collection of basis elements β is countable.*

Clearly a topological space which is second countable is also first countable. **R** with its standard topology is both T_4 and second countable so its topology has enough open sets to insure rather fine separation but few enough to accomplish that separation with a countable collection of basis elements.

4.1.3 Subspace and product topologies

Although constructing a topology can be quite laborious, sometimes we can cut down on our effort by using old topologies as building blocks for new. While the techniques we are about to discuss are quite general, we emphasize two concrete applications:

- Using the standard Euclidean topology for $\mathbf{R}$ to define a "compatible" topology for an arbitrary subset $S \subset \mathbf{R}$; and
- Using the standard Euclidean topology for $\mathbf{R}$ to define the standard Euclidean topology for $\mathbf{R}^{\mathbf{n}}$.

Suppose that we are given a topological space (X, τ), and we want to have the "same" topology on a proper subset $S \subset X$. Clearly, we should exclude from the new topology the open sets in τ that are disjoint from S and include those that are contained in S. The interesting question is what to do about the open sets in τ which overlap, but are not contained, in S. What seems natural is to take the intersection of such elements of τ with S as the open sets of the new topology, and in fact this is what we do.

Definition 4.6 *If (X, τ) is a topological space and $S \subset X$, then the* **subspace topology** *inherited by S is given by the collection of open sets*

$$\tau_S = \{\, G' \subset S \mid G' = G \cap S,\ G \in \tau \,\}.$$

We often refer to a topology constructed in this way as the **relative topology** of S and call S a **topological subspace**.

The standard topology on $\mathbf{R}$ gives a good illustration of the appropriateness of this procedure. Let $S = [0, 2)$ and consider the open set $(-1, 1)$ in the original topology for $\mathbf{R}$. $(-1, 1) \cap [0, 2) = [0, 1)$ is the corresponding open set in the subspace topology, and it perhaps no longer looks open because the endpoint 0 has been included. But in a certain sense the point 0 is no longer on the boundary of the interval $[0, 2)$ because all the points to the left of 0 have disappeared. The subspace topology behaves the way we should want it to.

The other example of building new topologies from old that we want to consider involves Cartesian products. Suppose we are given a collection of topological spaces $\{\, (X_\alpha, \tau_\alpha) \mid \alpha \in A \,\}$ where A is an arbitrary index set. The question we want to address is how to construct a topology for the Cartesian product $\prod_{\alpha \in A} X_\alpha$ which is "naturally" related to the topologies on the coordinate spaces X_α.

Since a topology τ_α is trivially a basis for itself, we can without loss of generality assume that each of the topologies τ_α is generated by a basis

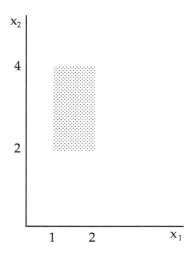

Fig. 4.2. Basis element for the product topology.

β_α. The natural procedure would be to construct a basis for the Cartesian product by taking the Cartesian products of the basis elements for each coordinate space: i.e., letting $\beta = \{\,\prod_{\alpha \in A} B_\alpha \mid B_\alpha \in \beta_\alpha\,\}$ define a basis for an appropriate topology on $\prod_{\alpha \in A} X_\alpha$. It is easy to check that this collection does satisfy the requirements for a basis. (See Munkres (1975), 113, if you really insist on seeing the details!) Thus, this basis generates a topology for the Cartesian product, often called the **box topology**.

When the index set A is finite, no one quarrels with the fact that the box topology is the natural topology, and so it is given a more official sounding name: the **product topology** for $\prod_{\alpha \in A} X_\alpha$. The standard topology for $\mathbf{R^n}$ provides a good illustration why this procedure for constructing a product topology is natural. Recall that the open intervals are a basis for the standard topology for $\mathbf{R}$. Taking $(1, 2)$ and $(2, 4)$ as typical, examine the corresponding basis element for $\mathbf{R} \times \mathbf{R}$. As shown in Figure 4.2, the result is a rectangle with sides excluded. The open rectangles constructed in this fashion (as they are called even when A is infinite!) are clearly a natural generalization of open intervals.

When the index set A is infinite, using the box topology for the Cartesian product space becomes more debatable — not because the basis elements fail to define a topology (of course they generate a topology since they are a basis) but because the resulting topology is too fine for certain purposes. Certain theorems with important applications in mathematics fail unless infinite product spaces are given a coarser topology than that provided by the box topology. The topology standardly used in place of the box topology, under which the key theorems are true and given the official title of the **product topology**, is generated by a basis that involves a simple modification of the basis elements for the box topology. The basis elements have the same form, $B = \prod_{\alpha \in A} B_\alpha$, but where $B_\alpha \in \beta_\alpha$ for a *finite* number of the indices α and $B_\alpha = X_\alpha$ for all the rest.

Definition 4.7 *Given a collection* $\{ (X_\alpha, \tau_\alpha \mid \alpha \in A \}$ *of topological spaces where* (X_α, τ_α) *has basis* β_α, *the* **product topology** *for* $\prod_{\alpha \in A} X_\alpha$ *is the topology with basis*

$$\beta := \Big\{ \prod_{\alpha \in A} B_\alpha \in \prod_{\alpha \in A} \beta_\alpha \mid B_\alpha = X_\alpha \quad if \quad \alpha \in A^* \Big\}$$

where $A^* \subset A$ *and* $A \backslash A^*$ *is finite.*

Our main use of the product topology will be for finite products where the distinction between the product and box topologies disappears, so in that sense this discussion is diversionary. But it does serve the useful purpose of offering at least the hint that some sets (e.g., an infinite Cartesian product of **R**) can have *more than one* useful topology.

4.1.4 Metric topologies

There is another way to define the standard topology on $\mathbf{R^n}$ which takes advantage of a somewhat special feature of this topology: it can be described in terms of a distance function ρ called a **metric**. Topological spaces of this type are said to be **metrizable** and the pairing (X, ρ) is referred to as a **metric space**. Metric spaces are somewhat special: e.g., they are necessarily T_4 and first countable (though not necessarily second countable). However, many useful topologies turn out to be metrizable and, when metrics are available, they often furnish an intuitively appealing description of the topology.

Definition 4.8 *A* **metric** *on* X *is a function* $\rho \colon X \times X \to \mathbf{R}_+$, $(x, y) \mapsto$ $\rho(x, y)$, *which satisfies the following conditions:*

(a) $\rho(x, y) = 0$ *iff* $x = y$;
(b) $\rho(x, y) = \rho(y, x)$ *for all* $x, y \in X$;
(c) $\rho(x, y) + \rho(y, z) \geq \rho(x, z)$ *for all* $x, y, z \in X$.

These conditions are meant to capture what one should require of a reasonable measure of the distance between points of a set:

(a) says that a point in X is always zero distance from itself, and that distinct points are always a positive distance apart;

(b) that the distance from x to y is the same as the distance from y to x; and

(c) (the "triangle inequality") that traveling an indirect route from x to y and then from y to z is never shorter than the direct route from x to z.

Once we have a suitable concept of distance, we can generate a topology consistent with the metric by using the metric to define a basis. For any point $x \in X$, we take as a typical basis element the set of all points lying closer than ϵ distance from x, $B_\rho(x, \epsilon) := \{\, y \in X \mid \rho(x, y) < \epsilon \,\}$, where $\epsilon > 0$. The set $B_\rho(x, \epsilon)$ is called the ϵ-**ball centered at** x. It is not too hard to show that the collection of balls

$$\beta = \{\, B \subset X \mid B = B_\rho(x, \epsilon),\ x \in X, \epsilon > 0 \,\}$$

satisfies the two requirements for a basis. A topology generated in this way is called a **metric topology** for X.

In $\mathbf{R^n}$ an obvious candidate for such a metric is **Euclidean distance**, defined by

$$\rho(x, y) = \left[\sum_{i=1}^{n}(x_i - y_i)^2\right]^{1/2} \quad \text{for} \quad x, y \in X.$$

In $\mathbf{R}$, $\mathbf{R}^2$, or $\mathbf{R}^3$ this metric is simply the length of the line segment connecting x and y, and in $\mathbf{R^n}$ we will interpret it the same way. You may have seen the same construct used in statistics or econometrics to measure how far a model departs from a perfect fit to the data. In $\mathbf{R}^2$ or $\mathbf{R}^3$ the ϵ balls centered at some point x constructed using the Euclidean metric *look* like balls: disks with center x and radius ϵ (excluding the circumference) in $\mathbf{R}^2$ and balls with center x and radius ϵ (with the surface excluded) in $\mathbf{R}^3$. In $\mathbf{R}$ the Euclidean balls collapse to open intervals of the form $(x - \epsilon, x + \epsilon)$ which we have already encountered as a basis for the standard topology of the real line.

One feature of this metric topology that you may find puzzling is that the basis elements for $n > 1$ are different from those we constructed earlier for the product topology for $\mathbf{R^n}$ since the latter were rectangular in shape, not round. This might lead you (incorrectly) to conjecture that the Euclidean metric topology for $\mathbf{R^n}$ is somehow different from its standard topology. Before considering this question suppose that we introduce an alternative metric for $\mathbf{R^n}$ whose balls take the form of open rectangles. The metric is defined in terms of a supremum and hence is called the **sup metric**, defined by

$$\rho(x,y) = \sup\{\, |x_i - y_i| \mid i = 1, \ldots, n \,\} \quad \text{for} \quad x, y \in X.$$

It is not too difficult to prove that the function ρ satisfies the conditions required of a metric. Because the ϵ-ball centered at x under this metric is an open rectangle (with sides having length 2ϵ), the metric topology generated by this metric has the same basis as the product topology and is, therefore, equivalent to the standard topology for $\mathbf{R^n}$.

The obvious question to ask at this point is whether the topology generated by the Euclidean metric is somehow different from the standard, at least when $n > 1$. We already know how to answer this question. Two topologies τ and τ' are equal if $\tau \subset \tau'$ and $\tau' \subset \tau$. Furthermore, if β is a basis for τ and β' a basis for τ', we can verify the two set inclusions simply by checking basis elements. To be precise, $\tau \subset \tau'$ if for each $x \in X$ and $B \in \beta$ containing x we can find a basis element $B' \in \beta'$ which fits inside B and contains x. A parallel statement holds for $\tau' \subset \tau$. Applying this idea to the current context, if we take a typical open rectangle in the basis for the sup topology and any x in that rectangle, then clearly we can center one of the balls for the Euclidean metric at x and, by choosing its radius to be sufficiently small, fit the ball entirely within the rectangle. Thus, the topology generated by the sup metric is coarser than that generated by the Euclidean metric. But we can just as easily fit the open rectangles of the sup metric inside the balls of the Euclidean metric, and so the Euclidean metric must generate a topology coarser than that generated by the sup metric. We conclude, therefore, that the two metric topologies are equivalent. Since the sup metric has the same basis as the product topology, the metric topologies are also equivalent to the product topology as defined in the preceding section. Fortunately, all these approaches lead to the same standard topology for $\mathbf{R^n}$.

This construction is worth describing in such detail because it begins to give a suggestion of the power implicit in the abstract definition of a topology. We now have several alternative ways to describe the standard Euclidean topology on $\mathbf{R^n}$ and, depending on the circumstances, each has its value. But we now also know that, no matter how we describe the standard topology and whether we take advantage of one of the metrics generating this topology or not, from a topological point of view the answers we obtain will be the same. It is about as nice an illustration of the virtues of mathematical abstraction as one could ask for.

4.1.5 Convergence

One useful interpretation of topology is that it provides a way to describe when points of a set are close to one another and when points are coming closer together. In this section we will see how convergence, the notion of coming closer, can be captured formally through the use of open sets.

The intuitive idea is the following. Consider a point x belonging to a topological space (X, τ) and a collection of points $\{ x^\alpha \mid \alpha \in A \}$ where A is an index set. To capture the notion that x^α converges to x as α "increases," we consider the collection of open sets in X which contain the point x. If for any choice of open neighborhood of x (no matter how small), the collection x^α eventually enters the neighborhood and stays there, then x^α converges to x.

To attach meaning to such a concept, we need first to impose a sense of direction to the index set A, thereby allowing us meaningfully to speak of α "increasing." We do this by assuming that A can be partially ordered by a binary relation.

Definition 4.9 $\succeq$ *is a* **binary relation** *on a set A if for any ordered pair $(\alpha, \alpha') \in A \times A$ it is always the case that either $\alpha \succeq \alpha'$ ("α is related to α'") or $\alpha \not\succeq \alpha'$ ("α is not related to α'").*

We have already encountered another example of a binary relation in the guise of *strict preference* $\succ$. All that is different here is the symbol we are using for the binary relation. As an economist you will almost instinctively want to interpret $\alpha \succeq \alpha'$ as "α is at least as good as α'," but try to be a little more open minded. When mathematicians see $\succeq$ used in this context the typical example which *they* have in mind is the relation $\subset$ applied to the set $A = 2^X$ of all subsets of some set X. For the moment, try to think like a mathematician! Recall also the definition of a partial ordering, introduced in Chapter 2.

Definition 4.10 *The binary relation $\succeq$ on A is a* **partial ordering** *on A if it is*

- **reflexive:** *$\alpha \succeq \alpha$ for all $\alpha \in A$;*
- **transitive:** *$\alpha \succeq \alpha'$ and $\alpha' \succeq \alpha''$ implies $\alpha \succeq \alpha''$ for all $\alpha, \alpha', \alpha'' \in A$; and*
- **antisymmetric:** *$\alpha \succeq \alpha'$ and $\alpha' \succeq \alpha$ implies $\alpha = \alpha'$ for all $\alpha, \alpha' \in A$.*

If in addition $\succeq$ is complete (i.e., $\alpha \succeq \alpha'$ or $\alpha' \succeq \alpha$ for all $\alpha, \alpha' \in A$), then it is called a **total ordering** *on A.*

You should have no difficulty verifying that the binary relation $\subset$ defined on 2^X is a partial ordering but "typically" not a total ordering.

Definition 4.11 *A set A is said to be* **directed** *by a binary relation $\succeq$ if*

- $\succeq$ *is a partial ordering on A and*
- *for each pair of indices $\alpha, \alpha' \in A$ there exists an element $\alpha'' \in A$ such that $\alpha'' \succeq \alpha$ and $\alpha'' \succeq \alpha'$.*

Definition 4.12 *A set $\{\, x^\alpha \in X \mid \alpha \in A \,\}$ indexed by a directed set A is called a* **net** *and denoted $\langle x^\alpha \mid \alpha \in A \rangle$ or simply as $\langle x^\alpha \rangle$ when the index set is clear from the context.*

After these preliminaries, we are finally ready to say what we mean by convergence.

Definition 4.13 *If (X, τ) is a topological space, a net $\langle x^\alpha \rangle$* **converges** *to a point x, written $x^\alpha \to x$, if for each neighborhood G_x of x there exists $\alpha^* \in A$ such that $x^\alpha \in G_x$ for all $\alpha \succeq \alpha^*$.*

Stated less formally, $x^\alpha \to x$ if, no matter how small we make the neighborhood G_x, the net eventually enters the neighborhood and stays there. As the neighborhoods collapse down onto the point x the net must approach x as well: the system of neighborhoods of x has snared the net.

Perhaps the most natural way to construct an example of a net converging to some point x is to use the open neighborhoods of x to index the net. Let β be a basis for some topology on X and β_x the collection of basis elements containing the point x. Label the basis elements by an index set A which is compatible with set inclusion in the following sense: $\alpha \succeq \alpha'$ iff $B^\alpha \subset B^{\alpha'}$ for $\alpha, \alpha' \in A$ and $B^\alpha, B^{\alpha'} \in \beta_x$. The binary relation $\succeq$ directs A because

- $\succeq$ is a partial order (since $\subset$ partially orders the collection β_x); and
- for any $\alpha, \alpha' \in A$ there exists an $\alpha'' \in A$ such that $\alpha'' \succeq \alpha$ and $\alpha'' \succeq \alpha'$ (since β is a basis and so for any $B^\alpha, B^{\alpha'} \in \beta_x$ there exists a basis element $B^{\alpha''} \in \beta_x$ such that $x \in B^{\alpha''} \subset B^\alpha \cap B^{\alpha'}$).

If we construct a net by choosing a representative x^α from each basis element B^α, then clearly $x^\alpha \to x$.

Often you will encounter a special case of a net, called a **sequence**, which uses the set of positive integers directed by $\geq$ as its index set A. Sequences are much more popular than nets because they seem less abstract. However, using sequences instead of nets can be dangerous. The topology of a set can always be described in terms of nets, but the same is not true of sequences.

For that reason, this book favors the use of nets over sequences. In much of the mathematical economics literature you will find sequences used instead of nets, a simplification which causes no problems when the topological space involved is $\mathbf{R^n}$ with its standard topology. However, in more general contexts nets should almost always be used instead of sequences.

Although a net in a topological set X may fail to converge to any point in the set, it is often possible to find a subset of the points in the net which do converge. To find such a subset, suppose that we have another directed index set Γ and a function $s\colon \Gamma \to A$ that picks out certain of the indices in A. In selecting these indices, we will require that $s(\gamma') \succeq s(\gamma)$ if $\gamma' \succeq \gamma$ and that the function s continues to select indices all the way through A in the sense that for each $\alpha \in A$ we can find an index $\gamma \in \Gamma$ such that $s(\gamma') \succeq \alpha$ for all $\gamma' \succeq \gamma$. A net $\left\langle x^{s(\gamma)} \mid \gamma \in \Gamma \right\rangle$ constructed in this way is called a **subnet** of the net $\langle x^\alpha \rangle$. If, given a net $\langle x^\alpha \rangle$, we can find a subnet converging to some point x, then x is said to be a **cluster point** of the original net $\langle x^\alpha \rangle$.

While these definitions are rather abstract, a few examples should convince you that the underlying concepts are quite simple and intuitive. Consider the real line with its Euclidean topology. (Note that, taking advantage of the special properties of $\mathbf{R}$, all of our nets are in fact sequences.) As a simple application of the definitions given above you should be able to prove that the net $\langle x^n = 1/n \mid n \in \mathbf{Z_{++}} \rangle$ converges to 0. A more interesting example is provided by the net

$$1, 0, -1, 1, 0, -1, 1, 0, -1, \ldots\ldots$$

This net does not converge but it does have cluster points: the subnet formed by selecting out the terms equal to 1 converges to 1, the subnet formed by selecting out the 0's converges to 0, and the subnet formed by selecting out the -1's converges to -1. (When applied to nets which are sequences, subnets are ordinarily called **subsequences**.) Thus, the net has $\{1, 0, -1\}$ as its set of cluster points. A final example on the real line should help resist the temptation to conclude that, if a net has but one cluster point, the net converges to that point. Consider the net

$$1, 1, 2, 1, 3, 1, 4, 1, 5, 1 \ldots\ldots$$

where the odd terms are the positive integers in ascending order and the even terms all equal 1. This net has 1 as its sole cluster point, but it has no limit.

You should have no difficulty coming up with examples in $\mathbf{R}^2$ or $\mathbf{R}^3$ of a similar nature. Considering nets in $\mathbf{R^n}$ raises an interesting and important question. Suppose that $\langle x^\alpha \mid \alpha \in A \rangle$ is a net in $\mathbf{R^n}$ converging to a limit

x. We can check convergence by establishing that $\rho(x^\alpha, x) \to 0$ where ρ is any metric for the standard topology on $\mathbf{R}^n$. However, we could also check convergence by examining each of the coordinates of the net: i.e., by checking whether $x_i^\alpha \to x_i$ for all $i = 1, \ldots, n$. Are these two types of convergence, convergence of the x^α and convergence coordinate by coordinate, related? If so, how? Fortunately, the answer to this question, asserted here without proof, is quite straightforward.

Theorem 4.14 *Let* $\{ (X_n, \tau_n) \mid n \in N \}$ *be a collection of topological spaces indexed by an arbitrary set* N. *A net* $\langle x^\alpha \rangle$ *in* $\prod_{n \in N} X_n$ *converges to* $x \in \prod_{n \in N} X_n$ *with the product topology iff* $x_n^\alpha \to x_n$ *for all* $n \in N$.

The preceding theorem establishes the equivalence between convergence in a product space and convergence coordinate by coordinate, certainly an "obvious" fact. The fascinating aspect of all this, however, is that the assertion is generally false when the index set is infinite if the product space is given the box rather than the product topology! The fact that the theorem is true when the box topology is replaced by the coarser product topology was historically one of the major reasons for the invention of the product topology. However, in this book we are primarily interested in finite Cartesian products where the distinction between the product and box topologies disappears. If all of this seems a bit mysterious, accept the conclusion of Theorem 4.14 as an obvious fact about $\mathbf{R}^n$ and wait until later to worry about infinite dimensions.

4.1.6 Interior, closure, and boundary

In our discussion thus far, we have been acting as though subsets of a topological space (X, τ) must be either open or closed (or perhaps both as in the case of the subsets $\emptyset$ and X). However, subsets frequently fail to be either open or closed. Fortunately, we can still establish some useful topological characteristics of such sets.

The intuition behind the definitions we are about to give is nicely illustrated by a half open interval in $\mathbf{R}$, say the interval $S = (a, b]$ where $a < b$, and we will use this example to illustrate the definitions as we go along.

Given a subset S of a topological space X, the **interior** of S is defined to be union of all the open sets contained in S and the **closure** as the intersection of all the closed sets containing S:

$$\text{int}\, S := \bigcup_{\substack{G \subseteq S \\ G \in \tau}} G \quad \text{and} \quad \text{cl}\, S := \bigcap_{\substack{F \supseteq S \\ X \setminus F \in \tau}} F.$$

Clearly int S is the largest open set contained in S and cl F the smallest closed set containing S. For the interval $(a, b]$, int $S = (a, b)$ and cl $S = [a, b]$.

A point $x \in X$ is said to be **topologically accessible** from S (or an **accumulation point** of S) if every open neighborhood of x has a nonempty intersection with the set $S \backslash \{ x \}$; i.e., the set of accumulation points for S is given by

$$\mathrm{acc}\, S := \{ x \in X \mid G_x \cap (S \backslash \{ x \}) \neq \emptyset \quad \forall\, G_x \in \tau \ni x \in G_x \}.$$

For the interval $(a, b]$, $\mathrm{acc}\, S = \mathrm{cl}\, S = [a, b]$. Note that while it is true for any set that $\mathrm{acc}\, S \subset \mathrm{cl}\, S$, the sets may not be equal (some points in S may be **isolated points** — i.e., not accessible as the limit of a net of points in S consisting of points other than x itself).

Finally, a point x is said to be in the boundary of S if x is topologically accessible both to S and to the complement of S. The **boundary** of S is the set $\mathrm{bd}\, S := \mathrm{cl}\, S \cap \mathrm{cl}(X \backslash S)$. For the interval $(a, b]$, we have $\mathrm{bd}\, S = \{ a, b \}$, but this example is somewhat misleading. Points on the "edge" of a set need not be on the boundary: to be on the boundary, they must be topologically close not only to S but to its complement as well. For example, if we consider the interval $S = [0, 1)$ as a subset of the set $\mathbf{R}_+$ with its (relative) Euclidean topology, then $\mathrm{bd}\, S = \{ 1 \}$. The point 0 is not in the boundary because there are no points in the complement of S which are close to it.

The following theorem, stated without proof, summarizes some of the useful characterizations of the concepts introduced above both in terms of open sets and in terms of nets.

Theorem 4.15 *If S is a subset of a topological space (X, τ), then:*

- *$x \in \mathrm{cl}\, S$ iff either (a) $G_x \cap S \neq \emptyset$ for every open neighborhood G_x of x; or (b) there exists a net $\langle x_\alpha \rangle$ in S which converges to x.*
- *$x \in \mathrm{acc}\, S$ iff either (a) $G_x \cap (S \backslash \{x\}) \neq \emptyset$ for every open neighborhood G_x of x; or (b) there exists a net in $S \backslash \{x\}$ which converges to x.*
- *$x \in \mathrm{int}\, S$ iff either (a) there is an open neighborhood G_x of x which is contained in S; or (b) there is no net $\langle x_\alpha \rangle$ contained in $X \backslash S$ which converges to x.*
- *$x \in \mathrm{bd}\, S$ iff either (a) $x \in \mathrm{cl}\, S \cap \mathrm{cl}(X \backslash S)$; or (b) there are nets $\langle x_\alpha \rangle$ in S and $\langle y_\beta \rangle$ in $X \backslash S$ which both converge to x.*

A set $D \subset X$, where X is a topological space, is said to be **dense** in X if $\mathrm{cl}\, D = X$. A topological space which contains a *countable* dense subset is often called **separable**. If X is metrizable, there is an important and plausible connection between the existence of a countable dense subset and the existence of a countable basis for a topology: a metrizable space (X, τ) is separable iff X is second countable.[5]

$\mathbf{R^n}$ with its standard topology provides an important illustration of this theorem. As a consequence of the fact that every open interval in $\mathbf{R}$ contains a rational number $r \in \mathbf{Q}$ (and every open ball in $\mathbf{R^n}$ defined by the Euclidean metric contains a vector in $\mathbf{Q^n}$), the set $\mathbf{Q}$ is dense in $\mathbf{R}$ (and $\mathbf{Q^n}$ is dense in $\mathbf{R^n}$), which permits the construction of a countable basis for the standard topology.

It is worth seeing how the presence of a dense subset permits the construction of a countable basis for any metrizable space (and, in particular, for the standard topology of $\mathbf{R^n}$). In Exercise 4.5 you are asked to demonstrate that metric spaces are always first countable: balls centered at x with *rational* (and strictly positive) radius form a countable basis at x for the metric topology induced by ρ. In general, metric spaces need not be second countable, but they will have a countable basis if they are separable. Suppose that D is a countable dense subset of the metric space X and consider the collection of balls with positive rational radius centered at the various points $x \in D$. By restricting the centers to lie in D, rather than in all of X, we obtain a countable collection. It is easy to check that this collection is a basis for the metric topology.

4.1.7 Continuity

In a very fundamental sense, topology is the study of continuity and, more specifically, a generalization to more abstract settings of the "delta-epsilon" construct used to define continuity of real-valued functions of a single real variable, $f \colon \mathbf{R} \to \mathbf{R}$, within the first week or two of a beginning calculus course. Topology provides a way to generalize the simple notion of continuity introduced in calculus courses to general functions, $f \colon X \to Y$, where X and Y are arbitrary sets with associated topologies τ_X and τ_Y respectively.

Definition 4.16 *If (X, τ_X) and (Y, τ_Y) are topological spaces and f a function $f \colon X \to Y$, then f is*

- **continuous at** $x \in X$ *if the inverse image of every open neighborhood $G_{f(x)} \in \tau_Y$ of $f(x)$ is open in τ_X (i.e., $f^{-1}(G_{f(x)}) \in \tau_X$);*

---

5 Note that the definition of separability has nothing to do with the separation axioms described at the beginning of this chapter. The use of the same word in two unrelated contexts is regrettable, but unfortunately highly standard.

- **continuous** *if f is continuous for all $x \in X$ or, equivalently, if the inverse image of every set $G \subset Y$ open in the topology for Y is an open set in the topology for X.*

This definition is a natural generalization of the δ-ϵ definition familiar from beginning calculus courses. Since the inverse image $f^{-1}(G_{f(x)})$ is open, the point x (which, of course, belongs to this set) must have an open neighborhood G_x contained in the inverse image. The fact that $G_x \subset f^{-1}(G_{f(x)})$ implies immediately that

$$f(G_x) \subset G_{f(x)}. \tag{$*$}$$

If we assume that X and Y are metric spaces with metrics ρ and ρ' respectively, then we can assume that the open neighborhoods G_x and $G_{f(x)}$ are balls centered at x and $f(x)$ respectively, say $G_x = B_\rho(x, \delta)$ and $G_{f(x)} = B_{\rho'}(f(x), \epsilon)$ with $\delta, \epsilon > 0$. But then the assertion that for any neighborhood $G_{f(x)}$ there is a neighborhood G_x satisfying condition $(*)$ is nothing more than the claim that

$$\forall\, \epsilon > 0 \, \exists\, \delta > 0 \quad \text{such that} \quad f(B_\rho(x, \delta)) \subset B_{\rho'}(f(x), \epsilon),$$

which says that, for delta sufficiently small, we can find a ball around x whose image lies entirely in the ϵ-ball around $f(x)$. Specializing even further to the case $X = Y = \mathbf{R}$ where both spaces have the standard Euclidean metric, the condition further reduces to

$$\forall\, \epsilon > 0 \, \exists\, \delta > 0 \quad \text{such that} \quad |f(x') - f(x)| < \epsilon \, \forall\, x' \in X \ni |x' - x| < \delta,$$

which is nothing more than the standard δ-ϵ criterion for continuity at x.

The following theorem provides a collection of equivalent criteria for a function to be continuous. The proof, an easy application of the basic definitions, has been omitted.

Theorem 4.17 *Let (X, τ_X) and (Y, τ_Y) be topological spaces. The following conditions on a function $f\colon X \to Y$ are equivalent:*

(a) *f is continuous;*
(b) *$f^{-1}(G) \in \tau_X$ for every $G \in \tau_Y$;*
(c) *$f^{-1}(F)$ is closed for every closed subset $F \subset Y$;*
(d) *the net $f(x^\alpha) \to f(x)$ for every net $x^\alpha \to x$ in X.*

Furthermore, if β_Y is a basis or γ_Y a subbasis for the topology τ_Y, then the following two conditions are also equivalent to the above:

(e) *$f^{-1}(B) \in \tau$ for every basis element $B \in \beta_Y$;*
(f) *$f^{-1}(B) \in \tau$ for every subbasis element $B \in \gamma_Y$.*

Criterion (d) uses nets to provide an intuitive characterization of continuity: if a net $\langle x^\alpha \rangle$ converges to some point x, then the net formed by the images $\langle f(x^\alpha) \rangle$ converges to $f(x)$. Criteria (b) and (c) say that a function is continuous iff the inverse image of every open (*resp.* closed) set is open (*resp.* closed), and criteria (e) and (f) say that to establish continuity it suffices to check that the inverse images of all basis (or even simply of all subbasis) elements are open.

To illustrate the great simplification the latter criteria permit, recall that the set of open intervals of the form $(-\infty, a)$ and (a, ∞) for $a \in \mathbf{R}$ constitute a subbasis for the Euclidean topology of $\mathbf{R}$. As a consequence, a function $f: \mathbf{R} \to \mathbf{R}$ is continuous iff the sets $f^{-1}(-\infty, a)$ and $f^{-1}(a, -\infty)$ are open sets in $\mathbf{R}$ for all $a \in \mathbf{R}$.

The following theorems assert that (i) restricting the domain of a continuous function preserves the continuity of a function and (ii) the Cartesian product of continuous functions is a continuous function. The proofs, which are omitted, follow almost immediately from the definition of the relative and product topologies respectively.

Theorem 4.18 *If $f: X \to Y$ is continuous and $S \subset X$, then the function $f_S: S \to Y$, $x \mapsto f_S(x) := f(x)$ is continuous with S given the relative topology inherited from X.*

The function f_S is called the **restriction** of f to S.

Theorem 4.19 *Consider the collection of functions $\{ f_\alpha: X \to Y_\alpha \mid \alpha \in A \}$ where A is an arbitrary index set and $Y := \prod_{\alpha \in A} Y_\alpha$. Define $f: X \to Y$, $x \mapsto f(x) := \prod_{\alpha \in A} f_\alpha(x)$. Provided that Y is given the product topology, the function f is continuous if and only if f_α is continuous for all $\alpha \in A$.*

The functions f_α are called the **coordinate functions** of f.

To illustrate the interpretation of the latter result, suppose that the demand set $\phi_i(p) \subset \mathbf{R}^\mathbf{m}$ of consumer i is singleton valued. Then ϕ_i is a continuous function of p if and only if the demand functions ϕ_{ij} for each of the commodities $j = 1, \ldots, m$ are continuous in p.

4.1.8 Homeomorphisms

The impact of continuity on the preservation of topological structure is typically a one way street. If a function is continuous, inverse images of open sets are open and inverse images of closed sets are closed, but the image of an open set need not be open and that of a closed set need not be closed.

For some other topological concepts, the flow goes the other way. As we will shortly see, continuous functions map compact sets into compact sets and connected sets into connected sets, but inverse images need not preserve these properties.

There is, however, an important circumstance in which matters become much simpler. If a function $f: X \to Y$ is bijective (so that it possesses an inverse $f^{-1}: Y \to X$) and if *both* f and f^{-1} are continuous, then f is a **homeomorphism**. Homeomorphisms preserve all topological properties going either way. If a homeomorphism exists between two topological spaces X and Y, then the spaces are said to be **homeomorphic**. Since any operation on open subsets of one of the spaces will be mirrored exactly by the images of the open subsets in the other space, for topological purposes the two spaces can be regarded as completely equivalent.

Later in this chapter, we will see that all finite dimensional vector spaces with "decent" topologies are homeomorphic to $\mathbf{R^n}$. Establishing that two topological spaces are homeomorphic is often a very subtle affair, but that is of no concern to us. What it means for two spaces to be homeomorphic is easily understood and, as we will see, equally easy to use to advantage.

4.1.9 Connectedness and compactness

Two topological properties of particular importance are connectedness and, most important for our applications, compactness.

Although we will not make much use of connectedness, the concept is worth describing for the simple practice it provides in using the concepts and definitions of topology. A topological space is connected if it is not composed of topologically isolated pieces. As this loose definition suggests, the easiest way to define connectedness is to define what it means for a space not to be connected.

Definition 4.20 *A topological space (X, τ) is* **disconnected** *if X can be partitioned into two disjoint, nonempty, open sets: i.e., $X = S_1 \cup S_2$ where $S_1 \cap S_2 = \emptyset$, $S_1, S_2 \in \tau$, and $S_1, S_2 \neq \emptyset$. X is* **connected** *if it is not disconnected.*

If X is disconnected with partition $X = S_1 \cup S_2$, then the topological isolation of the sets S_1 and S_2 is reflected in the fact that they are necessarily closed as well as open — a condition sometimes rather humorously referred to as **clopen**. When X is connected, the only clopen subsets are the empty set and X itself. $\mathbf{R^n}$ with its standard topology is an example of a connected topological space.

The sets S_1 and S_2 used to describe a disconnected topological space may themselves be disconnected, and if so then each disconnected subset can be further decomposed into a pair of disjoint nonempty open subsets. If this process has gone as far as it can go, so that $X = \bigcup_{\alpha \in A} S_\alpha$ is the finest possible partition of X into disjoint open sets, the subsets S_α are called the (connected) **components** of X. **R** with the discrete topology provides an extreme example in which each one point set $\{x\}$ is a component, hence clopen and topologically isolated from every other point in the set. (It is probably hard for you to think of the real numbers in this way because we are conditioned to view **R** in terms of its standard topology.)

In contrast to connectedness, the concept of compactness will play a crucial role throughout this book. To define compactness, we first need to introduce the preliminary notions of an open cover, a subcover, and a finite subcover of a topological space (X, τ).

Definition 4.21 *If* $\Gamma = \{ G_\alpha \in \tau \mid \alpha \in A \}$ *is a collection of open sets in* (X, τ) *where A is an arbitrary index set, then Γ is said to* **cover** *X and Γ is called an* **open cover** *of X provided that* $\bigcup_{\alpha \in A} G_\alpha = X$.

The grammar used here is poor, but entirely traditional, and sometimes causes confusion: The phrase "open cover" does not mean that the cover itself is being declared open in some sense or other. What is meant is that the sets making up the collection Γ are open sets.

Definition 4.22 *Given an open cover Γ of X indexed by A and a subset* $A^* \subset A$, *the corresponding subcollection of* Γ, $\Gamma^* = \{ G_\alpha \in \tau \mid \alpha \in A^* \}$, *is called a* **subcover** *of X if it also covers X. When A^* is finite, such a subcover is called a* **finite subcover**.

With these definitions, we can now give a very concise definition of compactness.

Definition 4.23 *A topological space (X, τ) is* **compact** *if every open cover of X has a finite subcover.*

This definition of compactness has an equivalent reformulation which is so useful that it is worth explaining in some detail. The key ideas in obtaining the reformulation are (i) the fact that the complement of an open set is a closed set and (ii) an identity from set theory known as DeMorgan's Law:

$$X \setminus \bigcup_{\alpha \in A} S_\alpha = \bigcap_{\alpha \in A} (X \setminus S_\alpha)$$

where A is an arbitrary index set and the S_α are arbitrary subsets of X. In reformulating the definition of compactness, we apply DeMorgan's Law to the subsets G_α of an open cover with the subsets G_α replacing the S_α.

The condition given above for compactness says the following:

$$\text{``}\Gamma \text{ is an open cover''} \quad \Rightarrow \quad \text{``}\Gamma \text{ contains a finite subcover,''} \qquad (*)$$

and the (logically equivalent) contrapositive of this statement is

$$\text{``}\Gamma \text{ contains no finite subcover''} \quad \Rightarrow \quad \text{``}\Gamma \text{ does not cover X.''}$$

Translating the contrapositive into more formal terms, we have

$$\bigcup_{\alpha \in A^*} G_\alpha \subset\subset X \quad \forall \text{ finite } A^* \subset A \quad \Rightarrow \quad \bigcup_{\alpha \in A} G_\alpha \subset\subset X$$

where "$\subset\subset$" indicates that the sets are not equal (i.e., the inclusion is "proper" so that part of the set X is left uncovered). This assertion is in turn equivalent to the claim

$$X \backslash \bigcup_{\alpha \in A^*} G_\alpha \neq \emptyset \quad \forall \text{ finite } A^* \subset A \quad \Rightarrow \quad X \backslash \bigcup_{\alpha \in A} G_\alpha \neq \emptyset.$$

Using DeMorgan's Law, this translates immediately into the statement that

$$\bigcap_{\alpha \in A^*} (X \backslash G_\alpha) \neq \emptyset \quad \forall \text{ finite } A^* \subset A \quad \Rightarrow \quad \bigcap_{\alpha \in A} (X \backslash G_\alpha) \neq \emptyset.$$

But each of the sets $X \backslash G_\alpha$ is, as the complement of an open set, closed. If we let $X \backslash G_\alpha = F_\alpha$ where F_α is a closed set, our condition for compactness now reads:

$$\bigcap_{\alpha \in A^*} F_\alpha \neq \emptyset \quad \forall \text{ finite } A^* \subset A \quad \Rightarrow \quad \bigcap_{\alpha \in A} F_\alpha \neq \emptyset, \qquad (**)$$

and we have shown that $(**)$ is logically equivalent to $(*)$.

Definition 4.24 *An indexed collection of closed subsets of a set X has the* **finite intersection property** *(FIP) if every finite subcollection of the collection has a nonempty intersection.*

From condition $(**)$ we conclude that X is compact iff any collection of closed sets having the FIP has a nonempty intersection. Thus, we obtain the following equivalent definition of compactness:

Definition 4.25 *A topological space (X, τ) is* **compact** *if every collection of closed subsets having the FIP has a nonempty intersection.*

The definition of compactness for a topological space extends directly to a subset $Y \subset X$ provided that Y is given the relative topology inherited from X.

Definition 4.26 *A collection* $\{ G_\alpha \in \tau \mid \alpha \in A \}$ *is an* **open cover of** $Y \subset X$ *iff* $Y \subset \bigcup_{\alpha \in A} G_\alpha$.

Definition 4.27 Y *is a* **compact subset** *of* X *if either:*

- *every open cover of* Y *contains a finite subcover; or*
- *every collection of closed subsets of* Y *having the FIP has a nonempty intersection.*

In $\mathbf{R^n}$ there is a simple criterion for recognizing when a subset is compact: $Y \subset \mathbf{R^n}$ is compact iff Y is closed and bounded (where we take bounded to mean that $\rho(x, y) < \infty$ for all $x, y \in Y$ with ρ the Euclidean metric). While this equivalence is typically false in more general topological spaces, even in metric spaces, it is a very helpful rule in $\mathbf{R^n}$. Thus, $\mathbf{R}$ or $\mathbf{R^n}$ is not compact; closed and bounded intervals of the form $[a, b]$ are compact; and open, half open, or unbounded intervals such as (a, b), $[a, b)$, or $[a, \infty)$ are noncompact. To illustrate the definitions given above for compactness, consider for example the noncompact half open interval $[0, 1)$. The collection $\{ [0, 1 - \epsilon) \mid 0 < \epsilon < 1 \}$ is an open cover of $[0, 1)$, where each $[0, 1 - \epsilon)$ is open in the relative topology of $[0, 1)$, and this cover contains no finite subcover. Taking complements, $\{ [1 - \epsilon, 1) \mid 0 < \epsilon < 1 \}$ is a collection of subsets closed in the relative topology of $[0, 1)$. This collection has the FIP (i.e, any finite subcollection has a nonempty intersection), but the collection itself has empty intersection.

Although the identification of compact subsets with subsets that are closed and bounded must be regarded as a feature peculiar to $\mathbf{R^n}$, the connection between sets that are compact and those that are closed is rather close:

Theorem 4.28 *Assume that* F *and* K *are subsets of a topological space* (X, τ).

- *(a) If* $F \subset K$ *with* F *closed and* K *compact, then* F *is compact.*
- *(b) If* K *is compact and* (X, τ) *is Hausdorff, then* K *is closed.*

Proof See Munkres (1975), 165-166. □

Perhaps the single most important result about compactness for our purposes is the **Tychonoff Theorem**, which asserts that, provided Cartesian product spaces are given the product topology, the product of compact spaces is compact.

Theorem 4.29 (Tychonoff) *If $X = \prod_{\alpha \in A} X_\alpha$ is given the product topology and each coordinate space X_α is compact, then X is compact.*

4.2 Topologies on vector spaces

The first three chapters of this book discussed vector spaces without mentioning topology while the preceding section focused on topology without mention of vector spaces. What more can be said when we have a set L which is *both* a vector space *and* a topological space?

4.2.1 Topological vector spaces

Continuity is the central concept of topology, and this immediately suggests the natural link to vector spaces. Vector spaces are, by definition, sets on which two functions have been defined: vector addition and multiplication of a vector by a scalar. To be of much use, a topology on a vector space should make these functions continuous.

Definition 4.30 *Let L be a vector space[6] with topology τ. τ is a* **linear topology** *and L a* **linear topological vector space** *if τ is T_1 and the vector space operations $+\colon L \times L \to L$, $(x, y) \mapsto x + y$, and $\colon \mathbf{R} \times L \to L$, $(\lambda, x) \mapsto \lambda x$, are continuous functions.*

Since the only topologies worth considering on a vector space are linear, the phrase **linear topological vector space** is usually shortened to **topological vector space** and abbreviated as TVS. In applying this definition, the scalar field $\mathbf{R}$ is given its standard topology and the products $L \times L$ and $\mathbf{R} \times L$ the respective product topologies. Note that the "function" representing scalar multiplication has no corresponding symbol since, while we represent vector addition as $x + y$, there is no symbol lying between λ and x in the product λx. Nevertheless, to have a linear topology this "invisible" function must be continuous.

To be useful a linear topology should also satisfy the Hausdorff (T_2) separation axiom so that, among other things, nets will have unique limits. In

---

6 As usual in this book, by "vector space" we mean a real vector space (i.e., a vector space defined over the scalar field R).

our definition of a TVS we have assumed that the topology is T_1 (or, equivalently, that singleton sets $\{x\}$ are closed), which in turn implies that the TVS is also Hausdorff (Rudin (1973), 10).[7]

Perhaps the most dramatic impact of requiring a topology on a vector space L to be linear is that, as a direct consequence of the continuity of the vector space operations, the topology must be **translation invariant**: i.e., a subset $G \subset L$ is open iff the translate $x + G$ is open for every $x \in L$. The implications of this for the net trade diagram should be transparent. Translation of, say, a strict preference set will preserve not only its linear structure (e.g., its convexity) but its topological structure as well (e.g., its openness).

The translation invariance of a linear topology greatly simplifies the task of characterizing the topology in terms of a basis: it suffices to describe the basis at any point in the vector space. An obvious choice for the point is the origin of the vector space, so you will often see a TVS characterized in terms of a basis at 0 (or a **local base** at 0 as it is usually called). Thus, if β_0 is a local base at 0 for a TVS, then a local base at x is given by translation:

$$\beta_x = \{\, B_x \subset L \mid B_x = x + B_0,\ B_0 \in \beta_0 \,\}.$$

The collection of all such local bases as x varies over L then gives a basis for the topology.

As you no doubt have anticipated, the vector space $\mathbf{R^n}$ with its standard topology is a TVS. What is much more surprising is that, in a precise sense, it is the *only* instance of a finite dimensional TVS.

Theorem 4.31 *Let L be an arbitrary n-dimensional real (Hausdorff) TVS and let $\mathbf{R^n}$ have its standard topology. There exists a bijection $h\colon \mathbf{R^n} \to L$ which is both linear and a homeomorphism.*

Proof Rudin (1973), 16. □

Finite dimensional real vector spaces may look different on the surface and, in fact, taking advantage of the surface differences may be very useful for creating applications. But what this theorem tells us is that every such vector space is equivalent to Euclidean space of the same dimension from the vector space point of view (because h is a linear bijection) and from a topological point of view (because h is a homeomorphism). Every "linear topological" theorem that can be proved for the arbitrary vector space can be proved for $\mathbf{R^n}$ and conversely.

---

7 Books on functional analysis often do not require the T_1 axiom of a TVS. I follow Rudin (1973) in building the T_1 axiom, and hence the Hausdorff property, into the definition of a TVS.

The following theorem summarizes the key facts about invariance of linear topologies to translation or to multiplication by a nonzero scalar:

Theorem 4.32 *Let G be any open subset and F any closed subset of a TVS L. Let $x \in L$ and $\lambda \in \mathbf{R}$ with $\lambda \neq 0$. Then*

- $G + x$ *is open and* $F + x$ *is closed.*
- λG *is open and* λF *is closed.*

Proof The proof, which can be found in any standard book on functional analysis, follows directly from the continuity of the vector space operations.

$\square$

The standard Euclidean topology for $\mathbf{R}^n$ has another property shared by most TVS's encountered in economics and mathematics: it can be defined in terms of a basis whose elements are convex sets.

Definition 4.33 *A linear topology is* **locally convex** *if it has a basis whose elements are convex sets. A TVS which is locally convex is called a* **locally convex topological vector space***, abbreviated as LCTVS.*

The local convexity of the standard Euclidean topology for $\mathbf{R}^n$ follows immediately from the fact that this topology can be characterized by a norm.

Definition 4.34 *Let L be a real vector space. A* **norm** *on L is a real-valued function which assigns to each vector $x \in L$ a nonnegative number $\|x\|$ called the norm of x. In order to qualify as a norm, the function must satisfy the following conditions:*

- $\|x\| = 0$ *if and only if* $x = 0$;
- $\|\alpha x\| = |\alpha| \, \|x\|$ *for every $x \in L$ and for every $\alpha \in \mathbf{R}$;*
- $\|x + y\| \leq \|x\| + \|y\|$ *for all* $x, y \in L$.

A vector space equipped with a norm is said to be a **normed space***.*

If a vector space is normed, then the norm automatically defines a metric ρ via the definition: $\rho(x, y) := \|x - y\|$. Checking that ρ satisfies the requirements for a metric is left as an easy exercise. Therefore, we can use a norm to define a **norm topology** in exactly the same way that we used a metric to define a **metric topology**.

Definition 4.35 *If L is a normed space, the* **open balls** $\{ x \in L \mid \|x\| < \epsilon \}$ *for $x \in L$ and $\epsilon > 0$ are a local base for a topology, called the* **norm topology** *of L.*

In this definition it suffices to consider only balls centered at 0 (a **local basis** for the topology) because every normed vector space is necessarily a TVS under its norm topology and, hence, the topology is translation invariant. Using the definition of a norm, it is easy to see that these open balls are convex sets and, hence, that a normed TVS is always an LCTVS.

The vector space $\mathbf{R^n}$ is a normed space under a variety of norms including, for example, the **Euclidean norm**

$$\|x\|_2 := \left[\sum_{i=1}^{n}(x_i)^2\right]^{1/2}$$

or the **sup norm** $\|x\|_\infty = \sup\{\,|x_i| \in \mathbf{R_+} \mid i = 1,\ldots,n\,\}$. From our earlier discussion of metric spaces, we know that both of these norms yield the same norm topology for $\mathbf{R^n}$, the standard Euclidean topology.

Although this book deals almost exclusively with finite dimensions, infinite dimensional vector spaces are beginning to receive considerable attention in the economics literature. As noted above, $\mathbf{R^n}$ with its standard Euclidean topology is the only finite dimensional TVS. I have, nevertheless, presented this topology in a more general setting to increase your awareness of how the finite dimensional results connect to those for infinite dimensions. In infinite dimensions, no "canonical" TVS exists that is linearly and topologically isomorphic to all of the rest, and the choice of an appropriate topology becomes a central issue. But, however chosen, useful topologies on infinite dimensional vector spaces will always be TVS's.

4.2.2 Topological taxonomy for TVS's

Since a TVS is, by definition, a topological space, the topological notions of open and closed, closure and interior, and so forth introduced earlier apply to TVS's as well. However, because TVS's are also vector spaces, it is possible to say a little more. The following theorem assembles some of the useful facts for later reference.

Theorem 4.36 *Let A, B be arbitrary subsets of a TVS L.*

(a) If A is convex, then $\operatorname{int} A$ and $\operatorname{cl} A$ are convex.

(b) If $A \subset B$ and B is closed, then $\operatorname{cl} A \subset B$.

(c) If $A \cup B = L$ and $A \cap B = \emptyset$ then $\operatorname{cl} A = L \backslash \operatorname{int} B$ and $\operatorname{int} A = L \backslash \operatorname{cl} B$.

(d) $\operatorname{cl} A + \operatorname{cl} B \subset \operatorname{cl}(A + B)$.

(e) More generally, if $\{\, A_i \subset L \mid i = 1,\ldots,n \,\}$ is any collection of subsets, then $\sum_{i=1}^{n} \operatorname{cl} A_i \subset \operatorname{cl}\sum_{i=1}^{n} A_i$.

(f) For any $x \in L$, $\mathrm{cl}(A + x) = \mathrm{cl}\, A + x$ and $\mathrm{int}(A + x) = \mathrm{int}\, A + x$.

(g) For any $\lambda \in \mathbf{R}$ such that $\lambda \neq 0$, $\mathrm{cl}(\lambda A) = \lambda\, \mathrm{cl}\, A$ and $\mathrm{int}(\lambda A) = \lambda\, \mathrm{int}\, A$.

Proof

(a) See Choquet (1969), Volume 1, 335.

(b) This is a standard result of topology, true whether or not L is a vector space.

(c) Again a standard result of topology, true whether or not L is a vector space.

(d) Given $a \in \mathrm{cl}\, A$ and $b \in \mathrm{cl}\, B$, there exists a net $\langle a^{\alpha} \rangle$ in A converging to a and a net $\langle b^{\beta} \rangle$ in B converging to b. By continuity of addition in a TVS, $a^{\alpha} + b^{\beta} \to a + b$ so $a + b \in \mathrm{cl}(A + B)$.

(e) Modify the proof in (d).

(f) Implied by continuity of addition in a TVS. See Choquet (1969), Volume 1, 271–272.

(g) Implied by continuity of scalar multiplication in a TVS. See Choquet (1969), Volume 1, 272.

$\square$

Note that the inclusions in parts (d) and (e) may be strict. Part (f) represents another manifestation of the translation invariance of linear topologies: if we translate a set A, then the interior and closure of A are translated in the same way.

There is another, more primitive way of looking at the topology of vector spaces which is simple to use and illuminating. The "primitive" concepts we are about to introduce are indeed primitive in the sense that they are not powerful enough to define a topology for a vector space. However, they are simple and they apply in the same way regardless of any topology we might want to put on the vector space, two virtues which make their introduction highly worthwhile.

The primitive approach to the topology of vector spaces capitalizes on the notion that if $z = \lambda x + (1 - \lambda)y$ where x and y belong to a vector space L and $\lambda \in \mathbf{R}$, then as λ approaches 1 the vector z approaches x. So even without mentioning an explicit topology for L we have a crude notion of what it means for vectors to be "close" or "getting closer."

First we establish the following notation:

Definition 4.37 *For any $x, y \in L$, where L is a vector space, let*

$$[x, y] = \{\, z \in L \mid z = \lambda x + (1 - \lambda)y, \ \lambda \in [0, 1] \,\}$$

$$(x, y) = \{\, z \in L \mid z = \lambda x + (1 - \lambda)y, \ \lambda \in (0, 1) \,\}$$

$$[x, y) = \{\, z \in L \mid z = \lambda x + (1 - \lambda)y, \ \lambda \in (0, 1] \,\}$$

We will refer to $[x, y]$ as a **linearly closed line segment** and (x, y) as a **linearly open line segment**. Note that a subset $C \subset L$ is convex iff $[x, y] \subset C$ for all $x, y \in C$.

We now define some primitive concepts for a vector space whose names are chosen to suggest an obvious analogy with the official topological concepts introduced earlier.[8]

Definition 4.38 *Let A be an arbitrary subset of a vector space L. The* **linear interior** *of A is the set*

$$\operatorname{lint} A := \{\, a \in A \mid \forall\, x \in L \backslash \{a\} \ \exists\, y \in (a, x) \ \ni \ [a, y) \subset A \,\}.$$

The set of points in L **linearly accessible** *from A is*

$$\operatorname{lacc} A := \{\, x \in L \mid \exists\, a \in A \ \ni \ [a, x) \subset A \,\}$$

and the **linear closure** *of A is $\operatorname{lcl} A := A \cup \operatorname{lacc} A$. A is said to be* **linearly open** *if $\operatorname{lint} A = A$,* **linearly closed** *if $\operatorname{lcl} A = A$, and* **linearly dense** *(or* **ubiquitous***) in L if $\operatorname{lcl} A = L$.*

This formal definition makes these concepts seem more complicated than they really are. Stated less formally,

- a is in the linear interior of A if, given any direction, you can move some "distance" from a along a straight line in the given direction while still remaining in A.
- A vector x is linearly accessible from A if there is a half open interval $[a, x)$ contained in A which connects x to a.
- A vector is in the linear closure of A if it is in A or at least linearly accessible from A.

---

8 The terminology I have adopted here is not standard. What I have called the linear interior is called the algebraic interior or, more commonly, the core and denoted cor A. The linear closure is referred to as the algebraic closure, denoted lin A. Most authors refer to the points in lacc A as linearly accessible, but use the notation linac A. I have chosen to adopt somewhat different terminology for a number of reasons: (a) by emphasizing the obvious parallel with the official topological concepts, the notation adopted here seems easier to remember; (b) "linear" is more specific than "algebraic"; and (c) economists and game theorists use the word "core" to refer to an entirely different concept.

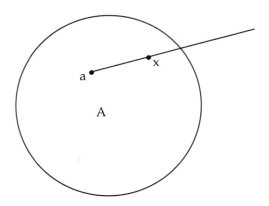

Fig. 4.3. Primitive topological concepts.

The definitions of the primitive topological concepts for vector spaces are illustrated in Figure 4.3 for the set

$$A = \{\, x \in \mathbf{R}^2 \mid x = (x_1, x_2),\ x_1^2 + x_2^2 \le 1 \,\}.$$

Clearly, lint A coincides with the inside of the disk while lacc A and lcl A equal the entire disk A.

The main fact which makes these primitive topological concepts useful to us is that, when applied to convex subsets of a *finite* dimensional vector space, the primitive linear concepts coincide with their parallel official topological counterparts:

Theorem 4.39 *If A is a convex subset of a finite dimensional TVS, then* int $A = $ lint A *and* cl $A = $ lcl A.

Proof Holmes (1975), 59, or van Tiel (1984), 29–30.   □

4.2.3 Topological dual spaces

Linear functionals are basic to vector space theory and, as we have already seen, they are of fundamental importance to economics. For us, they represent price systems. In Chapter 1 we introduced the concept of the dual space L', the set of all linear functionals on the vector space L, and in that earlier discussion we dealt only with the vector space properties of a vector space and its dual. Now that we are able to treat the topological as well as the linear aspects of a vector space, we are in a position to reconsider the dual and, as you might expect, the primary issue is whether the linear functionals in L' are continuous. Every linear functional on a finite dimensional TVS is necessarily continuous, but (is this a surprise any longer?) in infinite dimensions continuity of linear functionals is a major issue. For that reason, even though $L' = L^*$ in finite dimensions, it is important to distinguish carefully between the dual space L' and those linear functionals $L^* \subset L'$ which are continuous. In the interests of precision, we can no longer refer to L' as "the" dual: instead, L' is called the **algebraic dual space** of L (since its definition involves only linear algebra and no topology) and L^* the **topological dual space** of L (since it contains those linear functionals which are also continuous).

Continuity of linear functionals has immediate implications for the topological characteristics of hyperplanes and halfspaces which will prove of critical importance later on.

Theorem 4.40 *Let p be a linear functional on a TVS L. If $p \neq 0$, then the following assertions are equivalent:*

- *p is continuous.*

- *$H(p, \alpha)$ is closed for all $\alpha \in \mathbf{R}$;*

- *$H^+(p, \alpha)$ and $H^-(p, \alpha)$ are closed for all $\alpha \in \mathbf{R}$;*

- *$H_o^+(p, \alpha)$ and $H_o^-(p, \alpha)$ are open for all $\alpha \in \mathbf{R}$.*

Proof Exercise 4.24. □

When $L = \mathbf{R^n}$, all linear functionals are continuous ($L' = L^*$) and, as a consequence, hyperplanes are always closed sets, "closed" halfspaces are closed sets, and "open" halfspaces are open sets. In infinite dimensions, on the other hand, life becomes much more complex (and also more interesting!). As noted earlier, no single TVS emerges as canonical when vector spaces are infinite dimensional. Furthermore, natural choices of topology for L (e.g., a norm topology of some sort) frequently imply that L^* is a *proper* subset of L' (not all linear functional are continuous). The choice of appropriate topologies for L then becomes a major concern.

4.2.4 Separation and support by hyperplanes

For an economist perhaps the most important consequence of the interaction between the topological and algebraic properties of a vector space is its impact on the ability of hyperplanes to separate or support convex sets. The type of separation we are looking for can be more or less strong.

Definition 4.41 *Let A and B be nonempty subsets of a vector space L and $H(p, \alpha)$ a hyperplane defined by a linear functional $p \in L^*$.*

- *A and B are **separated** by the hyperplane if A and B lie in opposite closed halfspaces defined by $H(p, \alpha)$.*
- *A and B are **strictly separated** by the hyperplane if A and B lie in opposite open halfspaces defined by $H(p, \alpha)$.*
- *A and B are **strongly separated** by the hyperplane if A and B lie in opposite closed sets of the form $H^-(p, \alpha - \epsilon)$ and $H^+(p, \alpha + \epsilon)$ for some $\epsilon > 0$.*

Although the proofs of the fundamental results concerning separation and support are easy to understand and fun to prove, the proofs will not be given here: I have nothing to add to the beautiful expositions in Choquet (1969, Volume 2), Giles (1982), Holmes (1975), and van Tiel (1984). The discussion here focuses instead on organizing the results in an intuitive and easily remembered way.

Separation theorems address the following question: given two sets A and B in a vector space L, what properties of A and B will guarantee that these sets can be separated (strictly separated, strongly separated) by a hyperplane? Most of the issues involved can be easily illustrated in $\mathbf{R}^2$. For example, if either A or B is nonconvex, then — as shown in Figure 4.4 — there are situations in which the sets cannot be separated. On the other hand, if A and B are nonempty, convex, and disjoint subsets of $\mathbf{R}^2$, then "obviously" they can be separated. These conditions are all that is needed to obtain the result for any finite dimensional vector space.[9]

Theorem 4.42 *If A and B are nonempty, disjoint, convex subsets of a finite dimensional vector space L, then A and B can be separated by a hyperplane.*

Proof See Holmes (1975), 15, 63.   □

---

9 The infinite dimensional case is complicated by the possibility of hyperplanes which are dense in L, a situation in which separation cannot be expected. However, if at least one of the sets A or B has a nonempty interior, then, since the hyperplane does not enter the interior of A or B, the hyperplane *cannot* be dense. This supplementary "nonempty interior" condition is all that is needed to extend the separation result to infinite dimensions.

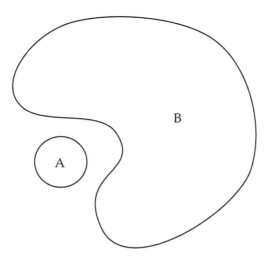

Fig. 4.4. Nonseparability: nonconvexity.

Simple examples in $\mathbf{R}^2$ also suggest that disjointness of A and B can be dispensed with provided that the convex sets in question "barely touch" (e.g., consider two disks in $\mathbf{R}^2$: they can be separated even if they touch on their "boundaries"), but separation is impossible if the interior of one of the sets intersects the other set. Thus, we have:

Theorem 4.43 *If A and B are nonempty, convex subsets of a finite dimensional vector space L and* int $A \neq \emptyset$, *then A and B can be separated by a hyperplane iff* (int A) $\cap B = \emptyset$.

Proof See Holmes (1975), 15, 63. □

In many applications it is useful to weaken the nonempty interior condition by reformulating the separation results in terms of a **relative interior** defined relative to the affine hulls of the convex sets involved.

Definition 4.44 *If A is a subset of a TVS L, then the **relative interior** of A, denoted* rint A, *is the topological interior of A in* cl(aff A) *where* cl(aff A) *is given the relative topology which it inherits from L.*

We use cl(aff A) rather than aff A in the definition of the relative interior because subspaces of infinite dimensional vector spaces need not be closed.

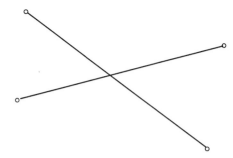

Fig. 4.5. Nonseparability: overlapping rint's.

However, subspaces of finite dimensional vector spaces are always closed so that, in that context, cl(aff A) may be replaced by aff A.

All of this sounds more complicated than it is. Consider, for example, a line segment in $\mathbf{R}^2$, say the closed interval $A = [x, y]$. This set has an empty interior, but its relative interior (relative to the line aff A which contains it) is just the open interval (x, y).

Figure 4.5 illustrates two intervals in $\mathbf{R}^2$ which cannot be separated because their relative interiors intersect. Ruling this out leads to a useful variation of the separation theorem.

Theorem 4.45 *If A and B are nonempty, convex subsets of a finite dimensional vector space L and* rint $A \cap$ rint $B = \emptyset$, *then A and B can be separated by a hyperplane. Furthermore, the hyperplane will not contain $A \cup B$.*

Proof See Giles (1982), 31.   □

Another useful variation provides conditions for obtaining strong separation. Even in $\mathbf{R}^2$ it is easy to construct examples of convex sets which can be separated but not strongly separated when the conditions of this theorem are not met.

Theorem 4.46 *Let A and B be nonempty, disjoint, convex subsets of an LCTVS L. If A is compact and B is closed, then A and B can be strongly separated by a closed hyperplane.*

Proof See Giles (1982), 70.   □

Recall that every finite dimensional TVS is locally convex.

Equally useful to economics is the collection of results dealing with support of a set by a hyperplane. The picture to have in mind is a disk in $\mathbf{R}^2$ with a hyperplane touching the disk at some point on its boundary. The hyperplane is said to support the disk, and a point where they touch is called a support point for the disk.

Definition 4.47 *Let A be a subset of a vector space L and $H(p, \alpha)$ a hyperplane defined by a linear functional $p \in L^*$.*

- *If A lies in one of the two closed halfspaces defined by $H(p, \alpha)$ and $A \cap H(p, \alpha) \neq \emptyset$, then $H(p, \alpha)$ is called a* **supporting hyperplane** *for A.*
- *If $H(p, \alpha)$ is a supporting hyperplane for A, then a point $\widehat{x} \in A \cap H(p, \alpha)$ is called a* **support point** *of A.*
- *If $\widehat{x}$ is a support point for A and A is not entirely contained in $H(p, \alpha)$, then $\widehat{x}$ is a* **proper** *support point of A.*

Theorem 4.48 *If A is a nonempty, convex subset of a finite dimensional vector space L, then*

- *x is a support point of A if and only if $x \in A \backslash \operatorname{rint} A$; and*
- *each of the points in $A \backslash \operatorname{rint} A$ is a proper support point of A.*

Proof See Giles (1982), 29–30, 67. □

We end with a result which has profound implications for the applications of duality theory in economics. Again an illustration using a disk in $\mathbf{R}^2$ makes the conclusion seem obvious.

Theorem 4.49 *If A is a nonempty, closed, convex subset of an LCTVS, then A equals the intersection of all the closed halfspaces which contain it.*

Proof See Giles (1982), 70. □

4.3 Summary

Don't try to absorb all of the details of this chapter on first reading. Particular facts can always be looked up later when the need arises. The main message to carry away is an appreciation of the special role of the Euclidean topology on $\mathbf{R^n}$, its inevitability in finite dimensional vector spaces, and the competition it faces in infinite dimensions.

Once you have learned to think of the Euclidean topology in more general terms, feel free to exploit any of its special properties throughout the rest of the book. The most important notions for now are openness and closedness, interior and boundary, continuity, compactness, the continuity of linear functionals (on finite dimensional vector spaces), and separating and supporting hyperplanes.

Exercises

4.1   Show that:

(a) $T_4 \Rightarrow T_3 \Rightarrow T_2 \Rightarrow T_1$ (so that, for example, a topology which is T_3 is automatically T_2 and T_1).

(b) If X has the discrete topology, then it is T_4.

(c) If X has the indiscrete topology and contains more than one point, then it is not T_1. Verify that in this case one point sets are not closed.

4.2   Verify that the collection of open intervals in $\mathbf{R}$ meets the requirements for a topological basis.

4.3   (a) Prove that $\bigcap_{\alpha \in \mathbf{R}_+} [-\alpha, \alpha]$ is a closed set.

(b) Is $\bigcap_{\alpha \in \mathbf{R}_{++}} (-\alpha, \alpha)$ an open set? A G_δ set? A Borel set?

4.4   Show that a subbasis for the product topology is given by the sets of the form $\prod_{\alpha \in A} B_\alpha$ where exactly one of the B_α is a subbasis element for the topology on X_α and $B_\alpha = X_\alpha$ for *all of the other* $\alpha \in A$. (*Hint:* All that you need to show is that a typical basis element can be expressed as a finite intersection of these subbasis elements.) Illustrate the procedure by showing how an arbitrary open rectangle in $\mathbf{R}^2$ can be expressed as the intersection of two subbasis elements of this form.

4.5   Let $\mathbf{Q}$ denote the set of rational numbers in $\mathbf{R}$ (i.e., those real numbers which are expressible as the ratio of two integers) and let $\mathbf{Q}_{++}$ be the set of rationals which are strictly positive. Show that for any metric space (X, ρ), the collection of balls centered at x with radius $\epsilon \in \mathbf{Q}_{++}$ constitutes a basis for the metric topology (and, hence, conclude that every metric space is first countable). Observe that you could even restrict the collection of basis elements at x to be those balls with radius $1/n$ where $n \in \mathbf{Z}_{++}$.

4.6   Let $\mathcal{S}$ be a collection of subsets of a set X.

(a) Verify that $\subset$ is a partial ordering of $\mathcal{S}$.

(b) Give an example of a collection $\mathcal{S}$ for which $\subset$ is not a total ordering; an example where $\subset$ is a total ordering.

4.7   Since the discrete topology is the finest possible topology on a set, convergence relative to this topology should be very strong. At the opposite extreme, since the indiscrete topology is the coarsest topology on a set, convergence should be very weak.

   (a) Prove that if X has the discrete topology then a net $x^\alpha \to x$ iff there exists an α^* such that $x^\alpha = x$ for all $\alpha \succeq \alpha^*$.

   (b) Show that if X has the indiscrete topology then any net in X converges to every point in X!

4.8   Let S be an arbitrary subset of a topological space (X, τ).

   (a) Prove that the set int S is open and the set cl S is closed.

   (b) Prove that (i) S is closed iff $S = \mathrm{cl}\,S$ and (ii) S is open iff $S = \mathrm{int}\,S$.

   (c) Show that cl $S = S \cup \mathrm{acc}\,S$.

4.9   Suppose that the point x in a topological space (X, τ) is an isolated point as defined above: i.e., x is not accessible as the limit of a net of points in X other than x itself.

   (a) Show that $\{\, x \,\}$ is both open and closed.

   (b) Let S be a set containing x. Show that $x \notin \mathrm{acc}\,S$.

4.10   Draw some pictures of sets in $\mathbf{R}^2$ which are neither open nor closed. Describe the interior, closure, boundary, and set of accumulation points for each of the sets you have drawn.

4.11   Using the fact that every open interval contains a rational number, prove that $\mathbf{Q}$ is a dense subset of $\mathbf{R}$ under the standard topology.

4.12   Show that a function $f : \mathbf{R} \to \mathbf{R}$ is continuous iff the sets $f^{-1}(-\infty, a]$ and $f^{-1}[a, -\infty)$ are closed in $\mathbf{R}$ for every $a \in \mathbf{R}$. Verify that the function $f : \mathbf{R} \to \mathbf{R}$, $f : x \mapsto x^2$ is continuous.

4.13   Let X, Y, and Z be topological spaces and assume that the functions $f : X \to Y$ and $g : Y \to Z$ are continuous. Prove that the composite function $f \circ g : X \to Z$ is continuous. (*Hint:* First show that $f^{-1}(g^{-1}(G)) = (g \circ f)^{-1}(G)$ for any $G \subset Z$ whether G is open or not.)

4.14   (a) A function $f : X \to Y$ is called an **open map** if it maps every open set in X to an open set in Y and a **closed map** if it maps every closed set in X to a closed set in Y. Provide an example of a function $f : \mathbf{R} \to \mathbf{R}$ which is continuous but not open and one which is continuous but not closed.

   (b) Prove that if a function $f : X \to Y$ is bijective and open, then it is also closed, and that if it is bijective and closed it must also be open.

4.15 Let S_1 and S_2 be any two subsets of $\mathbf{R}^2$ whose closures in $\mathbf{R}^2$ are disjoint. Prove that $Y = S_1 \cup S_2$ is disconnected even though S_1 and S_2 are not necessarily open in the topology of $\mathbf{R}^2$.

4.16 Prove that if (X, τ) is a topological space with the discrete topology, then X is compact iff it contains a finite number of elements.

4.17 Prove DeMorgan's Law.

4.18 Let $f: X \to Y$ be a continuous function from a topological space X to a topological space Y.

 (a) Prove that the image $f(C)$ of a connected set C is connected and that the image $f(K)$ of a compact set K is compact.

 (b) Using a continuous function $f: \mathbf{R} \to \mathbf{R}$, provide examples illustrating that the inverse image $f^{-1}(C)$ of a connected set C need not be connected and that the inverse image $f^{-1}(K)$ of a compact set need not be compact.

4.19 (a) Show that the Cartesian product of compact topological spaces is compact if the product is given any topology weaker than the product topology.

 (b) Show that, unless all but a finite number of the coordinate spaces have the trivial topology, the Tychonoff Theorem fails if the box topology is used in place of the product topology and the index set A is not finite. (*Hint:* For each $\alpha \in A$ let B_α^* be an open *proper* subset of X_α and consider sets of the form $\widetilde{B}_{\alpha'} = \prod_{\alpha \in A} B_\alpha$ where $B_\alpha = B_\alpha^*$ for all but one $\alpha \, (= \alpha')$ for which $B_{\alpha'} = X_\alpha$. Show that the collection $\{\, \widetilde{B}_\alpha \mid \alpha \in A \,\}$ is an open cover of $X = \prod_{\alpha \in A} X_\alpha$ with the box topology and that this cover has no finite subcover.)

4.20 As noted in Section 4.2.1, any linear topology can be completely described in terms of a local base at 0. It is tempting to conclude that this proves that any first countable TVS is immediately second countable, but this is false. Why?

4.21 Illustrate translation invariance in $\mathbf{R}^2$ using the Euclidean metric; the sup metric. Verify that the basis elements for each of these metric topologies in $\mathbf{R^n}$ are convex sets.

4.22 A subset of a vector space L is called a **line** if it is a one-dimensional subspace or a translate of a one-dimensional subspace. Let $A \subset L$ and suppose that $a \in A$. Prove that $a \in \operatorname{lint} A$ if and only if every line S containing a contains a linearly open interval $(x, y) \subset A \cap S$ such that $a \in (x, y)$.

4.23 Give an example of two convex sets $A, B \in \mathbf{R}^2$ for which $\operatorname{cl} A + \operatorname{cl} B \subset \operatorname{cl}(A + B)$ but $\operatorname{cl} A + \operatorname{cl} B \neq \operatorname{cl}(A + B)$. (*Hint:* Since A and B are convex, you may find it convenient to replace $\operatorname{cl} A$, $\operatorname{cl} B$, and $\operatorname{cl}(A+B)$ by their equivalent linear counterparts: $\operatorname{lcl} A$, $\operatorname{lcl} B$, and $\operatorname{lcl}(A + B)$.)

4.24 Prove Theorem 4.40.

4.25 Show that the linear functional $0 \in L'$ belongs to L^* whatever the topology on L. (*Hint:* Note that the inverse image of any open set containing the point 0 equals L and the inverse image of any open set not containing 0 is empty.)

4.26 Give an example of two disjoint, closed, convex subsets of $\mathbf{R}^2$ which can be separated but not strictly or strongly separated by a hyperplane. (*Hint:* One of the sets must be noncompact.)

4.27 Show that if A is a nonempty, convex, and open subset of a TVS, then it has no support points. What are the support points for $\operatorname{cl} A$?

5

Best response

The first part of this book stresses broad concepts and examples, the second rigorous theory. Topology allows us to make the transition. Why does topology play this critical role? Essentially because topology allows us to make headway in characterizing *qualitative* properties of a model when *quantitative* information is missing. Why not seek better quantitative information instead? This goes to the heart of the matter, to the basic question of what competitive theory is really about. In modeling a competitive economy we want to assume as little as possible about what consumers and firms are like because it is the absence of such information which renders planners impotent and markets worth having. At least that is what we, as economists, have claimed from Adam Smith on. Modern general equilibrium theory can be faulted for not going far enough in this direction, but it certainly does try.

This chapter looks at individual consumers and firms in isolation, ignoring for now how they interact with one another. The main issues concern their response to prices and other aspects of their environment. The questions we ask are deliberately qualitative, not quantitative. Not what formula describes the demand of a consumer with Cobb-Douglas utility, but rather: Does the consumer have a best response to her environment? If the best response is not unique, what more can we say about the set of best responses? Does the response vary continuously when the environment changes? Without topology we cannot get far in addressing these questions. With topology we can say quite a lot.

The first section introduces some basic facts about preferences while the second explores what is required for best responses to exist. The third section tackles the issue of continuity of best response, culminating in a proof of the celebrated Maximum Theorem. The final section ties up some loose ends.

5.1 Preferences

Recall the solution to the consumer's decision problem. Given a strict preference relation $\succ_i$ defined on $X_i \times X_i$ and budget set $\beta_i(p)$, the demand set (or best response) of consumer i to prices p is given by

$$\phi_i(p) = \{\, x_i \in \beta_i(p) \mid P_i(x_i) \cap \beta_i(p) = \emptyset \,\}.$$

As we saw in Chapter 2, the supply set for a firm (or, under constant returns, the aggregate supply set) can be characterized in much the same way. Our goal in this chapter is to investigate more closely the properties of demand and supply sets. Under what circumstances are they nonempty? How do they vary in response to changes in the price vector p?

Our first order of business is to streamline notation. Since this chapter studies consumers in isolation, the subscript i is dropped throughout. In particular, we replace X_i by X, $\succ_i$ by $\succ$, $P_i(x)$ by $P(x)$, $\beta_i(p)$ by $\beta(p)$, and so on. We also want our notation to be a little less tied to the specifics of the consumer, a little more abstract. Therefore, in place of p and $\beta(p)$ we use e (for the **environment**) and $K(e)$ (for the **constraint set**). Since initially we hold the environment fixed, we delete reference to e throughout this section and write the constraint set $K(e)$ simply as K with the understanding always that $K \subset X$. Using this new notation, the demand set takes the form

$$B(K) := \{\, x \in K \mid P(x) \cap K = \emptyset \,\}$$

with "B" suggesting the generic concept **best response**.

This change of notation is meant to highlight the generality of the results we are about to present. They apply to very general problems of rational choice, not just the consumer. For concreteness the consumer will be used to illustrate and motivate most of the discussion with extensions to the firm indicated as we go along. Later chapters apply the results to the players in a noncooperative game and to the Walrasian Auctioneer as well!

Throughout this chapter when I assume that a set X (or, more properly, (X, τ)) is a topological space, I am tacitly assuming that the topology is Hausdorff. When needed, stronger conditions on the topology will be explicitly stated.

5.1.1 *Binary relations and orderings*

Up to now I have emphasized almost exclusively the strict preference relation $\succ$. This emphasis was deliberate, intended to discourage the traditional (and, I believe, misguided) habit of viewing weak preference $\succeq$ as the natural

Table 5.1. *Properties of binary relations.*

Property	Definition
reflexive	$x\rho x \quad \forall x \in X$
irreflexive	$x \neg \rho x \quad \forall x \in X$
complete	$(x\rho y) \vee (y\rho x) \quad \forall x, y \in X \ni x \neq y$
transitive	$(x\rho y) \wedge (y\rho z) \Rightarrow x\rho z \quad \forall x, y, z \in X$
negatively transitive	$(x\neg\rho y) \wedge (y\neg\rho z) \Rightarrow x\neg\rho z \quad \forall x, y, z \in X$
symmetric	$x\rho y \Rightarrow y\rho x \quad \forall x, y \in X$
asymmetric	$x\rho y \Rightarrow y\neg\rho x \quad \forall x, y \in X$
antisymmetric	$(x\rho y) \wedge (y\rho x) \Rightarrow x = y \quad \forall x, y \in X$

primitive on which to base a theory of choice. But the time has now come to make contact with the more traditional point of view.

Definition 5.1 *The binary relations* $\succ, \succeq, \sim$ *on* $X \times X$ *are given the following interpretation:*

- *$y \succ x$ means "y is **strictly preferred** to x";*
- *$y \succeq x$ means "y is **at least as good** as x";*
- *$y \sim x$ means "y is **indifferent** to x."*

Definition 5.2 *For each* $x \in X$ *define*

- *the **strict upper contour set**, $P(x) := \{ y \in X \mid y \succ x \}$;*
- *the **strict lower contour set**, $P^{-1}(x) := \{ y \in X \mid x \succ y \}$;*
- *the **upper contour set**, $R(x) := \{ y \in X \mid y \succeq x \}$;*
- *the **lower contour set**, $R^{-1}(x) := \{ y \in X \mid x \succeq y \}$;*
- *the **indifference set**, $I(x) := \{ y \in X \mid y \sim x \}$.*

We have used the term binary relation without formally defining what this means. The standard definition, though a bit abstract, is not complicated.

Definition 5.3 *Any nonempty subset* $S \subset X \times X$ *defines a* **binary relation** *on* X *with the interpretation:*

- *If $(y, x) \in S$, then "y is related to x."*
- *If $(y, x) \notin S$ then "y is not related to x."*

Often we prefer to use an alternative notation which most people find more natural. If $S \subset X \times X$ represents a relation ρ, then

Table 5.2. *Examples of binary relations.*

Property	$=$	$>$	$\geq$	$\subset$
reflexive	yes	no	yes	yes
irreflexive	no	yes	no	no
complete	no	yes	yes	no
transitive	yes	yes	yes	yes
negatively transitive	no	yes	yes	no
symmetric	yes	no	no	no
asymmetric	no	yes	no	no
antisymmetric	yes	yes*	yes	yes

* True by vacuous implication.

- $y\rho x$ indicates that y is related to x, and
- $y\neg\rho x$ indicates that y is not related to x.

With preference relations we write $\not\succ$ rather than $\neg \succ$ and $\not\succeq$ rather than $\neg \succeq$. While relations can represent many different kinds of relationships (e.g., "is a daughter of"), we ordinarily have preference relations in mind.

Along with binary relations comes a bewildering array of definitions which can be difficult to remember and keep straight. Don't bother! Tables 5.1–5.3, which summarize the main facts, can be used as a reference.[1] You should go carefully through the tables making sure you understand what they say, but you do not need to memorize them. With practice and experience you will find yourself referring to the tables less and less often.

Table 5.1 describes some of the properties that a binary relation can have. The standard symbols $\wedge$ and $\vee$ are used for "and" and "or" respectively. For example, the definition of transitivity reads: a binary relation ρ on a set X is transitive if "$x\rho y$ and $y\rho z$ implies $x\rho z$ for all $x, y, z \in X$." Table 5.2 illustrates these basic properties in terms of several well-known binary relations: $=, >, \geq$ defined on $\mathbf{R}$ and $\subset$ defined on the set of subsets of an arbitrary set X. A "yes" indicates that the binary relation has the property in question, a "no" that it does not. Finally, Table 5.3 defines some of the most frequently used types of binary relations in economics and mathemat-

---

1 Unfortunately, the terminology used to describe properties of a binary relation and types of binary relations is not completely standardized. Irreflexive binary relations are sometimes called nonreflexive, and complete relations are often described as total. Preorderings are often called quasi-orderings and total orderings are also referred to as linear or simple orderings.

Table 5.3. *Types of binary relations.*

Property	Equivalence relation	Preordering	Complete preordering
reflexive	*	*	*
irreflexive			
complete			*
transitive	*	*	*
negatively transitive			
symmetric	*		
asymmetric			
antisymmetric			

Property	Weak ordering	Partial ordering	Total ordering
reflexive		*	*
irreflexive	†		
complete			*
transitive	†	*	*
negatively transitive	*		
symmetric			
asymmetric	*		
antisymmetric		*	*

† These properties can be derived from the others.

ics where an asterisk indicates that the binary relation is assumed to have the property listed at the top of the column.

Comparing Tables 5.2 and 5.3 it is easy to see that $=$ is an equivalence relation and $\geq$ a total ordering on $\mathbf{R}$ and that $\subset$ is a partial ordering on 2^X.

5.1.2 Neoclassical preferences

The flexibility which binary relations provide can be quite overwhelming and, in fact, you are likely to find the literature on this subject very confusing. To provide a clearer picture of what is going on, we begin on familiar ground with the "standard" case of a preference relation which can be represented by a utility function.

Definition 5.4 *A strict preference relation $\succ$ defined on X can be **represented by a utility function** if there exists a function $u: X \to \mathbf{R}$ such that either:*

$\quad$ *(a) $y \succ x$ iff $u(y) > u(x)$ for all $x, y \in X$; or*
$\quad$ *(b) $y \not\succ x$ iff $u(y) \leq u(x)$ for all $x, y \in X$.*

The equivalence of (a) and (b) is immediate: Negate both sides of (a) to obtain (b), and negate both sides of (b) to obtain (a). (Do you see how this follows from the equivalence of a proposition and its contrapositive?)

Theorem 5.5 *If a strict preference relation $\succ$ defined on X can be represented by a utility function, then $\not\succ$ is a complete preordering and $\succ$ a weak ordering.*

Proof Use the properties of the ordering $\geq$ on $\mathbf{R}$ to show that, since $y \not\succ x$ iff $u(y) \leq u(x)$, the preference relation $\not\succ$ is complete, reflexive, and transitive. Since $\not\succ$ is transitive, by definition $\succ$ is negatively transitive. Finally, since $y \succ x$ iff $u(y) > u(x)$, the asymmetry of $>$ on $\mathbf{R}$ implies the asymmetry of $\succ$ on X. $\qquad\square$

As you would expect, it is easily established that $\not\succ$ is a complete preordering if and only if $\succ$ is a weak ordering.

$\quad$ We now examine some of the consequences which follow if $\succ$ is a weak ordering (or, equivalently, $\not\succ$ a complete preordering).

Definition 5.6 *If $\succ$ is a weak ordering on X, then (a) $y \succeq x$ iff $x \not\succ y$ and (b) $y \sim x$ iff $x \not\succ y$ and $y \not\succ x$.*

Theorem 5.7 *If $\succ$ is a weak ordering on X, then $\succeq$ is a complete preordering and $\sim$ is an equivalence relation.*

Proof The first part is trivial, and the second follows immediately from the definitions. $\qquad\square$

Theorem 5.8 *If $\sim$ is an equivalence relation on X, then (a) $I(x) = I(y)$ iff $x \sim y$ and (b) $\cup_{x \in X} I(x) = X$.*

Proof Exercise 5.5. □

Thus, the indifference relation partitions X into disjoint indifference sets, and the collection of indifference sets collectively covers X.[2]

Theorem 5.9 *If* $\succ$ *is a weak ordering on* X, *then each of the families* $\{\, R(x) \mid x \in X \,\}$, $\{\, R^{-1}(x) \mid x \in X \,\}$, $\{\, P(x) \mid x \in X \,\}$, *and* $\{\, P^{-1}(x) \mid x \in X \,\}$ *is totally ordered by set inclusion.*

Proof Exercise 5.5. □

Stated less formally, the members of these families are nested one inside another, just as in elementary price theory textbooks.

According to Theorem 5.5, existence of a representing utility function implies that $\succ$ is a weak ordering and $\succeq$ a complete preordering. As we have just seen, the fact that $\succ$ is a weak ordering (or, equivalently, that $\not\succ$ is a complete preordering) is a very powerful hypothesis. What about the converse to Theorem 5.5? Is the property of being a weak ordering sufficiently powerful to guarantee that a preference relation $\succ$ can be represented by a utility function? Remarkably enough the answer is "No." The standard counterexample is provided by lexicographic preference.

Definition 5.10 (Lexicographic preference on $\mathbf{R}_+^2$) $y \succ x$ *if either (a)* $y_1 > x_1$ *or (b)* $y_1 = x_1$ *and* $y_2 > x_2$ *for each pair of commodity bundles* $x = (x_1, x_2)$ *and* $y = (y_1, y_2)$ *in* $\mathbf{R}_+^2$.

With this preference ordering, differences in commodity one always come first. Only when commodity bundles differ not at all in the quantity of the first commodity are differences in the amount of the second commodity allowed to influence preference. Preferences of this sort are not as far-fetched as they might seem. An alcoholic or a person of principle might prefer commodity 1 (alcohol or a matter of principle) to commodity 2 "no matter what."

A typical strict upper contour set $P(x)$, illustrated in Figure 5.1, consists of all the points lying to the right of x and the points on the solid line above x, but *none* of the points lying on the dotted line below x. For these preferences each point in X is its own equivalence class (i.e., $I(x) = \{\, x \,\}$ for all $x \in X$), so the indifference sets are much smaller than is typical in economics. Since existence of a representing utility function clearly requires that the equivalence classes be in one-to-one correspondence with some subset of the

---

2 This is a standard result true of *any* equivalence relation. Of course, mathematicians use a different terminology: indifference sets are called equivalence classes.

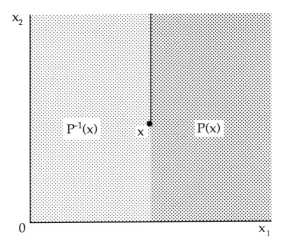

Fig. 5.1. Lexicographic preference.

real line, the equivalence classes for lexicographic preferences may seem too numerous for this to be true. However, that is not really the nub of the problem since it is a basic fact of mathematics that $\mathbf{R}^2$ can be put into one-to-one correspondence with $\mathbf{R}$. Thus, the fact that lexicographic preferences cannot be represented by a utility function is a more subtle matter, and it is genuinely surprising.

Theorem 5.11 *There exists no representing utility function for lexicographic preferences on* $\mathbf{R}^2_+$.

Proof We will assume that there exists a representing utility function $u \colon \mathbf{R}^2_+ \to \mathbf{R}$ and obtain a contradiction. Consider two points on the same vertical line, say $x = (a, b_1)$ and $y = (a, b_2)$ where $b_2 > b_1$ (Figure 5.2(a)). Since $y \succ x$, we must have $u(y) > u(x)$. Repeating this procedure for another pair of points $x' = (a', b_1')$ and $y' = (a', b_2')$ where $b_2' > b_1'$, we conclude that $u(y') > u(x')$. Letting (x, y) denote the line segment which has x and y as endpoints (excluding the endpoints themselves) and letting (x', y') denote the corresponding set of points lying between x' and y', lexicographic preference requires that the utility assigned to points in (x, y) belong to the open interval $(u(x), u(y))$ and the utility assigned to points in (x', y') belong to the open interval $(u(x'), u(y'))$. Furthermore, if $a' > a$ then the second open interval must lie to the right of the first interval (see Figure 5.2(b))

a: The points x and y.

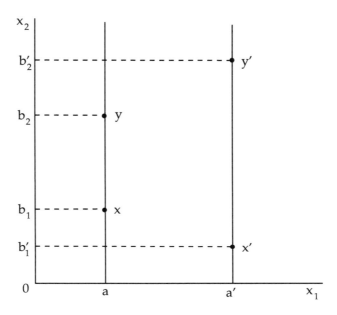

b: Corresponding utility intervals.

Fig. 5.2. Theorem 5.11.

while if $a' < a$ then it must lie to the left (in the figure, we assume $a' > a$). In either case, if $a \neq a'$ the corresponding intervals must be disjoint.

Thus, for each $a \in \mathbf{R}_+$ we must be able to fit an open interval into the real line in such a way that the intervals do not overlap, and the question is whether this is possible. It is not because there can be at most only countably many such disjoint open intervals (*Proof:* Each open interval must contain a distinct rational number, and $\mathbf{Q}$ is countably infinite), and we require uncountably many (one for each $a \in \mathbf{R}$). We conclude that the construction of a representing utility function is impossible. □

The key aspect of lexicographic preference which destroys the chances for representation by a utility function is the absence of continuity. In Figure 5.1

the boundary between $P(x)$ and $P^{-1}(x)$ is not the typical indifference set disjoint from $P(x)$ and $P^{-1}(x)$ that we expect to see in economics: each of these boundary points belongs either to $P(x)$ or to $P^{-1}(x)$. The strict upper and lower contour sets abut one another directly without the cushioning effect of an indifference set in between, allowing abrupt changes in preference ranking when the border is crossed.

Phrased in topological terms, the pathology exhibited by lexicographic preference is that the sets $P(x)$ and $P^{-1}(x)$ are not open.

Definition 5.12 *A preference relation on (X, τ) is* **continuous** *if the sets $P(x)$ and $P^{-1}(x)$ are open for all $x \in X$.*

Recalling that a function $u: X \to \mathbf{R}$ is continuous if the inverse images of the standard subbasis elements (i.e., $u^{-1}(-\infty, a)$ and $u^{-1}(a, \infty)$) are open for all $a \in \mathbf{R}$, there seems reason to hope for a close connection between continuous weak orderings and continuous representing utility functions.

Theorem 5.13 (Debreu) *Let $\succ$ be a binary relation defined on (X, τ), assumed second countable. $\succ$ is representable by a continuous utility function if and only if $\succ$ is a continuous weak ordering.*

Proof

($\Rightarrow$)   By Theorem 5.5, if $\succ$ is represented by a utility function u, then $\succ$ is necessarily a weak ordering. All that remains is to demonstrate that continuity of the utility function implies continuity of the preference relation. But this follows immediately from the fact that

$$P(x) = \{\, y \in X \mid y \succ x \,\} = \{\, y \in X \mid u(y) > u(x) \,\} = u^{-1}(u(x), \infty)$$

and

$$P^{-1}(x) = \{\, y \in X \mid x \succ y \,\} = \{\, y \in X \mid u(y) < u(x) \,\} = u^{-1}(-\infty, u(x)).$$

($\Leftarrow$)   Since expositions of this result are readily available [Bowen (1968) or Hildenbrand and Kirman (1976)], I will only sketch the proof. Let β be a countable basis for the topology of X indexed by A. Since the basis is countable, we can take $A = \mathbf{Z}_{++}$. For each strict lower contour set P^{-1}, let

$$\Gamma(x) = \{\, B_\alpha \in \beta \mid B_\alpha \subset P^{-1}(x) \,\}, \quad A(x) = \{\, \alpha \in A \mid B_\alpha \in \Gamma(x) \,\},$$

and define the utility function u by $u(x) = \sum_{\alpha \in A(x)} (1/2)^\alpha$. Thus, $u(x)$ counts the basis elements contained in the lower contour set $P^{-1}(x)$ with

(1/2) used in the summation to guarantee that the sum converges.[3] Notice that

(a) $y \succ x$ iff $u(y) > u(x)$ (Because the lower contour sets are nested); and

(b) $P^{-1}(x) = \bigcup_{B_\alpha \in \Gamma(x)} B_\alpha$ (Because β is a basis for the topology on X).

Part (a) says that u is a representing utility function, so all that remains is to show that it is continuous. Part (b) immediately implies that u is *uppersemicontinuous* (i.e., $u^{-1}(-\infty, a)$ is open for all $a \in \mathbf{R}$), but u need not be *lowersemicontinuous* (which requires that $u^{-1}(a, \infty)$ be open for all $a \in \mathbf{R}$) and, hence, u may fail to be continuous. Since we used only the openness of the strict lower contour sets in constructing u and not the openness of the strict upper contour sets, the fact that u need only be uppersemicontinuous is not surprising. Taking advantage of the assumption that the sets $P(x)$ are open, it is straightforward to demonstrate the existence of a function $f \colon \mathbf{R} \to \mathbf{R}$ which is strictly increasing and such that $u^* := f \circ u$ is continuous (see Bowen (1968) for the details). Because f is strictly increasing, the continuous function u^* represents $\succ$. □

Remark 5.14 *This theorem applies in particular to any set $X \subset \mathbf{R^n}$ provided that X is given the relative Euclidean topology which it inherits as a subspace of $\mathbf{R^n}$. (Because $\mathbf{R^n}$ is second countable, X with the relative topology is clearly second countable.)*

5.2 Existence of best response

Under what conditions do best responses exist? The following lemma, which requires no assumptions, is a useful first step.

Lemma 5.15 *The set of best responses in the feasible set K is given by*

$$B(K) = K \backslash \bigcup_{x \in K} P^{-1}(x).$$

Proof

$$
\begin{aligned}
K \backslash \bigcup_{x \in K} P^{-1}(x) &= \{ y \in K \mid y \notin P^{-1}(x) \; \forall x \in K \} \\
&= \{ y \in K \mid x \notin P(y) \; \forall x \in K \} \\
&= \{ y \in K \mid P(y) \cap K = \emptyset \} \\
&= B(K)
\end{aligned}
$$

3 The terms are nonnegative and the sum is bounded above by $\sum_{\alpha \in \mathbf{Z}_{++}} (1/2)^\alpha = 1$.

as claimed.   □

You should illustrate this result by drawing a sketch. All that is involved
is the intuitive claim that, if you throw away all elements of K which are
dominated by some element of K, what is left over must be undominated
(maximal).

Why does this lemma leave our opening question unanswered? Because
$B(K)$ might be empty, and the lemma does not preclude that possibility!
Remarkably enough, while the desired result does require some assumptions,
$\succ$ need not be a weak ordering.

Theorem 5.16 *Let $\succ$ be an irreflexive and transitive preference relation on
(X, τ), and K a nonempty, compact subset of X. If $P^{-1}(x)$ is open for all
$x \in K$, then $B(K)$ is nonempty and compact.*

Proof If $B(K) = \emptyset$, then by the lemma $K \subset \bigcup_{x \in K} P^{-1}(x)$ and so $\{ P^{-1}(x) \mid$
$x \in K \}$ is an open covering of K. Since K is compact, there exists a
finite set $\widetilde{K} = \{ x_1, \ldots, x_n \mid x_i \in K \}$ such that $\{ P^{-1}(x) \mid x \in \widetilde{K} \}$ covers
K. By transitivity, $\widetilde{K}$ has a maximal element, say x_n: i.e., $x_n \notin P^{-1}(x_i)$
for $i = 1, \ldots, n-1$. But $x_n \notin P^{-1}(x_n)$ because $\succ$ is irreflexive and so
the collection $\{ P^{-1}(x) \mid x \in \widetilde{K} \}$ does not cover K, a contradiction. We
conclude that $B(K) \neq \emptyset$.

By the lemma, $B(K) = K \backslash \bigcup_{x \in K} P^{-1}(x)$. Since each set $P^{-1}(x)$ is open,
the union $\bigcup_{x \in K} P^{-1}(x)$ is open and so

$$ K \cap \left(X \backslash \bigcup_{x \in K} P^{-1}(x) \right) = K \backslash \bigcup_{x \in K} P^{-1}(x) $$

is closed by Theorem 4.28(b). (Note that here we are employing the assumption, tacit throughout the chapter, that (X, τ) is Hausdorff.) Therefore, $B(K)$, a closed subset of the compact set K, is itself compact (Theorem 4.28(a)).   □

Of course, this result implies the existence of a best response under the
more restrictive conditions of neoclassical preference.

Corollary 5.17 *If $\succ$ can be represented by a continuous utility function on
(X, τ) and $K \subset X$ is nonempty and compact, then $B(K)$ is nonempty and
compact.*

Proof The existence of a representing utility function guarantees that $\succ$ is irreflexive and transitive. The fact that the utility function is continuous implies that the sets $P^{-1}(x)$ are open for all $x \in K$. $\square$

What does the theorem imply within the usual context of a consumer or firm?

- For the standard consumer, the demand set

$$\phi(p) := \{\, x \in \beta(p) \mid P(x) \cap \beta(p) = \emptyset \,\},$$

  where $\beta(p) := \{\, x \in X \mid p \cdot x \le p \cdot w \,\}$, is nonempty and compact if $\succ$ is a weak ordering, $\emptyset \ne X \subset \mathbf{R}^m$ (which implies that X is Hausdorff), and either (a) $p >> 0$ and $X \subset \mathbf{R}_+^m$ (which implies that $\beta(p)$ is compact); or (b) X is compact.
- For the standard firm[4] with technology set Y, the supply set

$$\eta(p) := \{\, y \in Y \mid H_o^+(p, p \cdot y) \cap Y = \emptyset \,\}$$

  is nonempty and compact provided that Y is a compact subset of $\mathbf{R}^m$. (Note that the lower contour sets $H_o^-(p, p \cdot y)$ for the firm are open since the linear functional p is continuous on $\mathbf{R}^m$.)

However, the theorem is more general than either of these typical applications suggests:

- The commodity space does not have to be finite dimensional (recall that, by our definition, topological vector spaces are always Hausdorff); and
- The preference relation $\not\succ$ need not be complete or transitive.

In particular, Theorem 5.16 guarantees existence of a best response even if preferences cannot be represented by a utility function.

A simple, but illuminating, example of an incomplete preference relation is provided by the vector ordering preference relation.

Definition 5.18 (Weak vector ordering on $\mathbf{R}_+^m$) *For $x, y \in \mathbf{R}_+^m$, (a) $y \succeq x$ iff $y \ge x$ and (b) $y \succ x$ iff $y > x$.*

In this definition, $\succeq$ is taken as primitive with $\succ$ derived from it in the usual way, $y \succ x$ iff $y \succeq x$ and $x \not\succeq y$, which reduces to $y \succ x$ iff $y > x$ in this special case. Notice that $\succeq$ is transitive as well as reflexive and so $\sim$ is an equivalence relation.[5] However, the weak vector ordering preference relation is not complete: in $\mathbf{R}^2$, for example, the vectors $(1, 2)$ and $(2, 1)$

---

4 Just as for the consumer, we suppress the subscripts indexing the firms.
5 The indifference classes are one-point sets.

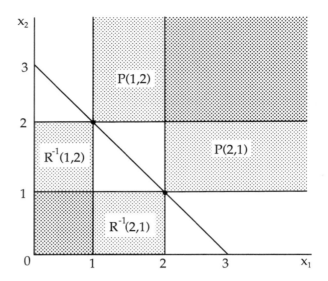

Fig. 5.3. Maximal elements, not best.

cannot be compared since neither $(1,2) \succeq (2,1)$ nor $(2,1) \succeq (1,2)$ is true. Consider now the feasible set

$$K = \{\, x \in \mathbf{R}_+^2 \mid x_1 + x_2 \le 3 \,\}$$

illustrated in Figure 5.3. The weak vector ordering does not satisfy the requirements of Theorem 5.16 since the lower strict contour sets $P^{-1}(x)$ are not open. Nevertheless, the set of maximal elements in K is nonempty, given by

$$B(K) = \{\, x \in \mathbf{R}_+^2 \mid x_1 + x_2 = 3 \,\}.$$

Figure 5.3 portrays the strict upper contour sets for two of the maximal elements, $(1,2)$ and $(2,1)$. Notice that for any $x \in B(K)$, $P(x) \cap K = \emptyset$ so that the elements of $B(K)$ are indeed maximal (best responses).

If we were to use instead a more traditional definition of best response, the best response set would be empty. The traditional (classical) definition defines the best response to be

$$B^c(K) := \{\, x \in K \mid K \subset R^{-1}(x) \,\} :$$

i.e., an element $x \in B^c(K)$ is "at least as good" as any other feasible alternative. Figure 5.3 illustrates the lower contour sets $R^{-1}(x)$ for the commodity bundles $(1,2)$ and $(2,1)$. Note that for these choices of x, and in fact for any $x \in B$, it is *not* true that $K \subset R^{-1}(x)$. There are no best elements in B in this classical sense.

In the literature, the set $B^c(K)$ is often called the set of *best elements* of K and $B(K)$ the set of *maximal elements*. Fortunately, the relationship between the two concepts is easy to characterize.

Theorem 5.19 *Let $\succeq$ be a binary relation on X and define $\succ$ as follows:* $y \succ x$ *iff* $y \succeq x$ *and* $x \not\succeq y$.

    (a) *For any feasible set of alternatives $K \subset X$, $B^c(K) \subset B(K)$;*

    (b) *If $\succeq$ (equivalently, $\not\succ$) is complete on X, then $B^c(K) = B(K)$.*

Proof

    (a) If $x \in B^c(K)$, then $K \subset R^{-1}(x)$ and, by definition of $\succ$, $P(x) \cap R^{-1}(x) = \emptyset$. Therefore, $P(x) \cap K = \emptyset$ which proves that $x \in B(K)$.

    (b) Because of part (a), it suffices to prove that $B(K) \subset B^c(K)$. If $x \in B(K)$, then $P(x) \cap K = \emptyset$. Since $\succeq$ is complete, $R^{-1}(x) = X \backslash P(x)$ and so $K \subset R^{-1}(x)$, which means that $x \in B^c(K)$.

$\square$

In our example of the weak vector ordering preference relation, $B^c(K)$ is empty so the conclusion $B^c(K) \subset B(K)$ of the theorem does hold!

Intuitively, the reason why the weak vector ordering preference relation is incomplete is that the consumer is unwilling to make tradeoffs. A consumer with such preferences would only be willing to say that one commodity bundle is at least as good as another if each of the components of the one is at least as large as the corresponding components of the other. If a vector y offers more of some components and less of others than the vector x, then y and x are incomparable.

Representing preferences by vector ordering is, of course, an extreme case, and one that would be rejected by most economists as unrealistic. The ability to make tradeoffs, to compare, is fundamental to the economist's view of the world. However, we should not jump to the conclusion that preferences should, therefore, always be assumed complete. Allowing for incompleteness permits economic models to recognize that, in asking a consumer to rank two alternatives, a permissible response is: "I don't know."

For example, a resident of Los Angeles living meagerly on a $5,000 annual income could be asked to compare the commodity bundle currently enjoyed in Los Angeles with the lifestyle possible upon accepting a $50,000 a year job in Alaska. The consumer might jump at the prospect, but it seems at least possible that, when contemplating life in a cold and unknown setting, the

consumer would respond that she is not sure. Describing this consumer's
equilibrium in terms of maximal elements, as defined in this book and the
modern mathematical economics literature, requires only the assertion that
the consumer will remain in Los Angeles if the Alaska alternative is not
regarded as strictly better. In contrast to the traditional definition of best
elements, we do not require the consumer to know that her well-being in Los
Angeles is at least as good as it would be in Alaska. If by some chance the
consumer were transported to Alaska, she might decide to stay there: the
Alaska alternative might also be maximal so that, viewed from an Alaskan
perspective, life in Los Angeles might not seem better and, in fact, might
even seem worse!

Although the modern definition of maximal elements seems better in most
respects, the traditional formulation has merit in contexts where $\succ$ is a weak
ordering. Fortunately, as Theorem 5.19(b) demonstrates, in that case the
two definitions of best (maximal) response coincide. The main virtue of the
traditional definition manifests itself in situations where we want to establish
that the best response set is convex. To show how this is done, we begin
with a lemma paralleling the earlier Lemma 5.15 for maximal elements.

Lemma 5.20 *If $\succ$ is a weak ordering on X, then the set of best elements
in the feasible set K is given by $B(K) = \bigcap_{x \in K}(K \cap R(x))$.*

Proof By Lemma 5.15 we have $B(K) = K \backslash \bigcup_{x \in K} P^{-1}(x)$. Applying one of
DeMorgan's Laws,

$$K \backslash \bigcup_{x \in K} P^{-1}(x) = \bigcap_{x \in K}(K \backslash P^{-1}(x)).$$

But, since $\not\succ$ is complete, $X \backslash P^{-1}(x) = R(x)$. Because $K \subset X$, we conclude
that $K \backslash P^{-1}(x) = K \cap (X \backslash P^{-1}(x)) = K \cap R(x)$, which establishes the desired
result.   □

Theorem 5.21 *If $\succ$ is a weak ordering on X, the feasible set K is convex,
and the upper contour sets $R(x)$ are convex for all $x \in K$, then the best
response $B(K)$ is convex.*

Proof By the preceding lemma, $B(K) = \bigcap_{x \in K}(K \cap R(x))$. Since K is
convex and $R(x)$ is convex for each $x \in K$, the intersection $K \cap R(x)$ is
convex. Therefore, the intersection $\bigcap_{x \in K}(K \cap R(x))$ is convex.   □

Example 1 (consumer). In a pure exchange economy, a consumer's de-
mand set is given by $\phi(p) := \{ x \in \beta(p) \mid P(x) \cap \beta(p) = \emptyset \}$ with budget

set $\beta(p) := \{\, x \in X \mid p \cdot x \le p \cdot w \,\}$. If the consumption set X is convex, the feasible (budget) set $\beta(p)$ will be convex. Therefore, if preferences are convex (i.e., $R(x)$ is convex for all $x \in X$) and $\succ$ is a weak ordering, then the demand set $\phi(p)$ is convex.

Example 2 (firm). In a production economy, supply sets (for the firm or the economy) take the form

$$\eta(p) = \{\, y \in Y \mid H_o^+(p, p \cdot y) \cap Y = \emptyset \,\}.$$

Therefore, if the technology set Y is convex, then the supply set $\eta(p)$ will be convex.

5.3 Continuity of best response

Up to now we have looked at best response only in an unchanging environment. We now ask: How does best response change when the decision-maker's environment changes? Figure 5.7 (which appears a few pages hence) provides a schematic representation of how the problem is posed. Our model of the consumer involves mappings from an environment $e \in E$ to the consumption set X, a subset of the commodity space L. The environment affects both the feasible set, through a constraint mapping $K\colon E \to 2^X$, $e \mapsto K(e)$, and the choice of a best response, through a best response mapping $B\colon E \to 2^X$, $e \mapsto B(e) \subset K(e)$. Our main goal is to establish conditions under which best response is a continuous function of the environment, a property critical to existence of a Walrasian equilibrium.

5.3.1 Graph of a preference relation

We begin by introducing a new concept, the graph of a preference relation.

Definition 5.22 *If $\succ$ is a preference relation on X, then*

- *the graph of $\succ$ is the set $\Gamma(\succ) = \{\, (x, y) \in X \times X \mid y \succ x \,\}$; and*
- *the graph of $\nsucc$ is the set $\Gamma(\nsucc) = \{\, (x, y) \in X \times X \mid y \nsucc x \,\} = (X \times X) \backslash \Gamma(\succ)$.*

Requiring $\succ$ to have open graph provides an alternative (and very powerful) way to characterize preferences as continuous.

Definition 5.23 *If $\succ$ is a preference relation on (X, τ), then*

- *$\succ$ has **open graph** if $\Gamma(\succ)$ is an open subset of $X \times X$, and*
- *$\nsucc$ has **closed graph** if $\Gamma(\nsucc)$ is a closed subset of $X \times X$*

where, of course, $X \times X$ is given the product topology.

Because $\Gamma(\not\succ)$ is the complement of $\Gamma(\succ)$ in $X \times X$, clearly $\succ$ has open graph if and only if $\not\succ$ has closed graph.

What is the connection between this open graph condition and the definition of continuity given earlier in this chapter? Recall that, according to that definition, a preference relation $\succ$ is continuous if the strict upper and strict lower contour sets (sections) $P(x) = \{y \in X \mid y \succ x\}$ and $P^{-1}(x) = \{y \in X \mid x \succ y\}$ are open subsets of X. For brevity we refer to this characterization of continuity as **open sections**.

In one direction, the relationship between open graph and open sections is quite straightforward.

Theorem 5.24 *If the preference relation $\succ$ on (X, τ) has open graph, then it has open sections.*

Proof This is an easy application of the definition of the product topology applied to $X \times X$. I will prove that $P(x)$ is open, leaving the similar proof that $P^{-1}(x)$ is open to you.

Choose $x \in X$ arbitrarily. If $y \in P(x)$, then $(x, y) \in \Gamma(\succ)$. Because $\Gamma(\succ)$ is an open set, there exist open neighborhoods G_x and G_y of x and y respectively such that $G_x \times G_y \subset \Gamma(\succ)$. But this implies that $G_y \in P(x)$. Therefore, every point $y \in P(x)$ is an interior point: i.e., $P(x)$ is an open set. $\qquad\square$

The following corollary provides a very intuitive picture of what open graph means: if y is strictly preferred to x and the graph of $\succ$ is open, then any commodity bundle close to y will also be strictly preferred to any commodity bundle close to x.

Corollary 5.25 *If the preference relation $\succ$ on (X, τ) has open graph, then there exist open neighborhoods G_x and G_y of x and y respectively such that $y' \succ x'$ for all $y' \in G_y$ and for all $x' \in G_x$.*

Proof Exercise 5.11. $\qquad\square$

While the converse of Theorem 5.24 is false, open sections do imply open graph under reasonable conditions.

Definition 5.26 *A preference relation $\succ$ on X is **order dense** if for any $(x, y) \in \Gamma(\succ)$ there exists a $z \in X$ such that $y \succ z$ and $z \succ x$.*

Theorem 5.27 *If a preference relation $\succ$ on X has open sections, then it has open graph provided any one of the following conditions is satisfied:*

- $\succ$ *is transitive and order dense;*
- $\succ$ *and $\not\succ$ are transitive;*
- $\succ$ *is a weak ordering;*
- $\not\succ$ *is a complete preordering;*
- *X is a subset of a finite dimensional TVS and $P(x)$ is convex for all $x \in X$.*

Proof See Bergstrom, Parks, and Rader (1976). □

Open graph, though stronger than open sections, seems no less palatable, but it may seem less intuitive. Geometric illustration, in particular, seems nearly impossible: since the smallest commodity space which typically makes sense to an economist is $\mathbf{R}^2$, displaying graphs requires at least dimension four. However, there is a way to view preferences on $\mathbf{R}$ in economic terms. Doing so yields considerable insight into the general case.

Consider a situation in which a consumer must choose a single point on the real line, say in the consumption set $X = [0, 1]$. To provide motivation, you might interpret the problem in political terms with $[0, 1]$ representing a spectrum of policies from "left" to "right." Suppose that the preferences of the consumer are represented by a "single-peaked" utility function as illustrated in Figure 5.4(a). Assume that the feasible set for this consumer is an interval $K = [.2, .8]$ and that the point x^* which maximizes the utility function lies in K.

Figure 5.4(b) shows the graph of the strict preference relation induced by the utility function and Figure 5.4(a) the strict upper contour set $P(x)$ corresponding to a commodity bundle $x \neq x^*$. In Figure 5.4(b) this strict preference set becomes a vertical cross-section of $\Gamma(\succ)$.

Recall the definition of best response:

$$B(K) := \{\, x \in K \mid P(x) \cap K = \emptyset \,\}.$$

Since $B(K) = \{\, x^* \,\}$, this means that the graph $\Gamma(\succ)$ in Figure 5.4(b) has a tiny hole lying above the best response x^*. Thus, a commodity bundle x^* is a best response if (i) it lies in the feasible set K and (ii) the vertical cross-section of the graph $\Gamma(\succ)$ lying above x^* contains no point in K.

Also recall our characterization of best response[6] (Lemma 5.15): $B(K) = K \backslash \bigcup_{y \in K} P^{-1}(y)$. This says we can locate the "hole" in $\Gamma(\succ)$ by plotting the *horizontal* cross-sections $P^{-1}(y) \times \{\, y \,\}$. For a hole (best response) in

6 I have changed the dummy variable from x to y to clarify its interpretation in the diagram.

a: Graph of utility function.

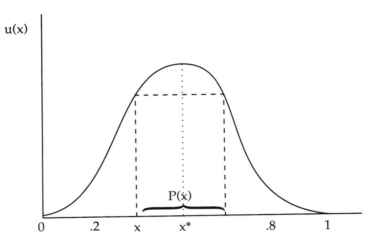

b: Graph of strict preference.

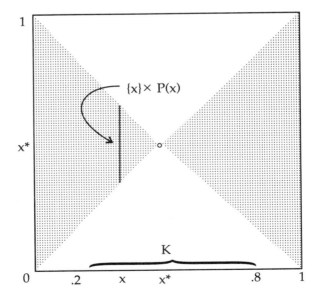

Fig. 5.4. Single-peaked utility.

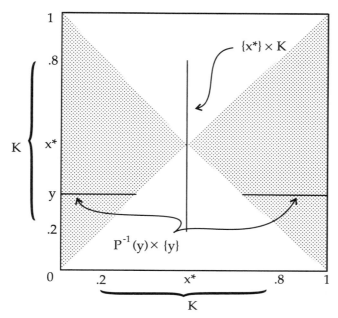

Fig. 5.5. Illustration of Lemma 5.15.

$\Gamma(\succ)$ to exist at the point x^*, the horizontal cross-sections for *every* point $y \in K$ must fail to intersect the vertical slice $\{x^*\} \times K$ (see Figure 5.5).

This construction suggests the possibility of a proof of the existence of maximal elements under more general conditions than we have obtained thus far, a possibility which will be realized in Chapter 7. Exploring the properties of the graph of a preference relation along the lines of the above example will yield rich dividends. Exercise 5.9 suggests some possibilities for that exploration.

5.3.2 Topologies on spaces of subsets

The problem we are addressing — "When will best response vary continuously with changes in the environment?" — poses an immediate difficulty. What topology are we going to use on the codomain of the best response mapping B? Recall that the codomain is 2^X, the **space of subsets** of the consumption set X. We certainly are willing to assume that X itself is a topological space with relative topology inherited from the TVS L. In this book L is simply $\mathbf{R}^m$ with the standard Euclidean topology. But what meaning can we attach to the notion that two subsets of X are close? Even contemplating what it means for subsets of X to be "points" of some larger space of subsets seems hard to fathom. So we must now ask: What is an appropriate topology on the set 2^X when (X, τ) is a topological space?

Two candidates for such a topology which we now explore are provided by the **Hausdorff metric topology** and by the **exponential topology**. The discussion will be simplified enormously, with no loss for the applications we have in mind, by restricting attention to the family of *nonempty, closed* subsets of a topological space (X, τ).

Definition 5.28 *If (X, τ) is a topological space, let $(2^X)_o^F$ denote the collection of all nonempty, closed subsets of X.*

We begin with the Hausdorff metric topology because it is the easiest to understand. Suppose that X is a compact metric space with metric ρ, a measure of the distance between the *points* of X (e.g., X could be a closed and bounded subset of $\mathbf{R}^n$ with the Euclidean metric). Prior to defining a distance between *subsets* of X, we start with a simple measure of the distance between a point and a set.

Definition 5.29 *If (X, ρ) is a compact metric space, then define the distance between a point $x \in X$ and a subset $S \subset X$ as* $\mathrm{dist}(x, S) := \inf_{y \in S} \rho(x, y)$.

A simple sketch should convince you that this definition makes sense. The following result should also seem quite obvious.

Theorem 5.30 *The distance function* $\mathrm{dist} \colon X \times (2^X)_o^F \to \mathbf{R}_+$ *satisfies the following properties:*

- $\mathrm{dist}(x, \{y\}) = \rho(x, y)$ *for all $x, y \in X$;*
- *For a fixed set $S \subset X$, $\mathrm{dist}(x, S)$ is a continuous function of x.*

Proof See Kuratowski (1966), 209.   □

We now use this measure of distance to define Hausdorff distance.

Definition 5.31 *If (X, ρ) is a compact metric space, then the **Hausdorff distance** between nonempty, closed subsets $A, B \subset X$ is given by*

$$\delta(A, B) := \max \Big\{ \sup_{x \in A} \mathrm{dist}(x, B), \sup_{y \in B} \mathrm{dist}(y, A) \Big\}.$$

To provide some interpretation, we generalize the definitions of open and closed balls of Chapter 4 to allow balls centered on a subset rather than a point.

Definition 5.32 *If (X, ρ) is a compact metric space and S is a nonempty, closed subset of X, then for any $\epsilon > 0$ define*

- *the* **open ϵ-ball** *with center S, $B(S, \epsilon) := \{ x \in X \mid \text{dist}(x, S) < \epsilon \}$;*
- *the* **closed ϵ-ball** *with center S, $\overline{B}(S, \epsilon) := \{ x \in X \mid \text{dist}(x, S) \leq \epsilon \}$.*

Thus, two subsets A and B of (X, ρ) are within ϵ Hausdorff distance of one another if

- A lies in a closed ϵ-ball centered at B; and
- B lies in a closed ϵ-ball centered at A.

Although Hausdorff distance seems a reasonable measure of distance between subsets, it is not a metric on 2^X. Consider, for example, an open set $A \subset X$ and its closure $\text{cl}\, A$. The Hausdorff distance between these two sets is zero, but they are not the same element of 2^X (thereby violating one of the basic conditions for a metric space). However, when attention is restricted to the space $(2^X)_o^F$ of nonempty, closed subsets of X, all difficulties disappear.

Theorem 5.33 *If (X, ρ) is a compact metric space, then $((2^X)_o^F, \delta)$ is a compact metric space.*

Proof See Kuratowski (1966), 214, and Kuratowski (1968), 45. □

While the metric topology induced by Hausdorff has the advantage of easy interpretation, it is not the most useful way to put a topology on a space of subsets. An alternative, called the **exponential topology**, defines a topology by characterizing its subbasis:

Definition 5.34 *If (X, τ) is a topological space, then the* **exponential topology** τ_e *on $(2^X)_o^F$ is the coarsest topology such that the following sets are open for every open set $V \subset X$:*

- *the upper subbasis elements $\beta^u(V) := \{ F \in (2^X)_o^F \mid F \subset V \}$;*
- *the lower subbasis elements $\beta^\ell(V) := \{ F \in (2^X)_o^F \mid F \cap V \neq \emptyset \}$.*

Although this definition looks rather abstract, the topology it describes coincides with the Hausdorff metric topology in the contexts we care about.

Theorem 5.35 *If X is a compact metric space, then the topological spaces $((2^X)_o^F, \delta)$ and $((2^X)_o^F, \tau_e)$ are homeomorphic.*

Proof Kuratowski (1968), 47. □

The point of view adopted here is that, while Hausdorff distance gives a useful guide to intuition, the abstract definition of the exponential topology provides the best way to characterize continuity of best response.

5.3.3 Continuity of correspondences

Suppose we are given a correspondence[7] $B: E \to (2^X)_o^F$. As the notation suggests, we have in mind best response correspondences from the environment to the set of (nonempty, closed) subsets of the consumption set. But the discussion which follows applies to *any* correspondence of this form.

To define continuity of the correspondence B we apply the standard definition of continuity, as set forth in Chapter 4, using $\beta^u(V)$ and $\beta^\ell(V)$ as the subbasis elements.

Definition 5.36 *Assume that (E, τ_E) and (X, τ_X) are topological spaces. The correspondence $B: E \to (2^X)_o^F$ is* **continuous at** $e \in E$ *if for every subbasis element β such that $B(e) \in \beta$ there exists an open set U in E such that $B(e') \in \beta$ for all $e' \in U$. If B is continuous for each $e \in E$, then B is simply said to be continuous.*

All we are doing is applying the standard definition of continuity using this particular choice of topology. The problem is understanding what it means. Since two different types of subbasis element are involved, it makes sense to examine each in turn.

We start with the upper subbasis elements. Since

$$\beta^u(V) = \{\, F \in (2^X)_o^F \mid F \subset V \,\},$$

where V is an arbitrary open subset of X, we conclude that $B(e) \in \beta^u(V)$ iff $B(e) \subset V$. Applying Definition 5.36 using *only* the upper subbasis elements characterizes a property called **upperhemicontinuity**.

Definition 5.37 *Assume that (E, τ_E) and (X, τ_X) are topological spaces. The correspondence $B: E \to (2^X)_o^F$ is* **upperhemicontinuous (uhc)** *at $e \in E$ if for every open set $V \subset X$ such that $B(e) \subset V$ there exists an open neighborhood U of e such that $B(e') \subset V$ for every $e' \in U$. If B is uhc for all $e \in E$, then it is simply said to be uhc.*

Next we use the lower subbasis in the same way. Since

$$\beta^\ell(V) = \{\, F \in (2^X)_o^F \mid F \cap V \neq \emptyset \,\},$$

---

7 Following the standard tradition in economics, we often use this terminology for functions which are "set-valued" but not "empty-set-valued": i.e., which have codomain contained in $(2^X)_o$, the collection of all subsets of X except for the empty set.

where V is an arbitrary open subset of X, we conclude that $B(e) \in \beta^\ell(V)$ iff $B(e) \cap V \neq \emptyset$. Applying Definition 5.36 using *only* the lower subbasis elements yields the property called **lowerhemicontinuity**.

Definition 5.38 *Assume that (E, τ_E) and (X, τ_X) are topological spaces. The correspondence $B\colon E \to (2^X)_o^F$ is* **lowerhemicontinuous (lhc)** *at $e \in E$ if for every open set $V \subset X$ such that $B(e) \cap V \neq \emptyset$ there exists an open neighborhood U of e such that $B(e') \cap V \neq \emptyset$ for every $e' \in U$. If B is lhc for all $e \in E$, then it is simply said to be lhc.*

Of course, correspondences which satisfy both forms of hemicontinuity are continuous.

Theorem 5.39 *Assume that (E, τ_E) and (X, τ_X) are topological spaces. The correspondence $B\colon E \to (2^X)_o^F$ is continuous at $e \in E$ iff it is both uhc and lhc at $e \in E$. B is continuous iff it is continuous for all $e \in E$.*

Proof Immediate from the definitions. $\qquad\square$

Corollary 5.40 *Assume that (E, τ_E) and (X, τ_X) are topological spaces. If the correspondence $B\colon E \to (2^X)_o^F$ is singleton-valued for all $e \in E$ and either uhc or lhc, then it is continuous.*

Proof In this case the correspondence B can be viewed as a function $B\colon E \to X$. The conditions $B(e) \subset V$ (for uhc) or $B(e) \cap V \neq \emptyset$ (for lhc) reduce to the familiar condition $B(e) \in V$, and both the definition of uhc and the definition of lhc become nothing more than the ordinary definition of continuity. $\qquad\square$

Figure 5.6, which illustrates the interpretation of these different forms of continuity, should seem largely self-explanatory.

- In panel (a) the correspondence B is uhc at e because for every open set V containing $B(e)$ we can find a neighborhood U of e such that the images $B(e')$ remain in V for all $e' \in U$.
- In panel (b) the image $B(e)$ excludes the dotted line. The correspondence B is not uhc at e: perturbing e to any point e' to the right of e, no matter how close to e, yields an image which does *not* fit inside V.
- In panel (d) (meant to look just like panel (b)) the correspondence is lhc at e because for every open set V which intersects $B(e)$ we can find a neighborhood U of e such that the images $B(e')$ continue to intersect V for all $e' \in U$.

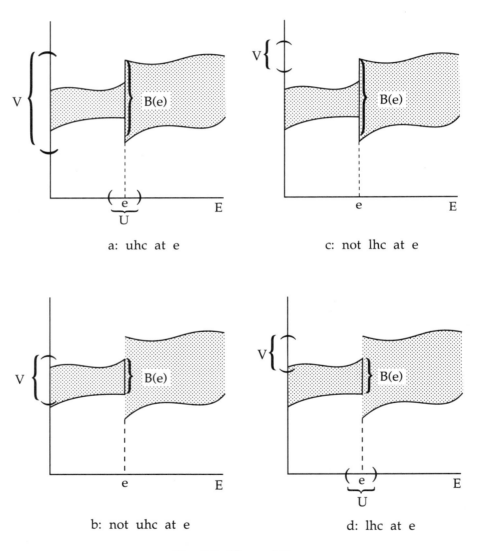

a: uhc at e   c: not lhc at e

b: not uhc at e   d: lhc at e

Fig. 5.6. Uhc and lhc.

- In panel (c) (meant to be the same as (a)) the image $B(e)$ includes the points formerly on the dotted line. The correspondence B is not lhc at e: when e is perturbed to any point e' to the left of e, no matter how slightly, the image $B(e')$ fails to intersect V.

5.3.4 Uhc and closed graph

The following notion is often used as a substitute for upperhemicontinuity.

Definition 5.41 *Assume that (E, τ_E) and (X, τ_X) are topological spaces. A correspondence $B \colon E \to (2^X)_o^F$ has* **closed graph** *if the graph*

$$\Gamma(B) := \{\, (e, x) \in E \times X \mid x \in B(e) \,\}$$

is a closed subset of $E \times X$ where this product space is given the product topology.

The closed graph property is obviously a close relative of upperhemicontinuity. In Figure 5.6(a), for example, the graph of the uhc correspondence is closed while in Figure 5.6(b) (where the correspondence is not uhc) the graph is not closed. There are circumstances, however, in which the two concepts can differ. Consider, for example, the correspondence defined by

$$B(e) = \begin{cases} \{\, -1/x, 0 \,\} & \text{for } x < 0; \\ \{\, 0 \,\} & \text{for } x \geq 0. \end{cases}$$

The graph of this correspondence is closed, but, as you can easily verify, B is not uhc at 0. However, provided that X is a compact Hausdorff space, the setting appropriate for all of our applications, the two concepts are equivalent.

Theorem 5.42 *Assume that E is a Hausdorff topological space and X a compact Hausdorff space. Then a correspondence $B \colon E \to (2^X)_o^F$ is uhc iff it has closed graph.*

Proof Exercise 5.15. (Or see Kuratowski (1968), 58.) $\qquad\square$

Warning 5.43 *For this reason, in the economics literature you will often see closed graph taken as the definition of upperhemicontinuity.*

The closed graph characterization of upperhemicontinuity is even more useful when given a local definition (corresponding to our definition of uhc at a point $e \in E$).

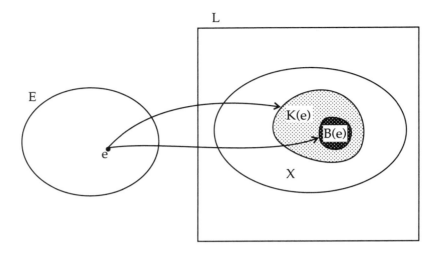

Fig. 5.7. The Maximum Theorem.

Definition 5.44 *Assume that (E, τ_E) and (X, τ_X) are topological spaces. A correspondence $B: E \to (2^X)_o^F$ is* **closed** *at $e \in E$ if for any $x \notin B(e)$ there exist open sets $U \subset E$ and $V \subset X$ such that $(e, x) \in U \times V$ and $V \cap B(e') = \emptyset$ for all $e' \in U$.*

Theorem 5.45 *Assume that E is a Hausdorff topological space and X a compact Hausdorff space. Then a correspondence $B: E \to (2^X)_o^F$ is uhc at $e \in E$ iff it is closed at e.*

Proof Exercise 5.16.   □

5.3.5 The Maximum Theorem

We arrive finally at the topic which is our main concern, establishing conditions under which best response varies upperhemicontinuously as a function of the environment. We consider a very general formulation of the problem, illustrated in Figure 5.7.

The basic ingredients are as follows:

- an **environment** E, a topological space;
- a **consumption set** $X \subset L$, where the commodity space L is a topological vector space;
- a **constraint correspondence**, $K: E \to (2^X)_o^F$, $e \mapsto K(e) \subset X$;

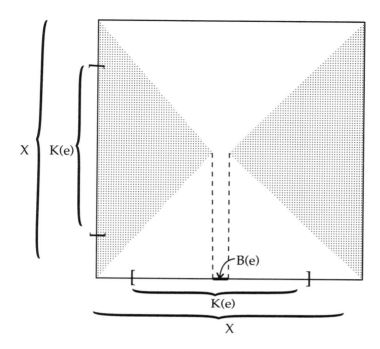

Fig. 5.8. Cross-section for fixed e.

- a family $\{\succ^e |\ e \in E\}$ of **strict preference relations** on X indexed by the environment E; and
- a **best response correspondence**, $B: E \to (2^X)_o^F$, $e \mapsto B(e) \subset K(e)$.

Because the environment can affect preferences, we must modify the definition of the strict preference mapping P and its graph:

Definition 5.46 *Given a family of strict preference relations* $\{\succ^e |\ e \in E\}$ *indexed by the environment* E, *the* **strict preference mapping** *is given by the function* $P: E \times X \to 2^X$, $(e, x) \mapsto P(e, x) := \{\,x' \in X \mid x' \succ^e x\,\}$. *The* **graph** *of* P *is the set* $\Gamma(P) = \{\,(e, x, y) \in E \times X \times X \mid y \succ^e x\,\}$.

Recall the graphical interpretation of best response developed earlier in this chapter. For a *fixed* environment e, the best response set $B(e)$ includes exactly those commodity bundles $x^* \in K(e)$ for which the corresponding vertical cross-sections of the graph $\Gamma(\succ^e)$ are empty (see Figure 5.5 and Figure 5.8). Now we vary the environment, obtaining the "three-dimensional"[8]

---

8 "Three-dimensional" is in quotes because, of course, the spaces E and L will themselves each typically be high dimensional vector spaces.

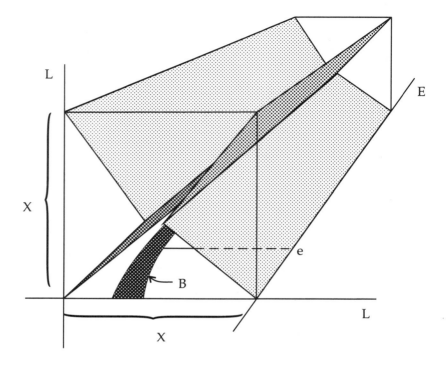

Fig. 5.9. Varying the environment.

picture portrayed in Figure 5.9. Each of the cross-sections such as Figure 5.8 is a slice of Figure 5.9. The best response correspondence is represented by the shaded area lying on the "floor" of this diagram.

We observed earlier that passing from the open sections to the open graph characterization of continuity represented a strengthening of the concept (in the sense that open graph implies open sections but not conversely). Allowing for the possibility that the environment will vary leads to a further strengthening of the continuity requirement. We are going to assume that $\Gamma(P)$ is open in $E \times X \times X$. The intuitive interpretation is similar to that given earlier for open graph with a fixed environment:

if $y \succ^e x$ and $\Gamma(P)$ is open in $E \times X \times X$, then there exist open neighborhoods G_e, G_x, G_y such that $y' \succ^{e'} x'$ for all $e' \in G_e, x' \in G_x, y' \in G_y$.

or, less formally,

if the commodity bundle y is strictly preferred to the commodity bundle x when the environment is e, then any commodity bundle "sufficiently close" to y is preferred to any commodity bundle "sufficiently close" to x for any environment "sufficiently close" to e.

All in all, a very natural characterization of continuity.

The following theorem is the main result of this chapter.

Theorem 5.47 (Maximum Theorem) *Assume that*

(a) *the commodity space L is a topological vector space;*

(b) *the consumption set X is compact;*

(c) *the environment E is a Hausdorff topological space;*

(d) *the constraint correspondence K is continuous at $e \in E$;*

(e) *the graph $\Gamma(P)$ of the strict preference mapping P is open in $E \times X \times X$; and*

(f) *the best response $B(e)$ is nonempty in the environment e.*

Then the best response correspondence B is upperhemicontinuous at e.

Proof Since $B(e)$ is contained in the compact set X for all $e \in E$, the best response correspondence is uhc at e iff it is closed at e. Therefore, we will prove that B is closed at e: i.e., if $x \notin B(e)$, we want to show that there exist open neighborhoods G_e of e and G_x of x such that $B(e') \cap G_x = \emptyset$ for all $e' \in G_e$. We consider two cases:

Case 1: $x \notin K(e)$.

Because K is continuous at e, it is uhc at e and hence has closed graph. But $x \notin K(e)$ then implies there exist open neighborhoods G_e of e and G_x of x such that $K(e') \cap G_x = \emptyset$ for all $e' \in G_e$. However, $B(e') \subset K(e')$ for all $e' \in E$ and so certainly for all $e' \in G_e$. Therefore, $B(e') \cap G_x = \emptyset$ for all $e' \in G_e$.

Case 2: $x \in K(e)$.

Because $x \notin B(e)$, there exists a point $y \in K(e)$ such that $y \succ^e x$: i.e., $(e, x, y) \in \Gamma(P)$. Since $\Gamma(P)$ is open in $E \times X \times X$, there is an open rectangle $G'_e \times G_x \times G_y$ containing (e, x, y) such that $y' \succ^{e'} x'$ for all $(e', x', y') \in G'_e \times G_x \times G_y$. However, G_y is an open set for which $K(e) \cap G_y \neq \emptyset$ because $y \in K(e)$ and $y \in G_y$. Since K is lhc (note!), there exists an open neighborhood G''_e of e such that $K(e') \cap G_y \neq \emptyset$ for all $e' \in G''_e$. Let $G_e := G'_e \cap G''_e$. Then for any $e' \in G_e$ and for any $x' \in G_x$, there exists a $y' \in G_y$ such that $y' \succ^{e'} x'$ and $y' \in K(e')$, which implies that $x' \notin B(e')$. Therefore, $B(e') \cap G_x = \emptyset$ for all $e' \in G_e$. $\qquad \square$

Corollary 5.48 *Suppose that the conditions of Theorem 5.47 are satisfied* *and that, in addition, the best response correspondence is singleton-valued for all $e \in E$. Then the best response is continuous.*

Proof Apply Corollary 5.40.   □

Since we are now allowing preferences to depend on the environment, we need to modify the definition of a representing utility function accordingly.

Definition 5.49 *A strict preference mapping* $P: E \times X \rightarrow 2^X$ *is represented by a utility function if there exists a function* $u: E \times X \rightarrow \mathbf{R}$, $(e, x) \mapsto u(e, x)$ *such that, for all* $e \in E$ *and for all* $x, y \in X$, $y \succ^e x$ *iff* $u(e, y) > u(e, x)$.

Corollary 5.50 *Assume that assumptions (a)–(d) and (f) of Theorem 5.47 hold and that, in place of assumption (e), we are given that the strict preference mapping* $P: E \times X \rightarrow 2^X$ *is represented by a continuous utility function* u. *Then the best response correspondence* B *is upperhemicontinuous.*

Proof All that is required is to prove that $\Gamma(P)$ is open in $E \times X \times X$. But

$$
\begin{aligned}
\Gamma(P) &= \{ (e, x, y) \in \mathcal{X} \mid y \succ^e x \} \\
&= \{ (e, x, y) \in \mathcal{X} \mid u(e, y) > u(e, x) \} \\
&= \{ (e, x, y) \in \mathcal{X} \mid u(e, y) - u(e, x) > 0 \} \\
&= f^{-1}(0, \infty)
\end{aligned}
$$

where the function f is defined by $f(e, x, y) := u(e, y) - u(e, x)$. The function f is continuous as the difference of two continuous functions, so the inverse image $f^{-1}(0, \infty)$ of the open interval $(0, \infty)$ is open.   □

5.3.6 Applying the Maximum Theorem

Figure 5.10 portrays the best response of a consumer in three different situations and the best response of a firm. In panels (a)–(c), which apply to the consumer, the endowment is always $w = (1, 3)$, the consumption set $X = [0, 10^6] \times [0, 10^6]$ (or any suitably large but closed and bounded — hence compact — box), and the environment the set of possible price vectors p.

- Panel (a) illustrates the best response when preferences are strictly convex (i.e., indifference contours have no "flat spots"). The best response is then a continuous function of the "environment" p.

- Panel (b) illustrates the best response when preferences are convex but not strictly convex. When the budget line coincides with a flat, the best response becomes "multi-valued" but in an uhc way.

- Panel (c) shows the nonconvex case. The best response becomes "multi-valued" when two dips in the indifference curves are both tangent to the budget line, but the best response is still uhc.

- Panel (d) illustrates a technology set for a firm operating under constant returns up to a maximum capacity output level y^*. One unit of input is required for each unit of output. The best response is

$$\eta(p) = \begin{cases} 0 & \text{if } p_2 < p_1; \\ [0, y^*] & \text{if } p_2 = p_1; \\ y^* & \text{if } p_2 > p_1; \end{cases}$$

which is uhc in p.

In applying the Maximum Theorem, most of the conditions required of the theorem are typically regarded as "automatic." The modeler simply assumes them to be true for the problem at hand. The exceptions to this rule involve the constraint correspondence, typically the main source of trouble. Figure 5.11 provides an example of what can go wrong. The consumer featured in this figure has consumption set $X = [0, 3]^2$ and well-behaved preferences represented by the indifference contours shown there. The consumer's endowment is $w = (1, 0)$. Normalizing prices to sum to one, the best response of this consumer is given by

$$\phi(p) = \begin{cases} (1, 0) & \text{if } p_1 > 0; \\ (3, 0) & \text{if } p_1 = 0; \end{cases}$$

which fails to be uhc at $p = (0, 1)$.

Why does the Maximum Theorem fail in this example? Tracing through the steps of the proof is a very instructive exercise. You will find that the proof fails in the middle, precisely at the point where we use the assumption that the constraint correspondence is lowerhemicontinuous: when p_1 reaches 0, the budget set "suddenly" collapses from a two-dimensional area to the one-dimensional line segment $[0, 3]$ on the horizontal axis. The constraint correspondence fails to be continuous at that price vector and, as a consequence, the best response is not uhc.

Note that this problem does not arise for the standard model of the firm with fixed constraint correspondence (equal to the technology set Y). If the technological possibilities do vary with the environment (because of external effects, for example), then continuity of the constraint is no longer automatic.

a:

c:

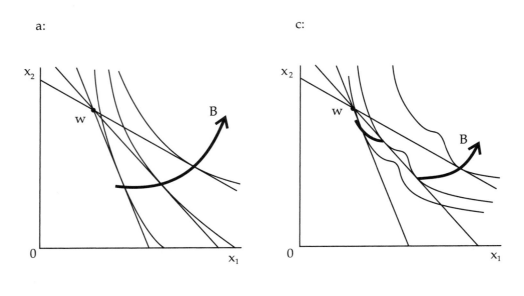

b:

d:

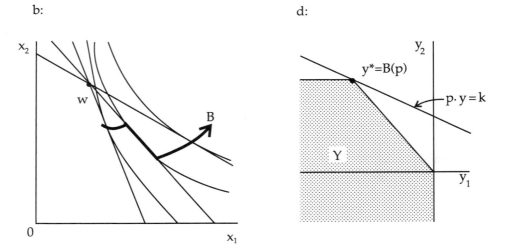

Fig. 5.10. Best response.

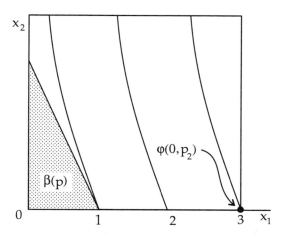

Fig. 5.11. A non-uhc best response.

The following theorem gives the main result on continuity of consumer budget correspondences which we will use in later chapters. Let $\omega(p)$ represent consumer wealth at prices p.

Theorem 5.51 *If the consumption set $X \subset \mathbf{R}^m$ is nonempty, compact, and convex, then the budget correspondence defined by $\beta(p) := \{ x \in X \mid p \cdot x \leq \omega(p) \}$ is continuous at every $p \neq 0$ for which ω is continuous and $\omega(p) > \inf p \cdot X$.*

Proof Because X is compact, upperhemicontinuity is equivalent to closed graph. I will show that the complement of $\Gamma(\beta)$ is open. If $(p, x) \notin \Gamma(\beta)$, then by definition $p \cdot x > \omega(p)$. Because $p \cdot x$ is continuous in p and x and because $\omega(p)$ is continuous in p, there exist open neighborhoods G_p and G_x of p and x respectively such that $p' \cdot x' > \omega(p')$ for all $(p', x') \in G_p \times G_x$. Therefore, $(p, x) \in G_p \times G_x \subset (E \times X) \backslash \Gamma(\beta)$, which proves that $\Gamma(\beta)$ is closed.

To prove that β is lhc at p, let $V \subset X$ be any open set such that $\beta(p) \cap V \neq \emptyset$. Since $\omega(p) > \inf p \cdot X$ and X is convex,[9] there exists an $x \in \beta(p) \cap V$ such that $\omega(p) > p \cdot x$. Because $p \cdot x$ and ω are continuous in p, there exists an open neighborhood U of p such that $\omega(p') > p' \cdot x$ and hence $x \in \beta(p') \cap V$

9 See Exercise 5.21(b) for an example where lhc of β fails because X is not convex.

for all $p' \in U$. Therefore, $\beta(p') \cap V \neq \emptyset$ for all $p' \in U$, which establishes that β is lhc at p. □

For example, in the pure exchange case with $\omega(p) = p \cdot w$, a (very strong) sufficient condition guaranteeing $p \cdot w > \inf p \cdot X$ for all $p > 0$ is to require $X = \mathbf{R}_+^\mathbf{m}$ and $w \gg 0$. Clearly this condition is not very realistic, but more realistic conditions tend to be fairly complicated. The general idea is to find some condition which guarantees that each consumer has sufficient wealth so that her budget set has nonempty interior.[10]

The current attitude among general equilibrium theorists is that, because failure of continuity of the budget correspondence is not a very important issue in the "standard" (finite dimensional, convex) setting, strong sufficient conditions of this type are acceptable. But the issue can sometimes be critical — especially when consumption sets are nonconvex or the commodity space is infinite dimensional. Unfortunately, conditions ruling out discontinuity of the constraint correspondence are necessarily rather model specific.

5.4 Miscellany

Continuity, upperhemicontinuity, or lowerhemicontinuity of a correspondence — once established — is preserved under a variety of useful mathematical operations: composition, union, intersection, product, summation, and the taking of convex hulls. Some of these results depend in a rather delicate way on the topology of the space X used to define the codomain 2^X of the correspondences and on whether or not the codomain is confined to the nonempty, closed subsets of X. However, if we restrict attention to codomain $(2^X)_o^F$ with X compact (which gives us all we need in this book), then the complications disappear.

Theorem 5.52 *Let E, X, Y be topological spaces and $F_1 \colon E \to (2^X)_o^F$, $F_2 \colon X \to (2^Y)_o^F$ correspondences. Define the composition $F_2 \circ F_1$ as the correspondence*

$$F_2 \circ F_1 \colon E \to (2^Y)_o^F, \quad e \mapsto \{\, F_2(x) \mid x \in F_1(e) \,\}.$$

If F_1 and F_2 are uhc (resp. lhc, continuous), then the composition $F_2 \circ F_1$ is uhc (resp. lhc, continuous).

Proof See Klein and Thompson (1984), 87, Theorem 7.3.11. □

---

10 See, for example, the concept of indirect resource relatedness in Arrow and Hahn (1971) for a much more general condition.

Theorem 5.53 *Let E and X be topological spaces, X compact, and $F_1 \colon E \to$ $(2^X)_o^F$, $F_2 \colon E \to (2^X)_o^F$ correspondences. Define the correspondences*

$$F_1 \cup F_2 \colon E \to (2^X)_o^F, \quad e \mapsto F_1(e) \cup F_2(e)$$

and

$$F_1 \cap F_2 \colon E \to (2^X)_o^F, \quad e \mapsto F_1(e) \cap F_2(e).$$

(a) *If F_1 and F_2 are uhc (resp. lhc, continuous) at $e \in E$, then $F_1 \cup F_2$ is uhc (resp. lhc, continuous).*
(b) *If F_1 and F_2 are uhc and $F_1(e) \cap F_2(e) \neq \emptyset$, then $F_1 \cap F_2$ is uhc at e.*

Proof

(a) See Klein and Thompson (1984), 86, Theorem 7.3.8, or Kuratowski (1966), 178–179, Theorems 1 and 2.
(b) See Klein and Thompson (1984), 86, Theorem 7.3.10, or Kuratowski (1966), 180, Theorem 1.

$\square$

Remark 5.54 *As the omission suggests, lhc (and hence continuity) of the intersection of correspondences is a much more delicate issue. See Hildenbrand (1974), 35, Problem 6, Klein and Thompson (1984), 86, Theorem 7.3.10, or Kuratowski (1966), 180–181, for some results on this.*

Cartesian products cause no problems.

Theorem 5.55 *Let $\{ F_\alpha \colon E \to (2^{X_\alpha})_o^F \mid \alpha \in A \}$ be a collection of correspondences from a topological space E to compact topological spaces X_α. The correspondence $F := \prod_{\alpha \in A} F_\alpha$ from E to $\prod_{\alpha \in A} X_\alpha$ (with the product topology) defined by $F(e) := \prod_{\alpha \in A} F_\alpha(e)$ is uhc (resp. lhc, continuous) if each F_α is uhc (resp. lhc, continuous).*

Proof Klein and Thompson (1984), 87–88, Theorems 7.3.12 and 7.3.14. $\square$

Combining Theorem 5.55 with Theorem 5.52 and the fact that addition in a TVS is continuous gives an immediate proof of the following result concerning sums of correspondences (which, of course, makes sense only for correspondences into vector spaces).

Theorem 5.56 *Let $\{ F_i \colon E \to (2^{X_i})_o^F \mid i \in I \}$ be a finite collection of correspondences from a topological space E to compact subsets X_i of a TVS*

L. The correspondence $F := \sum_{i \in I} F_i$ from E to $X := \sum_{i \in I} X_i$ is uhc (resp. lhc, continuous) if each F_i is uhc (resp. lhc, continuous).

Proof Use Klein and Thompson (1984), 89, Theorem 7.3.15, and the usual induction argument.   □

The final result we want to report concerns convex hulls.

Theorem 5.57 *If $F \colon E \to (2^X)_o^F$ is a correspondence from a topological space E to a compact subset X of a finite dimensional TVS L, then the correspondence $\mathrm{co}\, F$ defined by $e \mapsto \mathrm{co}\, F(e)$ is uhc (resp. lhc, continuous) if F is uhc (resp. lhc, continuous).*

Proof See Klein and Thompson (1984), 89, Theorem 7.3.17. (Although they state their result for an arbitrary Banach space, the proof they give is not correct. Their theorem is correct if $\mathrm{co}\, F(e)$ is replaced by its closure.)   □

5.5 Summary

I trust by now you are convinced that topology is a quite remarkable tool. The main results of this chapter are readily summarized. Under fairly general conditions we can show that the best responses of consumers and firms are nonempty and compact-valued (and, if we want to strengthen the assumptions, convex-valued as well). Given nonempty best responses, the Maximum Theorem provides a powerful engine for demonstrating a type of continuity (upperhemicontinuity) of these best responses which we will need in proving existence of a Walrasian equilibrium. The rest is detail, the infrastructure needed to make sense of preferences, continuity, and the like. The fact that the various types of continuity are preserved under a wide range of operations on correspondences allows us to generalize from individual responses to the economy as a whole.

Exercises

5.1   Verify the entries in Table 5.2.
5.2   Which, if any, of the relations $>, \geq$ and $=$ on $\mathbf{R}$ and $\subset$ on 2^X is a preordering? a weak ordering?
5.3   Prove that if $\succ$ is a weak ordering on X (i.e., negatively transitive and asymmetric), then $\succ$ is irreflexive and transitive.
5.4   Prove that $\not\succ$ is a complete preordering iff $\succ$ is a weak ordering.
5.5   Prove Theorems 5.8 and 5.9.

5.6   Formulate and prove a version of Theorem 5.19 in which $\succ$ rather than $\succeq$ is taken as primitive with $\succeq$ defined by $y \succeq x$ iff $x \not\succ y$.

5.7   Verify that in Example 2 concluding Section 5.2 the implicit preferences of the firm are convex weak orderings.

5.8   For the four blood groups O, A, B, and AB consider the binary relation "is a possible donor for." O can donate to any of the other blood groups, A or B can donate to AB, and each group can donate to itself. There are no other relationships between blood groups. For the set $T = \{\, O, A, B, AB \,\}$ let $\succeq$ denote the weak relation "is a possible donor for." Define (i) $y \succ x$ iff $y \succeq x$ and $x \not\succeq y$ and (ii) $y \sim x$ iff $y \succeq x$ and $x \succeq y$.

(a) Do equivalence classes exist? Why or why not? If they do exist, what are they?

(b) Is there a set of best elements for the set $\{\, O, A, B, AB \,\}$ in the classical sense? A set of maximal elements?

(c) Is there a set of best elements for the set $\{\, A, B, AB \,\}$ in the classical sense? A set of maximal elements?

5.9   Extend the example of Section 5.3.1 to cover the following cases. In each case, I have indicated parenthetically the interpretation to be given to the modification.

(a) A feasible set K which does not contain the point x^* which maximizes the utility function over $[0, 1]$ (the constraint is binding).

(b) A utility function with a flat interval for the maximum (preferences are convex, but not strictly convex).

(c) A utility function with two maxima, say one at $x^* = .3$ and the other at $x^{**} = .6$ (preferences are nonconvex).

5.10   Come up with some variations of the preceding exercise on your own!

5.11   Prove Corollary 5.25.

5.12   Describe the open and closed ϵ-balls centered on each of the following:

(a) A disk in $\mathbf{R}^2$ with center $(0, 0)$ and radius one.

(b) A square in $\mathbf{R}^2$ with center $(2, 2)$ and sides of length one.

5.13   Compute the Hausdorff distance between two disks in $\mathbf{R}^2$ of radius one, the first centered at $(0, 0)$ and the other at $(3, 4)$.

5.14   Let $B\colon E \to (2^X)_o^F$ where E and X are topological spaces and X is compact. Within this context, the following "sequential" definitions of uhc and lhc are often employed:[11]

---

11 See Hildenbrand (1974), 24-25, 27.

(a) B is uhc at e if, given any net $e^\alpha \to e$ and given any net $x^\alpha \to x$ selected from[12] $\langle B(e^\alpha) \rangle$, it is the case that $x \in B(e)$.

(b) B is lhc at e if, given any $x \in B(e)$ and given any net $e^\alpha \to e$, there exists a net $\langle x^\alpha \rangle$ selected from $\langle B(e^\alpha) \rangle$ such that $x^\alpha \to x$.

Illustrate each of these definitions using the correspondences graphed in Figure 5.6, showing what happens both when B is uhc (*resp.* lhc) at e and when it is not.

5.15   Prove Theorem 5.42.

5.16   Prove Theorem 5.45.

5.17   Prove that if a correspondence $B \colon E \to (2^X)^F_o$ is closed for all $e \in E$, then it has closed graph.

5.18   Let $B \colon E \to (2^X)^F_o$ where E and X are topological spaces and X is compact. Prove that B is uhc iff for any net $(e^\alpha, x^\alpha) \to (e, x)$ where $(e^\alpha, x^\alpha) \in \Gamma(B)$ for all α the limit $(e, x) \in \Gamma(B)$. Show that the condition just given is equivalent to the "sequential" definition of uhc given in Exercise 5.14.

5.19   State a version of Corollary 5.50 appropriate for a constrained **minimization** problem and prove it.

5.20   For each of the examples displayed in Figure 5.10, draw typical open sets U and V and verify the assertion that the best responses are uhc in p.

5.21   Illustrate how the Maximum Theorem can fail in the following situations.

(a) The consumer's consumption set is $X = \{\, x \in \mathbf{R}^2_+ \mid x_1 + 2x_2 \geq 2 \,\}$ and endowment $w = (1, 1)$. Preferences are represented by the utility function $u(x) := \max\{\, \min\{\, x_1, 2x_2 \,\}, \min\{\, 2x_1, x_2 \,\} \,\}$.

(b) The consumer's consumption set is $X = \mathbf{R}_+ \times \{\, 0, 1 \,\}$ and endowment $w = (1, 0)$. Preferences are represented by the utility function

  (i) $u(x) = x_1 + 2x_2$;
  (ii) $u(x) = x_1 + x_2$;
  (iii) $u(x) = 2x_1 + x_2$.

(Analyze the situation for each of these preferences.)

5.22   Consider the standard textbook consumer with consumption set $X = \mathbf{R}^2_+$ and Cobb-Douglas preferences represented by the utility function $u \colon X \to \mathbf{R}$, $x \mapsto x_1^\alpha x_2^{1-\alpha}$ where $0 < \alpha < 1$. Assume that this consumer has endowment $w = (b, b) \gg 0$, and restrict prices to lie in the simplex $\Delta := \{\, p \in \mathbf{R}^2_+ \mid p_1 + p_2 = 1 \,\}$.

---

12 In other words, $x^\alpha \in B(e^\alpha)$ for all α.

Therefore, wealth equals b while demand is given by $\phi\colon \Delta \to X$, $p \mapsto \phi(p) = (\alpha b/p_1, (1-\alpha)b/p_2)$. The utility function u is clearly continuous on X and the condition $p \cdot w > \inf p \cdot X = 0$ is satisfied for all $p \in \Delta$. Since for singleton-valued correspondences upperhemicontinuity is equivalent to continuity, the Maximum Theorem leads us to expect ϕ to be continuous. Clearly it is not: as p_j approaches zero, demand for commodity j increases without bound. But continuous functions defined on compact sets (which Δ certainly is) are necessarily bounded.

What went wrong? How can the specification of this consumer be altered, while still retaining Cobb-Douglas utility, to obtain a uhc demand correspondence?

6

Clearing markets

Why bother with existence? Doubts on this score are too commonplace among economists to be dismissed out of hand. So let us face the issue squarely. What makes existence proofs unappealing? A typical reaction might be:

What is the point of reading the proof, much less trying to understand it? The fact that equilibrium exists is really quite obvious from an intuitive, economic point of view. I suppose it is good that someone has worked out the math, but I would rather be spared the gory details. Let's get on to the more interesting parts of economics!

The problem with this reaction is that it fails to realize what proving existence is all about. If validation of standard operating procedure were the major contribution of existence proofs, then most of us would probably be more than happy to learn that our models pass the test and to leave the details to specialists. But in fact the conclusion reported in an existence proof is of secondary importance. What really matters is the understanding gained in proving the result.

The fact that insight is what we are after is why we are going to prove existence in several different ways, spread over two different chapters. It also explains why we will not strive for the most general results possible. The settings I have chosen for exploring existence are complex enough to bring out the important issues, but not so complex that they obscure what is going on. This chapter focuses on two major ways of establishing existence of Walrasian equilibrium, the excess demand approach and the algorithmic, while the next deals with another approach closely linked with the theory of noncooperative games. As we will see, each produces its own distinctive insights into the nature of competitive equilibrium.

The chapter begins with a discussion of homogeneity and the normalization of prices. The second section proves existence of Walrasian equilibrium within the particularly simple context of a pure exchange economy with singleton-valued demand. Using this context as motivation, the third section develops an algorithmic approach to computing equilibria. In the fourth section, I digress to report on a remarkable result known as the Excess Demand Theorem. The chapter concludes by introducing the Kakutani Fixed Point Theorem, the main tool needed in Chapter 7.

6.1 Homogeneity

We begin by deriving some simple but important facts about demand functions. In contrast to the preceding chapter, we again employ subscripts to distinguish among consumers. Thus,

$$\beta_i(p) := \{\, x_i \in X_i \mid p \cdot x_i \leq p \cdot w_i \,\}$$

is the budget set and

$$\phi_i(p) := \{\, x_i \in X_i \mid P_i(x_i) \cap \beta_i(p) = \emptyset \,\}$$

the demand set for consumer i in an exchange economy $\mathcal{E}$.

Definition 6.1 *Let X and Y be vector spaces and C a cone contained in X. A function $f\colon C \to 2^Y$ is **positively homogeneous of degree 0 on C** if $f(\lambda x) = f(x)$ for all $\lambda > 0$ and for all $x \in C$.*

Theorem 6.2 *Let $\mathcal{E}$ be an exchange economy with commodity space L and C a cone contained in the dual space L'. The demand correspondence $\phi_i\colon C \to 2^L$ for consumer $i \in I$ is positively homogeneous of degree 0 on C.*

Proof $\beta_i\colon C \to 2^L$ is positively homogeneous of degree 0 in p since

$$
\begin{aligned}
\beta_i(\lambda p) &= \{\, x_i \in X_i \mid \lambda p \cdot x_i \leq \lambda p \cdot w_i \,\} \\
&= \{\, x_i \in X_i \mid p \cdot x_i \leq p \cdot w_i \,\} \\
&= \beta_i(p)
\end{aligned}
$$

for all $\lambda > 0$ and $p \in C$. Therefore,

$$
\begin{aligned}
\phi_i(\lambda p) &= \{\, x_i \in X_i \mid P_i(x_i) \cap \beta_i(\lambda p) = \emptyset \,\} \\
&= \{\, x_i \in X_i \mid P_i(x_i) \cap \beta_i(p) = \emptyset \,\} \\
&= \phi_i(p).
\end{aligned}
$$

$\square$

Corollary 6.3 *Under the conditions described in the preceding theorem, the excess demand correspondence $\Delta_w \phi_i$ for consumer $i \in I$ is also positively homogeneous of degree 0 on C.*

Proof Exercise 6.2. □

We go from individual demand functions to market demand functions by summing over consumers.

Definition 6.4 *Let $\mathcal{E}$ be an exchange economy with a finite set of consumers I and a finite dimensional commodity space L. Given a domain $C \subset L'$, the* **market demand correspondence** *and the* **market excess demand correspondence** *are defined by setting $\Phi(p) := \sum_{i \in I} \phi_i(p)$ and $\Delta_w \Phi(p) := \sum_{i \in I} \Delta_w \phi_i(p)$ respectively for each $p \in C$.*

Theorem 6.5 *Let $\mathcal{E}$ be an exchange economy with a finite set of consumers and a finite dimensional commodity space L, and let $C \subset L'$ be a cone. The market demand correspondence Φ and the market excess demand correspondence $\Delta_w \Phi$ are positively homogeneous of degree 0 on C.*

Proof Exercise 6.3. □

One of the important consequences of homogeneity in prices is that Walrasian equilibrium prices are not uniquely determined: only relative prices matter.

Theorem 6.6 *If $p \in \mathrm{WE}^p(\mathcal{E})$ for an exchange economy $\mathcal{E}$, then $\lambda p \in \mathrm{WE}^p(\mathcal{E})$ for all $\lambda > 0$.*

Proof By definition, $(x, p) \in \mathrm{WE}(\mathcal{E})$ iff $x \in \mathrm{F}(\mathcal{E}, I)$ and $x_i \in \phi_i(p)$ for all $i \in I$. But then $x_i \in \phi_i(\lambda p)$ for all $\lambda > 0$ by Theorem 6.2. □

Thus, the set of Walrasian equilibrium prices in an exchange economy is a cone. If p is an equilibrium price, then so is any price vector on the open halfline running through p: $\{\, p' \in L' \mid p' = \lambda p, \ \lambda > 0 \,\}$. For that reason, it is often convenient to **normalize** prices by choosing a single price vector to represent each such halfline. Provided that prices are nonnegative, the three **normalization rules** most often employed are the following:

- choosing a **numéraire** (say the first commodity), $p_1 = 1$,
- restricting prices to the **unit simplex**, $\{\, p \in \mathbf{R}_+^{\mathbf{m}} \mid \sum_{j \in J} p_j = 1 \,\}$, and
- restricting prices to the **unit sphere**, $\{\, p \in \mathbf{R}_+^{\mathbf{m}} \mid \sum_{j \in J} p_j^2 = 1 \,\}$,

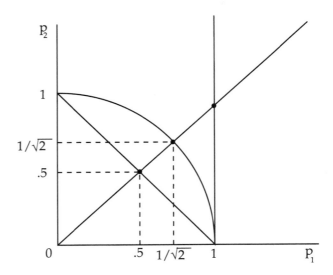

Fig. 6.1. Normalization rules.

where $J := \{1, \ldots, m\}$ indexes the set of commodities.

Figure 6.1 applies these normalization rules to the halfline

$$\{p \in \mathbf{R}^2 \mid p = \lambda(2,2), \ \lambda > 0\},$$

resulting in the normalized price vector $(1,1)$ when the first commodity serves as *numéraire*; $(.5, .5)$ in the unit simplex; and $(1/\sqrt{2}, 1/\sqrt{2})$ in the unit sphere.

Each normalization has its advantages and disadvantages. Choosing a *numéraire* is simple, but this method fails if the equilibrium price of the *numéraire* commodity is zero. The unit simplex is convex (a convenience when using fixed point theorems) and allows for zero prices, but it is inappropriate if we want to allow some prices to be negative. Finally, the unit sphere, favored in approaches emphasizing the use of calculus, is not convex. In this book, we almost always normalize prices by using the simplex.

Homogeneity also has another important implication, known as Walras' Law.

Theorem 6.7 (Weak Form of Walras' Law) *In an exchange economy $\mathcal{E}$ with finite dimensional commodity space L, $p \cdot \Delta_w \Phi(p) \leq 0$ for every price functional $p \in L'$.*

Proof If $z \in \Delta_w \Phi(p)$, then $z = \sum_{i \in I} \Delta_w y_i$ with $\Delta_w y_i \in \Delta_w \phi_i(p)$ for all $i \in I$. But $\Delta_w y_i \in \Delta_w \phi_i(p)$ implies $p \cdot \Delta_w y_i \leq 0$ by definition of the demand set, so $p \cdot z = p \cdot \sum_{i \in I} \Delta_w y_i = \sum_{i \in I} p \cdot \Delta_w y_i \leq 0$. $\qquad \square$

It is worth emphasizing that this result holds for *any* price functional p, not just for equilibrium price functionals. The reasoning is very simple. Because no consumer can spend more than the amount of her wealth on consumption, the total value of expenditures on consumption must be less than or equal to the total value of initial endowments.

If consumers spend all of their wealth on consumption, then the inequality in Theorem 6.7 becomes an equality. Consumers will spend all of their wealth on consumption provided that they are not satiated — crudely speaking, if their indifference sets are not thick. We capture this property in the following way:

Definition 6.8 *A strict preference relation $\succ_i$ on X_i is **locally nonsatiated (lns)** at x_i if $x_i \in \operatorname{cl} P_i(x_i)$. If $\succ_i$ is lns at x_i for all $x_i \in X_i$, then the preference relation $\succ_i$ (or the consumer i) is simply said to be lns.*

Theorem 6.9 (Strong Form of Walras' Law) *Let $\mathcal{E}$ be an exchange economy with finite dimensional commodity space L. If every consumer in $\mathcal{E}$ is locally nonsatiated, then $p \cdot \Delta_w \Phi(p) = 0$ for every price functional $p \in L'$.*

Proof In proving the weak form of Walras' Law, we argued that $z \in \Delta_w \Phi(p)$ implies $z = \sum_{i \in I} \Delta_w y_i$ where $\Delta_w y_i \in \Delta_w \phi_i(p)$ and $p \cdot \Delta_w y_i \leq 0$ for all $i \in I$. But if consumer i is locally nonsatiated and $p \cdot \Delta_w y_i < 0$, there must exist a net trade $\Delta_w y_i' \in \Delta_w X_i$ such that $\Delta_w y_i' \in \Delta_w P_i(z_i)$ and $p \cdot \Delta_w y_i' \leq 0$. This would imply that $\Delta_w y_i' \in \Delta_w P_i(y_i) \cap \Delta_w \beta_i(p)$, contradicting the assumption that $\Delta_w y_i \in \Delta_w \phi_i(p)$. We conclude that $p \cdot \Delta_w y_i = 0$ for all $i \in I$ and therefore that $p \cdot z = p \cdot \sum_{i \in I} \Delta_w y_i = \sum_{i \in I} p \cdot \Delta_w y_i = 0$. $\qquad \square$

6.2 Existence of Walrasian equilibrium

Our goal in this section is to prove existence of Walrasian equilibrium under the simplifying assumption that consumer demand functions are singleton-valued. We will discuss two different but closely related approaches, one based on Brouwer's Fixed Point Theorem and the other on the KKM Theorem.

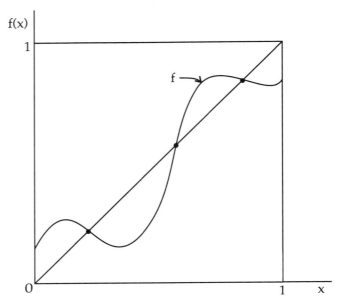

Fig. 6.2. The Brouwer Theorem.

6.2.1 The Brouwer Fixed Point Theorem

We begin with the definition of a fixed point.

Definition 6.10 *If f is a function which maps a set K into itself, then a point $x \in K$ is a* **fixed point** *of f if $f(x) = x$.*

Fixed point theorems are, naturally enough, theorems which guarantee the existence of a fixed point. Perhaps the best known version is due to Brouwer.

Theorem 6.11 (Brouwer) *If $f: K \to K$ is a continuous function from a nonempty, compact, convex subset K of a finite dimensional TVS into itself, then f has a fixed point.*

Deferring a proof of the Brouwer Theorem until later, we will be content for now to demonstrate a special case. If we let $K = [0,1] \subset \mathbf{R}$, then, as suggested in Figure 6.2, the Brouwer Theorem advances the claim — obvious in this context — that there is no way to draw a continuous curve (the graph of f) from the left hand edge of the box to the right which fails to cross the 45° line. But any point where f meets that line is, by definition, a fixed point!

Suppose now that we want to use the Brouwer Theorem to establish existence of a solution to a system of equations: i.e., a vector x^* such that

$$f(x^*) = 0 \quad \text{where} \quad f \colon \mathbf{R^n} \to \mathbf{R^n}. \tag{$*$}$$

At first glance it is far from apparent how the solution to a problem such as $(*)$ involves fixed points. However, if we define another function $\psi \colon \mathbf{R^n} \to \mathbf{R^n}$ which maps $x \mapsto x + f(x)$, then

$$\psi(x^*) = x^* \quad \text{iff} \quad x^* = x^* + f(x^*) \quad \text{iff} \quad f(x^*) = 0.$$

We conclude that problem $(*)$ has a solution x^* if and only if x^* is a fixed point of the function ψ.

We still face a major difficulty. The Brouwer Theorem does not apply directly to this problem because $\mathbf{R^n}$ is not compact. However, if f is restricted to a nonempty, compact, convex subset of $\mathbf{R^n}$ (and if f is a continuous map from K into itself), then the Brouwer Theorem can be used. To see more clearly what is involved, we turn now to the problem of establishing existence of a Walrasian equilibrium in an exchange economy.

Consider an exchange economy with a market excess demand function $\Delta_w \Phi$ which is singleton-valued, continuous, and satisfies the strong form of Walras' Law. We adopt the normalization which restricts price vectors to the unit simplex $\Delta := \{\, p \in \mathbf{R_+^m} \mid \sum_{j \in J} p_j = 1 \,\}$, a set which is nonempty, compact, and convex. If, following the strategy outlined above, we define $\psi(p) := p + \Delta_w \Phi(p)$, then $\Delta_w \Phi(p^*) = 0$ iff $\psi(p^*) = p^*$. The function ψ does not satisfy the requirements of the Brouwer Theorem because the image $\psi(p)$ need not lie in the unit simplex. Note that the function ψ maps $p \mapsto (p_1 + \Delta_w \Phi_1(p), \ldots, p_m + \Delta_w \Phi_m(p))$. If we replace each component $\Delta_w \Phi_j(p)$ by $\max(0, \Delta_w \Phi_j(p))$, then the image will have nonnegative components though they need not sum to one. The natural way to force this image back into the simplex is to divide by the sum of the components. Thus, if we replace ψ by a function $\Psi \colon \Delta \to \Delta$ such that

$$\Psi_j(p) = \frac{p_j + \max(0, \Delta_w \Phi_j(p))}{c(p)} \quad \text{for each} \quad j \in J$$

where

$$c(p) := \sum_{j \in J} (p_j + \max(0, \Delta_w \Phi_j(p))) = 1 + \sum_{j \in J} \max(0, \Delta_w \Phi_j(p)),$$

then, provided that Ψ is continuous, we have a function to which the Brouwer Theorem applies. Because each of the functions $\Delta_w \Phi_j(p)$ is continuous, Ψ will be continuous provided that the denominator $c(p)$ does not vanish. This is the case since clearly $c(p) \geq 1$.

Theorem 6.12 *Assume that the market excess demand function $\Delta_w \Phi$ of an exchange economy is singleton-valued, continuous, and satisfies the strong form of Walras' Law. There exists a price vector $p^* \in \Delta$ such that (a) $\Delta_w \Phi(p^*) \leq 0$ and (b) $\Delta_w \Phi_j(p^*) = 0$ whenever $p_j^* > 0$.*

Proof By the Brouwer Theorem, Ψ has a fixed point p^* such that

$$p_j^* = \Psi_j(p^*) = \frac{p_j^* + \max(0, \Delta_w \Phi_j(p^*))}{c(p^*)} \quad \text{for all} \quad j \in J. \tag{$\dagger$}$$

We know that $c(p^*) \geq 1$, and we want to show that in fact $c(p^*) = 1$. Rewriting equation ($\dagger$), we obtain $(c(p^*) - 1)p_j^* = \max(0, \Delta_w \Phi_j(p^*))$ for all $j \in J$. Consequently, if we suppose that $c(p^*) - 1 > 0$, then $\Delta_w \Phi_j(p^*) > 0$ for all j such that $p_j^* > 0$. But, since at least one $p_j^* > 0$ (why?), this in turn implies that $p^* \cdot \Delta_w \Phi(p^*) > 0$, contradicting Walras' Law. We conclude that $c(p^*) = 1$. Therefore, our fixed point condition ($\dagger$) simplifies to $p_j^* = p_j^* + \max(0, \Delta_w \Phi_j(p^*))$ for all $j \in J$ which implies that $\Delta_w \Phi_j(p^*) \leq 0$ for all $j \in J$ or, when expressed as a vector inequality,

$$\Delta_w \Phi(p^*) \leq 0, \tag{$*$}$$

which is part (a). The strong form of Walras' Law imposes the restriction

$$p^* \cdot \Delta_w \Phi(p^*) = \sum_{j \in J} p_j^* \Delta_w \Phi_j(p^*) = 0. \tag{$**$}$$

Using ($*$) and the fact that $p_j^* \geq 0$, we conclude that *each term* in the sum ($**$) is equal to zero. Thus, we conclude that $\Delta_w \Phi_j(p^*) = 0$ whenever $p_j^* > 0$. $\qquad\square$

6.2.2 Free disposal

While we have just proved that an equilibrium exists, it is not the sort of equilibrium which we originally had in mind. Recall that we require of a Walrasian equilibrium that

$$\sum_{i \in I} x_{ij}^* = \sum_{i \in I} w_{ij}$$

for all commodities $j \in J$. If $p_j^* > 0$ for all $j \in J$, then the equilibrium whose existence we have just established does meet this requirement, but our result leaves open the possibility that

$$\sum_{i \in I} x_{ij}^* < \sum_{i \in I} w_{ij}$$

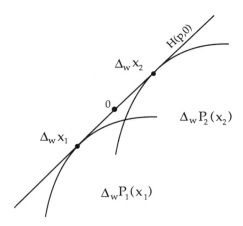

Fig. 6.3. Equilibrium with a "bad."

in markets where the equilibrium price p_j^* equals zero. From an economist's perspective, this makes sense. Because $p_j^* = 0$ means that the jth commodity is worthless, it is no surprise that demand falls short of the amount available.

Why did our use of the Brouwer Theorem lead to this result? Recall that we began with the fact that $\Delta_w\Phi(p^*) = 0$ iff $\psi(p^*) = p^*$ where $\psi(p) = p + \Delta_w\Phi(p)$. But to use the Brouwer Theorem, we were forced to modify the definition of ψ to guarantee a mapping from the price simplex back into itself, and it is this modification which produced a result different from what we expected.

To gain a little more insight into why this comes about, consider an economy with two consumers and two commodities where commodity 1 is a "good" and commodity 2 a "bad." You worked through an example of such an economy in Exercise 1.16, finding an equilibrium price vector $p^* = (1, -1)$ and an equilibrium allocation

$$\Delta_w x_i^* = \begin{cases} (-1.5, -1.5) & \text{for consumer 1;} \\ (1.5, 1.5) & \text{for consumer 2.} \end{cases}$$

The true equilibrium for this economy is portrayed in the net trade diagram of Figure 6.3. Notice that the price of the second commodity is negative, so that p^* does not lie in the simplex. Furthermore, the prices sum to zero, not one!

What happens when, as in Theorem 6.12, we force equilibrium prices to lie in the unit simplex? The resulting **free disposal equilibrium**, as it is called in the literature, puts $p_1 = 1$ (as expensive as the "good" can be) and $p_2 = 0$ (as cheap as the "bad" can be). Each consumer consumes his initial endowment of the first commodity and "throws away" his endowment of the second. The only way for this to make economic sense, of course, is if such disposal is free.

In a world increasingly concerned with problems of pollution and waste disposal, this cavalier treatment is unwarranted. Why have we found ourselves in this difficulty? The problem is not that the Brouwer Theorem is restricted to the unit simplex. Any set homeomorphic to the unit simplex will do as well.

Theorem 6.13 (Modified Brouwer) *Let K be a set homeomorphic to a nonempty, compact, convex subset of a finite dimensional TVS. If $f: K \to K$ is continuous, then f has a fixed point.*

Proof Denote the nonempty, compact, convex set referenced in the theorem by Δ (in fact, without loss of generality we can assume this set to be a simplex). Let $h: \Delta \to K$ be a homeomorphism, and define the composite map $g: \Delta \to \Delta$ by $g = h^{-1} \circ f \circ h$. The function g is continuous, because it is the composition of continuous functions. Therefore, according to Theorem 6.11, it has a fixed point: i.e., a point $x^* \in \Delta$ such that $g(x^*) = x^*$. Substituting in the definition of g gives $h^{-1}(f(h(x^*)) = x^*$ or, equivalently, $f(h(x^*)) = h(x^*)$. We conclude that $h(x^*)$ is a fixed point of f.   □

Of course, this restatement of the Brouwer Theorem leaves open the question of which sets are homeomorphic to a nonempty, compact, convex set, a rather complicated issue. As suggested in the course of proving Theorem 6.13, any nonempty, compact, convex subset of a finite dimensional TVS is homeomorphic to a simplex. However, convexity is not required. For example, the alternative set for normalizing prices suggested earlier, the unit sphere restricted to the positive orthant $\{ p \in \mathbf{R}^{\mathbf{m}}_+ \mid \sum_{j \in J} p_j^2 = 1 \}$, is also homeomorphic to the $m - 1$ dimensional unit simplex.[1]

At this point, you should be wondering why we do not simply use the *entire* unit sphere, $\{ p \in \mathbf{R}^{\mathbf{m}} \mid \sum_{j \in J} p_j^2 = 1 \}$, rather than restricting ourselves to the portion of the sphere contained in the positive orthant. If we did take the entire sphere, then the equilibrium price vector for the economy portrayed in Figure 6.3 would be represented by the point $(1/\sqrt{2}, -1/\sqrt{2})$. However, the unit sphere is *not* homeomorphic to a simplex and, as a consequence,

---

1 Crudely speaking, you can continuously deform this part of a sphere into a simplex by flattening it out and then pulling the flattened object into the shape of a "triangle."

the Brouwer Theorem is not applicable. In fact, it is quite possible to have continuous functions mapping the unit sphere to itself which have no fixed point. Consider, for example, the unit sphere S in two dimensions, which is just a circle of radius one with center at the origin. The function $f \colon S \to S$ which maps each point $x \in S$ to the point $-x$ opposite is clearly continuous and, just as clearly, has no fixed point.

While allowing for "bads" does, therefore, raise difficulties, in practice there is no problem. We can certainly agree to rule out the possibility that *every* commodity is bad. If we delete the set

$$\mathbf{R^m_{--}} := \{\, p \in \mathbf{R^m} \mid p_j < 0 \; \forall j \in J \,\}$$

from the unit sphere, under the plausible hypothesis that not all prices will be negative, we obtain the set $\{\, p \in \mathbf{R^m} \backslash \mathbf{R^m_{--}} \mid \sum_{j \in J} p_j^2 = 1 \,\}$, which is homeomorphic to the unit simplex in $\mathbf{R^m}$ and hence a proper subject for the modified form of the Brouwer Theorem.

With this rather complicated digression behind us, we can return to the conveniently simple assumption that prices are restricted to the unit simplex with the understanding that — if the occasion arises where we want to model bads — the results can be easily adapted to the modified price set described above.

6.2.3 Simplices

In preparation for looking at this existence question from another perspective, we need to take a closer look at the price simplex. With a view toward other applications later in the chapter, our discussion of simplices will be more general than seems appropriate at first glance.

We begin by recalling our discussion of linear, affine, and convex combinations in Chapter 2.

Definition 6.14 *Given a pair of vectors* v^1, v^2 *in a vector space* L, *the combination* $\alpha_1 v^1 + \alpha_2 v^2$ *with* $\alpha_1, \alpha_2 \in \mathbf{R}$ *is called*

- *a* **linear combination** *if no further restrictions are placed on the scalars* α_i;
- *an* **affine combination** *if we also require* $\alpha_1 + \alpha_2 = 1$; *and*
- *a* **convex combination** *if we add the requirement that the* α_i's *be nonnegative.*

This definition generalizes in the obvious way to combinations of any finite number of vectors $\{\, v^1, \ldots, v^n \,\}$ in L (or, equivalently, to any collection of vectors provided that only a finite number of the scalars α_i are nonzero). In particular, $\sum_{i=1}^{n} \alpha_i v^i$ is an affine combination of the vectors $\{\, v^i \in L \mid i = 1, \ldots, n \,\}$ provided that $\sum_{i=1}^{n} \alpha_i = 1$.

Many of the concepts involving linear combinations introduced in Chapter 2 have direct analogs for affine combinations. In particular:

Definition 6.15 *A subset $V = \{\, v^1, \ldots, v^n \,\}$ of a vector space is* **affinely independent** *if $v^i \notin \mathrm{aff}(V \setminus \{v^i\})$ for all $v^i \in V$.*

In words, the set V is affinely independent if no member of V can be expressed as an affine combination of the remaining members of V.

Definition 6.16 *A subset S of a vector space is an* **affine subspace** *if it includes all possible affine combinations of the elements in S: i.e., $S = \mathrm{aff}\, S$.*

Affine subspaces are not linear subspaces unless they include the zero vector, but they are translations of linear subspaces:

Theorem 6.17 *If S is an affine subspace of a vector space L, then there exists a vector x and a linear subspace M such that $S = x + M$. Furthermore, the linear subspace M is uniquely determined independent of the choice of the vector x.*

Proof See Rockafellar (1970), Theorem 1.2.   □

This in turn gives us a natural way to define the dimension of an affine subspace:

Definition 6.18 *The* **dimension** *of an affine subspace is the dimension of the (uniquely determined) linear subspace which is its translate.*

With these preliminaries out of the way, we are finally able to give a proper definition of a simplex.

Definition 6.19 *If $V = \{\, v^1, \ldots, v^n \,\}$ is an affinely independent subset of a vector space, then $\mathrm{co}\, V$ is called an ($n - 1$* **dimensional**) **simplex**. *The vectors v^i are called the* **vertices** *of the simplex.*

Definition 6.20 *If $V = \{\, e^1, \ldots, e^n \,\}$, where e^i is the ith unit vector of $\mathbf{R}^{\mathbf{n}}$, then $\Delta := \mathrm{co}\, V$ is called the* **unit simplex**.

As a direct consequence of our assumption that the vertices of a simplex are affinely independent, each simplex has a natural coordinate system associated with it.

Theorem 6.21 *If $S = \text{co}\, V$ is a simplex with vertices $V = \{\, v^1, \ldots, v^n \,\}$, then any point $x \in S$ can be uniquely expressed as a convex combination of the vertices: i.e., $x = \sum_{i=1}^n \alpha_i v^i$ where $\sum_{i=1}^n \alpha_i = 1$ and $\alpha_i \geq 0$ for $i = 1, \ldots, n$.*

Proof Suppose that $x = \sum_{i=1}^n \alpha_i v^i = \sum_{i=1}^n \alpha_i' v^i$ and $\alpha_i \neq \alpha_i'$ for some i, say $\alpha_n \neq \alpha_n'$. Since $\sum_{i=1}^n (\alpha_i - \alpha_i') v^i = 0$, we conclude that

$$v^n = \sum_{i=1}^{n-1} \left(\frac{\alpha_i - \alpha_i'}{\alpha_n' - \alpha_n} \right) v^i$$

which contradicts the assumption that the set V is affinely independent. $\square$

Definition 6.22 *The coefficients α_i appearing in the preceding theorem are called the* **barycentric coordinates** *of x.*

To gain some familiarity with barycentric coordinates, consider the two-dimensional simplex in $\mathbf{R}^2$ with vertices $V = \{\, (2,2), (2,3), (1,2) \,\}$. Examining a few typical points in the simplex $\text{co}\, V$ should convince you that each can be expressed in one and only one way as an affine combination of the vertices. If we add the point $(1,1)$, then the resulting set $V' = \{\, (2,2), (2,3), (1,2), (1,1) \,\}$ is not affinely independent and so $\text{co}\, V'$ is not a simplex. Experimenting with a few points in $\text{co}\, V'$ should convince you that typically each can be expressed *in more than one way* as affine combinations of the elements of V'.

Figure 6.4(a) portrays the 2-dimensional unit simplex in $\mathbf{R}^3$ generated by the vertices $V = \{\, e^1, e^2, e^3 \,\}$. Since the simplex itself is only two dimensional, ordinarily we display it in two rather than three dimensions as shown in Figure 6.4(b).

When the unit simplex is regarded as a set of normalized prices, barycentric coordinates have a simple and familiar interpretation. Recall that the $m - 1$ dimensional unit simplex is given by

$$\Delta = \left\{ x \in \mathbf{R^m} \mid x = \sum_{j \in J} \alpha_j e^j, \ \alpha_j \geq 0, \ \sum_{j \in J} \alpha_j = 1 \right\}$$

a: In three dimensions.

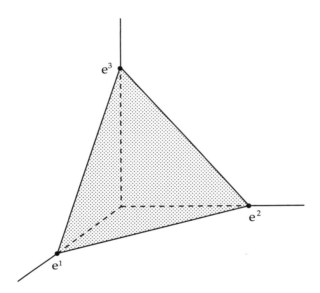

b: In two dimensions.

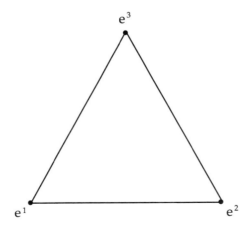

Fig. 6.4. The 2D unit simplex.

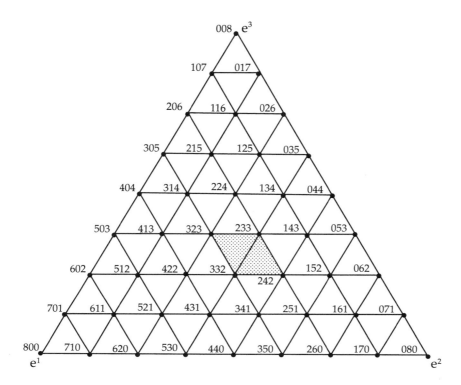

Fig. 6.5. Barycentric coordinates for Δ.

where $J = \{1, \ldots, m\}$. Replacing x by p and α_j by p_j, we obtain

$$\Delta = \left\{p \in \mathbf{R}^{\mathbf{m}} \mid p = \sum_{j \in J} p_j e^j, \ p_j \geq 0, \ \sum_{j \in J} p_j = 1\right\}$$

$$= \left\{p \in \mathbf{R}^{\mathbf{m}}_+ \mid \sum_{j \in J} p_j = 1\right\}$$

so that the barycentric coordinate p_j is nothing but the normalized price of the jth commodity.

Figure 6.5 displays the barycentric coordinate system for fractional prices measured in eighths: i.e., we let $p = (\pi_1/8, \pi_2/8, \pi_3/8)$. The figure shows all of the points in the simplex for which the π_j's are nonnegative integers summing to 8. To ease the notational burden, only the numerators of the fractions are shown in the picture. The vertices e^1, e^2, and e^3 correspond to the corner points $(8, 0, 0)$, $(0, 8, 0)$, and $(0, 0, 8)$ respectively. Once you become used to this coordinate system, it becomes second nature. Moving

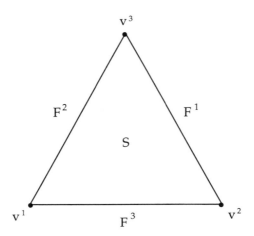

Fig. 6.6. Faces and facets.

away from the vertex e^j corresponds to a fall in the price of the jth commodity. For example, as the price of the first commodity falls, we move away from the corner $(8, 0, 0)$ until, when the price reaches zero, we reach the face of the simplex opposite e^1.

The concept "face" alluded to in the preceding paragraph can be defined in a way which applies to simplices of arbitrary dimension.

Definition 6.23 *Let V be an affinely independent set of vectors in a vector space L and $S := \mathrm{co}\, V$ the corresponding simplex. If $V' \subset V$, then the simplex $\mathrm{co}\, V'$ is called a **face** of S. A face obtained by deleting only a single vertex, $F^j := \mathrm{co}(V \backslash \{v^j\})$ where $v^j \in V$, is called the **facet of S opposite** v^j.*

Figure 6.6 illustrates the basic idea for a two-dimensional simplex S: the vertices $\{v^1, v^2, v^3\}$ are the one-dimensional faces of S; the simplices $\{F^1, F^2, F^3\}$ are the two-dimensional facets of S; and the simplex S itself is the sole three-dimensional face of S.

6.2.4 The KKM Theorem

To soften what otherwise would be a rather abstract presentation of the KKM Theorem, we first develop a simple example of equilibrium in an exchange economy.

Table 6.1. *Data for the economy.*

Type	μ_t	a_{t1}	a_{t2}	a_{t3}	$p \cdot w_t$
1	μ_1	α	$(1-\alpha)/2$	$(1-\alpha)/2$	b
2	μ_2	$(1-\alpha)/2$	α	$(1-\alpha)/2$	b
3	μ_3	$(1-\alpha)/2$	$(1-\alpha)/2$	α	b

Assume that there are three types of consumers in the economy, and a total of n consumers. Let n_t denote the number of consumers of type t ($t = 1, 2, 3$), and $\mu_t := n_t/n$ the fraction of consumers of type t.[2] Each consumer of type t has Cobb-Douglas utility $u_t(x_t) = x_{t1}^{a_{t1}} x_{t2}^{a_{t2}} x_{t3}^{a_{t3}}$ and endowment $w_t = (b, b, b)$ where x_{tj} denotes the quantity of the jth commodity consumed by each consumer of type t and b is a positive constant (assumed the same for consumers regardless of type). Because we restrict prices to lie in the unit simplex, all consumers have the same wealth $p \cdot w_t = \sum_{j=1}^{3} p_j w_{tj} = b$.

The fundamental data for this economy are summarized in Table 6.1. The taste parameters have been chosen symmetrically to simplify calculations while retaining a fair amount of flexibility in the equilibrium prices which result.

Computing the market demand for the jth commodity, we obtain

$$\Phi_j(p) = \sum_{t=1}^{3} \frac{a_{tj} \, p \cdot w_t}{p_j} n_t.$$

The total endowment of commodity j is nb. Therefore, excess demand per capita is given by

$$\frac{\Delta_w \Phi_j(p)}{n} = \sum_{t=1}^{3} \frac{a_{tj} b}{p_j} \mu_t - b.$$

Substituting the data for the economy, we obtain

$$\frac{\Delta_w \Phi_1(p)}{n} = \frac{b}{p_1} [\alpha\mu_1 + (1/2)(1-\alpha)\mu_2 + (1/2)(1-\alpha)\mu_3] - b$$

$$\frac{\Delta_w \Phi_2(p)}{n} = \frac{b}{p_2} [(1/2)(1-\alpha)\mu_1 + \alpha\mu_2 + (1/2)(1-\alpha)\mu_3] - b$$

$$\frac{\Delta_w \Phi_3(p)}{n} = \frac{b}{p_3} [(1/2)(1-\alpha)\mu_1 + (1/2)(1-\alpha)\mu_2 + \alpha\mu_3] - b.$$

2 If you wish, you may regard this as a continuum of consumers model with the measure of the set of agents of type t equal to μ_t.

Our goal is to find an equilibrium price vector p^* such that

$$\frac{\Delta_w \Phi_j(p^*)}{n} \leq 0 \quad \text{for} \quad j = 1, 2, 3.$$

Because preferences are clearly nonsatiated, these inequalities will hold with equality. Clearing the market for the first commodity and using the fact that the fractions μ_t sum to one yields

$$
\begin{aligned}
p_1^* &= \alpha\mu_1 + (1/2)(1-\alpha)(\mu_2 + \mu_3) \\
&= \alpha\mu_1 + (1/2)(1-\alpha)(1-\mu_1) \\
&= \frac{1-\alpha}{2} + \left[\frac{3\alpha-1}{2}\right]\mu_1
\end{aligned}
$$

so that, by symmetry, the equilibrium price vector is given by

$$
\begin{aligned}
p_1^* &= \frac{1-\alpha}{2} + \left[\frac{3\alpha-1}{2}\right]\mu_1 \\
p_2^* &= \frac{1-\alpha}{2} + \left[\frac{3\alpha-1}{2}\right]\mu_2 \\
p_3^* &= \frac{1-\alpha}{2} + \left[\frac{3\alpha-1}{2}\right]\mu_3.
\end{aligned}
$$

As a simple check whether this solution makes sense, note that $\mu_j = 1/3$ for $j = 1, 2, 3$ implies $p_j^* = 1/3$ for $j = 1, 2, 3$, which is clearly correct.

We now want to reexamine the mapping we used when we applied the Brouwer Theorem to prove existence of Walrasian equilibrium for an exchange economy:

$$\Psi_j(p) = \frac{p_j + \max(0, \Delta_w \Phi_j(p))}{c(p)} \quad (j \in J := \{1, \ldots, m\}). \qquad (*)$$

To interpret the expression $\max(0, \Delta_w \Phi_j(p))$ define the set

$$M_j := \{p \in \Delta \mid \Delta_w \Phi_j(p) \leq 0\}.$$

Recall that if p^* is a fixed point of Ψ, then $c(p^*) = 1$. Therefore, $p^* = \Psi(p^*)$ implies that $p_j^* \in M_j$ for all $j \in J$. Conversely, if $p_j^* \in M_j$ for all $j \in J$, then $c(p^*) = 1$ and $(*)$ maps $p_j^* \mapsto p_j^*$ for all $j \in J$; i.e., p^* is a fixed point of Ψ. Thus, we conclude that $\Psi(p^*) = p^*$ iff $\Delta_w \Phi(p^*) \leq 0$ iff $p^* \in \bigcap_{j \in J} M_j$.

To make this relationship more concrete, consider the simple economy described above with equal numbers of consumers of each type: $\mu_1 = \mu_2 = \mu_3 = 1/3$. The per capita excess demand for the jth commodity is then

$$\frac{\Delta_w \Phi_j(p)}{n} = \frac{b}{3p_j}\left[\alpha + \frac{1}{2}(1-\alpha) + \frac{1}{2}(1-\alpha)\right] - b = \frac{b}{3p_j} - b.$$

Consequently,

$$
\begin{aligned}
M_j &= \{\, p \in \Delta \mid \Delta_w \Phi_j(p) \le 0 \,\} = \{\, p \in \Delta \mid (b/3p_j) - b \le 0 \,\} \\
&= \{\, p \in \Delta \mid p_j \ge 1/3 \,\},
\end{aligned}
$$

and we conclude that $\mathrm{WE}^p(\mathcal{E}) = \{p^*\} = \bigcap_{j \in J} M_j = \{\,(1/3, 1/3, 1/3)\,\}$.

As we will see, this characterization of the set of equilibrium prices holds quite generally. The KKM[3] Theorem, known to be equivalent to the Brouwer Fixed Point Theorem, provides conditions guaranteeing that this equilibrium price set is nonempty.

Theorem 6.24 (KKM) *Suppose that $\{\, M_j \mid j = 1, \ldots, n \,\}$ is a covering of a simplex $S = \mathrm{co}\{\, v^1, \ldots, v^n \,\}$ by closed sets M_j satisfying the property*

$$
\mathrm{co}\{\, v^j \mid j \in T \,\} \subset \bigcup_{j \in T} M_j \quad \text{for all} \quad \emptyset \ne T \subset \{\, 1, \ldots, n \,\}.
$$

Then $\bigcap_{j=1}^n M_j \ne \emptyset$.

As with the Brouwer Theorem, we defer a proof of the KKM Theorem until later in this chapter. What we want to do now is to show how it can be used to provide an alternative proof of the existence of free disposal equilibrium for an exchange economy. All that is necessary is to verify that the sets M_j appropriate to this context satisfy the requirements of the KKM Theorem.

Theorem 6.25 *Assume that the market excess demand function $\Delta_w \Phi$ of an exchange economy is singleton-valued, continuous, and satisfies the strong form of Walras' Law. Then there exists a price vector $p^* \in \Delta$ such that (a) $\Delta_w \Phi(p^*) \le 0$ and (b) $\Delta_w \Phi_j(p^*) = 0$ whenever $p_j^* > 0$.*

Proof Because the excess demand function is continuous, we conclude immediately that each set

$$
M_j = \{\, p \in \Delta \mid \Delta_w \Phi_j(p) \le 0 \,\} = (\Delta_w \Phi_j)^{-1}(-\infty, 0]
$$

is closed as the inverse image of the closed set $(-\infty, 0]$. All that remains is to verify the other requirement of the KKM Theorem:

$$
\mathrm{co}\{\, e^j \mid j \in T \,\} \subset \bigcup_{j \in T} M_j \quad \text{for all} \quad \emptyset \ne T \subset J.
$$

---

3 A standard acronym for the authors of this theorem: Knaster, Kuratowski, and Mazurkiewitz.

If $T = \{j\}$, then $\mathrm{co}\{e^j\} = \{e^j\} \in M_j$ because $p = e^j$ implies

$$\sum_{k \in J} p_k \Delta_w \Phi_k(p) = \Delta_w \Phi_j(p) = 0$$

by Walras' Law, and $\Delta_w \Phi_j(p) = 0$ implies $p \in M_j$ by the definition of M_j. In the general case, if $p = \sum_{j \in T} p_j e^j$ and $p \notin \bigcup_{j \in T} M_j$, then $\Delta_w \Phi_j(p) > 0$ for all $j \in T$ by the definition of M_j. But this would imply $\sum_{j \in J} p_j \Delta_w \Phi_j(p) > 0$ since all of the remaining terms in the sum are zero, contradicting Walras' Law.

The remainder of the proof is identical to that of Theorem 6.12. □

Notice that, in particular, $\Delta := \mathrm{co}\{e^1, \ldots, e^m\} \subset \bigcup_{j \in J} M_j$ so that the M_j cover the price simplex.

6.3 Computation of equilibria

Although the proofs given above guarantee the existence of Walrasian equilibria, they give no clue how one might go about finding a particular equilibrium. This section surveys some aspects of the remarkable circle of ideas associated with the "Scarf algorithm" for computing approximate fixed points. I rely heavily on the remarkably lucid expository article by Scarf (1982), which should be read in conjunction with this section.

6.3.1 Simplicial subdivisions and Sperner's Lemma

One way to find an approximate equilibrium using a computer is to select a suitably large number, say $D = 10^6$, and to evaluate excess demands for each possible price vector $p = (\pi_1/D, \ldots, \pi_m/D)$ where $\sum_{i=1}^{l} \pi_j = D$ and $\pi_j \geq 0$ for all $j \in J$. However, this brute force method of **exhaustive search** is clearly very wasteful of computer resources. Scarf's algorithm implements a much more efficient and purposeful method of locating an approximate equilibrium.

We begin by recognizing that the price grid described in the preceding paragraph can also be used to subdivide the simplex into a collection of subsimplices.

Definition 6.26 *Given a set $S \subset L$, where L is an n-dimensional vector space, a collection of n-dimensional simplices $\{\sigma_i \mid i \in I\}$ indexed by the set I is called a* **simplicial subdivision** *of S if*

(a) $S \subset \bigcup_{i \in I} \sigma_i$; and
(b) for all $i, j \in I$, $i \neq j$, either

(i) $\sigma_i \cap \sigma_j = \emptyset$ *or*

(ii) $\sigma_i \cap \sigma_j$ *is a face of both* σ_i *and* σ_j.

If S is a simplex, the simplices σ_i are often called subsimplices.

Figure 6.7 gives some idea of collections of simplices which qualify as simplicial subdivisions, panel(a), and those which do not. In panel (b), $\sigma_1 \cap \sigma_2$ is a face of neither σ_1 nor σ_2. In panel (c), neither $\sigma_1 \cap \sigma_2$ nor $\sigma_1 \cap \sigma_3$ is a face of σ_1.

Constructing a simplicial subdivision of a two-dimensional simplex is quite easy, and in fact Figure 6.5 already displays a version. The lines which we drew earlier form the boundaries of the subsimplices, the smaller "triangles" which subdivide the larger unit simplex. Using the jargon of the trade, what we did was:

- choose a **grid denominator** D (or, equivalently, a **mesh size** $1/D$);
- construct a **grid** of points (price vectors) in the price simplex of the form $v = (\pi_1/D, \pi_2/D, \pi_3/D)$;
- connect the vertices of the grid with straight lines, forming the simplicial subdivision.

When generalized to an arbitrary $n-1$ dimensional simplex, this subdivision is known as the **Kuhn simplicial subdivision**. Of course, to characterize this subdivision, we can no longer rely on pictures and instead must resort to an algebraic description.

As in the two-dimensional case, we choose a grid denominator D, which serves as the denominator of the vectors in our grid. Let

$$b = \begin{pmatrix} b_1 \\ \vdots \\ b_n \end{pmatrix}$$

give the numerators of the components of an arbitrary vector in the grid (which we will call the **base vertex**). Let

$$\tilde{e}^1 = \begin{pmatrix} 1 \\ -1 \\ 0 \\ 0 \\ \vdots \\ 0 \\ 0 \end{pmatrix}, \quad \tilde{e}^2 = \begin{pmatrix} 0 \\ 1 \\ -1 \\ 0 \\ \vdots \\ 0 \\ 0 \end{pmatrix}, \quad \ldots \tilde{e}^{n-1} = \begin{pmatrix} 0 \\ 0 \\ 0 \\ 0 \\ \vdots \\ 1 \\ -1 \end{pmatrix}$$

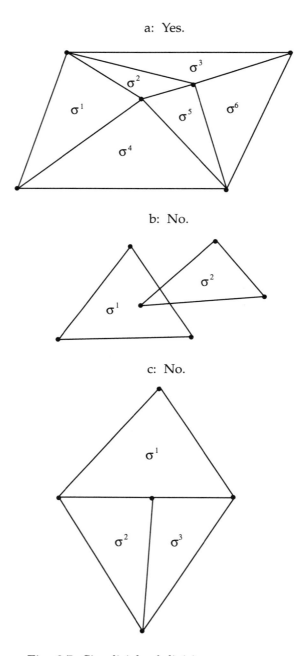

Fig. 6.7. Simplicial subdivisions: yes or no.

denote transformed versions of the standard basis vectors.[4] Finally, let

$$\psi: \{\, 1, \ldots, n-1 \,\} \rightarrow \{\, 1, \ldots, n-1 \,\}$$

denote a **permutation** (i.e., bijection) of the integers $\{\, 1, \ldots, n-1 \,\}$. In the discussion to follow, it will be convenient to represent a particular permutation in tabular form as

$$\begin{pmatrix} 1 & 2 & \ldots & n-1 \\ \psi(1) & \psi(2) & \ldots & \psi(n-1) \end{pmatrix}$$

to indicate that 1 maps to $\psi(1)$, 2 to $\psi(2)$, and so on. For each base vertex b and permutation ψ we define $\sigma(b, \psi)$ to be the simplex with vertices

$$\begin{aligned} \tilde{v}^1 &= b \\ \tilde{v}^2 &= \tilde{v}^1 + \tilde{e}^{\psi(1)} \end{aligned}$$

$$\ldots$$

$$\tilde{v}^n = \tilde{v}^{n-1} + \tilde{e}^{\psi(n-1)}.$$

To illustrate this procedure in the two-dimensional case, let the grid denominator $D = 8$ and choose

$$b = \begin{pmatrix} 2 \\ 3 \\ 3 \end{pmatrix}$$

for the base vertex. Then the permutation

$$\psi = \begin{pmatrix} 1 & 2 \\ 1 & 2 \end{pmatrix}$$

generates the subsimplex with vertices

$$\tilde{v}^1 = \begin{pmatrix} 2 \\ 3 \\ 3 \end{pmatrix}, \quad \tilde{v}^2 = \begin{pmatrix} 3 \\ 2 \\ 3 \end{pmatrix}, \quad \tilde{v}^3 = \begin{pmatrix} 3 \\ 3 \\ 2 \end{pmatrix}$$

while the permutation

$$\psi = \begin{pmatrix} 1 & 2 \\ 2 & 1 \end{pmatrix}$$

generates the subsimplex with vertices

$$\tilde{v}^1 = \begin{pmatrix} 2 \\ 3 \\ 3 \end{pmatrix}, \quad \tilde{v}^2 = \begin{pmatrix} 2 \\ 4 \\ 2 \end{pmatrix}, \quad \tilde{v}^3 = \begin{pmatrix} 3 \\ 3 \\ 2 \end{pmatrix}.$$

These two subsimplices are shown as the shaded triangles in Figure 6.5.

4 See Scarf (1982) for details on how the vectors $\tilde{e}^j$ are related to the standard basis vectors e^j.

Theorem 6.27 *The Kuhn subdivision is a simplicial subdivision of the $n-1$ dimensional unit simplex.*

Proof See Scarf (1982), Theorem 5.4.   □

Suppose that we have a simplicial subdivision of the $n-1$ dimensional unit simplex and that we attach labels $\ell(v) \in \{1, \ldots, n\}$ to each vertex in the grid subject only to the following **labeling rule**: $\ell(v) \neq j$ if $v \in F^j$ where F^j is the facet opposite e^j.

Definition 6.28 *Let $\{\sigma_i \mid i \in I\}$ be a simplicial subdivision of a simplex S. A subsimplex σ_i is said to be* **completely labeled** *if its vertices bear all of the labels $\{1, \ldots, n\}$.*

Lemma 6.29 (Sperner) *If the vertices of a simplicial subdivision of a simplex are labeled subject to the restrictions of the labeling rule, then the number of completely labeled subsimplices is odd.*

Proof Scarf (1982, Theorem 3.4) gives a simple proof that there is at least one completely labeled subsimplex. See Tompkins (1964) for a proof that there must be an odd number.   □

6.3.2 An algorithm

The interesting feature of Scarf's proof of Sperner's Lemma is that it involves an algorithm which traces a path from an "almost completely labeled" subsimplex (which is easy to find) to a completely labeled subsimplex. Figure 6.8, which contains three completely labeled subsimplices, illustrates the basic idea. An **almost completely labeled subsimplex** bears all distinct labels except for one pair of vertices which have the same label. The path labeled A shows a path from an almost completely labeled simplex on the boundary to one which is completely labeled. The rules for following the path are:

- When starting with the almost completely labeled subsimplex, flip across the facet of the subsimplex opposite the label on the boundary which matches the label in the interior (a label 2 in this example).
- From then on, find the pair of labels in the subsimplex which match, and flip across the facet opposite the vertex of this pair which has been around the longest.[5]

---

5 In accounting terminology, it is a FIFO rule: "first in, first out."

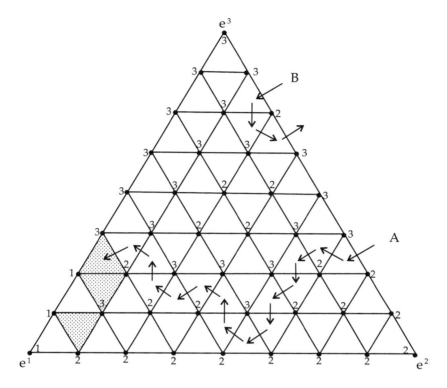

Fig. 6.8. A path which escapes.

It is easy to see that, provided that one starts at the edge of the simplex, the path can never cycle. However, it is possible to defeat this attempt to reach a completely labeled subsimplex by escaping from the simplex as shown by path B. Scarf avoids this difficulty by adding an artificial layer to the simplex as shown in Figure 6.9 with the labels on the artificial layer chosen to avoid escape.[6]

Specifically, we start with a subsimplex with one vertex (base vertex)

$$b = \begin{pmatrix} 0 \\ b_2 \\ \vdots \\ b_n \end{pmatrix}$$

6 Figure 6.9 also shows the coordinates for the added vertices.

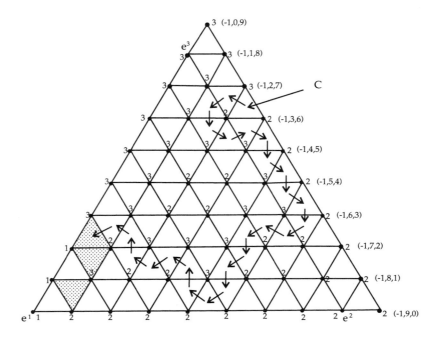

Fig. 6.9. No escape.

of the subsimplex lying in the facet F^1 of the main simplex opposite[7] v^1 and the remaining vertices of the subsimplex lying on the artificial facet. Then we label each vertex of the subsimplex

$$v^k = \begin{pmatrix} v_1^k \\ \vdots \\ v_n^k \end{pmatrix}$$

lying on the artificial facet by the smallest integer j such that $v_j^k > b_j$. Path C in Figure 6.9 starts at about the same place as path B in Figure 6.8, but now succeeds in reaching one of the completely labeled subsimplices. With a little thought, you should be able to see that any such path will be successful:

---

7 We could just as well add an artificial layer to any face of the main simplex. I have chosen the face opposite the first vertex for purposes of illustration.

- Escape through the other facets of the main simplex is impossible because of the labeling rule.

- The path continues from almost completely labeled subsimplex to almost completely labeled subsimplex unless it reaches a completely labeled subsimplex.

- Since the path cannot cycle and since the number of subsimplices to visit is finite, the path must eventually reach a completely labeled subsimplex.

How can this be converted to an algorithm suitable for implementation on a computer? We certainly cannot tell the computer "flip across the opposite facet," at least not in so many words. However, the idea is easily converted into algebra.[8] Suppose that we are currently visiting a subsimplex with vertices $(\tilde{v}^1, \ldots, \tilde{v}^n)$. To remove vertex $\tilde{v}^j$ and flip across the opposite facet, replace the vertex $\tilde{v}^j$ by

$$\widehat{v}^j := \tilde{v}^{j-1} + \tilde{v}^{j+1} - \tilde{v}^j \qquad (\text{mod } n)$$

where mod n (short for modulo n) is an instruction to "wrap around the ends" if $j = 1$ or $j = n$: i.e., the rule becomes

$$\begin{aligned}
\widehat{v}^1 &= \tilde{v}^n + \tilde{v}^2 - \tilde{v}^1 & \text{when} \quad j = 1; \quad \text{and} \\
\widehat{v}^n &= \tilde{v}^{n-1} + \tilde{v}^1 - \tilde{v}^n & \text{when} \quad j = n.
\end{aligned}$$

Working through the example illustrated by path C in Figure 6.9, we take

$$b = \begin{pmatrix} 0 \\ 2 \\ 6 \end{pmatrix}$$

as the base vertex and

$$\begin{matrix} 3 & 2 & 2 \end{matrix}$$
$$\begin{pmatrix} -1 & -1 & 0 \\ 2 & 3 & 2 \\ 7 & 6 & 6 \end{pmatrix}$$

---

8 See Scarf (1982), Theorem 5.2, for a proof that this rule generates the Kuhn simplicial subdivision.

as the starting subsimplex[9] where the labels attached to each vertex (column) are shown in the first row.

Using the replacement rule, the next five subsimplices visited are represented by the matrices[10]

$$
\begin{matrix} 3 & 3 & 2 \end{matrix} \qquad \begin{matrix} 3 & 3 & 2 \end{matrix} \qquad \begin{matrix} 3 & 3 & 2 \end{matrix}
$$
$$
\begin{pmatrix} -1 & 0 & 0 \\ 2 & 1 & 2 \\ 7 & 7 & 6 \end{pmatrix} \rightarrow \begin{pmatrix} 1 & 0 & 0 \\ 1 & 1 & 2 \\ 6 & 7 & 6 \end{pmatrix} \rightarrow \begin{pmatrix} 1 & 1 & 0 \\ 1 & 2 & 2 \\ 6 & 5 & 6 \end{pmatrix} \rightarrow
$$

$$
\begin{matrix} 3 & 3 & 2 \end{matrix} \qquad \begin{matrix} 3 & 2 & 2 \end{matrix}
$$
$$
\begin{pmatrix} 0 & 1 & 0 \\ 3 & 2 & 2 \\ 5 & 5 & 6 \end{pmatrix} \rightarrow \begin{pmatrix} 0 & -1 & 0 \\ 3 & 3 & 2 \\ 5 & 6 & 6 \end{pmatrix}
$$

as the path enters the main simplex, circles around, and heads back out to the artificial layer. After creeping along the artificial layer for seven more iterations, the path finally reaches the beginning of path A (see Figure 6.8) with corresponding matrix

$$
\begin{matrix} 2 & 2 & 3 \end{matrix}
$$
$$
\begin{pmatrix} 0 & 1 & 0 \\ 6 & 5 & 5 \\ 2 & 2 & 3 \end{pmatrix}.
$$

After 14 more iterations, it finally reaches the goal, a completely labeled subsimplex, with terminal matrix

$$
\begin{matrix} 1 & 3 & 2 \end{matrix}
$$
$$
\begin{pmatrix} 6 & 5 & 5 \\ 0 & 0 & 1 \\ 2 & 3 & 2 \end{pmatrix}.
$$

9 In the general case of an $n - 1$ dimensional simplex, the starting subsimplex takes the form

$$
\begin{matrix} n & n-1 & \ldots & 2 & \ell(b) \end{matrix}
$$
$$
\begin{pmatrix} -1 & -1 & \ldots & -1 & 0 \\ b_2 & b_2 & \ldots & b_2+1 & b_2 \\ b_3 & b_3 & \ldots & b_3 & b_3 \\ \vdots & \vdots & \vdots & \vdots & \vdots \\ b_{n-1} & b_{n-1}+1 & \ldots & b_{n-1} & b_{n-1} \\ b_n+1 & b_n & b_n & b_n & b_n \end{pmatrix}.
$$

where $\ell(b)$ is the label assigned to the base vertex b.

10 Those of you tempted to follow the algebra will find the coordinates listed in Figure 6.5 to be helpful.

6.3.3 Choosing labels

Why are we interested in finding a completely labeled subsimplex? Recall that, apart from the boundary, we are quite free to choose any labels we wish. By choosing labels cleverly, we can solve for an approximate Walrasian equilibrium (or an approximate fixed point, or whatever).

How do we choose an appropriate set of labels to solve for an approximate Walrasian equilibrium? The KKM Theorem provides the key insight. Recall that, in applying the KKM Theorem to an exchange economy, we defined the sets $M_j = \{ p \in \Delta \mid \Delta_w \Phi_j(p) \leq 0 \}$ for $j \in J := \{ 1, \ldots, m \}$. All we need do is select a label for each v^k in our simplicial subdivision from among the integers $j \in J$ indexing the sets M_j which cover the vertex: $\ell(v^k) \in \{ j \in J \mid v^k \in M_j \}$.

Of course, we have to check that, in selecting labels in this way, we satisfy the labeling rule of Sperner's Lemma. But, in effect, we already know this to be true. In proving Theorem 6.25, we verified that the basic requirement of the KKM Theorem,

$$\mathrm{co}\{ e^j \mid j \in T \} \subset \bigcup_{j \in T} M_j \quad \forall \emptyset \neq T \subset J \qquad (*)$$

is satisfied. But, if we select labels as proposed above, then $\ell(v^k) \neq j$ if $v^k \in F^j$ because by definition $F^j := \mathrm{co}\{ e^1, \ldots, e^{j-1}, e^{j+1}, e^m \}$ so that, by $(*)$, the label j corresponding to the missing vertex e^j is not allowed. Thus, the "strange" labeling rule appearing in the statement of Sperner's Lemma and the "strange" condition imposed by the KKM Theorem turn out to be equivalent and, since they follow from Walras' Law, perhaps seem not so strange after all.

We have not yet said quite enough to permit this labeling rule to be implemented on a computer because it is ambiguous. What do we do if a vertex is covered by *more than one* of the sets M_j? However, this is easily resolved by any arbitrary rule breaking the tie. The following rule is standard in this context:

- select the label j from among the indices of the covering sets M_j which corresponds to the most negative excess demand; and

- if two or more commodities are tied for most negative, pick the smallest j.

To make this discussion less abstract, we return to our simple exchange economy with equal numbers of consumers of each type. Recall that the per

a: M_j for an exchange economy.

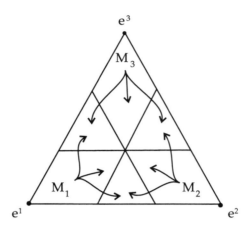

b: The labels.

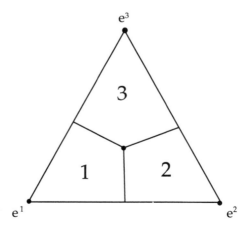

Fig. 6.10. Choosing labels.

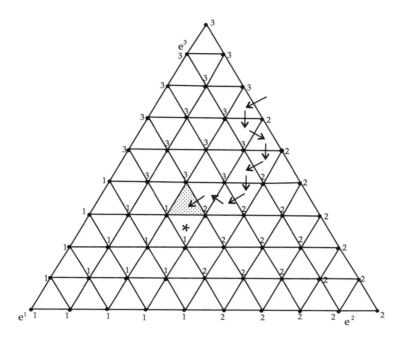

Fig. 6.11. A path to equilibrium.

capita excess demand for commodity j was given by

$$\frac{\Delta_w \Phi_j(p)}{n} = \frac{b}{3p_j} - b.$$

Therefore, comparing the per capita excess demands for commodities j and k, we conclude that $\Delta_w \Phi_j(p) < \Delta_w \Phi_k(p)$ iff $p_j > p_k$.

Figure 6.10(a) exhibits the sets M_j for this economy. Imposing the tie-breaking rule described above yields the regions in Figure 6.10(b) showing where vertices are to be labeled 1, 2, or 3 respectively (with the understanding that, on the boundaries between regions, the lowest number is chosen).

All that remains to construct an algorithm is to impose the simplicial subdivision and add an artificial layer. Figure 6.11 gives the final setup. Start with an initial estimate (base vertex) for the price vector,

$$b = \begin{pmatrix} 0 \\ \pi_2 \\ \pi_3 \end{pmatrix},$$

and follow the path. Notice how the path hugs along the boundary between the sets labeled 2 and 3. This example gives some hint concerning why, in practice, the Scarf algorithm typically seems rather efficient. If each of the labeled regions M_j is a solid region with a very regular "coastline," the path will never enter the interior of those regions (because no "almost completely labeled" subsimplices are to be found). In contrast, when labels are chosen more arbitrarily as in Figure 6.9, the path to a completely labeled subsimplex can meander all over the place.

In what sense can a completely labeled subsimplex be regarded as an approximate equilibrium? Consider what it means for a subsimplex to be completely labeled within the context of our exchange economy. For any commodity j, there is exactly one price vector (vertex) where the excess demand for j is the most negative. By Walras' Law, if at any such price vector some excess demands are strictly negative, then others must be positive. Therefore, since each commodity "gets its turn" to be negative for some vertex and since the excess demand function is continuous, all of the excess demands must be nearly zero (so that at some vertices they can be negative while at others they are positive). Thus, by choosing a sufficiently fine mesh (i.e., a high value for D), we can make the deviation from exact market clearing as small as we wish.[11] While all of this can be given a precise formulation, we will not bother with the details — it should seem obvious enough. In any case, for most practitioners the proof of the pudding is in the eating: the algorithm performs very well in actual applications.

6.3.4 Proof of KKM and Brouwer

We can now make good on our promise to prove the KKM and Brouwer Theorems.

Proof [**KKM Theorem**] Without loss of generality, we assume that the simplex referenced in the statement of the theorem is the unit simplex. Consider a sequence of simplicial subdivisions of the simplex with mesh tending to zero: for simplicity, assume that the grid denominator $D_k = k \in \mathbf{Z}_+$ for the kth subdivision in this sequence. For a given subdivision, label each vertex of the subdivision by the smallest integer j such that the set M_j covers the vertex. It is easily verified that this labeling rule satisfies the labeling rule required for Sperner's Lemma. Therefore, corresponding to each subdivision there exists a completely labeled subsimplex.

---

11 In practice, modelers who use the Scarf algorithm often select the midpoint (barycenter) of the completely labeled subsimplex as the approximation to the equilibrium price vector.

For the kth subdivision, select a completely labeled subsimplex, and let v_k^j denote the vertex of the completely labeled subsimplex which bears the label j. As k increases to infinity, the sequence of vertices labeled 1 contains a subsequence converging to a limit, say $v_k^1 \to v_*^1$, because the simplex is compact.[12] Furthermore, because the set M_1 is closed and each $v_k^1 \in M_1$, the limit $v_*^1 \in M_1$. Similarly, from the sequence of vertices labeled 2 in this subsequence of completely labeled subsimplices we can extract a subsequence $v_k^2 \to v_*^2 \in M_2$.[13] Continuing in this way through the label n, we eventually obtain a sequence (actually a subsequence of a subsequence ... of the original sequence) of completely labeled subsimplices for which $v_k^j \to v_*^j$ for all $j = 1, \ldots, m$. But since the mesh size is going to zero as k increases to infinity, each of the converging sequences of vertices, corresponding to labels $j = 1, \ldots, m$, must be converging to the same limit point v_*. This in turn implies that $v_* \in \cap_{j \in J} M_j$, which means that the intersection of the sets M_j is nonempty. $\qquad \square$

Proof [**Brouwer Fixed Point Theorem**] Without loss of generality, we can assume that the nonempty, compact, convex set is the unit simplex. Let $M_i := \{ x \in \Delta \mid f_i(x) - x_i \leq 0 \}$. It is easily verified that the sets M_i satisfy all of the requirements of the KKM Theorem. By the KKM Theorem, $\cap_{i=1}^n M_i \neq \emptyset$. Therefore, there exists an $x^* \in \Delta$ such that $f_i(x^*) \leq x_i^*$ for all $i = 1, \ldots, n$. But $\sum_{i=1}^n (f_i(x_i^*) - x_i^*) = 0$ (since both x^* and $f(x^*)$ lie in the simplex), so $f_i(x^*) = x_i^*$ for all $i = 1, \ldots, n$. Thus, $f(x^*) = x^*$, which means that x^* is a fixed point. $\qquad \square$

6.3.5 The Merrill restart algorithm

Scarf's algorithm seems quite efficient: once the path emerges from the artificial layer into the true simplex, it heads straight for a completely labeled subsimplex. Our example is somewhat deceptive, however: if the destination is far from the starting edge and D is large, a large number of "flips" will be required to follow the path from beginning to end. Fortunately, a simple variation on Scarf's algorithm due to Merrill (1972) avoids this difficulty by allowing the path to start from anywhere within the simplex.

Illustrating how Merrill's algorithm works will be much easier if we reduce the number of commodities in our exchange economy example from three to two. All consumers have Cobb-Douglas preferences of the form $u_t(x_t) =$

---

12 To avoid notational complexity, we label this subsequence $\langle v_k^1 \rangle$ rather than the more cumbersome $\langle v_{k_n}^1 \rangle$.

13 Once again we relabel this "subsequence of a subsequence" as simply $\langle v_k^2 \rangle$.

a: Per capita excess demand for commodity one.

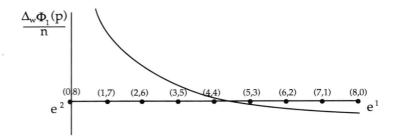

b: Scarf's algorithm.

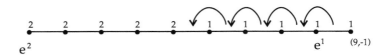

Fig. 6.12. The Scarf algorithm in one dimension.

$x_{t1}^{a_t} x_{t2}^{1-a_t}$, a fraction μ with $a_t = \alpha$ and the rest with $a_t = 1 - \alpha$. All have initial endowment $w_t = (b, b)$ and, hence, wealth $p \cdot w_t = b$. If the total number of consumers is n, then per capita excess demands for commodities 1 and 2 are given by

$$\frac{\Delta_w \Phi_1(p)}{n} = \frac{b}{p_1}[1 - \mu - \alpha + 2\alpha\mu] - b$$

and

$$\frac{\Delta_w \Phi_2(p)}{n} = \frac{b}{p_2}[\mu + \alpha - 2\alpha\mu] - b.$$

Consequently, the equilibrium prices are given by $p_1 = 1 - \mu - \alpha + 2\alpha\mu$ and $p_2 = 1 - p_1$. For specificity we let $\alpha = \mu = 1/3$ and $b = 9$, yielding per capita excess demand

$$\frac{\Delta_w \Phi_1(p)}{n} = \frac{5}{p_1} - 9 \quad \text{and} \quad \frac{\Delta_w \Phi_1(p)}{n} = \frac{4}{p_2} - 9$$

and equilibrium prices $(p_1, p_2) = (5/9, 4/9)$. Figure 6.12(a) shows a plot of per capita excess demand for the first commodity against its price along with the barycentric coordinates corresponding to the Kuhn simplicial subdivision with $D = 8$.[14] The arrows in Figure 6.12(b) trace the path which Scarf's algorithm follows in moving from the artificial layer to the right of e^1 to a completely labeled subsimplex.[15]

Implementing Merrill's algorithm proceeds in several steps:

- First, we imbed our one-dimensional simplex in $\mathbf{R}^2$ where, as indicated in Figure 6.13(a), it becomes the line segment co$\{\,e^1, e^2\,\}$. The figure also shows the vertices along with their coordinates in the simplicial subdivision with $D = 8$. As usual, only the numerators of the coordinates are exhibited, expressed as (π_1, π_2) where $\pi_1 + \pi_2 = 8$ and $\pi_1, \pi_2 \in \mathbf{Z}_+$.
- Next we add a vertex $e^0 = (0,0)$ to form a two-dimensional simplex co$\{\,e^0, e^1, e^2\,\}$ which has the original one-dimensional simplex as the facet opposite e^0 (see Figure 6.13(b)).
- Using the grid denominator $D = 8$, we subdivide the two-dimensional simplex co$\{\,e^0, e^1, e^2\,\}$ using the Kuhn subdivision. Vertices on the facet opposite e^0 coincide with the subdivision of the original one-dimensional simplex, but with barycentric coordinates $(\pi_0, \pi_1, \pi_2) = (0, \pi_1, \pi_2)$ where, just as before, $\pi_1 + \pi_2 = 8$ and $\pi_1, \pi_2 \in \mathbf{Z}_+$. Figure 6.13(b) shows the resulting subdivision for the "sandwich" lying between the original simplex and the adjacent "artificial layer" whose vertices have coordinates $(\pi_0, \pi_1, \pi_2) = (1, \pi_1, \pi_2)$ with $\pi_1 + \pi_2 = 7$ and $\pi_1, \pi_2 \in \mathbf{Z}_+$.
- The labels for vertices on the upper layer of the sandwich are determined by the original problem (compare Figures 6.12(b) and 6.14(a)).
- The labels for vertices on the artificial layer of the sandwich are determined by the initial guess (π_1^*, π_2^*). Given that guess, we label each of the vertices (π_1^k, π_2^k) in the artificial layer with the lowest index j such that $\pi_j^k > \pi_j^* - 1$. As Figure 6.14(a) suggests, this choice of labels will prevent the path from escaping through either end of the sandwich.

Starting with the initial guess $(\pi_1^*, \pi_2^*) = (6, 2)$, we begin with the almost completely labeled subsimplex

$$\begin{pmatrix} 0 & 1 & 1 \\ \pi_1^* & \pi_1^* - 1 & \pi_1^* \\ \pi_2^* & \pi_2^* & \pi_2^* - 1 \end{pmatrix} = \begin{pmatrix} 0 & 1 & 1 \\ 6 & 5 & 6 \\ 2 & 2 & 1 \end{pmatrix}$$

corresponding to the shaded subsimplex in Figure 6.14(a). Columns of the

---

14 Warning: the vertex e^1 appears on the right and e^2 on the left, opposite perhaps from what you were expecting.

15 Paralleling our earlier implementation of Scarf's algorithm, I have added an "artificial" vertex to the right of e^1 with coordinates $(9, -1)$.

a: The original simplex imbedded in R^2.

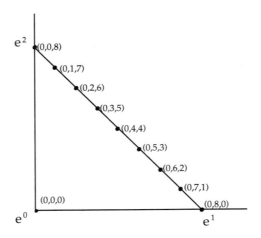

b: Constructing the sandwich.

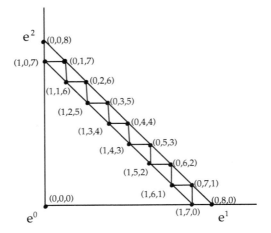

Fig. 6.13. Implementing Merrill's algorithm.

a: D = 8.

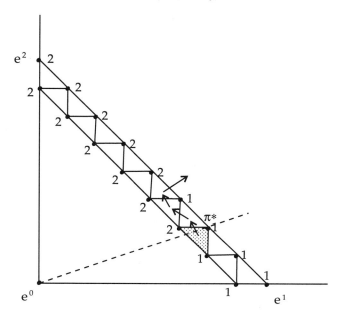

b: D = 64.

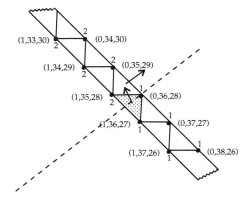

Fig. 6.14. Merrill's algorithm.

matrix with a 0 in the first row correspond to vertices on the layer representing the original simplex, those with a 1 to vertices on the artificial layer. Using exactly the same procedure that we used for the original Scarf algorithm, we follow the path shown in Figure 6.14(a), flipping across facets until we eject through a completely labeled subsimplex on the top layer.

The sequence of matrices tracing this path is[16]

$$
\begin{array}{ccc} 1 & 2 & 1 \end{array} \qquad \begin{array}{ccc} 1 & 2 & 1 \end{array} \qquad \begin{array}{ccc} 2 & 2 & 1 \end{array} \qquad \begin{array}{ccc} 2 & 2 & 1 \end{array}
$$
$$
\begin{pmatrix} 0 & 1 & 1 \\ 6 & 5 & 6 \\ 2 & 2 & 1 \end{pmatrix} \rightarrow \begin{pmatrix} 0 & 1 & 0 \\ 6 & 5 & 5 \\ 2 & 2 & 3 \end{pmatrix} \rightarrow \begin{pmatrix} 1 & 1 & 0 \\ 4 & 5 & 5 \\ 3 & 2 & 3 \end{pmatrix} \rightarrow \begin{pmatrix} 1 & 0 & 0 \\ 4 & 4 & 5 \\ 3 & 4 & 3 \end{pmatrix},
$$

ending with the completely labeled subsimplex we are looking for (identified by the two columns with leading zeros).

Merrill's algorithm breaks the task of estimating a fixed point into many smaller steps, each successive step building on the results of the last until results with sufficient accuracy have been obtained. In our example with $D = 8$ we obtained a completely labeled subsimplex with vertices $(4, 4)$ and $(5, 3)$, which averages to $(4.5, 3.5)$. At that average, per capita excess demand computes to $\Delta_w \Phi(p) = (-1/9, 1/7)$ rather than the desired $(0, 0)$, an "error" amounting to about 1.2% of per capita endowment for commodity one and 1.6% for commodity two. If these results do not seem accurate enough, we can run the Merrill algorithm once again with the above estimate of prices as a starting value and a higher value for the grid denominator D, say $D = 64$. Figure 6.14(b) shows the relevant part of the new sandwich with starting subsimplex determined by the initial estimate $8(4.5, 3.5) = (36, 28)$. The sequence from beginning to end,

$$
\begin{array}{ccc} 1 & 2 & 1 \end{array} \qquad \qquad \begin{array}{ccc} 1 & 2 & 2 \end{array}
$$
$$
\begin{pmatrix} 0 & 1 & 1 \\ 36 & 35 & 36 \\ 28 & 28 & 27 \end{pmatrix} \rightarrow \begin{pmatrix} 0 & 1 & 0 \\ 36 & 35 & 35 \\ 28 & 28 & 29 \end{pmatrix},
$$

reaches a completely labeled subsimplex in a single step! Averaging the vertices $(36, 28)$ and $(35, 29)$ yields $(35.5, 28.5)$, implying per capita excess demands $\Delta_w \Phi(p) = (1/71, -1/51)$ with errors around 0.16% and 0.20% for commodities one and two respectively. If this does not seem accurate enough, we can use this improved estimate as the starting point for yet another round of the Merrill algorithm and, by iterating in this fashion, achieve any degree of accuracy short of absolute perfection.

16 As before, labels are shown in the row above the matrix.

Implementing Merrill's algorithm in the general case is a straightforward extension of the specialized two-commodity version described above. Starting with $(\pi_1^*, \pi_2^*, \ldots, \pi_m^*)$ as the initial estimate where $\sum_{j \in J} \pi_j^* = D$, we initiate the algorithm at the almost completely labeled subsimplex

$$
\begin{array}{ccccc}
& 2 & 3 & \cdots & m & 1 \\
\begin{pmatrix}
0 & 1 & 1 & \cdots & 1 & 1 \\
\pi_1^* & \pi_1^* - 1 & \pi_1^* & \cdots & \pi_1^* & \pi_1^* \\
\pi_2^* & \pi_2^* & \pi_2^* - 1 & \cdots & \pi_2^* & \pi_2^* \\
\vdots & \vdots & \vdots & \ddots & \vdots & \vdots \\
\pi_{m-1}^* & \pi_{m-1}^* & \pi_{m-1}^* & \cdots & \pi_{m-1}^* - 1 & \pi_{m-1}^* \\
\pi_m^* & \pi_m^* & \pi_m^* & \cdots & \pi_m^* & \pi_m^* - 1
\end{pmatrix}
\end{array}
$$

with labels for vertices on the artificial layer shown above the matrix. The label assigned to any other vertex on the artificial layer[17] is the smallest index j such that $\pi_j^k > \pi_j^*$. Vertices on the layer representing the original simplex are assigned labels just as with the Scarf algorithm.

6.3.6 Some myths about Scarf's algorithm

Although Scarf's algorithm is truly an object of beauty, there are a few commonly held myths about its significance which should be dispelled.

Myth 1: The Scarf algorithm provides a constructive proof of the Brouwer Fixed Point Theorem and a constructive proof that Walrasian equilibrium exists.

Some years after proving his theorem, Brouwer sought to disown it on the grounds that the proof was nonconstructive. What bothered Brouwer (and what concerns mathematicians seeking constructive proofs in mathematics) is that the proof of his fixed point theorem cannot be verified in a finite number of steps: the convergent subsequences alluded to in the proof need converge only "at infinity." If taken seriously, constructivist critiques of this sort affect a large number of conventional proofs in real analysis, and a number of mathematicians who take these matters seriously have attempted to provide constructive alternatives to the usual fare. Scarf's algorithm is sometimes characterized as a "constructive proof of the Brouwer Theorem." However, this is false. What Scarf's algorithm provides is a constructive

---

17 Treating the vertices on the artificial layer differently if they happen to be in the starting subsimplex is necessary in order to guarantee that the starting simplex is (i) almost completely labeled and (ii) the only simplex in the sandwich with m vertices on the artificial layer bearing m distinct labels. If (ii) were not true, the path could exit through the lower, artificial layer of the sandwich.

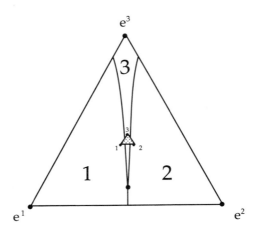

Fig. 6.15. Far from a fixed point!

alternative to the Brouwer Theorem: in a finite number of steps, the algorithm finds a point x^* which is "nearly fixed" in the sense that $f(x^*) \approx x^*$ with some specified degree of accuracy. But there is no guarantee of the existence of a true fixed point, a point x^{**} such that $f(x^{**}) = x^{**}$ *exactly*, unless one accepts the nonconstructive "pass to the limit" just as in the proof of the Brouwer Theorem that we gave.

Myth 2: The Scarf algorithm finds an approximation to a fixed point or an approximation to a market clearing price.

A common misapprehension on the part of those encountering Scarf's algorithm is that, once the algorithm has located a completely labeled subsimplex, a fixed point or equilibrium price vector lies somewhere within that subsimplex. Thus, in Figure 6.11 the equilibrium price vector $(3/8, 3/8, 3/8)$, denoted by an asterisk, is the barycenter of the subsimplex lying directly below the completely labeled subsimplex located by the Scarf algorithm. The point is that Scarf's algorithm can find points x^* or p^* such that $f(x^*) \approx x^*$ (an approximate fixed point) or $\Delta_w \Phi(p^*) \approx 0$ (an approximate equilibrium price vector), but not an x^* near to a true fixed point x^{**} or a p^* near to a true equilibrium price vector p^{**}. Furthermore, as Figure 6.15 is meant to suggest, a completely labeled subsimplex may remain far away from a true equilibrium price vector p^* (or a true fixed point) even when the mesh size becomes very small.

6.4 The Excess Demand Theorem

The connection between the Brouwer Theorem and existence of Walrasian equilibrium seems remarkably close, leading to the conjecture that they are essentially equivalent. Uzawa (1962b) confirmed that intuition by establishing what is in effect the converse to Theorem 6.12: if a continuous function which maps the simplex to itself and satisfies Walras' Law always has a "free disposal equilibrium," then the Brouwer Theorem is valid. It remained to Sonnenschein (1973a) to extract from this observation a matter of economic substance. Uzawa's observation tacitly assumes that continuity and Walras' Law exhaust what economics has to say about market excess demand. But is that so? Debreu (1974a) established what Shafer and Sonnenschein (1982) characterize as the "state of the art" response to Sonnenschein's query. Before stating Debreu's result, we need to introduce a few definitions.

Throughout this chapter I have adopted the normalization which restricts prices to the unit simplex. However, the literature on the Excess Demand Theorem favors $S_{++} := \{ p \in \mathbf{R}_{++}^m \mid \sum_{j \in J} p_j^2 = 1 \}$, that portion of the unit sphere in which all prices are strictly positive: the results reported below translate directly to the unit simplex. However, since I am sending you to the literature for the proofs, I will stick with the normalization favored in that literature. To bound prices away from the axes, we also need to define for $\epsilon > 0$ the set $S_\epsilon := \{ p \in S_{++} \mid p_j \geq \epsilon \; \forall j \in J \}$. Finally, we introduce some additional terminology about preferences.

Definition 6.30 *Let $\succ_i$ be a weak ordering defined on the consumption set $X_i = \mathbf{R}_+^m$.*

- *$\succ_i$ is **strictly convex** if for any $\alpha \in (0,1)$ and for any $x_i, x_i' \in X_i$ such that $x_i \nsucc x_i'$ and $x_i \neq x_i'$ we have*

$$\alpha x_i + (1 - \alpha) x_i' \succ_i x_i.$$

- *$\succ_i$ is **monotonic** if $x_i' \succ_i x_i$ whenever $x_{ij}' > x_{ij}$ for all $j \in J$.*
- *$\succ_i$ is **homothetic** if it is representable by a utility function which is homogeneous of degree one.*

Loosely speaking, strict convexity says that indifference contours have no flat spots; monotonicity that more is better; and homotheticity that Engel curves are rays through the origin.

The results I am about to give are all drawn from the excellent review of the literature by Shafer and Sonnenschein (1982).

Theorem 6.31 (Debreu) *Let $f: S_{++} \to \mathbf{R}^m$ be any continuous function* *satisfying Walras' Law.*[18] *For every $\epsilon > 0$ there exists an m-consumer exchange economy $\mathcal{E} = \{\, X_i, \succ_i, w_i \mid i \in I \,\}$ whose market excess demand function $\Delta_w \Phi$ coincides with f on S_ϵ. For each consumer i in this economy $\mathcal{E}$ we can assume that $X_i{}' = \mathbf{R}_+^m$ and $\succ_i$ is a continuous, strictly convex, monotonic, weak ordering.*

Proof See Debreu (1974a). $\qquad\qquad\qquad\qquad\qquad\qquad\qquad\qquad$ $\square$

Those who like to think that an economy is like a (representative) consumer could object: perhaps Debreu's result will go away if we require differentiability and rule out perverse income effects. Not so.

Theorem 6.32 (Mantel) *Let $f\colon S_{++} \to \mathbf{R}^m$ be any continuously differentiable (C^1) function satisfying Walras' Law. For every $\epsilon > 0$ such that f has bounded second partial derivatives on S_ϵ, there exists an m-consumer exchange economy $\mathcal{E} = \{\, X_i, \succ_i, w_i \mid i \in I \,\}$ whose market excess demand function $\Delta_w \Phi$ coincides with f on S_ϵ. For each consumer i in this economy $\mathcal{E}$ we can assume that $X_i = \mathbf{R}_+^m$ and that $\succ_i$ is strictly convex, monotonic, homothetic, and representable by a continuous utility function.*

Proof See Mantel (1979). $\qquad\qquad\qquad\qquad\qquad\qquad\qquad\qquad\qquad$ $\square$

The message conveyed by these results is rather devastating to current economic practice. One consumer per market is certainly a bare minimum when we are talking about competition. In economies meeting that minimal standard, all of the hard work which economists put into studying responses of individual consumers washes out in the aggregate. This does not mean that putting additional restrictions on market excess demand is somehow undesirable. Without doing so, market excess demand functions have no economic content apart from budget balance. However, adding content requires a serious attempt to describe appropriate distributions of consumer endowments and preferences (see Hildenbrand (1983) for developments along those lines). Wishful thinking is not enough!

6.5 Kakutani Fixed Point Theorem

Throughout this chapter we have assumed demand functions are singleton-valued. Relaxing this assumption requires a fixed point theorem different from Brouwer, a fixed point theorem for correspondences. We begin by modifying what we mean by a fixed point.

18 Throughout this section, when I say "Walras' Law" I mean the strong form.

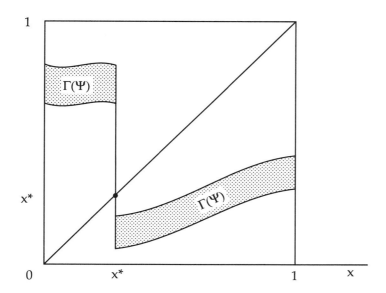

Fig. 6.16. The Kakutani Fixed Point Theorem.

Definition 6.33 *A point* $x \in K$ *is a* **fixed point** *of the mapping* $\Psi \colon K \to 2^K$ *if* $x \in \Psi(x)$.

The fixed point theorem we are seeking is due to Kakutani (1941).

Theorem 6.34 (Kakutani) *Let* K *be a nonempty, compact, convex subset of a finite dimensional TVS. If* $\Psi \colon K \to (2^K)_o^F$ *is convex-valued and uhc, then* Ψ *has a fixed point.*

Proof See Kakutani (1941) or Hildenbrand and Kirman (1988), Mathematical Appendix IV. □

Figure 6.16 illustrates the main idea: letting $K = [0,1]$, fixed points x^* of $\Psi \colon K \to (2^K)_o^F$ correspond to points (x^*, x^*) where the graph of Ψ intersects the diagonal.

As preparation for the main existence result, we first establish a basic fact about market demand correspondences.

Theorem 6.35 *In any economy* $\mathcal{E}$*, if individual demand correspondences* ϕ_i *are convex-valued and uhc, then the market demand correspondence* Φ *is convex-valued and uhc and, if individual excess demand correspondences* ϕ_i

are convex-valued and uhc, then the market excess demand correspondence $\Delta_w \Phi$ is convex-valued and uhc.

Proof By definition, $\Phi(p) = \sum_{i \in I} \phi_i(p)$ and $\Delta_w \Phi(p) = \sum_{i \in I} \Delta_w \phi_i(p)$. Preservation of convex-valuedness follows from Theorem 2.4 and preservation of uhc from Theorem 5.56. $\qquad\square$

Theorem 6.36 *Let $\mathcal{E}$ be a pure exchange economy and K a nonempty, compact, convex subset of the commodity space L large enough to contain all feasible net trades. Assume that market excess demand $\Delta_w \Phi \colon \Delta \to (2^K)_o^F$ is convex-valued, uhc, and satisfies the strong form of Walras Law. Then the economy $\mathcal{E}$ has a free disposal equilibrium: i.e., a price vector $p^* \in \Delta$ and an excess demand vector $z^* \in \Delta_w \Phi$ such that $z^* \leq 0$ and $z_j^* = 0$ whenever $p_j^* > 0$.*

Proof To force market clearing, we introduce a fictitious actor, the Auctioneer, whose utility function $u \colon \Delta \times K \to \mathbf{R}$ maps $(p, z) \mapsto u(p, z) := p \cdot z$ and best response $\alpha \colon K \to 2^\Delta$ maps

$$z \mapsto \alpha(z) := \left\{ p \in \Delta \mid p \cdot z = \sup_{p \in \Delta} u(p, z) \right\}.$$

Thus, the Auctioneer chooses a price vector p which maximizes the value of excess demand. Define

$$\Psi \colon \Delta \times K \to (2^{\Delta \times K})_o^F, \quad (p, z) \mapsto \Psi(p, z) := \alpha(z) \times \Delta_w \Phi(p).$$

We want to show that Ψ satisfies the requirements of the Kakutani Theorem:

- Because both Δ and K are nonempty, compact, and convex, their Cartesian product $\Delta \times K$ inherits the same properties (Theorem 2.3 and Theorem 4.29).
- Since the constraint set Δ and the upper contour sets

$$R(p, z) := \{ p' \in \Delta \mid u(p', z) \geq u(p, z) \}$$

  of the Auctioneer are convex, her best response $\alpha(z)$ is convex for any $z \in K$ (Theorem 5.21).
- Because the Auctioneer's utility function is continuous in both p and z and her constraint correspondence is constant (and, therefore, trivially continuous), her best response α is uhc in z (Corollary 5.50).
- By assumption, the excess demand correspondence $\Delta_w \Phi$ is convex-valued and uhc. We conclude that Ψ, the product of α and $\Delta_w \Phi$, is convex-valued and uhc (Theorems 2.3 and 5.55).

Therefore, Ψ satisfies the requirements of the Kakutani Theorem, and so there exists a fixed point $(p^*, z^*) \in \Psi(p^*, z^*) := \alpha(z^*) \times \Delta_w \Phi(p^*)$ or, equivalently, $p^* \in \alpha(z^*)$ and $z^* \in \Delta_w \Phi(p^*)$. $p^* \in \alpha(z^*)$ implies that $p \cdot z^* \leq p^* \cdot z^*$ for all $p \in \Delta$. Since this economy satisfies the strong form of Walras' Law, $z^* \in \Delta_w \Phi(p^*)$ implies that $p^* \cdot z^* = 0$. Therefore, $p \cdot z^* \leq 0$ for all $p \in \Delta$, which in turn implies that $z^* \leq 0$. Because $p^* \cdot z^* := \sum_{j \in J} p_j^* z_j^* = 0$ and each term in the sum is nonpositive, each term must equal zero. We conclude that $z_j^* = 0$ whenever $p_j^* > 0$. $\square$

Remark 6.37 *Buried in the proof of Theorem 6.36 is a simplified form of a result known as the Gale-Debreu-Nikaido Lemma. With relatively minor changes, the same proof can be used to establish existence of a free disposal equilibrium for an economy with production. See Debreu (1982), 717–719, Theorem 7, for more details.*

6.6 Summary

Clearing markets involves much more than counting equations and unknowns. If market demand is singleton-valued, then establishing existence of a Walrasian equilibrium is essentially equivalent to the Brouwer Theorem or the KKM Theorem. Viewing the existence problem from the perspective of the KKM Theorem leads naturally to a powerful algorithm for computing economic equilibria, the Scarf algorithm. Our discussion has emphasized the special case of singleton-valued demand and focused on pure exchange. As suggested in the final section, the excess demand approach can be extended to cover economies with production and set-valued demand or supply correspondences. However, since those topics are treated, albeit differently, in the next chapter, I have omitted them here.

Exercises

6.1   Prove that $\Delta_w \Phi(p) = \Phi(p) - \sum_{i \in I} w_i$.

6.2   Prove Corollary 6.3.

6.3   Prove Theorem 6.5.

6.4   Extend the results of Section 6.1 to a constant returns to scale production economy. To an Arrow-Debreu production economy.

6.5   Find all of the fixed points of $f : [0, 1] \to [0, 1]$ for

    (a) $f : x \mapsto x^2$;
    (b) $f : x \mapsto \sqrt{x}$;
    (c) $f : x \mapsto 1/(1 + x)$.

6.6   For $\emptyset \neq S \subset [0, 1]$, provide an example where $f \colon S \to S$ fails to have a fixed point because:

(a) S is compact and convex, but f is not continuous;
(b) f is continuous and S is compact, but S is not convex;
(c) f is continuous and S is convex, but S is not compact.

6.7   Using a net trade diagram, illustrate the free disposal equilibrium for the economy portrayed in Figure 6.3.

6.8   Let $V = \{\, (0,0), (1,0), (1,1), (0,1) \,\} \subset \mathbf{R}^2$ and $S = \operatorname{co} V$. Show that the midpoint of the square S is expressible in more than one way as an affine combination of the vertices of S. Which points in S, if any, are uniquely expressible as an affine combination of its vertices?

6.9   For appropriate choices of the parameters, can any $p \in \Delta$ be attained as a solution to the model described in Table 6.1?

6.10   Illustrate the sets M_j in a drawing of the simplex for the example economy of Section 6.2.4 with $\mu_1 = \mu_2 = \mu_3 = 1/3$, and verify that they satisfy the requirements of the KKM Theorem. Experiment with some alternative values for the μ_t.

6.11   Complete the proof of Theorem 6.25.

6.12   For $V = \{\, (0,0), (1,0), (0,1) \,\} \subset \mathbf{R}^2$ and $S = \operatorname{co} V$, give examples where the conclusion of Theorem 6.24 fails to hold because

(a) the sets M_j are not closed;
(b) the sets M_j do not cover S;
(c) the condition $\operatorname{co}\{\, v^j \in V \mid j \in T \,\} \subset \cup_{j \in T} M_j$ for all nonempty $T \subset \{\, 1, \ldots, n \,\}$ is not satisfied.

6.13   How many distinct permutations are there of the form

$$\begin{pmatrix} 1 & 2 & \ldots & n-1 \\ \psi(1) & \psi(2) & \ldots & \psi(n-1) \end{pmatrix}?$$

6.14   Let

$$b = \begin{pmatrix} 5 \\ 4 \\ 3 \\ 4 \end{pmatrix}$$

be a base vertex in the 4-dimensional unit simplex with grid denominator $D = 16$. Describe the vertices of the subsimplex generated by this base vertex and the permutation

$$\psi = \begin{pmatrix} 1 & 2 & 3 \\ 2 & 1 & 3 \end{pmatrix}.$$

6.15 Sperner's Lemma has all of the makings of an excellent parlor game. Give a friend a copy of Figure 6.5 and tell the friend that she is free to attach labels 1, 2, or 3 to any of the vertices subject only to the restrictions that:

- the three main vertices corresponding to e^1, e^2, and e^3 must have labels 1, 2, and 3 respectively; and
- the vertices along the main facets must have labels (a) 2 or 3 if opposite the main vertex labeled 1; (b) 1 or 3 if opposite the main vertex labeled 2; and (c) 1 or 2 if opposite the main vertex labeled 3.

Wager that, however she chooses the labels inside the main triangle, there will always be an odd number of small triangles which are completely labeled. You can't lose!

6.16 Consider the Kuhn simplicial subdivision for the three-dimensional unit simplex with $D = 2$. There are ten vertices of the form

$$(\pi_1/2, \pi_2/2, \pi_3/2, \pi_4/2) \qquad \left(\sum_{i=1}^{4} \pi_i = 2\right)$$

to which are attached the following labels:

Vertex	Coordinates	Label
A	(2,0,0,0)	1
B	(0,2,0,0)	2
C	(0,0,2,0)	3
D	(0,0,0,2)	4
E	(1,1,0,0)	2
F	(0,1,1,0)	2
G	(0,0,1,1)	4
H	(1,0,1,0)	3
I	(0,1,0,1)	4
J	(1,0,0,1)	1

(a) Illustrate this simplex as a pyramid in $\mathbf{R}^3$ with vertices A, B, C as the base and D as the top. Indicate on the diagram the positions of the remaining vertices.

(b) Verify that this labeling satisfies the labeling rule of Sperner's Lemma.

(c) Starting with the base vertex

$$A = \begin{pmatrix} 2 \\ 0 \\ 0 \\ 0 \end{pmatrix}$$

and each possible permutation $\psi: \{1, 2, 3\} \rightarrow \{1, 2, 3\}$, find all of the subsimplices contained in the main simplex which have A as a base.

(d) Repeat the procedure of part (c) for each of the remaining vertices B, C, D, E, F, G, H, I, and J (as in part (c), you need only determine the subsimplices contained in the main simplex).

(e) List the subsimplices determined in parts (c) and (d), and illustrate the simplicial subdivision in your diagram.

(f) Starting with the base vertex

$$\begin{pmatrix} 2 \\ 0 \\ 0 \\ 0 \end{pmatrix}$$

compute the path to a completely labeled subsimplex. Illustrate the path in your diagram.

6.17 Suppose that in Figure 6.9 you start at some almost completely labeled subsimplex not on the boundary. Is it possible to cycle?

6.18 Compute the matrices corresponding to the path to an approximate equilibrium illustrated in Figure 6.11. Compute the excess demands for each of the three commodities at each of the three vertices of the completely labeled subsimplex, letting the endowment parameter $b = 10$.

6.19 Verify the claim in the proof of the KKM Theorem that the labeling satisfies the requirements of Sperner's Lemma.

6.20 Use the Brouwer Theorem to prove the KKM Theorem. You may use without proof the following fact about "partitions of unity": if $\{G_i \subset \Delta \mid i = 1, \ldots, n\}$ is an opening covering of the simplex Δ, then there exists a collection of functions $f_i: \Delta \rightarrow [0, 1]$ such that (a) $f_i(x) > 0$ if $x \in G_i$ and $f_i(x) = 0$ if $x \notin G_i$; and (b) $\sum_{i=1}^{n} f_i(x) = 1$ for all $x \in \Delta$.

6.21 Suppose that a pure exchange economy with two types of commodity has the market excess demand function for the first commodity illustrated below. The figure lists the barycentric coordinates of each point where $\Delta_w \Phi_1$ cuts the axis.

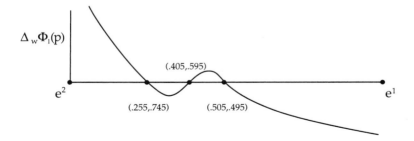

(a) Apply Merrill's algorithm to this economy with $D = 100$ and a starting estimate $\pi^* = (48, 52)$. Illustrate your results in a diagram similar to Figure 6.14.

(b) Repeat part (a) with the initial estimate $\pi^* = (39, 61)$, and illustrate your results in a diagram.

(c) Is there any way to use the Merrill algorithm to reach the third equilibrium point?

6.22 Letting $D = 9$ and taking $\pi = (3, 3, 3)$ as a starting estimate, use a diagram like that of Figure 6.5 to show the labels assigned by Merrill's algorithm to the vertices on the artificial layer. Verify that the 2-dimensional simplex on the artificial layer defined by the starting 3-dimensional simplex is the only 2-dimensional simplex on the artificial layer which is completely labeled. Why is this important to the successful functioning of Merrill's algorithm?

6.23 Letting $D = 8$ and taking $\pi^* = (3, 2, 3)$ as the starting estimate, apply Merrill's algorithm to the simplex illustrated in Figure 6.8. Give a rough sketch of the Merrill sandwich for this case. Is there any way that you can get the algorithm to find the other two completely labeled subsimplices in Figure 6.8?

6.24 Practical applications of the Scarf algorithm usually involve production. Assuming constant returns and the absence of intermediate production, it is possible to solve for equilibrium in such models by iterating through a low dimensional simplex even though the number of produced commodities is very large. This exercise gives a flavor of such applications.

Consider an economy with four commodities and a single consumer. Commodities 1 and 2 are produced subject to constant returns to scale with a Cobb-Douglas production function using commodities 3 and 4 as inputs. Average cost of production for commodities 1 and 2 is given by $p_3^\beta p_4^{1-\beta}$ and $p_3^{1-\beta} p_4^\beta$ respectively where $0 < \beta < 1$. The consumer has initial endowment $w = (0, 0, b, b)$, $b > 0$, of commodities 3 and 4, which she is willing to supply perfectly inelastically. Adopting the normalization $p_3 + p_4 = 1$, we conclude that consumer wealth equals b. The consumer's preferences are described by a Cobb-Douglas utility function $x_1^\alpha x_2^{1-\alpha}$, $0 < \alpha < 1$, for commodities 1 and 2. (Commodities 3 and 4 are not desired by the consumer, which explains why her supply of these input commodities is perfectly inelastic.)

(a) Show that, in solving for equilibrium, it suffices to clear only one of the markets for the "primary factors" (i.e., either commodity 3 or commodity 4) rather than three out of four markets as would be the case in pure exchange. Find the Walrasian equilibrium prices for commodities 3 and 4 as functions of the parameters α and β.

(b) Letting $\alpha = \beta = 1/4$, solve for the equilibrium prices for all four commodities.

(c) Focusing solely on the prices of the primary factors, illustrate the Merrill algorithm for this economy using a grid denominator $D = 8$ and initial estimate $(\pi_3, \pi_4) = (7, 1)$. Show how the path through the simplex can be represented by a series of matrices with the movement from matrix to matrix governed by the Kuhn replacement method.

(d) If the consumer's utility is an arbitrary quasi-concave function of all four commodities, does it still suffice to clear the markets for commodities 3 and 4? If not, what more needs to be assumed for this procedure to suffice?

6.25   Let $K \subset [0, 1]$ and $\Psi : K \to (2^K)_o^F$. Give an example where Ψ has no fixed point because:

(a) Ψ satisfies the conditions of Theorem 6.34, K is compact, but K is not convex;

(b) Ψ satisfies the conditions of Theorem 6.34, K is convex, but K is not compact;

(c) $K = [0, 1]$ and Ψ is uhc, but Ψ is not convex-valued;

(d) $K = [0, 1]$ and Ψ is convex-valued, but Ψ is not uhc.

7

Walras meets Nash

The preceding chapter approached the question of existence of Walrasian equilibrium by searching for prices which clear markets. This chapter explores an alternative approach, no less intuitive, which relies not on the summation of best responses but rather on their Cartesian product. Although the method is most directly associated with the work of Nash on noncooperative games, its roots reach back to Cournot in the early part of the nineteenth century.

The first section presents some basic concepts and existence proofs for equilibria of a noncooperative game and its close relative, an abstract economy. The second section applies these notions to proving existence for the traditional Arrow-Debreu economy. The remaining three sections pursue applications with a more exotic flavor involving equilibrium in the presence of externalities, nonconvexities, and nonordered preferences.

7.1 Noncooperative game theory

7.1.1 Nash equilibrium

We begin with a very selective presentation of some features of noncooperative game theory which are relevant to our present purpose.

Game theory has its own particular vocabulary which is rather different from that used to describe a Walrasian economy. The participants in a (noncooperative) game are called **players**, the choices they make **strategies**, and the benefits they derive from playing the game **payoffs**. While the terminology is quite different, by a judicious choice of notation we can highlight the similarities between the description of a game and a Walrasian economy.

Let $I = \{1, \ldots, n\}$ denote the **set of players** in the game. Each player $i \in I$ selects a **strategy** s_i from a fixed **strategy set** $S_i \subset L$ where L is a finite dimensional topological vector space. Let $S = \prod_{i \in I} S_i$ with typical element $s = (s_1, \ldots, s_n)$. The benefit derived by player i depends both on her choice of strategy s_i and on the strategies

$$s_{-i} := (s_1, \ldots, s_{i-1}, s_{i+1}, \ldots, s_n)$$

chosen by all of the other players. In the standard treatment of noncooperative games, this benefit is represented by a **payoff function** $u_i \colon S \to \mathbf{R}$, $s \mapsto u_i(s)$. The essential idea is that the payoff of player i depends not only on the response s_i, the strategy which she chooses, but also on the environment s_{-i}, the strategies selected by the other players.[1]

Although the use of payoff functions is rather standard in the game theoretic literature, the connection with Walrasian equilibrium will be more transparent if we use preference relations instead. For each choice of environment s_{-i}, let $\succ_i^{s_{-i}}$ denote the **strict preference relation of player i when the environment is s_{-i}** where $s_i' \succ_i^{s_{-i}} s_i$ has the interpretation "the strategy s_i' is strictly preferred to the strategy s_i provided that the other players are choosing the strategies s_{-i}."[2] Define the **strict preference mapping**

$$P_i \colon S \to 2^{S_i}, \quad s \mapsto P_i(s) := \{\, s_i' \in S_i \mid s_i' \succ_i^{s_{-i}} s_i \,\}$$

where the set $P_i(s)$ represents the set of all strategies s_i' preferred to strategy s_i by player i when the environment is s_{-i}. The **graph of the strict preference mapping** P_i is then

$$\Gamma(P_i) := \{\, (s, s_i') \in S \times S_i \mid s_i' \in P_i(s) \,\}.$$

Continuing our analogy with the consumer, the **best response** of player i is defined in the obvious way,[3]

$$B_i(s) := \{\, s_i \in S_i \mid P_i(s) \cap S_i = \emptyset \,\}$$

with essentially the same interpretation we gave to the best responses of consumers or firms in a Walrasian economy: the strategy s_i is a best response for player i to the environment s_{-i} if there is no other strategy available to the player which is preferred to s_i in that environment.

An n-tuple of strategies $(s_1^*, \ldots, s_n^*)$ is a **Nash equilibrium** if each individual strategy s_i^* is a best response to the strategies chosen by the other

---

1 While the usage is admittedly a little unusual, I will continue throughout this chapter to refer to the strategies of the other players as "the environment s_{-i}."

2 Writing the strategy n-tuple s as (s_i, s_{-i}) helps to clarify the connection between payoff functions and preferences. Defining $s_i' \succ_i^{s_{-i}} s_i$ iff $u_i(s_i', s_{-i}) > u_i(s_i, s_{-i})$ establishes the connection.

3 Despite appearances, $B_i(s)$ depends only on s_{-i} and not on s_i. If this does not seem clear, try replacing s_i by s_i' and s by (s_i', s_{-i}) on the right hand side.

players: i.e., $s_i^* \in B_i(s^*)$ for all $i \in I$. This condition can be expressed even more elegantly if we combine the individual best response correspondences into a single best response correspondence for the game as a whole, the Cartesian product of the individual best responses $B(s^*) = \prod_{i \in I} B_i(s^*)$.

Definition 7.1 *An n-tuple $(s_1^*, \ldots, s_n^*)$ is a* **Nash equilibrium** *for the n-person game $G = \{ S_i, P_i \mid i \in I \}$ if $s^* \in B(s^*)$.*

Thus, a Nash equilibrium is simply a fixed point of the best response correspondence. Kakutani's fixed point theorem cannot be far behind!

7.1.2 Cournot oligopoly

Although the idea of Nash equilibrium seems straightforward enough, the concept is rather abstract. We detour briefly to consider a simple illustration of the basic idea, the oligopoly model of Cournot (1838). Though not a very satisfactory theory of oligopolistic behavior, Cournot's work was remarkably advanced for the time. For our purposes, its main virtue is its simplicity.

Cournot's model is partial equilibrium in spirit. The player set $I = \{ 1, \ldots, n \}$ represents a collection of firms each producing the same commodity. Each firm supplies a quantity s_i of the commodity to the same market. Letting $Q = \sum_{i \in I} s_i$ denote the total quantity supplied, market price is determined by the demand function

$$p = \max\{ a - bQ, 0 \} \tag{7.1}$$

where a and b are positive constants. Each of the firms is able to produce the commodity at constant cost with marginal (and average) cost equal to the positive constant c. The goal of the analysis is to determine the quantities which each firm will supply.

Translating this model into the framework of the preceding section, we first observe that no firm will supply more than the quantity a/b since, according to equation (7.1), if $Q \geq a/b$ then the market clearing price is zero. We can, therefore, take as the strategy set of player (firm) i the set $S_i = [0, a/b]$. Letting $s = (s_1, \ldots, s_n)$ represent the n-tuple of strategies chosen by the players, the payoff to player i is given by the profit function $u_i(s) = (a - bQ)s_i - cs_i = (a - b\sum_{j \in I} s_j)s_i - cs_i$. Setting the partial derivative of this function with respect to s_i equal to zero yields the first order condition for a maximum,

$$a - bQ - bs_i - c = 0. \tag{7.2}$$

Solving for s_i gives the (singleton-valued) best response correspondence for player i:

$$B_i(s) = \frac{a - c - b\sum_{j \neq i} s_j}{2b}. \tag{7.3}$$

Before investigating the properties of the Nash equilibrium for this model, consider some more conventional solutions suggested by standard economic theory. Suppose first that this market is controlled by a single firm, a monopolist. Solving the problem $\max_Q\{\,(a - bQ)Q - cQ\,\}$ yields the solution

$$Q^m = \frac{a - c}{2b} \quad \text{and} \quad p^m = \frac{a + c}{2}. \tag{7.4}$$

Going to the opposite extreme, if the industry is perfectly competitive, then

$$Q^{pc} = \frac{a - c}{b} \quad \text{and} \quad p^{pc} = c. \tag{7.5}$$

Returning now to the oligopolistic context, note that for $n = 1$ the best response function (7.3) yields the same result as the simple monopoly model. When $n = 2$ (the duopoly model) the definition of Nash equilibrium requires $s_1^* = B_1(s^*)$ and $s_2^* = B_2(s^*)$. Since the resulting equations $s_1^* = (a - c - bs_2^*)/2b$ and $s_2^* = (a - c - bs_1^*)/2b$ are linear, solving for the Nash equilibrium is easy.

Although the case for general n can be solved in exactly the same way, it is easier to use a trick. Summing each of the equations (7.2) over the set of players I, we obtain $n(a - bQ) - b\sum_{i \in I} s_i - nc = 0$ or

$$n(a - bQ) - bQ - nc = 0.$$

Thus, the Nash solution for an arbitrary number of players n becomes

$$Q_n^N = \left(\frac{n}{n+1}\right)\left[\frac{a - c}{b}\right] \quad \text{and} \quad p_n^N = \left(\frac{a + nc}{n+1}\right). \tag{7.6}$$

Since the firms are identical, the individual Nash strategies are all the same:

$$s_{ni}^N = \left(\frac{1}{n+1}\right)\left[\frac{a - c}{b}\right] \quad \text{for all} \quad i \in I. \tag{7.7}$$

Notice that $\lim_{n\to\infty} Q_n^N = (a - c)/b$ and $\lim_{n\to\infty} p_n^N = c$, the perfectly competitive solution!

Figure 7.1 illustrates the Cournot-Nash solution for the case $n = 2$ where I have chosen the parameters $a = 4$, $b = 1$, and $c = 0$. The best response (reaction) functions for players 1 and 2, labeled B_1 and B_2 respectively, intersect at the Nash equilibrium point NE. The line segment with endpoints $(0, 2)$ and $(2, 0)$ corresponds to strategies which maximize joint profit, the

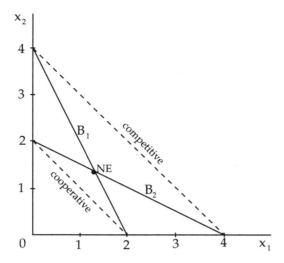

Fig. 7.1. The duopoly solution.

cooperative solution in which the two firms choose the total supply which would be chosen by a monopolist. The line segment with endpoints $(0, 4)$ and $(4, 0)$, on the other hand, represents strategies which are perfectly competitive (since production occurs under constant returns to scale, the amount contributed by each individual firm is indeterminate.)

7.1.3 Abstract economies

While appropriate for game theory, the assumption that strategy sets are fixed is not well-suited to Walrasian economics. Fortunately, the description of a game is easily modified to allow the sets of strategies available to a player to change in response to the strategies of the other players.

Keeping all other aspects of the description the same, we simply add a constraint correspondence $K_i \colon S \to (2^{S_i})_o^F$, $s \mapsto K_i(s) \subset S_i$ for each player $i \in I$ with the implicit understanding that, to avoid circularity, $K_i(s)$ depends only on s_{-i}, not s_i. The definition of the best response correspondence is modified accordingly:

$$B_i(s) := \{ s_i \in K_i(s) \mid P_i(s) \cap K_i(s) = \emptyset \}.$$

Definition 7.2 *An **abstract economy** $\mathcal{E} = \{ S_i, P_i, K_i \mid i \in I \}$ consists of a set of players $I = \{ 1, \dots, n \}$ and, for each $i \in I$,*

- *a **strategy set** $S_i \subset L$,*

- a **strict preference map** $P_i \colon S \to 2^{S_i}$, $s \mapsto P_i(s) \subset S_i$, and
- a **constraint correspondence** $K_i \colon S \to (2^{S_i})_o^F$, $s \mapsto K_i(s) \subset S_i$

where L is a finite dimensional TVS.

Abstract economies include the standard games defined earlier as a special case with each constraint correspondence K_i taking on the constant value S_i. Equilibrium for an abstract economy extends the Nash equilibrium concept in the obvious way.

Definition 7.3 *An n-tuple $(s_1^*, \ldots, s_n^*)$ is an* **equilibrium**[4] *for the abstract n-person economy $\mathcal{E} = \{ S_i, P_i, K_i \mid i \in I \}$ if $s^* \in B(s^*)$.*

7.1.4 Existence of equilibrium

Equilibrium without existence does not mean much. This section presents two existence theorems guaranteeing that the equilibrium of an abstract economy exists under quite general circumstances. The first result, which builds on the fundamental work of Nash (1950), is due to Debreu (1952). I preface the theorem with a lemma intended to clarify the role of Kakutani's fixed point theorem.

Lemma 7.4 *Let $\mathcal{E} = \{ S_i, P_i, K_i \mid i \in I \}$ be an abstract n-person economy. If for each player $i \in I$ the strategy set S_i is nonempty, compact, and convex and the best response correspondence B_i nonempty-valued, convex-valued, and upperhemicontinuous, then an equilibrium exists.*

Proof The proof is simply a verification that the best response correspondence B satisfies the requirements of the Kakutani Fixed Point Theorem.

Because each strategy set S_i is nonempty, compact, and convex, the set $S := \prod_{i \in I} S_i$ is nonempty, compact, and convex: nonemptyness is immediate; compactness follows from Theorem 4.29, the Tychonoff Theorem; convexity is implied by Theorem 2.3. Similarly, because each correspondence B_i is uhc, nonempty-valued, and convex-valued, the correspondence $B := \prod_{i \in I} B_i$ inherits the same properties (see Theorem 5.55). Therefore, by the Kakutani Fixed Point Theorem, there exists a fixed point $s^* \in B(s^*)$.

$\square$

While useful as a first step, the preceding lemma has one basic defect: some of its key assumptions involve the best response correspondences, which are derived constructs, rather than the model primitives S_i, P_i, and

4 Debreu (1952) calls this a social equilibrium.

K_i. We want instead to derive those properties from first principles. To that end we impose a traditional, though rather stringent, requirement on preferences: $\succ_i^{s-i}$ is a weak ordering, and hence $\succeq_i^{s-i}$ a complete preordering,[5] for all possible environments s_{-i} and for all $i \in I$. Adapting the notation of Chapter 5 to the present context, define the upper contour set $R_i(s) := \{\, s_i' \in S_i \mid s_i' \succeq_i^{s-i} s_i \,\}$. Also let $S_{-i} := \prod_{j \neq i} S_j$ denote the cartesian product of the strategy sets of all the players except for player i.

Theorem 7.5 *Let* $\mathcal{E} = \{\, S_i, P_i, K_i \mid i \in I \,\}$ *be an abstract n-person economy. If for each player* $i \in I$

- *the strategy set* S_i *is nonempty, compact, and convex,*
- *the constraint correspondence* K_i *is convex-valued and continuous,*
- *the binary relation* $\succ_i^{s-i}$ *underlying the strict preference map* P_i *is a weak ordering on* S_i *for each environment* $s_{-i} \in S_{-i}$,
- *the upper contour sets* $R_i(s)$ *are convex for all* $s \in S$,
- *the strict preference mapping* P_i *has open graph in* $S \times S_i$,

then an equilibrium exists.

Proof We only need to show that the best response correspondences B_i satisfy the requirements of Lemma 7.4.

For each $s \in S$, the sets $B_i(s)$ are nonempty, compact, and convex (Theorems 5.16 and 5.21). Since K_i is continuous and P_i has open graph, the correspondences B_i are uhc (the Maximum Theorem 5.47). Therefore, by the lemma, there exists a fixed point $s^* \in B(s^*)$. □

The other existence result presented in this section advances an almost unbelievable claim: existence of equilibrium when preferences are neither transitive nor complete. The proof given here, adapted from Shafer and Sonnenschein (1975b), is elegant but not very intuitive. That is the price we pay for allowing preferences to be so badly behaved, forcing the proof to circumvent direct use of the best response correspondence. The result is well worth the effort, however, as we will see when we talk about applications.

Theorem 7.6 *Let* $\mathcal{E} = \{\, S_i, P_i, K_i \mid i \in I \,\}$ *be an n-person abstract economy. If for each player* $i \in I$

(a) *the strategy set* S_i *is nonempty, compact, and convex,*

(b) *the constraint correspondence* K_i *is convex-valued and continuous,*

(c) *the strict preference map* P_i *has open graph in* $S \times S_i$, *and*

---

5 The preference relation $\succeq_i^{s-i}$ has the obvious interpretation: $s_i' \succeq_i^{s-i} s_i$ if, according to player i, "strategy s_i' is at least as good as strategy s_i when the environment is s_{-i}."

(d) $s_i \notin \operatorname{co} P_i(s)$ *for all* $s \in S$,

then an equilibrium exists.

Proof Let $g_i(s, s_i) := \operatorname{dist}((s, s_i), (S \times S_i) \backslash \Gamma(P_i))$. The graph $\Gamma(P_i)$ is open in $S \times S_i$; hence, g_i is continuous, $g_i(s, s_i) = 0$ on $(S \times S_i) \backslash \Gamma(P_i)$ and $g_i(s, s_i) > 0$ on $\Gamma(P_i)$. Define the correspondence $\widehat{B}_i : S \to (2^{S_i})^F_o$ which maps

$$s \mapsto \widehat{B}_i(s) := \left\{ s_i \in K_i(s) \mid g_i(s, s_i) = \max_{s_i' \in K_i(s)} g_i(s, s_i') \right\}.$$

The Maximum Theorem implies that $\widehat{B}_i$ is uhc, and so $\operatorname{co} \widehat{B}_i$ and hence $\prod_{i \in I} \operatorname{co} \widehat{B}_i$ is uhc. Therefore, by the Kakutani Fixed Point Theorem, the correspondence $\prod_{i \in I} \operatorname{co} \widehat{B}_i$ has a fixed point, say $s^* \in \prod_{i \in I} \operatorname{co} \widehat{B}_i(s^*)$, or equivalently $s_i^* \in \operatorname{co} \widehat{B}_i(s^*)$ for all $i \in I$.

It remains to show that $s_i^* \in B_i(s^*)$ (and not just that $s_i^* \in \widehat{B}_i(s^*)$). Since $\widehat{B}_i(s^*) \subset K_i(s^*)$ and $K_i(s^*)$ is convex, $\operatorname{co} \widehat{B}_i(s^*) \subset K_i(s^*)$ and so $s_i^* \in K_i(s^*)$ for all $i \in I$. If we can show that $P_i(s^*) \cap K_i(s^*) = \emptyset$ for all $i \in I$ then we are done. Suppose not, so that there exists $s_i' \in P_i(s^*) \cap K_i(s^*)$. Since $s_i' \in P_i(s^*)$, we have $(s^*, s_i') \in \Gamma(P_i)$ and so $g_i(s^*, s_i') > 0$. But it then must be the case that $g_i(s^*, s_i) > 0$ for every $s_i \in \widehat{B}_i(s^*)$ because $\widehat{B}_i(s^*)$ is the set of maximizers of g_i and we have just established that the maximum value is greater than zero. We conclude that $\widehat{B}_i(s^*) \subset P_i(s^*)$. However, $s_i^* \in \operatorname{co} \widehat{B}_i(s^*) \subset \operatorname{co} P_i(s^*)$, which means that $s_i^* \in \operatorname{co} P_i(s^*)$, contradicting hypothesis (d) of the theorem.   □

7.2 Walrasian equilibrium

7.2.1 *The Arrow-Debreu model*

In adapting the approach of Nash to proving existence of Walrasian equilibrium, the essential idea seems clear: treat consumers and firms as players in an abstract economy. We take as our setting the standard Arrow-Debreu model of Chapter 2. Table 7.1 transcribes the basic concepts of the Arrow-Debreu model into the game theoretic framework of the preceding section (ignore for the moment the second column, labeled "Auctioneer"). Each consumer $i \in I = \{1, \ldots, n\}$ chooses as her strategy a consumption vector x_i from the consumption set X_i. Likewise each firm $k \in K = \{1, \ldots, r\}$ chooses as its strategy an activity vector y_k from the technology set Y_k.

Most of the Walrasian concepts developed in earlier chapters translate easily into this new context. Eventually, however, we hit a snag: What are we to do with the market prices appearing as arguments in the best response correspondences of both consumers and firms? No single player determines

Table 7.1. *The Arrow-Debreu framework.*

	Auctioneer	Consumers	Firms
Strategies	p	$(x_1, \ldots, x_n)$	$(y_1, \ldots, y_r)$
Strategy sets	Δ	$(X_1, \ldots, X_n)$	$(Y_1, \ldots, Y_r)$
Constraints	Δ	$(\beta_1, \ldots, \beta_n)$	$(Y_1, \ldots, Y_r)$
Best responses	α	$(\phi_1, \ldots, \phi_n)$	$(\eta_1, \ldots, \eta_r)$

prices. Instead the Walrasian model assumes that consumers and firms act as price takers, treating prices as exogenous. But prices are also determined jointly by the actions these players take. Why should consumers and firms treat prices as given when, by their actions, they influence those prices? This involves an element of irrationality which game theory does not allow.

In applying Nash's idea to proving existence of Walrasian equilibrium, one of Debreu's key insights was the realization that we can "fake it" by adding a fictitious player whom we call the Auctioneer. Since the strategy of this player will be the price vector p, and since the other players in this pseudo-game will regard her strategy as part of their environment, in effect they act as price-takers!

Before proceeding further, we need to establish a little more notation. Let $X = \prod_{i \in I} X_i$ and $Y = \prod_{k \in K} Y_k$ denote the Cartesian product of the strategy spaces for the consumers and the firms[6] in the economy respectively with typical elements $x = (x_1, \ldots, x_n)$ and $y = (y_1, \ldots, y_r)$. The Auctioneer is assumed to choose the price vector p from the strategy space Δ, the unit simplex.[7] Thus, the joint strategy space for this entire $n+r+1$ player game is the product $S = \Delta \times X \times Y$ with typical element $s = (p, x, y)$.

Returning to our task of incorporating the Auctioneer into the abstract economy framework, all that remains is to choose for her a suitable payoff function. Since she is a fiction, we are free to ascribe to her a motivation that serves our purpose: choosing prices which clear markets. The environment faced by the Auctioneer is the $n + r$-tuple of strategies $(x, y) = (x_1, \ldots, x_n, y_1, \ldots, y_r)$. If each consumer $i \in I$ has endowment vector w_i,

---

6 Don't confuse this use of Y with the aggregate technology set $Y = \sum_{k \in K} Y_k$ of Chapter 2.

7 Restricting prices to the unit simplex makes the implicit assumption, which can easily be made explicit, that prices cannot all be zero. If $p = 0$ consumers would demand more than the economy can feasibly provide.

then excess demand is given by

$$Z(x, y) := \sum_{i \in I} x_i - \sum_{k \in K} y_k - \sum_{i \in I} w_i.$$

We define, therefore, the payoff for the Auctioneer as the function $u: S \to \mathbf{R}$ which maps $(p, x, y) =: s \mapsto u(s) := p \cdot Z(x, y)$, the value of excess demand at prices p. The best response of the Auctioneer consists of those price vectors which maximize the value of excess demand:

$$\alpha(p, x, y) := \left\{ p' \in \Delta \mid p' \cdot Z(x, y) = \sup_p u(p, x, y) \right\}.$$

The column of Table 7.1 labeled "Auctioneer" shows the strategy, strategy set, constraint correspondence, and best response of the Auctioneer.

Before stating the existence theorem, we first modify the specification of the Arrow-Debreu model in a direction suggested by Gale and Mas-Colell (1975). In a pure exchange model the wealth function of consumer i is given by $\omega_i(p) := p \cdot w_i$ where w_i is the consumer's endowment vector. In the standard Arrow-Debreu model, consumer i has wealth function $\omega_i(p) := p \cdot w_i + \sum_{k \in K} \theta_{ik} \pi_k(p)$ where θ_{ik} is the share of consumer i in the profit $\pi_k(p)$ of firm k. Following Gale and Mas-Colell, we generalize both these cases by allowing an arbitrary wealth function $\omega_i(p)$ for each consumer $i \in I$ subject to the obvious restriction that $\sum_{i \in I} \omega_i(p) = \sum_{i \in I} p \cdot w_i + \pi(p)$ for all $p \in \Delta$ where $\pi(p) := \sum_{k \in K} \pi_k(p)$ is the **aggregate profit function**. Consumer budget sets are modified in the obvious way, $\beta_i(p) := \{ x_i \in X_i \mid p \cdot x_i \le \omega_i(p) \}$.

With one more minor adjustment, we are ready to fit consumers and firms into the abstract economy framework. In earlier chapters, the best response correspondences of consumers and firms depended only on prices p and not on the entire strategy vector $s = (p, x, y)$. It does no harm, however, to extend the domain of definition to include x and y: they function simply as dummy variables with no effect on either the consumer or the firm.[8] Specifically, for each consumer $i \in I$ the **demand correspondence** becomes

$$\phi_i: S \to 2^{X_i}, \quad s \mapsto \phi_i(s) := \{ x_i \in X_i \mid P_i(x_i) \cap \beta_i(p) = \emptyset \},$$

and for each firm $k \in K$ the **supply correspondence** becomes

$$\eta_k: S \to 2^{Y_k}, \quad s \mapsto \eta_k(s) := \{ y_k \in Y_k \mid p \cdot y_k = \pi_k(p) \}.$$

---

8 At the risk of belaboring the obvious, the following analogy might help. Suppose that we are given a function $f: R \to R$ which maps $p \mapsto p^2$. We can extend the domain of f to R^3, with f regarded as a function of x and y as well as p, by defining $f(p, x, y) = p^2$ for all $(x, y) \in R^2$.

We begin with a lemma paralleling Lemma 7.4.

Lemma 7.7 *If $\mathcal{E} = (\{X_i, P_i, w_i, \omega_i \mid i \in I\}, \{Y_k \mid k \in K\})$ is an Arrow-Debreu economy for which*

- *the consumption set X_i is nonempty, compact, and convex for all $i \in I$,*
- *the technology set Y_k is nonempty, compact, and convex for all $k \in K$,*
- *the demand correspondence ϕ_i is nonempty-valued, convex-valued, and uhc for all $i \in I$,*
- *the supply correspondence η_k is nonempty-valued, convex-valued, and uhc for all $k \in K$,*
- *the Auctioneer's best response α is nonempty-valued, convex-valued, and uhc,*
- *$x_i \in \operatorname{cl} P_i(x_i)$ for every consumer $i \in I$ and for every allocation (x, y) for which excess demand $Z(x, y) \leq 0$,*

then a free disposal Walrasian equilibrium exists.

Proof Since this abstract economy satisfies the requirements of Lemma 7.4, there exists an $n + r + 1$-tuple of strategies

$$s^* \in \alpha(s^*) \times \prod_{i \in I} \phi_i(s^*) \times \prod_{k \in K} \eta_k(s^*)$$

or, equivalently, $p^* \in \alpha(s^*)$, $x_i^* \in \phi_i(s^*)$, and $y_k^* \in \eta_k(s^*)$ for all $i \in I$ and $k \in K$. Thus, consumers are maximizing "utility" and firms are maximizing profits. All that remains is to show that the allocation is feasible. However, just as in Chapter 6, the fact that we require equilibrium prices p^* to lie in the simplex means that we have to settle for a little less: a free disposal equilibrium.

From $x_i^* \in \phi_i^*(s^*)$ we conclude that $x_i^* \in \beta(p^*)$ and, hence, $p^* \cdot x_i^* \leq \omega_i(p^*)$ for all $i \in I$. Summing over I gives

$$\sum_{i \in I} p^* \cdot x_i^* \leq \sum_{i \in I} \omega_i(p^*) = \sum_{i \in I} p^* \cdot w_i + \pi(p^*).$$

For each firm $k \in K$, $y_k^* \in \eta_k(s^*)$ implies $p \cdot y_k^* = \pi_k(p^*)$ and so

$$\sum_{k \in K} p \cdot y_k^* = \sum_{k \in K} \pi_k(p^*) = \pi(p^*).$$

Therefore,

$$p^* \cdot \sum_{i \in I} x_i^* \leq p^* \cdot \sum_{i \in I} w_i + p^* \cdot \sum_{k \in K} y_k^*. \qquad (*)$$

Suppose that the excess demand for some commodity, say commodity j', is strictly positive:

$$Z_{j'}(x^*, y^*) := \sum_{i \in I} x^*_{ij'} - \sum_{k \in K} y^*_{kj'} - \sum_{i \in I} w_{ij'} > 0.$$

Since the Auctioneer maximizes her payoff, we must have

$$p^* \cdot Z(x^*, y^*) := \sum_{j \in J} p^*_j Z_j(x^*, y^*) > 0,$$

contradicting equation $(*)$. We conclude that $Z(x^*, y^*) \leq 0$. By assumption this implies that consumers are locally nonsatiated at the allocation (x^*, y^*) and hence (Exercise 7.5) that

$$p^* \cdot Z(x^*, y^*) := \sum_{j \in J} p^*_j Z_j(x^*, y^*) = 0.$$

Since every term in this sum is nonpositive and prices are nonnegative, we conclude that $Z_j(x^*, y^*) \leq 0$ for all $j \in J$ and $Z_j(x^*, y^*) = 0$ whenever $p^*_j > 0$; i.e., we have a free disposal Walrasian equilibrium. $\qquad\square$

We obtain our basic theorem by imposing enough restrictions on the model primitives to guarantee that best responses satisfy the requirements of the preceding lemma and that the free disposal equilibrium is a true equilibrium.

Theorem 7.8 *Let* $\mathcal{E} = (\{X_i, P_i, w_i, \omega_i \mid i \in I\}, \{Y_k \mid k \in K\})$ *be an Arrow-Debreu economy. For all consumers* $i \in I$, *assume that*

- X_i *is nonempty, compact, and convex;*
- $\succ_i$ *is a weak ordering with open graph in* $X_i \times X_i$;
- *the upper contour sets* $R_i(x_i)$ *are convex for all* $x_i \in X_i$;
- $x_i \in \operatorname{cl} P_i(x_i)$ *for every allocation* (x, y) *for which excess demand* $Z(x, y) \leq 0$,
- *the wealth function* ω_i *is continuous and satisfies the condition* $\omega_i(p) > \inf p \cdot X_i$ *for all* $p \in \Delta$.

For all firms $k \in K$, *assume that*

- Y_k *is nonempty, compact, and convex;*
- *if* $y \in \sum_{k \in K} Y_k$, *then* $-y^+ \in \sum_{k \in K} Y_k$ *(free disposal).*

A Walrasian equilibrium exists for the economy $\mathcal{E}$.

Proof The free disposal assumption guarantees that firms can eliminate any unwanted excess supply costlessly. Therefore, we can assume that an equilibrium established via Lemma 7.7 satisfies $\sum_{i \in I} x^*_i = \sum_{k \in K} y_k + \sum_{i \in I} w_i$.

All that remains is to prove that the best response correspondences satisfy the requirements of Lemma 7.7: i.e., each is nonempty-valued, convex-valued, and uhc. I will provide the main structure of the proof, leaving some of the details to the exercises.

- *Consumer $i \in I$:* Although we are now writing $\phi_i(s)$ rather than $\phi_i(p)$, it will probably be less confusing to revert temporarily to the earlier notation. Fixing $p \in \Delta$, we conclude that $\beta_i(p)$ is nonempty, compact, and convex (Exercise 7.6.). Since $\succ_i$ has open graph in $X_i \times X_i$, it has open sections (Theorem 5.24), which implies that $\phi_i(p)$ is nonempty and compact (Theorem 5.16). Because upper contour sets are convex, $\phi_i(p)$ is convex (Theorem 5.21). All that remains is to show that ϕ_i is uhc. Since X_i is nonempty, compact, and convex, $\omega_i(p) > \inf p \cdot X_i$ for all $p \in \Delta$, and ω_i is continuous in p, the budget constraint β_i is continuous in p (Theorem 5.51). Because p does not affect $\succ_i$, the fact that $\succ_i$ has open graph in $X_i \times X_i$ implies that $\succ_i$ has open graph in $\Delta \times X_i \times X_i$ (Exercise 7.7). Therefore, by the Maximum Theorem 5.47, ϕ_i is uhc in p. Finally, we need to show that these conclusions are preserved when we extend the domain from Δ to $\Delta \times X \times Y$. Since neither $\succ_i$ nor β_i depends on the actions of the other consumers, we conclude that $\phi_i(s)$ is nonempty, compact, and convex and that ϕ_i is uhc in s (Exercise 7.8).

- *Firm $k \in K$:* Just as for the consumer we will temporarily revert to earlier notation, writing $\eta_k(p)$ rather than $\eta_k(s)$ for the supply set of firm k. Firm k maximizes $p \cdot y_k$, which is continuous in y_k and has convex upper contour sets (Exercise 7.9). The constraint set Y_k is nonempty, compact, and convex. Therefore, $\eta_k(p)$ is nonempty and compact (Corollary 5.17) and convex (Theorem 5.21). Since the constraint correspondence for firm k is constant (i.e., it always equals Y_k), it is continuous in p. Because $p \cdot y_k$ is continuous in p as well as y_k, we conclude that η_k is uhc in p (Corollary 5.50). Finally, we extend the domain from Δ to $\Delta \times X \times Y$: since neither Y_k nor $p \cdot y_k$ depends on the other elements of the environment, y_{-k} or x, $\eta(s)$ is nonempty, compact, and convex and η_k is uhc in s.

- *The Auctioneer:* The constraint set Δ is nonempty, compact, and convex. The "utility function" $p \cdot Z(x, y)$ is continuous in p and, with x and y fixed, it has convex upper contour sets (Exercise 7.10). Therefore, $\alpha(s)$ is nonempty and compact (Corollary 5.17) and convex (Theorem 5.21). Since the constraint correspondence is constant (i.e., it always equals Δ), it is certainly continuous in s. The expression

being maximized, $p \cdot Z(x, y)$ is continuous in x and y as well as p
(Exercise 7.11). We conclude that α is uhc in s (Corollary 5.50).

$\square$

7.2.2 Elaborations

The literature contains many variations on Theorem 7.8 addressing issues
we have swept under the rug. One might object, for example, that assuming
consumption sets X_i and technology sets Y_k compact is not very natural:
consumers could consume unlimited quantities; firms could produce without
bound. "Obviously" the total resources of the universe put bounds on consumption and production, but perhaps what seems obvious needs deriving.
The following paraphrase of a theorem in Debreu (1982) gives the flavor of
results along these lines:

Theorem 7.9 *Let* $\mathcal{E} = (\{\, X_i, P_i, w_i, \omega_i \mid i \in I \,\}, \{\, Y_k \mid k \in K \,\})$ *be an
Arrow-Debreu economy. For all consumers* $i \in I$, *assume that*

- X_i *is nonempty, convex, and bounded from below;*
- $\succ_i$ *is a weak ordering with open graph in* $X_i \times X_i$;
- *the upper contour sets* $R_i(x_i)$ *are convex for all* $x_i \in X_i$;
- $x_i \in \operatorname{cl} P_i(x_i)$ *for every allocation* (x, y) *for which* $Z(x, y) \leq 0$.
- *the wealth function* ω_i *is continuous and satisfies the condition*
  $\omega_i(p) > \inf p \cdot X_i$ *for all* $p \in \Delta$.

For all firms $k \in K$, *assume that*

- Y_k *is nonempty, closed, and convex;*
- $\sum_{k \in K} Y_k \supset \mathbf{R}_-^m$;
- $\sum_{k \in K} Y_k \cap \mathbf{R}_+^m$ *is bounded from above.*

A Walrasian equilibrium exists for the economy $\mathcal{E}$.

Proof See Debreu (1982), 711, Theorem 5. $\square$

In contrast to Theorem 7.8, Theorem 7.9 no longer assumes that consumption sets and technology sets are compact. Although I am directing
you elsewhere for the details, discussing the essential idea behind Debreu's
proof seems worthwhile.

Relaxing the compactness assumptions causes no problems for an exchange economy. Letting $W_j := \sum_{i \in I} w_{ij}$ denote the total amount of commodity j available in the economy, we can certainly assume that consumption sets X_i are contained in the compact, convex box $\prod_{j \in J}[0, W_j]$. With
production, matters are somewhat more complex:

- If consumers could supply unlimited amounts of labor, scarcity could be eliminated and Walrasian equilibria fail to exist. We rule this out by bounding consumption sets from below: for each consumer $i \in I$ there exists a vector $b_i \in \mathbf{R^m}$ such that $X_i \geq b_i$.

- Scarcity could also be eliminated if outputs could be produced without using inputs: this possibility is eliminated by assuming that the intersection of the aggregate technology set with the positive orthant is bounded from above:[9] there exists a vector $c \in \mathbf{R^m}$ such that $\mathbf{R^m_+} \cap \sum_{k \in K} Y_k \leq c$.

With these two additional assumptions, the proof involves the construction of a "truncated" economy: artificial consumption sets and technology sets are constructed large enough to contain the equilibrium of the "true" economy. The truncated economy satisfies the assumptions of Theorem 7.8, guaranteeing existence of an equilibrium. Showing that this equilibrium is also an equilibrium for the true economy completes the proof.

Other variations on the standard theme include allowing for "bads" with negative prices and deriving the condition $\omega_i(p) > \inf p \cdot X_i$ required for budget correspondence continuity from more basic considerations. Rather than pursue those themes, we turn instead to some more exotic fare.

7.3 External effects

Our discussion of the Arrow-Debreu model complicated matters somewhat by pretending that best responses depend on the entire strategy vector s when in fact they depend only on prices p. We now reap the benefits of that artificial device: with only a slight twist, the same method of proof yields existence of a Walrasian equilibrium with external effects affecting both consumers and firms. And, as we will see, comparing equilibria with and without externalities leads to some interesting insights concerning the efficiency of competition.

Externalities impact consumers through preferences. As the notation suggests, the way consumer i ranks commodities, $\succ_i^{p,x_{-i},y}$, may depend on market prices p (e.g., "judging quality by price") as well as the consumption decisions of other consumers, x_{-i}, and the production decisions of firms, y. All of this potentially quite complex interaction is captured through specification of the strict preference map for consumer i,

$$P_i \colon S \to 2^{X_i}, \quad s \mapsto P_i(s) := \{\, x_i' \in X_i \mid x_i' \succ_i^{s_{-i}} x_i \,\}$$

where $s_{-i} := (p, x_{-i}, y)$ represents the consumer's environment. Writing

---

9 This assumption is adapted from Gale and Mas-Colell (1975).

$\omega_i(s)$ rather than $\omega_i(p)$ for the value of the consumer's wealth function, the budget correspondence becomes

$$\beta_i\colon S \to 2^{X_i}, \quad s \mapsto \beta_i(s) := \{\, x_i \in X_i \mid p \cdot x_i \le \omega_i(s) \,\}$$

and the demand correspondence

$$\phi_i\colon S \to 2^{X_i}, \quad s \mapsto \phi_i(s) := \{\, x_i \in X_i \mid P_i(s) \cap \beta_i(s) = \emptyset \,\}.$$

Externalities impact firms by altering technological possibilities. This we capture through the **technology correspondence**

$$Y_k^*\colon S \to (2^{Y_k})_o^F, \quad s \mapsto Y_k^*(s) \subset Y_k,$$

with the understanding that, to avoid circularity, $Y_k^*(s)$ actually depends only on $s_{-k} := (p, x, y_{-k})$. Y_k, which we continue to call the technology set, plays the same role for the firm as the consumption set X_i plays for the consumer. The supply correspondence of firm k is modified accordingly:

$$\eta_k\colon S \to (2_o^L)_o^F, \quad s \mapsto \eta_k(s) := \{\, y_k \in Y_k^*(s) \mid p \cdot y_k = \pi_k(s) \,\}.$$

where $\pi_k\colon S \to \mathbf{R}$, $s \mapsto \pi_k(s) := \sup p \cdot Y_k^*(s)$, is firm k's profit function, appropriately modified to account for the impact of external effects.

Finally, we link consumers with firms through the wealth functions

$$\omega_i\colon S \to \mathbf{R}, \quad s \mapsto \omega_i(s)$$

subject to the restriction $\sum_{i \in I} \omega_i(s) = \sum_{i \in I} p \cdot w_i + \pi(s)$ for all $s \in S$ where $\pi(s) := \sum_{k \in K} \pi_k(s)$ is the aggregate profit function.

7.3.1 Existence

A simple modification of Lemma 7.7 provides the existence result we are looking for:

Lemma 7.10 *If* $\mathcal{E} = (\{\, X_i, P_i, w_i, \omega_i \mid i \in I \,\}, \{\, Y_k, Y_k^* \mid k \in K \,\})$ *is an economy for which*

- *the consumption set* X_i *is nonempty, compact, and convex for all* $i \in I$,
- *the technology set* Y_k *is nonempty, compact, and convex for all* $k \in K$,
- *the demand correspondence* ϕ_i *is nonempty-valued, convex-valued, and uhc for all* $i \in I$,
- *the supply correspondence* η_k *is nonempty-valued, convex-valued, and uhc for all* $k \in K$,

- *the Auctioneer's best response α is nonempty-valued, convex-valued, and uhc,*
- $x_i \in \operatorname{cl} P_i(s)$ *for every* $s := (p, x, y)$ *for which* $Z(x, y) \leq 0$,

then a free disposal Walrasian equilibrium exists.

Proof Once again we have an abstract economy which satisfies the requirements of Lemma 7.4: There exists an $n + r + 1$-tuple of strategies s^* such that $p^* \in \alpha(s^*)$, $x_i^* \in \phi_i(s^*)$, and $y_k^* \in \eta_k(s^*)$ for all $i \in I$ and $k \in K$. The rest of the proof is identical to that of Lemma 7.7. $\qquad\square$

What is critical to this proof is the assumption that the constraint correspondences of consumers and firms are continuous and the best response correspondences upperhemicontinuous in s, not just in p: externalities, if present, must impact consumers and firms in a sufficiently "smooth" fashion. It is easier to see what is going on when we turn Lemma 7.10 into a theorem involving only the model primitives.

Theorem 7.11 *Let* $\mathcal{E} = (\{\, X_i, P_i, w_i, \omega_i \mid i \in I \,\}, \{\, Y_k, Y_k^* \mid k \in K \,\})$ *be an economy with externalities. For all consumers $i \in I$, assume that*

- X_i *is nonempty, compact, and convex;*
- $\succ_i^{s_{-i}}$ *is a weak ordering on X_i for every $s_{-i} \in S_{-i}$;*
- P_i *has open graph in $S \times X_i$;*
- *the upper contour sets $R_i(s) := \{\, x_i' \in X_i \mid x_i' \succeq_i^{s_{-i}} x_i \,\}$ are convex for all $s \in S$;*
- $x_i \in \operatorname{cl} P_i(s)$ *for every* $s := (p, x, y)$ *for which* $Z(x, y) \leq 0$,
- *the wealth function ω_i is continuous and satisfies the condition $\omega_i(s) > \inf p \cdot X_i$ for all $s \in \Delta \times X \times Y$.*

For all firms $k \in K$, assume that

- *the technology set Y_k is nonempty, compact, and convex,*
- *the correspondence Y_k^* is nonempty-valued, convex-valued, and continuous.*
- *if $y \in \sum_{k \in K} Y_k^*(s)$, then $-y^+ \in \sum_{k \in K} Y_k^*(s)$ for all $s \in S$.*

A Walrasian equilibrium exists for the economy $\mathcal{E}$.

Proof It suffices to prove that the best response correspondences satisfy the requirements of Lemma 7.10: i.e., each is nonempty-valued, convex-valued, and uhc. This is left as Exercise 7.13. $\qquad\square$

7.3.2 Bees and blossoms

Our first illustration of this construction is patterned after a famous parable due to James Meade (1952). In this economy farmers harvest two different crops, apples and honey, using labor as an input. Each industry is linked to the other by a positive externality: apple producers benefit from honey production (the apiary's bees pollinate the apple orchard) and honey producers benefit from apple production (the apple orchard provides the source of pollen). We label the three commodities a (apples), h (honey), and ℓ (labor[10]), numbered 1, 2, and 3 respectively.

Assume that all n consumers are identical with endowment $w_i = (0, 0, k)$ and utility function $u_i(x_i) := u_i(a_i, h_i, \ell_i) = a_i h_i$ with k strictly positive. Normalize prices by setting $p_\ell = 1$ so that consumer i has wealth k and, for $s = (p, x, y)$, demand $\phi_i(s) = (k/2p_a, k/2p_h, 0)$.

Since we assume that production of both apples and honey is subject to constant returns, we can think of each of these industries as a single firm.[11] For a fixed quantity of total honey production h, we assume that activity vectors for apple production lie in the set[12]

$$Y_a^*(s) := \left\{ y_a \in \mathbf{R}^3 \mid y_a = \lambda \left(1, 0, -\frac{\alpha(1+h)}{h} \right), \ \lambda \geq 0 \right\}$$

where $\alpha > 0$. Thus, if $h = 0$, no apples can be produced; if $h = 1$, then producing one unit of apples requires 2α units of labor; and as h increases to infinity, the input required to produce one unit of apples falls asymptotically to α. Similarly, we assume that given a fixed quantity of apple production a, activity vectors for honey production lie in the set

$$Y_h^*(s) := \left\{ y_h \in \mathbf{R}^3 \mid y_h = \lambda \left(0, 1, -\frac{\beta(1+a)}{a} \right), \ \lambda \geq 0 \right\}.$$

where $\beta > 0$.

Since each industry operates under constant returns to scale, zero profits must obtain in any equilibrium involving strictly positive amounts of production.[13] In the apple industry this means that

$$p \cdot \left(1, 0, -\frac{\alpha(1+h)}{h} \right) = p_a - \frac{\alpha(1+h)}{h} = 0$$

---

10 In Chapter 2, we followed Debreu in treating labor services as a negative quantity. Here we think of the endowment of labor k as a positive quantity which is used up in production.

11 More precisely, the firms making up an industry have no individual identity.

12 Technically, I am violating the assumptions of Theorem 7.11 because the correspondences Y_a^* and Y_h^* are empty-valued at $h = 0$ and $a = 0$ respectively. Also the sets $Y_a^*(s)$ and $Y_h^*(s)$ are not confined to a fixed compact set, a problem easily handled by truncation. My defense is that, by cheating a little, this example manages to convey a complicated idea very simply.

13 Although constant returns is conditional on the level of output of the other industry, the logic forcing zero profits is the same as in Chapter 2.

and in the honey industry

$$p \cdot \left(0, 1, -\frac{\beta(1+a)}{a}\right) = p_h - \frac{\beta(1+a)}{a} = 0,$$

and so

$$p_a = \frac{\alpha(1+h)}{h} \quad \text{and} \quad p_h = \frac{\beta(1+a)}{a}$$

if apples and honey are to be produced at all.

Assuming that positive amounts will be produced in equilibrium, market clearing for apples and honey requires

$$\frac{nk}{2}\left(\frac{h}{\alpha(1+h)}\right) = a \quad \text{and} \quad \frac{nk}{2}\left(\frac{a}{\beta(1+a)}\right) = h$$

respectively. In the symmetric case where $\alpha = \beta$, these equations are easily solved for the equilibrium levels of apples and honey production:[14] $a = h = nk/2\alpha - 1$. To illustrate, suppose that $\alpha = \beta = 1$, $k = 3$, and $n = 2$, implying that $a = h = 2$ and $p_a = p_h = 1.5$ in equilibrium. Each industry uses three units of labor input, and profits are zero. Somewhat remarkably the equilibrium is Pareto optimal, a direct consequence of the fact that labor is in perfectly inelastic supply.

Typically, of course, we associate externalities with Pareto inefficiency, and this model is no exception. Simply modify consumer utility to $u_i(x_i) = a_i h_i \ell_i$. Labor supply is no longer perfectly inelastic with consumer demand now taking the form $\phi_i(s) = (k/3p_a, k/3p_h, k/3p_\ell)$. Market clearing for apples and honey requires

$$\frac{nk}{3}\left(\frac{h}{\alpha(1+h)}\right) = a \quad \text{and} \quad \frac{nk}{3}\left(\frac{a}{\beta(1+a)}\right) = h,$$

which in the symmetric case $\alpha = \beta$ yields the equilibrium levels of production $a = h = nk/3\alpha - 1$. Letting $\alpha = \beta = 1$, $k = 3$, and $n = 2$ gives equilibrium production $a = h = 1$ with prices $p_a = p_h = 2$ (where once again we adopt the normalization $p_\ell = 1$). The equilibrium activity vectors $y_\ell^* = (1, 0, -2)$ and $y_h^* = (0, 1, -2)$ earn zero profits. Each consumer receives the commodity bundle $x_i = (.5, .5, 1)$ yielding utility $.25$.

In contrast to the first example, this equilibrium is not Pareto optimal. For instance, allocating to each consumer $a_i = h_i = \ell_i = 2/3$ is feasible[15] and yields utility $(2/3)^3$, which exceeds the equilibrium utility level $.25$.

---

14 If $nk/2\alpha \leq 1$, then no apples or honey is produced, and there is no trade in equilibrium.

15 As you can easily verify, the economy can produce any activity vector of the form $(q, q, -2(1 + q))$. Assuming that the consumers split both effort and output equally, each will receive utility $q^2(2-q)/4$, which is maximized at $q = 4/3$.

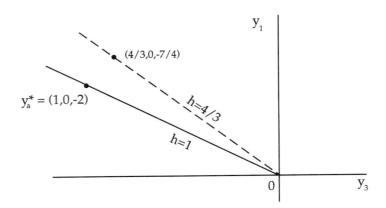

Fig. 7.2. Profit maximization with externalities.

Figure 7.2 illustrates profit maximization for the apple industry: the line labeled $h = 1$ gives the technology set $Y_a^*(s)$ when honey production equals 1 while that labeled $h = 4/3$ is the technology set that apple producers would enjoy if honey production were increased to the Pareto efficient level of $4/3$.

7.3.3 *Tragedy of the commons*

Our second illustration of this methodology returns to the setting of Samuelson's theory of pure public goods, but with a difference: the collective good enjoyed by all stems not from the action of government, but rather from the aggregation of individual responses. Examples to keep in mind include maintaining one's property, abstaining from littering, giving to charity, and preserving the commons.

On one level our economy resembles an economy of private goods. There are two commodities with the first used to produce the second. Production exhibits constant returns to scale with one unit of commodity one required to produce one unit of commodity two, captured by the technology set[16] $Y_2 = \{ y \in \mathbf{R}^2 \mid y = \lambda(-1, 1), \ \lambda \geq 0 \}$. Normalizing prices so that $p_1 = 1$, we conclude immediately that, unless it is not produced, the second commodity has price $p_2 = 1$ as well. Assume that all consumers are identical with endowment $w_i = (6, 0)$.

---

16 To fit within the framework of Theorem 7.11, Y_2 should be truncated to a compact set. To avoid cumbersome notation, I will not bother.

The complication to this otherwise conventional setting involves preferences. Consumer i attaches value to the amount x_{i1} she consumes of commodity one and to the average amount $\bar{x}_2$ which "society" consumes of commodity two (the collective, or public, good), represented by the utility function $u_i(x_{i1}, \bar{x}_2) = x_{i1}\bar{x}_2$ where $I = \{1, \ldots, n\}$ indexes the set of consumers and $\bar{x}_2 := \sum_{i \in I} x_{i2}/n$ denotes the average consumption of commodity two. In the terminology of this section, commodity two engenders a consumption externality.

Consumer i chooses x_{i1} and x_{i2} to maximize $u_i(x_i) = x_{i1}\bar{x}_2$ subject to $p \cdot x_i \leq p \cdot w_i$ or equivalently (since we know that $w_i = (6, 0)$ and equilibrium prices $p = (1, 1)$) $u_i(x_i) = x_{i1}\bar{x}_2$ subject to $x_{i1} + x_{i2} \leq 6$. Solving this constrained maximization problem in the usual way yields the first order conditions $x_{i1} = n\lambda$ and $\bar{x}_2 = \lambda$ where λ is a Lagrangian multiplier. Substituting one into the other gives $x_{i1} = n\bar{x}_2$, which, when in turn substituted into the budget constraint, gives

$$x_{i1} = \frac{6n}{n+1} \quad \text{and} \quad x_{i2} = \frac{6}{n+1} = \bar{x}_2 \quad \text{for} \quad i \in I$$

as the Walrasian equilibrium allocation in an economy in which the public good is voluntarily provided.

The equilibrium just calculated, though a Walrasian equilibrium in the sense of Theorem 7.11, is not Pareto optimal. The Samuelson necessary condition for Pareto optimality in this model (which you are asked to derive in Exercise 7.15), $\sum_{i \in I} \mathrm{MRS}_i(x_i) = n$ or, equivalently, $\sum_{i \in I} (x_{i1}/\bar{x}_2) = n$, when substituted into the technology constraint $\sum_{i \in I} x_{i1} + n\bar{x}_2 = 6n$ yields $\bar{x}_2 = 3$ as the unique Pareto optimal level for the collective commodity. Comparing this result with the Walrasian solution, we see that voluntary provision of the public good is Pareto optimal only when there is a single consumer: if $n > 1$, the public good is "underprovided."

7.3.4 A matter of optimality

The examples of the preceding two sections have deliberately glossed over a puzzling issue: though each example fits exactly into the framework of Theorem 7.11, the resulting allocations are typically inefficient in apparent violation of the First Fundamental Theorem of welfare economics.[17]

To deepen the mystery, we should first convince ourselves that the First

---

17 The overlapping generations model of Chapter 1 provided another instance where Walrasian equilibria could be Pareto inefficient. But in that case the cause for the failure of the First Fundamental Theorem could be traced to the infinite dimensional commodity space, an excuse not available here.

Fundamental Theorem of welfare economics applies to the world described by Theorem 7.11.

Theorem 7.12 *Even though* $\mathcal{E} = (\{X_i, P_i, w_i, \omega_i \mid i \in I\}, \{Y_k, Y_k^* \mid k \in K\})$ *is an economy with externalities,* $\mathrm{WE}^x(\mathcal{E}) \subset \mathrm{PO}(\mathcal{E})$.

Proof Suppose that $s := (p, x, y)$ is a Walrasian equilibrium, but $x \notin \mathrm{PO}(\mathcal{E})$. By the definition of Pareto optimality, there exists a feasible allocation x' such that

$$x_i' \succ_i^{s-i} x_i \quad \text{for all} \quad i \in I. \tag{\dag}$$

But then $x_i' \in P_i(s)$ and hence $p \cdot x_i' > \omega_i(s)$ for all $i \in I$. Summed over all consumers, this gives $\sum_{i \in I} p \cdot x_i' > \sum_{i \in I} \omega_i(s) := \sum_{i \in I} p \cdot w_i + \pi(s)$ or $p \cdot \sum_{i \in I}(x_i' - w_i) > \pi(s)$. However, feasibility of x' requires

$$\sum_{i \in I}(x_i' - w_i) \in \sum_{k \in K} Y_k^*(s) \tag{\ddag}$$

and so, by definition of $\pi(s)$, we have $p \cdot \sum_{i \in I}(x_i' - w_i) \leq \pi(s)$, a contradiction. $\qquad \square$

The faintly tongue in cheek way I phrased this theorem is meant to arouse your suspicions. And after all, we just gave two illustrations of equilibria which were not Pareto optimal. So what is going on?

Although there is nothing literally wrong with the theorem or its proof, appearances are deceiving. In the presence of externalities, Pareto optimal in the sense of Theorem 7.12 takes on a subtle new meaning: the optimality is *conditional* on the existing allocation — the status quo — and hence devoid of much meaning. The key steps of the proof where the conditionality is most evident are marked, appropriately enough, by daggers:

$$x_i' \succ_i^{s-i} x_i \quad \text{for all} \quad i \in I, \tag{\dag}$$

requiring x_i' to dominate x_i assuming everyone else continues behaving as before; and

$$\sum_{i \in I}(x_i' - w_i) \in \sum_{k \in K} Y_k^*(s), \tag{\ddag}$$

which requires the dominating net trades to be producible by firms acting under the supposition that the other firms will continue to act as before.

Our two examples can help to make this abstract point seem much more concrete. Recall that in each case we found that the Walrasian allocations

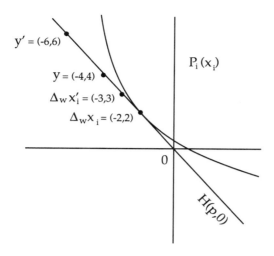

Fig. 7.3. Tragedy of the commons.

were Pareto dominated. Now we emphasize: these allocations are unconditionally Pareto dominated; conditioned by the status quo, they are Pareto optimal just as Theorem 7.12 asserts.

Consider the tragedy of the commons, for example, with $n = 2$. In the Walrasian equilibrium each consumer chooses $x_i = (4, 2)$, four units of the private good and two of the public, which translates to the net trade[18] $\Delta_w x_i = (-2, 2)$ exhibited in Figure 7.3 along with the activity vector $y = (-4, 4)$. The equilibrium hyperplane $H(p, 0)$ corresponding to prices $p = (1, 1)$ separates the consumer upper contour sets from the technology set Y_2 just as Theorem 7.12 says it must.

Where then is the failure of unconditional Pareto optimality? According to the calculations of the preceding section, each consumer should (if contributing equally) consume $x_i' = (3, 3)$ with corresponding net trade $\Delta_w x_i' = (-3, 3)$, also exhibited in Figure 7.3. Since the required production activity vector $y' = (-6, 6)$ lies in the technology Y_2, this allocation is feasible. And the allocation is preferred by each consumer to the Walrasian allocation: $u_i(3, 3) = 9 > 8 = u_i(4, 2)$. But within the context of Theorem 7.12, as consumer 1 evaluates the net trade $(-3, 3)$, she does so under the implicit assumption that consumer 2 will continue to select $\Delta_w x_2 = (-2, 2)$. Thus, for consumer 1 the utility of net trade

18 See Chapter 2.2 if you have forgotten how to construct net trade diagrams for constant returns to scale production economies.

$\Delta_w x_1' = (-3, 3)$ is only $u_1(x_1', (x_2' + x_2)/2) = u_1(3, (3 + 2)/2) = 7.5$, which is lower than that derived from the equilibrium net trade $\Delta_w x_1 = (-2, 2)$. For each consumer, the unconditionally dominating net trade $\Delta_w x_i' = (-3, 3)$ lies below the indifference curve passing through $\Delta_w x_i = (-2, 2)$ as shown in Figure 7.3.

The tragedy of the commons exhibits a consumption externality but not a production externality: indifference contours depend on the environment, but the technology set does not. Meade's example of apples and honey is just the reverse. Since the commodity space is three dimensional, a graphical illustration is not as straightforward as for the commons. Nevertheless, Figure 7.2, which we have already discussed, conveys the main idea. Firms stick with the unconditionally Pareto inefficient, but conditionally efficient, equilibrium allocation, producing one unit of output using two units of input, because each assumes that the other will produce only one unit of output. However, each could in fact produce a Pareto efficient 4/3 units of output using 7/4 units of inputs if each firm realized the complementaries which apple growers and honey producers enjoy.

7.4 Nonconvexity

As discussed in Chapter 3, a continuum of consumers eliminates some of the problems which we normally associate with nonconvexity. Is this an artifact of Aumann's special setting, or does something comparable happen in economies with a large but finite number of consumers? To address this question we begin by introducing a valuable piece of mathematics, the Shapley-Folkman Theorem.

7.4.1 The Shapley-Folkman Theorem

Preparatory to proving the main result we need to add to our stockpile of facts about convexity. Recall that, essentially by definition, the convex hull of any subset S of a vector space is equal to the set of all the convex combinations of the elements of S. In finite dimensional vector spaces, a much more remarkable fact is true.

Theorem 7.13 (Carathéodory) *If $S \subset \mathbf{R}^m$, then $x \in \operatorname{co} S$ if and only if x is equal to a convex combination of at most $m + 1$ points of S.*

Proof See Ichiishi (1983), Theorem 1.1.2, Rockafellar (1970), Theorem 17.1, or van Tiel (1984), Theorem 4.2. $\qquad\square$

This result says, for example, that any point in co S can be expressed as the convex combination of at most three points in S if $S \subset \mathbf{R}^2$, as the convex combination of at most four points in S if $S \subset \mathbf{R}^3$, and so forth. By drawing a few pictures, you should be able to convince yourself that the result cannot be improved (to, e.g., "at most m points of S").

In Chapter 2 we noted (Theorem 2.4) that a finite linear combination of convex sets is convex, a result which extends in a natural way to convex hulls.

Theorem 7.14 *For any finite collection* $\{\, S_i \subset \mathbf{R}^\mathbf{m} \mid i \in I \,\}$ *and scalars* $\alpha_i \in \mathbf{R}$, $\mathrm{co} \sum_{i \in I} \alpha_i S_i = \sum_{i \in I} \alpha_i \, \mathrm{co}\, S_i$.

Proof See Holmes (1975), 8. □

The proof of the Shapley-Folkman Theorem requires that we know when a convex set has extreme points.

Definition 7.15 *An element* x *of a convex set* C *is an* **extreme point** *of* C *if it is not the case that* $x = \alpha y + (1 - \alpha) z$ *for some* $y, z \in C$ *with* $y \neq z$ *and* $\alpha \in (0, 1)$.

The vertices of a simplex, the boundary points of disk in $\mathbf{R}^2$, or the corners of a cube in $\mathbf{R}^3$ are extreme points. Clearly not all convex sets have extreme points: $\mathbf{R}$ or $\mathbf{R}^2$, for example, are convex, but neither set has extreme points. Nor does an open interval in $\mathbf{R}$ which shows that boundedness is not enough. The basic result on existence of extreme points is the following:

Theorem 7.16 *Every nonempty, compact, convex subset of a locally convex TVS has at least one extreme point.*

Proof This is a direct consequence of the Krein-Milman Theorem which asserts that every nonempty, compact, convex subset of a locally convex TVS is the closed convex hull of its extreme points. See Rockafellar (1970), Corollary 18.5.3, for a proof of the result in $\mathbf{R}^\mathbf{m}$ and Yosida (1971, p. 362), for the general case. □

Before proving the Shapley-Folkman Theorem, we begin with a simple example involving the subsets $S_1 = \{\, 0, 1 \,\}$ and $S_2 = \{\, 2, 3 \,\}$ of the real line. Note that $S_1 + S_2 = \{\, 2, 3, 4 \,\}$ and $\mathrm{co}\{\, S_1 + S_2 \,\} = [2, 4]$ (see Figure 7.4). Now observe that any $x \in \mathrm{co}\{\, S_1 + S_2 \,\}$ can be expressed in the form $x = x_1 + x_2$ where $x_1 \in \mathrm{co}\, S_1$ and $x_2 \in \mathrm{co}\, S_2$ and *at most one* $x_i \notin S_i$. For example, if $x = 2.5$ then $x_1 = .5$ and $x_2 = 2$ (or $x_1 = 0$ and $x_2 = 2.5$) will serve the

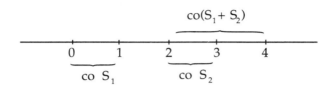

Fig. 7.4. The Shapley-Folkman Theorem.

purpose. The remarkable claim of the theorem we are about to introduce is that, no matter how many subsets S_i of $\mathbf{R}$ we summed in this example, we could decompose x in this fashion with at most one x_i belonging to co S_i but not S_i. Furthermore, the result generalizes to subsets of $\mathbf{R}^m$ in a natural way with at most m of the x_i belonging to co S_i but not S_i.

Returning to our simple example, the key idea of the proof is illustrated in Figure 7.5: we examine the Cartesian product of the sets co S_i. Adding the line $C(x) := \{\, (x_1, x_2) \in \mathbf{R}^2 \mid x_1 + x_2 = x \,\}$ to the figure (with x = 2.5), the two solutions described above correspond to extreme points of the convex set $C(x) \cap (\text{co } S_1 \times \text{co } S_2)$. With this illustration as guide, the general proof — adapted from Green and Heller's (1981) report of an unpublished result of Aubin and Ekelund (1974) — should be easy to follow.

Theorem 7.17 (Shapley-Folkman) *If $\{\, S_i \mid i \in I \,\}$ is a finite collection of nonempty subsets of $\mathbf{R}^m$ indexed by $I = \{\, 1, \ldots, n \,\}$, then any vector $x \in \text{co} \sum_{i \in I} S_i$ can be expressed in the form $x = \sum_{i \in I} x_i$ where $x_i \in \text{co } S_i$ for all $i \in I$ and $\#\{\, i \in I \mid x_i \notin S_i \,\} \leq m$.*

Proof Assume for now that each of the sets S_i is finite, an assumption to be relaxed shortly. Given $x \in \text{co} \sum_{i \in I} S_i$, define the sets

$$C(x) = \left\{ (x_1, \ldots, x_n) \in \mathbf{R}^{mn} \mid \sum_{i \in I} x_i = x \right\}$$

and $P(x) = C(x) \cap \prod_{i \in I} \text{co } S_i$. The set $C(x)$ is compact and convex. Because $\text{co} \sum_{i \in I} S_i = \sum_{i \in I} \text{co } S_i$, $P(x)$ is nonempty. Hence, by the preceding theorem, it has an extreme point, say $(z_1, \ldots, z_m)$. Since this point lies in $P(x)$, by definition $\sum_{i \in I} z_i = x$ and $z_i \in \text{co } S_i$ for all $i \in I$.

All that remains is to show that $z_i \in S_i$ for all but at most m of the z_i's. Suppose this is not true so that there exist $p > m$ indices, say the first p, such

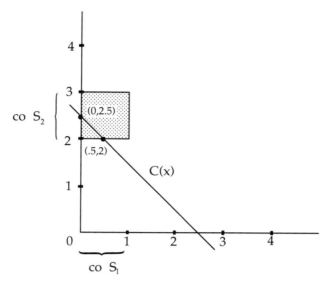

Fig. 7.5. Proof of Shapley-Folkman.

that $z_i \in (\text{co } S_i) \backslash S_i$ for $i = 1, \ldots, p$. For each such z_i there exists a nonzero vector $y_i \in \mathbf{R^m}$ such that[19] $z_i + y_i \in \text{co } S_i$ and $z_i - y_i \in \text{co } S_i$ for $i = 1, \ldots, p$. Because $p > m$ the vectors $\{ y_i \mid i = 1, \ldots, p \}$ are linearly dependent so there exist scalars μ_i, not all equal to zero, such that $\sum_{i=1}^{p} \mu_i y_i = 0$. With no loss of generality we can assume that $|\mu_i| \leq 1$ for $i = 1, \ldots, p$. (Just divide the equation in the preceding sentence by $\max_i |\mu_i|$.) The vectors

$$z^* = (z_1 + \mu_1 y_1, \ldots, z_p + \mu_p y_p, z_{p+1}, \ldots, z_n)$$

and

$$z^{**} = (z_1 - \mu_1 y_1, \ldots, z_p - \mu_p y_p, z_{p+1}, \ldots, z_n)$$

are in $P(x)$ and $(z_1, \ldots, z_n) = (1/2)z^* + (1/2)z^{**}$. However, this contradicts the assumption that $(z_1, \ldots, z_n)$ is an extreme point, proving the theorem when the S_i are finite.

Now suppose that the sets S_i are not necessarily finite. Given $x \in \text{co} \sum_{i \in I} S_i = \sum_{i \in I} \text{co } S_i$, let $x = \sum_{i \in I} x_i$ where $x_i \in \text{co } S_i$ for all $i \in I$. By the Carathéodory Theorem, each x_i can in turn be expressed in the form $x_i = \sum_{j \in J_i} x_{ij}$ where $x_{ij} \in S_i$ for all j in some finite set J_i. Let $\widetilde{S}_i = \{ x_{ij} \mid j \in J_i \}$. Since each $\widetilde{S}_i$ is finite and $x \in \text{co} \sum_{i \in I} \widetilde{S}_i$, we conclude by what has already been proved that $x = \sum_{i \in I} x_i$ where $x_i \in \text{co } \widetilde{S}_i$ for all

19 This follows since $z_i \in \text{co } S_i \backslash S_i$ implies that z_i is not an extreme point of S_i.

$i \in I$ and $\#\{ i \in I \mid x_i \notin \widetilde{S}_i \} \leq m$. But $\widetilde{S}_i \subset S_i$ for all $i \in I$, and so the theorem is proved. $\square$

7.4.2 Nonconvexity and equilibrium

Large numbers convexify supply and demand. This insight came from Starr (1969), building on earlier, less formal, results of Farrell (1959) and Rothenberg (1960).

   The method of approach adopted here, due to Hildenbrand, Schmeidler, and Zamir (1973), is quite straightforward. Given an economy $\mathcal{E}$ with nonconvexities, we eliminate the nonconvexities by passing to convex hulls, obtaining a **convexified economy** $\mathcal{E}^*$. Assuming that apart from the absence of convexity everything else remains the same, our earlier theorems guarantee that $\mathcal{E}^*$ will have a Walrasian equilibrium. Applying the Shapley-Folkman Theorem to this equilibrium, we conclude that there exists an **approximate equilibrium** for the original economy $\mathcal{E}$, an approximation which improves as the number of consumers and firms increases.

   For simplicity we will consider an Arrow-Debreu economy without externalities.

Definition 7.18 *Let* $\mathcal{E} = (\{ X_i, P_i, w_i, \omega_i \mid i \in I \}, \{ Y_k \mid k \in K \})$ *be an Arrow-Debreu economy in which the consumption sets* X_i *and the technology sets* Y_k *are not necessarily convex. The* **convexified economy** $\mathcal{E}^*$ *is obtained from* $\mathcal{E}$ *by replacing each consumption set* X_i *by* $\mathrm{co}\, X_i$, *each technology set* Y_k *by* $\mathrm{co}\, Y_k$, *each demand correspondence* ϕ_i *by*

$$\phi_i^*: S \to (2^{\mathrm{co}\, X_i})_o^F, \qquad \phi_i^*: s \mapsto \mathrm{co}\, \phi_i(s),$$

and each supply correspondence η_k *by*

$$\eta_k^*: S \to (2^{\mathrm{co}\, Y_k})_o^F, \qquad \eta_k^*: s \mapsto \mathrm{co}\, \eta_k(s).$$

Figure 7.6 illustrates the main idea. In panel (a), the demand set of consumer i at prices p consists of the two bundles x_i' and x_i''. In the convexified economy, $\phi_i(p) = \{ x_i', x_i'' \}$ is replaced by $\phi_i^*(p) = \mathrm{co}\{ x_i', x_i'' \}$, the line segment connecting x_i' to x_i''. In panel (b), the technology set Y_k of firm k exhibits a nonconvexity due to increasing returns. At prices p the firm is willing to supply either nothing or the activity vector y'. In the convexified economy, the supply set $\eta_k(p) = \{ 0, y' \}$ is replaced by $\eta_k^*(p) = \mathrm{co}\{ 0, y' \}$, the line segment connecting 0 to y'.

a: Consumer.   b: Firm.

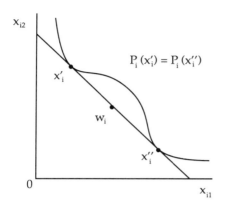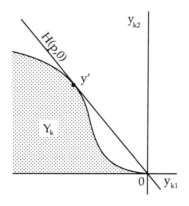

Fig. 7.6. Convexifying best responses.

Lemma 7.19 *Let* $\mathcal{E} = (\{\, X_i, P_i, w_i, \omega_i \mid i \in I \,\}, \{\, Y_k \mid k \in K \,\})$ *be an Arrow-Debreu economy for which*

- *the consumption set X_i is nonempty and compact for all $i \in I$,*
- *the technology set Y_k is nonempty and compact for all $k \in K$,*
- *the demand correspondence ϕ_i is nonempty-valued and uhc for all $i \in I$,*
- *the supply correspondence η_k is nonempty-valued and uhc for all $k \in K$,*
- *the Auctioneer's best response α is nonempty-valued, convex-valued, and uhc,*
- $x_i \in \mathrm{cl}\, P_i(x_i)$ *for every allocation (x, y) for which excess demand $Z(x, y) \leq 0$,*
- *if $y \in \sum_{k \in K} Y_k$, then $-y^+ \in \sum_{k \in K} Y_k$,*

and let $\mathcal{E}^* = (\{\, \mathrm{co}\, X_i, P_i, w_i, \omega_i \mid i \in I \,\}, \{\, \mathrm{co}\, Y_k \mid k \in K \,\})$ *be the convexified version of $\mathcal{E}$. The economy $\mathcal{E}^*$ has an equilibrium (p^*, x^*, y^*) in which*

$$\sum_{i \in I} x_k^* - \sum_{k \in K} y_k^* - \sum_{i \in I} w_i = 0$$

with

$$x_i^* \in \mathrm{co}\, \phi_i(p^*) \quad \text{for all} \quad i \in I, \quad y_k^* \in \mathrm{co}\, \eta_k(p^*) \quad \text{for all} \quad k \in K,$$

and

$$\#\{\,x_i^* \notin \phi_i(p^*)\,\} + \#\{\,y_k^* \notin \eta_k(p^*)\,\} \leq m.$$

Proof As suggested above, our first step is to verify that the convexified economy has an equilibrium. In order for Lemma 7.7 to apply, all that is required is to verify that the sets $\mathrm{co}\,X_i$ and $\mathrm{co}\,Y_k$ are nonempty, compact, and convex and that the correspondences ϕ_i^* and η_k^* are nonempty-valued, convex-valued, and uhc.

Nonemptyness and convexity of the sets $\mathrm{co}\,X_i$ and $\mathrm{co}\,Y_k$ is immediate while compactness follows from the fact that the convex hull of a compact subset of a finite dimensional TVS is compact (Rockafellar (1970), Theorem 17.2). For given s, the sets $\phi_i^*(s)$ and $\eta_k^*(s)$ are obviously nonempty and convex. Compactness follows once again from the fact that convex hulls of compact sets are compact in finite dimensional TVS's. Upperhemicontinuity of the correspondences ϕ_i and η_k implies upperhemicontinuity of ϕ_i^* and η_k^* (Theorem 5.57).

We conclude that the economy $\mathcal{E}^*$ has an equilibrium[20] (p^*, x, y) with $x_i \in \mathrm{co}\,\phi_i(p^*)$ for all $i \in I$, $y_k \in \mathrm{co}\,\eta_k(p^*)$ for all $k \in K$, and $\sum_{i \in I} x_i - \sum_{k \in K} y_k = \sum_{i \in I} w_i := w$. But by the Shapley-Folkman Theorem, since $w \in \sum_{i \in I} \mathrm{co}\,\phi_i(p^*) - \sum_{k \in K} \mathrm{co}\,\eta_k(p^*)$ we can write $w = \sum_{i \in I} x_i^* - \sum_{k \in K} y_k^*$ where $x_i^* \in \mathrm{co}\,\phi_i(p^*)$ for all $i \in I$, $y_k^* \in \mathrm{co}\,\eta_k(p^*)$ for all $k \in K$, and $\#\{\,x_i^* \notin \phi_i(p^*)\,\} + \#\{\,y_k^* \notin \eta_k(p^*)\,\} \leq m$. $\qquad\square$

Provided that the sets X_i are convex, turning this lemma into a full-fledged theorem is easy.

Theorem 7.20 *Let* $\mathcal{E} = (\{\,X_i, P_i, w_i, \omega_i \mid i \in I\,\}, \{\,Y_k \mid k \in K\,\})$ *be an Arrow-Debreu economy. For all consumers* $i \in I$, *assume that*

- X_i *is nonempty, compact, and convex;*
- $\succ_i$ *is a weak ordering with open graph in* $X_i \times X_i$;
- $x_i \in \mathrm{cl}\,P_i(x_i)$ *for every allocation* (x, y) *for which excess demand* $Z(x, y) \leq 0$,
- *the wealth function* ω_i *is continuous and satisfies the condition* $\omega_i(p) > \inf p \cdot X_i$ *for all* $p \in \Delta$.

For all firms $k \in K$, *assume that*

- Y_k *is nonempty and compact;*
- *if* $y \in \sum_{k \in K} Y_k$, *then* $-y^+ \in \sum_{k \in K} Y_k$.

---

[20] Since we have assumed free disposal, we can claim an equilibrium, not just a free disposal equilibrium.

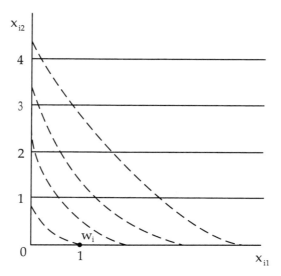

Fig. 7.7. A problem with indivisibility.

Let $\mathcal{E}^* = (\{\,\mathrm{co}\,X_i, P_i, w_i, \omega_i \mid i \in I\,\}, \{\,\mathrm{co}\,Y_k \mid k \in K\,\})$ *be the convexified version of* $\mathcal{E}$. *The economy* $\mathcal{E}^*$ *has an equilibrium* (p^*, x^*, y^*) *in which*

$$\sum_{i \in I} x_k^* - \sum_{k \in K} y_k^* - \sum_{i \in I} w_i = 0$$

with

$$x_i^* \in \mathrm{co}\,\phi_i(p^*) \quad \textit{for all} \quad i \in I, \quad y_k^* \in \mathrm{co}\,\eta_k(p^*) \quad \textit{for all} \quad k \in K,$$

and

$$\#\{\,x_i^* \notin \phi_i(p^*)\,\} + \#\{\,y_k^* \notin \eta_k(p^*)\,\} \le m.$$

Proof Just as in passing from Lemma 7.7 to Theorem 7.8, all that needs to be shown is that the correspondences ϕ_i^* and η_k^* are nonempty-valued, convex-valued, and uhc. Our proof in Theorem 7.8 that the best response correspondences ϕ_i and η_k are nonempty-valued and uhc required no convexity hypothesis apart from the convexity of X_i (used to establish continuity of the budget correspondence β_i). Therefore, ϕ_i and η_k are nonempty-valued and uhc in this context as well, and the result follows immediately from the preceding lemma. $\square$

Nonconvexity of the consumption set X_i, characteristic of economies with indivisibilities, raises a subtle complication: the condition $\omega_i(p) > \inf pX_i$ is no longer sufficient to guarantee continuity of the budget correspondence.

Figure 7.7 illustrates the nature of the problem. Consumer i has consumption set $X_i = \mathbf{R}_+ \times \mathbf{Z}_+$ and endowment $w_i = (1, 0)$. With the preferences shown,[21] the budget correspondence fails to be continuous and the demand correspondence uhc at $p = (1, 1)$. Getting around this difficulty is somewhat tricky, but it is surmountable.[22] Because such results are rather specialized, I will not report them here.

7.4.3 *The meaning of approximation*

The approximation results just described can and have been improved upon. Rather than saddling a few consumers and firms with nonoptimal choices, it is possible to allow everyone to optimize provided that demand and supply are no longer required to match exactly. However, I think these variations on basic Shapley-Folkman miss the point.

Walrasian equilibrium with a finite number of consumers is *always* an approximation to reality because, apart from some special cases, consumers and firms always have some monopoly power. By tying economic theory to convexity, neoclassical economics muddled the issues by making the two-person Edgeworth box look like a plausible version of competition. It is not a version of competition, of course, unless each of those consumers represents part of a continuum. Economies with indivisibilities or nonconvex preferences are not so prone to this confusion, encouraging the view that competition is meaningful only as a limiting case.

Nonconvexity raises a problem in economies with a finite number of consumers, but so does the hypothesis of pricetaking behavior. As Aumann said some time ago, we need to realize that perfect competition is an idealization, an abstraction no more realizable than a perfectly elastic collision between billiard balls. Economics does not have to apologize for offering abstractions — that's what models are for, in economics as in any other science — but we do need to recognize when we are abstracting. The neoclassical overemphasis on convexity reveals confusion on that score.

7.5 Nonordered preferences

Our final variation on the basic theme of this chapter takes us into terrain alien to most of economics, a world in which preferences need be neither

---

21 I have shown indifference curves with dotted lines to indicate that they are really not defined between the horizontal lines: you can't have preferences for half a car!

22 Generally, it requires at least one commodity to be perfectly divisible and that every consumer consumes at least a little bit of that commodity in equilibrium.

transitive nor complete. Without transitivity or completeness, utility functions do not exist and indifference contours lose their meaning. I begin by adapting Theorem 7.6 to an Arrow-Debreu type economy.

7.5.1 Existence

In proving existence it is actually a little easier to allow for external effects. Existence in the absence of externalities will, of course, be included as a special case. The notation used here is exactly as in Section 7.3. In particular, $S = \Delta \times X \times Y$ with typical element $s = (p, x, y)$.

Theorem 7.21 *Let $\mathcal{E} = (\{\, X_i, P_i, w_i, \omega_i \mid i \in I \,\}, \{\, Y_k, Y_k^* \mid k \in K \,\})$ be an economy with externalities. For all consumers $i \in I$, assume that*

- *the consumption set X_i is nonempty, compact, and convex;*
- *the budget constraint β_i is nonempty-valued, convex-valued, and continuous;*
- *the strict preference map P_i has open graph in $S \times X_i$;*
- $x_i \notin \operatorname{co} P_i(s)$ *for every $s \in S$.*

For all firms $k \in K$, assume that

- *the technology set Y_k is nonempty, compact, and convex,*
- *the correspondence Y_k^* is nonempty-valued, convex-valued, and continuous.*
- $x_i \in \operatorname{cl} P_i(s)$ *for every $s := (p, x, y)$ for which $Z(x, y) \le 0$;*
- *if $y \in \sum_{k \in K} Y_k^*(s)$, then $-y^+ \in \sum_{k \in K} Y_k^*(s)$ for all $s \in S$.*

A Walrasian equilibrium exists for the economy $\mathcal{E}$.

Proof Consumers satisfy all of the assumptions of Theorem 7.6. Firm k maximizes $p \cdot y_k$, which is continuous in $s := (p, x, y)$, and so its implicit "strict preference map"

$$P_k \colon S \to 2^{Y_k}, \quad s \mapsto P_k(s) := \{\, y_k' \in Y_k(s) \mid p \cdot y_k' > p \cdot y_k \,\}$$

has open graph in $S \times Y_k$. Since for any $s \in S$ the set $P_k(s)$ is convex, clearly $y_k \notin \operatorname{co} P_k(s)$ where y_k is the component of s corresponding to firm k. Therefore, the firms satisfy the assumptions of Theorem 7.6. Showing that the Walrasian Auctioneer also satisfies these conditions is similarly straightforward (Exercise 7.20). We conclude from Theorem 7.6 that this abstract economy has an equilibrium $s^* = (p^*, x^*, y^*)$ in the sense that $p^* \in \alpha(s^*)$, $x_i^* \in \phi_i(s^*)$, and $y_k^* \in \eta_k(s^*)$ for all consumers $i \in I$ and for all

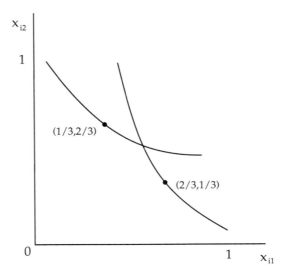

Fig. 7.8. Intransitive preferences.

firms $k \in K$. Using the local nonsatiation and free disposal assumptions, it follows that (p^*, x^*, y^*) is a Walrasian equilibrium for $\mathcal{E}$. $\qquad\square$

The only assumption which might look a little mysterious is the requirement that $x_i \notin \mathrm{co}\,P_i(s)$. If the strict upper contour set is convex, then $\mathrm{co}\,P_i(s) = P_i(s)$ and so the condition becomes $x_i \notin P_i(s)$ or, equivalently, $x_i \not\succ_i^{s-i} x_i$: i.e., strict preference is irreflexive, a very mild requirement. However, if $P_i(s)$ is not convex, this assumption is quite likely to fail.

7.5.2 Drugs and intransitivity

Markets for addictive substances such as alcohol or narcotics lead quite naturally to equilibria with nonordered preferences, specifically preferences which are intransitive. To provide a simple example, consider an economy with two commodities. Commodity one, leisure, can either be consumed directly or used to produce commodity two, narcotics. Production exhibits constant returns to scale with technology set[23]

$$Y_2 = \{\, y_2 \in \mathbf{R}^2 \mid y_2 = \lambda(-1, 1), \ \lambda \geq 0 \,\}.$$

---

23 I assume that there are no externalities, and so $Y_k^*(s) = Y_k$ for all $s \in S$. To fit within the context of the theorem, the set Y_k should be truncated to a compact set. However, I will not bother to do so.

I will assume that all consumers in this economy are identical with consumption set $X_i = [0,1]^2$ and endowment $w_i = (1,0)$: each owns one unit of leisure, which she may consume or use to buy drugs. Describing preferences represents more of a challenge.

Fixing a commodity bundle $\bar{x}_i \in X_i$, define

$$v_i(x_i, \bar{x}_i) := x_{i1}^{1-\lambda(\bar{x}_{i2})} x_{i2}^{\lambda(\bar{x}_{i2})} \tag{7.8}$$

where the function $\lambda: [0,1] \to [0,1]$, $x \mapsto \lambda(x)$, is assumed continuous. If, for example, $\bar{x}_i = (1/3, 2/3)$ and $\lambda(2/3) = 2/3$, equation (7.8) becomes $v_i(x_i, \bar{x}_i) = x_{i1}^{1/3} x_{i2}^{2/3}$, a "Cobb-Douglas" utility function whose "indifference contour" through the bundle $\bar{x}_i = (1/3, 2/3)$ is shown in Figure 7.8. If, on the other hand, we take $\bar{x}_i = (2/3, 1/3)$ with $\lambda(1/3) = 1/3$, equation (7.8) reduces to another "Cobb-Douglas" expression with different exponents: $v_i(x_i, \bar{x}_i) = x_{i1}^{2/3} x_{i2}^{1/3}$ whose "indifference contour" through the bundle $\bar{x}_i = (2/3, 1/3)$ is also shown in Figure 7.8. Notice how these "indifference contours" cross, impossible behavior with neoclassical preferences.

The function v_i is, of course, not a utility function: after all, we are trying to model preferences which are intransitive. But, as the diagram suggests, we can nevertheless use v_i to define strict upper contour sets[24] as $P_i(\bar{x}_i) = \{ x_i \in X_i \mid v_i(x_i, \bar{x}_i) > v_i(\bar{x}_i, \bar{x}_i) \}$ for each possible commodity bundle $\bar{x}_i \in X_i$. Provided that we assume that the function λ_i is continuous, the strict preference mapping P_i just defined will satisfy the requirements of Theorem 7.21.

The interpretation I want to give to these preferences is as follows. For low levels of drug consumption, say $\bar{x}_{i2} = 1/3$, the boundary of the strict preference set[25] is relatively steep: the consumer is unwilling to trade away much of commodity one for drugs. On the other hand, for high levels of drug consumption, say $\bar{x}_{i2} = 2/3$, the boundary of the corresponding strict preference set is relatively flat: the consumer has become addicted to the drug and will trade away much leisure to obtain it.

Making this all work requires an appropriate choice for the function λ, the function relating the preference parameter $\lambda(\bar{x}_{i2})$ in our ersatz utility function v_i to the reference level of drug consumption. Figure 7.9 suggests a likely shape for λ, a sigmoid generated by the logistic

$$\lambda(x) := \frac{e^{\alpha+\beta(x-.5)}}{1 + e^{\alpha+\beta(x-.5)}} \tag{7.9}$$

where α and β are constants. To facilitate numerical computation, it will

---

24 Since external effects are presumed absent, I will write $P_i(x_i)$ rather than $P_i(s)$.
25 What I referred to earlier as the "indifference contour," deliberately in quotes!

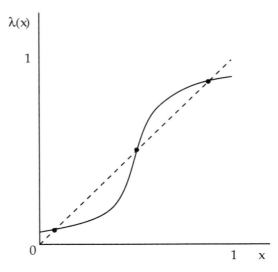

Fig. 7.9. The drug dependency function λ.

be convenient to replace e in this expression by 2:

$$\lambda(x) := \frac{2^{\alpha+\beta(x-.5)}}{1 + 2^{\alpha+\beta(x-.5)}}. \qquad (7.10)$$

Observe that with $\alpha = 0$ and $\beta = 6$, we obtain

$$\lambda(1/3) = \frac{1/2}{1 + 1/2} = 1/3 \quad \text{and} \quad \lambda(2/3) = \frac{2}{1+2} = 2/3,$$

which is how I generated the values displayed in Figure 7.8.

We consider next how these preferences can be used to characterize consumer equilibrium. Figure 7.10 suggests what we are looking for: a bundle $\bar{x}_i$ lying on the consumer budget line with the corresponding strict upper contour set $P_i(\bar{x}_i)$ above it or, more formally,[26]

$$\bar{x}_i \in \phi_i(p) := \{\, x_i \in \beta_i(p) \mid P_i(x_i) \cap \beta_i(p) = \emptyset \,\}.$$

Because preferences are intransitive, there may be other tangencies of this same budget line with strict upper contour sets,[27] but I have shown only one in order to preserve your sanity. We can describe the boundary of this equilibrium upper contour set by setting equation (7.8) equal to a constant,

---

26 Since there are no externalities, once again we revert to earlier notation in writing $\phi_i(p)$ rather than $\phi_i(s)$.

27 Remember that these strict upper contour sets are no longer nested, and so their boundary lines may cross. In the present instance there are in fact three tangencies!

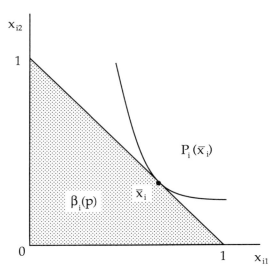

Fig. 7.10. A consumer equilibrium.

say $v_i(x_i, \bar{x}_i) = \bar{v}_i := v_i(\bar{x}_i, \bar{x}_i)$. Tangency can then be characterized by the familiar condition

$$\frac{\partial v_i(\bar{x}_i, \bar{x}_i)/\partial x_{i2}}{\partial v_i(\bar{x}_i, \bar{x}_i)/\partial x_{i1}} = \frac{p_2}{p_1},$$

which reduces to

$$\frac{p_2 \bar{x}_{i2}}{p_1 \bar{x}_{i1}} = \frac{\lambda_i(\bar{x}_{i2})}{1 - \lambda(\bar{x}_{i2})}.$$

Substituting into the budget constraint $p \cdot x_i = p \cdot w_i$ yields

$$\bar{x}_i = \left(\frac{(1 - \lambda(\bar{x}_{i2})) \, p \cdot w_i}{p_1}, \frac{\lambda(\bar{x}_{i2}) \, p \cdot w_i}{p_2} \right).$$

Assuming that drugs are in fact produced, the zero profit condition implies that in equilibrium $p^* = (1, 1)$, $p \cdot w_i = 1$, and so

$$\bar{x}_i = (1 - \lambda(\bar{x}_{i2}), \lambda(\bar{x}_{i2})).$$

Thus, our problem reduces to solving the fixed point problem[28]

$$\lambda(\bar{x}_{i2}) = \bar{x}_{i2}.$$

As indicated by the dotted 45° line in Figure 7.9, with a sigmoid-shaped

---

28 If $\lambda(\bar{x}_{i2}) = \bar{x}_{i2}$, then substitution into the budget constraint $x_{i1} + x_{i2} = 1$ yields $x_{i1} = 1 - \lambda(\bar{x}_{i2}) = \bar{x}_{i1}$.

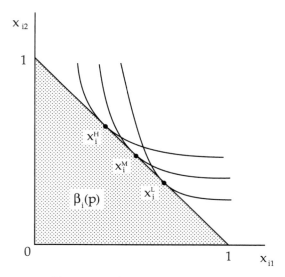

Fig. 7.11. Consumer equilibria.

λ we typically expect three fixed points. Substituting $\lambda(x) = x$ into equation (7.10) gives

$$x = \frac{2^{\alpha+\beta(x-.5)}}{1 + 2^{\alpha+\beta(x-.5)}},$$

which in turn implies that

$$\frac{x}{1-x} = 2^{\alpha+\beta(x-.5)}$$

and hence that

$$\log_2\left(\frac{x}{1-x}\right) = \alpha + \beta(x - .5). \tag{7.11}$$

To obtain the solutions given earlier, we simply work backward. Substituting $x = 2/3$ into equation (7.11) yields $1 = \alpha + \beta/6$ while substituting $x = 1/3$ gives $-1 = \alpha - \beta/6$. Solving these two equations simultaneously gives the solution $\alpha = 0$, $\beta = 6$, and hence

$$\lambda(x) = \frac{2^{6(x-.5)}}{1 + 2^{6(x-.5)}}$$

for the drug dependency equation generating as equilibria the bundles portrayed in Figure 7.8. As Figure 7.9 suggests, there should be a third equilibrium, and there is: $x = 1/2$ also solves equation (7.11) when $\alpha = 0$ and

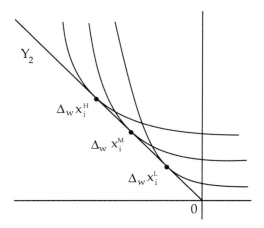

Fig. 7.12. Net trade diagram.

$\beta = 6$. Figure 7.11 exhibits the fruit of our labors, the three equilibria bundles

$$x_i^L = (2/3, 1/3), \quad x_i^M = (1/2, 1/2), \quad \text{and} \quad x_i^H = (1/3, 2/3),$$

which could be chosen for any one of our identical consumers at prices $p^* = (1, 1)$.

Figure 7.12 shows the net trade diagram for this economy. Each of the n consumers in the economy can choose any one of the three equilibria bundles, corresponding to light (L), moderate (M), and heavy (H) addiction,[29] and hence a total of 3^n equilibrium allocations. Note that each consumer, consuming at any one of the equilibrium bundles, regards each of the other bundles as inferior. Nevertheless, as the net trade diagram clearly shows, any of these equilibria is Pareto optimal. But this Pareto optimality is conditional on one's existing behavior, for essentially the same reasons we encountered in the presence of externalities in Section 7.3. Addicts don't want to be off drugs (otherwise, they would quit using the substance), but if forced to quit they would prefer being off drugs to being addicted.[30]

---

29 There are no teetotalers in this economy!
30 But in fairness I must add: those who haven't tried drugs, once addicted, won't want to quit!

7.5.3 *Unmasking a cusp catastrophe*

I have illustrated equilibrium in this market for drugs using particular values
for the parameters α and β. What happens when these parameters are
allowed to vary over their entire allowable range? As it turns out, the
equilibrium manifold takes the form of a **cusp catastrophe**, a concept
popularized by the mathematician René Thom (1975).

Regardless of the choice of parameters, consumers will always choose consumption bundles lying somewhere on the budget line stretching from $(0, 1)$
to $(1, 0)$. We can, therefore, simplify notation by writing a typical equilibrium bundle as $(1 - x, x)$ rather than (x_{i1}, x_{i2}). It will also be more
convenient to use version (7.9) of the drug dependency function rather than
version (7.10).[31] Defining

$$\psi(x) = \log_e \left(\frac{x}{1-x} \right) - \alpha - \beta x,$$

finding solutions to the fixed point condition $\lambda(x) = x$ is then equivalent to
finding zeros of the function ψ.

To examine the nature of the zero set of ψ, we first differentiate ψ twice,
obtaining the first and second derivatives

$$\psi'(x) = \frac{1}{x(1-x)} - \beta \quad \text{and} \quad \psi''(x) = \frac{2x - 1}{x^2(1-x)^2}$$

respectively. Since the graph of $1/x(1-x)$ is u-shaped, reaching its minimum
of 4 at $x = .5$, it follows that $\psi'(x) > 0$ and ψ is strictly increasing provided
that $\beta \leq 4$. Because ψ approaches $-\infty$ as x approaches zero and $+\infty$
as x approaches one, we conclude that under these circumstances ψ will
have exactly one zero and hence that the consumer will have exactly one
equilibrium point of tangency along the budget line. However, if β exceeds
4, then the first derivative of ψ can change sign, opening up the possibility
of multiple equilibria for the consumer.

Setting $\psi'(x) = 0$ yields as the critical points of ψ the solutions to the
quadratic $x^2 - x + 1/\beta = 0$, given by $x = .5 \pm .5\sqrt{1 - 4/\beta}$. Three distinct
cases emerge as possibilities, illustrated in Figure 7.13:

- $\beta < 4$: The expression under the radical sign is imaginary, and so there
  are no real roots. As observed above, ψ is strictly increasing, and $\psi(x) = 0$
  for exactly one value of x. (See panel (a) of Figure 7.13.)
- $\beta = 4$: In this knife-edge case, the expression under the radical sign equals
  zero corresponding to an inflection point of ψ. ψ continues to have exactly
  one zero. (See panel (b) of Figure 7.13.)

---

31 The two versions will be reconciled shortly.

a: β < 4.

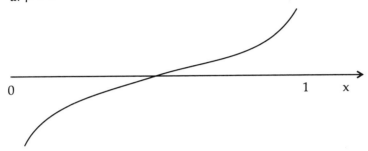

b: β = 4.

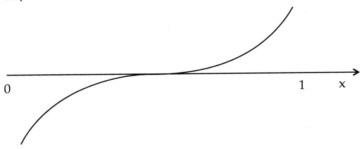

c: β > 4.

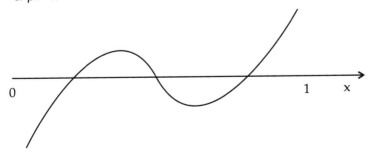

Fig. 7.13. Zeros of the ψ function.

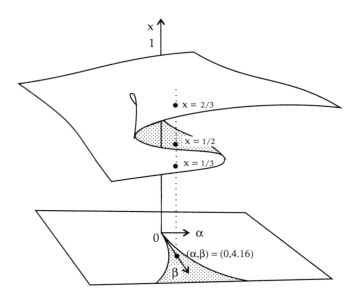

Fig. 7.14. The equilibrium manifold.

- $\beta > 4$: ψ has two critical points, with the lower value of x representing a maximum and the upper value a minimum. If α is either large or small, ψ continues to have only one zero. However, for intermediate values of α, lying in an interval $(\alpha^{\beta}_-, \alpha^{\beta}_+)$ which depends on β, ϕ will have three zeros and the consumer three equilibria. (See panel (c) of Figure 7.13.)

Figure 7.14 assembles the cross-sections of Figure 7.13 into an equilibrium manifold of three dimensions, a **cusp catastrophe**, with the x-axis now pointing up. The cusp gets its name from the shaded area in the $\alpha - \beta$ plane, a triangular region which tapers off to a "cusp" as β decreases to 4. This region, called the **bifurcation set**, corresponds to values for α and β which lead to multiple equilibria, reflected in the folding of the equilibrium manifold which lies above it.

The equilibrium described in the preceding section was generated by parameters $(\alpha, \beta) = (0, 6)$ defined in terms of equation (7.10) rather than equation (7.9). However, converting from base 2 to base e is easy. Letting

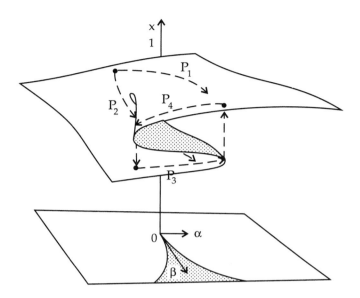

Fig. 7.15. Comparative statics of drug use.

$\alpha = \alpha^* \log_e(2)$ and $\beta = \beta^* \log_e(2)$ in equation (7.9) gives

$$\lambda(x) = \frac{e^{\alpha^* \log_e(2) + \beta^* \log_e(2)(x-.5)}}{1 + e^{\alpha^* \log_e(2) + \beta^* \log_e(2)(x-.5)}} = \frac{2^{\alpha^* + \beta^*(x-.5)}}{1 + 2^{\alpha^* + \beta^*(x-.5)}}.$$

When converted in this way, the parameters $(\alpha, \beta) = (0, 6)$ of the preceding section become $(0, 4.16)$, shown positioned under the equilibrium values $x = 1/3, 1/2, 2/3$ in Figure 7.14.

As demonstrated in Figure 7.15, comparative statics with this equilibrium manifold can be used to illustrate three themes popular in the literature on "catastrophe theory": divergence, abrupt changes in behavior, and hysteresis [see Zeeman (1977)].

- *Divergence.* Assume that the consumer starts with parameter values $(\alpha, \beta) = (0, 0)$, resulting in a moderate amount of drug use $x = .5$. Suppose now that β increases over time,[32] the consequence perhaps of habituation. If at the same time α increases slightly (the intrinsic attractiveness of the drug increases due, perhaps, to its increasing social appeal), then

---

32 Mention of "time" doesn't make much sense in this static context, so this discussion should be taken with several grains of salt. However, it seems far too interesting to let theoretical scruples get in our way!

the equilibrium moves onto the top fold of the sheet (path P_1), resulting in a high level of drug use. In contrast if α decreases slightly as β increases (the intrinsic attractiveness of the drug decreases due, perhaps, to increased taxation on its use), then the equilibrium moves onto the bottom fold with a low level of drug use (path P_2). Thus, small changes in the control parameter α can lead to big changes in drug use.

- *Abrupt change in behavior.* Fix β at some level exceeding the threshold $\beta = 4$ at which equilibria bifurcate. Let α increase from low to high (path P_3), reflecting perhaps the increasing availability of drugs. For low values of α, the consumer begins with a unique, low level of equilibrium drug use. As α increases, the level of drug use increases slowly as the control parameters move under the fold of the equilibrium manifold. Eventually, when the point (α, β) hits the far edge of the bifurcation set, the lower level of drug usage disappears as an equilibrium, leaving high usage as the only equilibrium: drug usage jumps dramatically as the moderate user becomes a full scale addict.

- *Hysteresis.* Continuing to hold β fixed, imagine that the addict is now exposed to a drug rehabilitation program which seeks to undo the damage. Unfortunately for our addict, the path which led to addiction is not reversible: as α decreases, he now moves onto the upper region of the manifold (Path P_4). In other words, preferences, once altered, exhibit some inertia. If α decreases sufficiently, eventually the upper equilibrium disappears: drug usage falls dramatically, leaving the former addict at the low level of usage at which he began.

Although too crude to serve as an adequate model of addiction, the model presented here does show how modern equilibrium theory can cope with varieties of economic "man" far removed from the standard textbook version. It should, in particular, serve as a useful antidote to the restrictive view of "rational" drug addiction advanced by Becker and Murphy (1988).

7.6 Summary

As suggested at the beginning of Chapter 6, the primary importance of proving existence lies in the process: going through the proofs helps us understand what equilibrium is all about. I hope this chapter has justified that claim. Establishing a link between Nash and Walrasian equilibrium connects two of the most active and productive areas of economic research of the past half century, general equilibrium theory and game theory. The abstract equilibrium approach greatly clarifies the relevance of fixed point theorems. Viewing the Auctioneer as an abstract player sheds new light on the pricetaking hypothesis. And finally, the "exotic" applications — modeling externalities, nonconvexities, and nonordered preferences — testify to the flexibility of the approach.

Exercises

7.1 Replacing s_i by x_i and s_{-i} by e, show that the definition of $\Gamma(P_i)$ in Section 7.1.1 is equivalent to the definition given in Chapter 5,

$$\Gamma(P_i) := \{ (e, x_i, x_i') \in E \times X_i \times X_i \mid x_i' \in P_i(e, x_i) \}.$$

7.2 Consider a two-person game in which player 1 has strategy set $S_1 = \{ U, D \}$ and player 2 strategy set $S_2 = \{ L, R \}$. Assume that payoffs are given by the following payoff matrix

$$
\begin{array}{ccc}
 & L & R \\
U & (5,5) & (-3,8) \\
D & (8,-3) & (0,0)
\end{array}
$$

with the interpretation $(u_1(D, L), u_2(D, L)) = (8, -3)$ for the lower left hand entry and so on. Determine $B_1(s)$ and $B_2(s)$ for $s = (U, L)$ and for $s = (D, R)$. Using the fixed point characterization, show that one of these strategy vectors is a Nash equilibrium and one is not.

7.3 Replacing s by (s_i, s_{-i}) and using the fact that K_i does not actually depend on s_i, show that $B_i(s)$ given in Section 7.1.3 does not depend on s_i. Conclude, therefore, that the definition of $B_i(s)$ is not circular.

7.4 Let $\{ S_i, P_i \mid i \in I \}$ be an ordinary game (not an abstract economy!) in which each of the strategy sets S_i is nonempty, compact, and convex. Assume that preferences of each player satisfy the assumptions listed in Theorem 7.5. Using Theorem 7.5 as a model, state and prove a theorem establishing existence of a Nash equilibrium for this game.

7.5 Under the conditions of Lemma 7.7 prove that if the fixed point $s^* = (p^*, x^*, y^*)$ satisfies $x_i^* \in \operatorname{cl} P_i(x^*)$ for all $i \in I$, then $p^* \cdot Z(x^*, y^*) = 0$. (*Hint:* Look at the proof of Theorem 6.9, the strong form of Walras' Law.)

7.6 Fixing $p \in \Delta$ and assuming that the conditions of Theorem 7.8 are satisfied, verify each of the following assertions about consumer $i \in I$:

(a) $\{ x_i \in L \mid p \cdot x_i \le \omega_i(p) \}$ is closed;

(b) $\beta_i(p) := X_i \cap \{ x_i \in L \mid p \cdot x_i \le \omega_i(p) \}$ is compact;

(c) $\{\, x_i \in L \mid p \cdot x_i \leq \omega_i(p) \,\}$ is convex;
(d) $\beta_i(p) := X_i \cap \{\, x_i \in L \mid p \cdot x_i \leq \omega_i(p) \,\}$ is convex;
(e) $\beta_i(p)$ is nonempty.

7.7   Show that if $\succ_i$ has open graph in $X_i \times X_i$ and $\succ_i$ is independent of p, then $\succ_i$ has open graph in $\Delta \times X_i \times X_i$.

7.8   Show that if $\phi_i(s) := \phi_i(p, x, y)$ is independent of x_{-i} and y and if ϕ_i is uhc in p, then ϕ_i is uhc in s.

7.9   Assuming that Y_k is convex, prove that the upper contour set $\{\, y_k' \in Y_k \mid p \cdot y_k' \geq p \cdot y_k \,\}$ is convex.

7.10   Prove that for fixed x and y, the upper contour set $\{\, p' \in \Delta \mid p' \cdot Z(x, y) \geq p \cdot Z(x, y) \,\}$ of the Auctioneer is convex.

7.11   Justify the assertion in Section 7.2.1 that $p \cdot Z(x, y)$ is continuous in p, x, and y.

7.12   Consider a two-person exchange economy. Consumer 1 has utility function $u_1(x_1) = \sqrt{x_{11}} + \sqrt{x_{12}}$ and endowment $w_1 = (2, 0)$. Consumer 2 has utility function $u_2(x_2) = \min\{\, 2x_{21}, x_{22} \,\}$ and endowment $w_2 = (2, 4)$. Consumption sets $X_1 = X_2 = [0, 10]^2$. Normalize prices so that $p_1 + p_2 = 1$.

   (a) Verify that consumer 1's budget correspondence is not continuous and his demand correspondence is not uhc at $p = (0, 1)$.
   (b) Does a Walrasian equilibrium exist for this economy?
   (c) Does your answer to (b) change if $u_2(x_2) = x_{22}$?
   (d) Does your answer to (b) change if $u_2(x_2) = x_{22}$ and $X_1 = X_2 = [0, 4]^2$?

7.13   Complete the proof of Theorem 7.11.

7.14   In the first version of the model presented in Section 7.3.2 with $\alpha = \beta$ and strictly positive production, justify the assertion that the equilibrium is Pareto optimal. Show explicitly that if $nk/2\alpha \leq 1$, then an equilibrium with no trade and no production does exist. (For greater specificity, take $n = 2$, $k = 1$, and $\alpha = \beta = 1$ if you wish.)

7.15   Using the Lagrangian

$$L = u_1(x_{11}, \bar{x}_2) + \sum_{i=2}^{n} \lambda_i \left(\bar{u}_i - u_i(x_{i1}, \bar{x}_2) \right) + \gamma \left(6n - \sum_{i=1}^{n} x_{i1} - n\bar{x}_2 \right),$$

   derive the Samuelson condition for the optimal provision of a pure public good: $\sum_{i \in I} \mathrm{MRS}_i(x_i) = n$.

7.16   Suppose that $S_1 = (0, 1)$ and $S_2 = (2, 3)$.

   (a) Letting $x = 3$ and using a diagram like Figure 7.5, illustrate the Shapley-Folkman Theorem.

(b) Again letting $x = 3$, find closed sets of the type $\tilde{S}_i$ described in the proof of the Shapley-Folkman Theorem.

7.17 Suppose that $S_i = \{0, 1\}$ for $i \in I = \{1, \ldots, 100\}$.

(a) Describe the sets $\sum_{i \in I} S_i$ and co $\sum_{i \in I} S_i$.

(b) Illustrate the Shapley-Folkman Theorem for $x = 42.3$.

7.18 Verify that the set $C(x)$ described in the proof of the Shapley-Folkman Theorem is nonempty, compact, and convex as claimed. Also verify that z^* and z^{**} belong to $P(x)$ as claimed.

7.19 Consider a production economy with three commodities: the first two are not produced while the third is produced using commodities one and two as inputs. Production is performed by an arbitrary number of identical firms each with cost function

$$c(p_1, p_2, y_3) = \sqrt{p_1 p_2}(1 + y_3^2)$$

where p_1 and p_2 are the prices of commodities one and two and y_3 the output of commodity three. Assume that consumers have strictly positive initial endowments of commodities one and two and that utility functions $u_i(x_i)$ are strictly monotonic and continuous.

(a) Compute the supply correspondence for a representative firm and demonstrate that for some prices it fails to be convex-valued.

(b) Describe the effect of "convexifying" this economy on the cost function of each of the firms.

(c) Assuming that an equilibrium exists for the convexified economy, apply the Shapley-Folkman Theorem to prove the existence of an approximate equilibrium for this economy: i.e., a price vector p such that all markets clear, every consumer receives a commodity bundle which maximizes utility subject to his or her budget constraint, and the production of all but three firms is both feasible and profit maximizing.

(d) Use the Shapley-Folkman Theorem to prove that the approximate equilibrium can allow all but *one* firm a profit maximizing, feasible production vector.

7.20 Show that the Walrasian Auctioneer satisfies the assumptions of Theorem 7.6.

7.21 Illustrate with an example in $\mathbf{R}^2$ that it is possible to have $x_i \notin P_i(s)$ (irreflexivity) but $x_i \in$ co $P_i(s)$.

7.22 Using equation (7.8), verify that the strict upper contour sets in Figure 7.8 are correct in depicting that $(2/3, 1/3) \notin P_i(1/3, 2/3)$

and $(1/3, 2/3) \notin P_i(2/3, 1/3)$. Demonstrate by example that these preferences are in fact intransitive.

8

What is competition?

We have learned that Walrasian equilibrium exists in a wide variety of circumstances. But establishing existence only partially validates the competitive hypothesis. The Edgeworth box notwithstanding, markets with two consumers are unlikely to be competitive. How then do we recognize settings in which the Walrasian model is appropriate, where price taking is the right thing to do? This is the question which this final chapter tries to address.

We cover a lot of ground. The chapter begins with a diversion, a proof of the Second Fundamental Theorem of welfare economics. Apart from its intrinsic interest, this theorem provides some useful background for material presented later. The second section addresses our major question in terms of core equivalence and core convergence. The third section looks at the issue of competition from another point of view, examining Walrasian equilibrium when the number of commodities is not finite. As I argue in the final section, allowing for a double infinity of consumers and commodities — the **large square economy** — provides the right setting for addressing the question: What is competition?

8.1 The Second Fundamental Theorem

All Walrasian equilibria are efficient. This familiar claim does not offer much solace to a starving person. The Second Fundamental Theorem of welfare economics is meant to put a kinder face on competition, suggesting that — with suitable taxes and transfers — the market can be induced to support any Pareto optimal allocation whatsoever. Although rather naive as a statement of social policy, proving the Second Fundamental Theorem is worthwhile nonetheless: not for its social content, but as a useful technical fact about the Walrasian model.

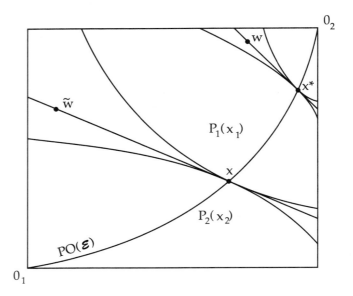

Fig. 8.1. The Second Fundamental Theorem.

8.1.1 Pure exchange

The essential idea behind the Second Fundamental Theorem is easily portrayed within the setting of the Edgeworth box (Figure 8.1). Suppose that the initial endowment distribution w results in a Walrasian allocation, x^*, which is simply terrible from consumer two's point of view. As social planners, we agree with this consumer and set our sights instead on the Pareto optimal allocation x. First we pass a budget line through x which separates the sets $P_1(x_1)$ and $P_2(x_2)$ of commodity bundles which consumer one and two respectively prefer to x. Selecting any point $\tilde{w}$ on this budget line, we compute the **lump sum transfer** $t := \tilde{w} - w$. Adding t to the initial endowment w yields a new endowment $\tilde{w}$ and, with that new endowment, the Walrasian equilibrium x.

The Second Fundamental Theorem, in contrast to the First, does require assumptions. Figure 8.2 illustrates what can go wrong if strict preference sets are nonconvex: there is no way to pass a budget line through x which separates the two strict preference sets, and therefore no way to support x as a market outcome. Absence of convexity is not all that can go wrong. However, before pursuing that question, we pause to introduce a geometric device more suited to the general case of many consumers and many commodities.

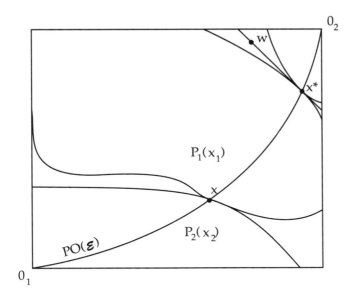

Fig. 8.2. Nonconvex preference sets.

The geometric device is our old friend, the net trade diagram, but with a difference: the targeted Pareto optimal allocation $x \in \mathrm{PO}(\mathcal{E})$ becomes the focus of attention with x_i rather than w_i used to translate the commodity space for each consumer $i \in I$. To keep these translations distinct, we will use Δ_x rather than Δ_w to denote our new net trade operator. The translated strict preference set for consumer i becomes $\Delta_x P_i(x_i) := P_i(x_i) - x_i$ with the other translated constructs defined accordingly. Just as before, the **net trade diagram** is constructed by superimposing the translated diagrams for each consumer with origins coinciding. Figure 8.3 shows the result of applying this procedure to the Edgeworth box of Figure 8.1.

On our way to a proof of the Second Fundamental Theorem, we begin by establishing a variation on the geometric characterization of Pareto optimality proved in Chapter 1 (Lemma 1.11):

Lemma 8.1 *For an exchange economy $\mathcal{E}$, $x \in \mathrm{PO}(\mathcal{E})$ iff $0 \notin \sum_{i \in I} \Delta_x P_i(x_i)$.*

Proof According to Lemma 1.11, $x \in \mathrm{PO}(\mathcal{E})$ iff $0 \notin \sum_{i \in I} \Delta_w P_i(x_i)$. But $x \in \mathrm{PO}(\mathcal{E})$ implies $x \in \mathrm{F}(\mathcal{E}, I)$ and hence $\sum_{i \in I} x_i = \sum_{i \in I} w_i$. Therefore,

$$\sum_{i \in I} \Delta_x P_i(x_i) = \sum_{i \in I} P_i(x_i) - \sum_{i \in I} x_i = \sum_{i \in I} P_i(x_i) - \sum_{i \in I} w_i = \sum_{i \in I} \Delta_w P_i(x_i)$$

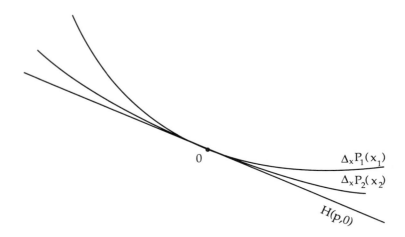

Fig. 8.3. Net trade diagram.

from which the desired result follows immediately.   □

Translated from Edgeworth box to net trade diagram, what the Second Fundamental Theorem asserts is the existence of a hyperplane $H(p,0)$ which puts every set $\Delta_x P_i(x_i)$ in the open halfspace above it. However, for the moment we settle for less, showing only that net strict preferred sets lie on or above the hyperplane and not necessarily strictly above it.

Definition 8.2 *An allocation* $x \in \mathrm{F}(\mathcal{E}, I)$ *and a linear functional* $p \neq 0$ *constitute a* **quasi-equilibrium** *for the exchange economy* $\mathcal{E}$ *if* $\Delta_x P_i(x_i) \subset H^+(p,0)$ *for all* $i \in I$.

Our first result asserts the existence of a quasi-equilibrium.

Lemma 8.3 *Let* $x \in \mathrm{PO}(\mathcal{E})$ *for the exchange economy* $\mathcal{E}$ *with finite dimensional commodity space* L. *If*

- $P_i(x_i)$ *is nonempty and convex for all* $i \in I$, *and*
- $x_i \in \mathrm{cl}\, P_i(x_i)$ *for all* $i \in I$,

then $\mathcal{E}$ *has a quasi-equilibrium* (x, p).

Proof Since each set $\Delta_x P_i(x_i)$ is convex, the sum $\sum_{i \in I} \Delta_x P_i(x_i)$ is convex

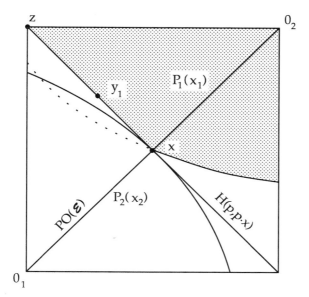

Fig. 8.4. Quasi-equilibrium.

(Theorems 2.4 and 2.8(a)). Because x is Pareto optimal, 0 does not belong to this sum (Lemma 8.1). Hence the sets $\{0\}$ and $\sum_{i \in I} \Delta_x P_i(x_i)$ are nonempty, disjoint, and convex and so, by Theorem 4.42, they can be separated by a hyperplane $H(p, \alpha)$ with $0 \in H^-(p, \alpha)$ and $\sum_{i \in I} \Delta_x P_i(x_i) \subset H^+(p, \alpha)$. Since $0 \in H(p, 0)$ and $H^+(p, \alpha) \subset H^+(p, 0)$ for any $\alpha \geq 0$, we conclude that $0 \in H^-(p, 0)$ and $\sum_{i \in I} \Delta_x P_i(x_i) \subset H^+(p, 0)$.

All that remains is to show that each set $\Delta_x P_i(x_i)$ lies in the upper halfspace. Since p is a continuous linear functional, the halfspace $H^+(p, 0)$ is a closed subset of L. Therefore, by Theorem 4.36(b),

$$\operatorname{cl} \sum_{i \in I} \Delta_x P_i(x_i) \subset H^+(p, 0),$$

and so, by Theorem 3.36(e),

$$\sum_{i \in I} \operatorname{cl} \Delta_x P_i(x_i) \subset H^+(p, 0). \tag{$*$}$$

Because consumers are locally nonsatiated at x, $0 \in \operatorname{cl} \Delta_x P_i(x_i)$ for all $i \in I$. Hence, equation $(*)$ implies $\operatorname{cl} \Delta_x P_i(x_i) \subset H^+(p, 0)$ and so $\Delta_x P_i(x_i) \subset H^+(p, 0)$ for all $i \in I$. $\qquad \square$

Unlike true equilibria, quasi-equilibria allow strict preference sets to intersect the separating hyperplane. Using an Edgeworth box, Figure 8.4

illustrates this possibility. The point x which allocates $x_1 = x_2 = (2,2)$ to the two consumers is assumed to be Pareto optimal: the preference sets $P_1(x_1)$ and $P_2(x_2)$ are separated by a hyperplane with prices $p = (1,1)$. Assume that, while consumer two has a consumption set $X_2 = \mathbf{R}_+^2$ of the usual sort, the consumption set of consumer one has the hyperplane as its lower boundary: i.e., $X_1 = \{\, x_1 \in \mathbf{R}_+^2 \mid x_{11} + x_{12} \geq 4 \,\}$. The strict preference set $P_2(x_2)$ is perfectly standard. Were it not for the constraint imposed by the consumption set, consumer one's preferences would be much the same. The dotted line indicates where the boundary of $P_1(x_1)$ "would like to go" but for the consumption set restriction. However, since by definition $P_1(x_1) := \{\, x_1' \in X_1 \mid x_1' \succ_1 x_1 \,\}$ is restricted to bundles lying in the consumer's consumption set, consumer one's preference set (shaded in Figure 8.4) does not in fact dip below the budget line and, as a consequence, $P_1(x_1)$ can intersect the hyperplane at some point y_1.[1] If this happens, then the conclusion of the Second Fundamental Theorem fails: using lump sum transfers to shift the endowment to some point $\widetilde{w}$ on the budget line will not support the Pareto optimal allocation x as a Walrasian equilibrium because for consumer one, $x_1 \notin \phi_1(p)$.

At this juncture you might argue:

If we assume as usual that preferences are continuous (which the preceding lemma did not do), the phenomenon just described cannot happen. Since the point y_1 lies on the hyperplane, and $P_1(x_1)$ by assumption does not dip below the hyperplane, y_1 must be a boundary point of the strict preference set. But if preferences are continuous and hence $P_1(x_1)$ open, then $P_1(x_1)$ can have no boundary points.

You would be wrong. Continuity of preferences implies that $P_1(x_1)$ is open in the *relative topology* of X_1, and in this subspace topology y_1 is not on the boundary!

Ruling out quasi-equilibria which are not equilibria requires something more than continuity of preferences.

Definition 8.4 *Given an exchange economy $\mathcal{E}$, a pair (x,p) consisting of an allocation $x \in \mathrm{F}(\mathcal{E}, I)$ and a linear functional $p \neq 0$ satisfies the **cheaper point property** if $y_i \in H(p,0) \cap \Delta_x P_i(x_i)$ implies $y_i \in \mathrm{cl}(X_i \cap H_o^-(p,0))$ for all $i \in I$.*

Buried beneath the formalism is a rather simple idea: the cheaper point property is satisfied if each consumer when offered x_i can find an alternative x_i^* which is cheaper but still in her consumption set (see Exercise 8.4). This seems a rather mild restriction, requiring in effect that at any Pareto

---

1 In fact, in Figure 8.4 $P_1(x_1)$ intersects the hyperplane along the entire interval from x to z.

optimum to be supported the consumer not be "reduced nearly to the point of starvation." We are now in position to prove our desired result, the **Second Fundamental Theorem** of welfare economics.

Theorem 8.5 *Let $\mathcal{E} := \{ X_i, P_i, w_i \mid i \in I \}$ be an exchange economy with commodity space the finite dimensional TVS L. If x is a Pareto optimal allocation for which*

- $P_i(x_i)$ *is nonempty and convex for all $i \in I$, and*
- $x_i \in \text{cl}\, P_i(x_i)$ *for all $i \in I$,*

then $\mathcal{E}$ has a quasi-equilibrium (x, p). If, in addition,

- $P_i(x_i)$ *is open (relative to X_i) for all $i \in I$, and*
- (x, p) *satisfies the cheaper point property,*

then there is an endowment distribution $\widetilde{w}$ satisfying the condition $\sum_{i \in I} \widetilde{w}_i = \sum_{i \in I} w_i$ such that $(x, p) \in \text{WE}^x(\widetilde{\mathcal{E}})$ where $\widetilde{\mathcal{E}}$ is the economy obtained from $\mathcal{E}$ by replacing w with $\widetilde{w}$.

Proof Lemma 8.3 establishes the first part of the theorem, existence of a quasi-equilibrium (x, p): i.e., a linear functional $p \neq 0$ such that $\Delta_x P_i(x_i) \subset H^+(p, 0)$ for all $i \in I$. Setting $\widetilde{w} = x$, it follows trivially that $\sum_{i \in I} \widetilde{w}_i = \sum_{i \in I} w_i$ and $\Delta_{\widetilde{w}} P_i(x_i) \subset H^+(p, 0)$ for all $i \in I$. All that remains is to show that $\Delta_{\widetilde{w}} P_i(x_i) \subset H_o^+(p, 0)$ for all $i \in I$. Suppose that $\Delta_{\widetilde{w}} y_i \in \Delta_{\widetilde{w}} P_i(x_i) \cap H(p, 0)$ for some consumer $i \in I$. Then, because $\Delta_{\widetilde{w}} P_i(x_i)$ is open and because the cheaper point property is satisfied, there exists a commodity bundle $\Delta_{\widetilde{w}} x_i^* \in \Delta_{\widetilde{w}} P_i(x_i) \cap H_o^-(p, 0)$, contradicting the fact that (x, p) is a quasi-equilibrium. Thus, each net trade set $\Delta_{\widetilde{w}} P_i(x_i)$ lies strictly above the hyperplane which, in conjunction with the fact that $\Delta_{\widetilde{w}} x_i = 0$, means that (x, p) is a Walrasian equilibrium. $\qquad \square$

The Walrasian equilibrium described in this proof is, of course, a trivial no-trade equilibrium: the lump sum transfer $t := \widetilde{w} - w$ gives each consumer $i \in I$ the desired Pareto allocation x_i as an initial endowment. To place a gloss on the result, note that we can also obtain x as a Walrasian allocation by choosing for each $i \in I$ any point $\widetilde{w}_i$ on the budget line $\{ y_i \in X_i \mid p \cdot y_i = p \cdot x_i \}$ subject to the constraint that $\sum_{i \in I} \widetilde{w}_i = \sum_{i \in I} w_i$. I prefer not to add the gloss since, in any case, lump sum taxes are largely a figment of the economist's imagination.

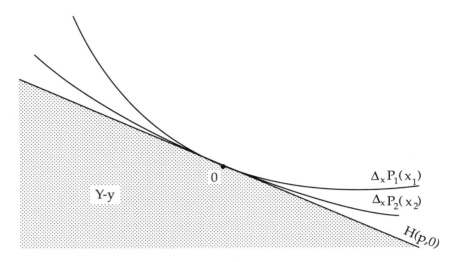

Fig. 8.5. Net trade diagram with production.

8.1.2 Production

Extending these results to economies with production is quite straightforward. To avoid the complication of distributing profits, I will restrict attention to economies where production exhibits constant returns to scale (CRS). We begin with a variation on the geometric characterization of Pareto optimality proved in Chapter 2 (Lemma 2.25).

Lemma 8.6 *For a CRS production economy* $\mathcal{E} := (\{\, X_i, P_i, w_i \mid i \in I \,\}, Y)$, $x \in \mathrm{PO}(\mathcal{E})$ *iff* $(Y - y) \cap \sum_{i \in I} \Delta_x P_i(x_i) = \emptyset$.

Proof Fix $x \in \mathrm{F}(\mathcal{E}, I)$ with $y := \sum_{i \in I}(x_i - w_i) \in Y$. It follows easily (Exercise 8.5) that $z \in (Y - y) \cap \sum_{i \in I} \Delta_x P_i(x_i)$ iff there exists $y' \in Y$ and $x' \in \mathrm{F}(\mathcal{E}, I)$ such that $y' = \sum_{i \in I}(x'_i - w_i)$ and $x'_i \succ_i x_i$ for all $i \in I$, which is in turn equivalent to $x \in \mathrm{Dom}(\mathcal{E}, I)$. Since by definition $\mathrm{PO}(\mathcal{E}) = \mathrm{F}(\mathcal{E}, I)\backslash\mathrm{Dom}(\mathcal{E}, I)$, the result is immediate. $\qquad\square$

Figure 8.5 depicts the net trade diagram with production. The Pareto optimal allocation to be supported is represented by the origin of the diagram. The Second Fundamental Theorem asserts the existence of a hyperplane $H(p, 0)$ passing through the origin which puts the net strict preference sets $\Delta_x P_i(x_i)$ in the open halfspace $H_o^+(p, 0)$ and the net technology set $Y - y$ in the closed halfspace $H^-(p,0)$. As in the case with pure exchange, we begin by settling for a little less.

Definition 8.7 *An allocation $x \in \mathrm{F}(\mathcal{E}, I)$ and a linear functional $p \neq 0$ constitute a* **quasi-equilibrium** *for the CRS production economy $\mathcal{E}$ if*

$$Y - y \subset H^-(p,0) \quad and \quad \Delta_x P_i(x_i) \subset H^+(p,0) \quad for \; all \quad i \in I$$

where $y := \sum_{i \in I}(x_i - w_i)$.

Existence of a quasi-equilibrium in a production economy is proved in much the same way as for pure exchange.

Lemma 8.8 *Let $x \in \mathrm{PO}(\mathcal{E})$ for the economy $\mathcal{E} := (\{X_i, P_i, w_i\}, Y)$ with finite dimensional commodity space L. If*

- *Y is a nonempty, convex cone,*
- *$P_i(x_i)$ is nonempty and convex for all $i \in I$, and*
- *$x_i \in \mathrm{cl}\, P_i(x_i)$ for all $i \in I$,*

then $\mathcal{E}$ has a quasi-equilibrium (x,p).

Proof Since $x \in \mathrm{PO}(\mathcal{E})$, Lemma 8.6 implies that the sets $Y - y$ and $\sum_{i \in I} \Delta_x P_i(x_i)$ are disjoint. They are also nonempty and convex (Theorems 2.4 and 2.8(a)). Therefore, by the Separating Hyperplane Theorem 4.42, there exists a $p \neq 0$ such that $Y - y \subset H^-(p,0)$ and $\sum_{i \in I} \Delta_x P_i(x_i) \subset H^+(p,0)$. All that remains is to show that each set $\Delta_x P_i(x_i)$ lies in the upper halfspace $H^+(p,0)$, which follows exactly as in the proof of Lemma 8.3. □

The **cheaper point property** for a production economy is identical to that for an exchange economy:

Definition 8.9 *Given a CRS production economy $\mathcal{E}$, a pair (x,p) consisting of an allocation $x \in \mathrm{F}(\mathcal{E}, I)$ and a linear functional $p \neq 0$ satisfies the* **cheaper point property** *if $y_i \in H(p,0) \cap \Delta_x P_i(x_i)$ implies $y_i \in \mathrm{cl}(X_i \cap H_o^-(p,0))$ for all $i \in I$.*

Proving the **Second Fundamental Theorem** of welfare economics for a CRS production economy then follows along much the same lines as the proof for the case of pure exchange:

Theorem 8.10 *Let $\mathcal{E} := (\{X_i, P_i, w_i\}, Y)$ be a production economy with commodity space a finite dimensional TVS L. If x is a Pareto optimal allocation for which*

- Y *is a nonempty, convex cone containing 0,*
- $P_i(x_i)$ *is nonempty and convex for all* $i \in I$, *and*
- $x_i \in \operatorname{cl} P_i(x_i)$ *for all* $i \in I$,

then $\mathcal{E}$ *has a quasi-equilibrium* (x, p). *If, in addition,*

- $P_i(x_i)$ *is open (relative to* X_i*) for all* $i \in I$, *and*
- (x, p) *satisfies the cheaper point property,*

then there is an endowment distribution $\widetilde{w}$ *satisfying the condition* $\sum_{i \in I} \widetilde{w}_i = \sum_{i \in I} w_i$ *such that* $(x, p) \in \mathrm{WE}^x(\widetilde{\mathcal{E}})$ *where* $\widetilde{\mathcal{E}}$ *is the economy obtained from* $\mathcal{E}$ *by replacing* w *by* $\widetilde{w}$.

Proof Exercise 8.6. $\square$

Once again the Walrasian equilibrium we have constructed involves no trade. However, we can also obtain the Pareto optimal allocation x as a Walrasian allocation by choosing for each $i \in I$ any point $\widetilde{w}_i$ on the budget line $\{\, x_i' \in X_i \mid p \cdot x_i' = p \cdot x_i \,\}$ subject to the constraint that $\sum_{i \in I} \widetilde{w}_i = \sum_{i \in I} w_i$.

8.2 Core equivalence

We are agreed, I hope, that two-person economies are not hospitable to competition. Neither consumer has any reason to act as a price-taker. Each has every reason to act strategically, bargaining vigorously over every morsel. To justify our focus on Walrasian equilibrium as a reasonable solution concept, we need to articulate what constitutes a truly competitive environment. Economists have long suspected what this takes: thick markets with lots of buyers and sellers. The core convergence and core equivalence theorems formalize this intuition by comparing core and Walrasian allocations as the size of the economy increases, arguing that in the right circumstances the set of core allocations shrinks to the set of Walrasian allocations with equality holding in the limit.

Our discussion of core equivalence will be confined to pure exchange. Most results extend readily to economies with CRS production, but, for reasons noted in Chapter 2, not to the Arrow-Debreu economy. Coalition production economies, designed with core analysis in mind, seem to me too much of a contrivance. In any case, pure exchange conveys most that is of interest.

8.2.1 The Debreu-Scarf Theorem

We begin with the ancestor of all core equivalence results, the Debreu-Scarf (1963) Core Equivalence Theorem. As described in Chapter 1, Debreu and Scarf conduct a very special thought experiment, replication of an economy an indefinite number of times. Consumers in this economy are characterized by their type, a triplet of characteristics $(X_t^*, \succ_t^*, w_t^*)$ indexed by the finite set T. We assume that for each type $t \in T$: the consumption set $X_t^* = \mathbf{R}_+^m$; the preference relation $\succ_t^*$ is a strictly convex, strongly monotonic, continuous weak ordering; and the endowment $w_t^* \gg 0$.

What I will call the **original economy**, denoted either as $\mathcal{E}$ or $\mathcal{E}^1$, contains exactly one consumer of each type. The replicated economy $\mathcal{E}^r$, on the other hand, contains r consumers of each type. More precisely:

Definition 8.11 *For each $r \geq 1$ an economy $\mathcal{E}^r := \{ X_i, P_i, w_i \mid i \in I^r \}$ is constructed as follows:*

- *The set of consumers is given by $I^r = \bigcup_{t \in T} I_t^r$ where $I_t^r \cap I_{t'}^r = \emptyset$ for all $t \neq t'$ and $\#I_t^r = r$ for all $t \in T$.*
- *For each consumer $i \in I_t^r$, $(X_i, \succeq_i, w_i) = (X_t^*, \succeq_t^*, w_t^*)$.*

The key fact which allowed Edgeworth to describe the effects of replication within a single box diagram is captured by the following lemma:

Lemma 8.12 (Equal Treatment) *In the economy $\mathcal{E}^r$:*

(a) If $(x, p) \in \mathrm{WE}(\mathcal{E}^r)$, then x is constant on I_t^r for all $t \in T$.

(b) If $x \in C(\mathcal{E}^r)$ and $r > 1$, then x is constant on I_t^r for all $t \in T$.

Proof To prove (a), observe that strict convexity implies that the demand set $\phi_i(p)$ for consumer i is singleton-valued (Exercise 8.7). Since consumers of the same type have identical characteristics, their demand sets are identical. Therefore, the equilibrium allocation must assign each the same commodity bundle.

The proof of (b) is somewhat more involved. Suppose that for some $r > 1$ the allocation $x \in C(\mathcal{E}^r)$ does not exhibit equal treatment. We want to construct a coalition S which can improve upon x. For each $t \in T$, define $\bar{x}_t = (1/r) \sum_{i \in I_t^r} x_i$, the average allocation received by consumers of type t. From each type $t \in T$ select a consumer $s(t) \in I_t^r$ treated no better than any other of that type: i.e., for whom $x_i \succeq_i x_{s(t)}$ for all $i \in I_t$. Assemble these ill-treated folk into a coalition $S = \{ s(t) \mid t \in T \}$ and define an allocation $y: I^r \to \mathbf{R}_+^m$ for the economy $\mathcal{E}^r$, which gives each member of S

the average of her type while giving each member of the complement $I^r \backslash S$ his endowment: i.e.,

$$y_i = \begin{cases} \bar{x}_t & \text{for } i \in S \cap I_t^r; \\ w_i & \text{for } i \notin S. \end{cases}$$

You can easily check that this allocation is feasible for the coalition S: i.e., $y \in F(\mathcal{E}^r, S)$. Because preferences are convex, $y_i \succeq_i x_i$ for all $i \in S$. Since by hypothesis consumers of at least one type t^* are unequally treated, strict convexity of preferences implies that $y_{i^*} \succ_{i^*} x_{i^*}$ for the representative $i^* := s(t^*)$ of that type. Under our strong assumptions,[2] this in turn implies the existence of an allocation y' feasible for S which every consumer in S prefers to the allocation x. We conclude that the allocation y' dominates x, contradicting the assumption that x is in the core of $\mathcal{E}^r$.   □

The Equal Treatment Lemma greatly simplified the task faced by Debreu and Scarf. Just as for Edgeworth, allocations in $C(\mathcal{E}^r)$ or $WE^x(\mathcal{E}^r)$ can be represented as allocations in $F(\mathcal{E}, I^1)$ by assigning the commodity bundle received by all consumers in I^r of type t to the sole representative of that type in I^1.

Given $r > 1$, let $\overline{C(\mathcal{E}^r)}$ and $\overline{WE^x(\mathcal{E}^r)}$ be the images under this mapping of $C(\mathcal{E}^r)$ and $WE^x(\mathcal{E}^r)$ respectively. Clearly, we have

$$WE^x(\mathcal{E}) = \overline{WE^x(\mathcal{E}^2)} = \cdots = \overline{WE^x(\mathcal{E}^r)} = \cdots$$

and

$$C(\mathcal{E}) \supset \overline{C(\mathcal{E}^2)} \supset \cdots \supset \overline{C(\mathcal{E}^r)} \supset \cdots$$

Only the latter claim requires any thought: the image of the core can only shrink, not expand, because any allocation which can be improved upon by some coalition S in the economy $\mathcal{E}^r$ can be improved by a coalition of the same size and composition in any larger economy $\mathcal{E}^{r'}$.

The First Fundamental Theorem guarantees that $WE^x(\mathcal{E}^r) \subset C(\mathcal{E}^r)$ and so $\overline{WE^x(\mathcal{E}^r)} \subset \overline{C(\mathcal{E}^r)}$. Putting all of the pieces together, we conclude that

$$C(\mathcal{E}) \supset \overline{C(\mathcal{E}^2)} \supset \cdots \supset \overline{C(\mathcal{E}^r)} \supset \cdots \supset WE^x(\mathcal{E}).$$

The assumptions we have made about this economy are quite strong, strong enough to guarantee that the set of Walrasian equilibria is not empty. Thus, replication gives us a chain of cores with each link contained in the last and

---

2 Debreu and Scarf adopt a weaker definition of domination: the coalition S dominates x with the allocation $y \in F(\mathcal{E}, S)$ if (a) $y_i \succeq_i x_i$ for all $i \in S$ and (b) $y_i \succ_i x_i$ for some $i \in S$. Consequently, they are able to prove equal treatment without assuming that preferences are strongly monotonic.

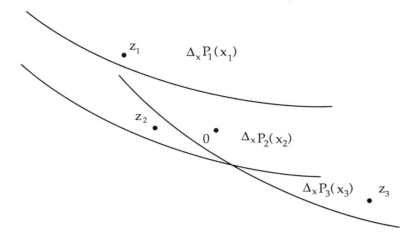

Fig. 8.6. Proof of Lemma 8.15.

the Walrasian allocations at the tail. Our task is to prove that in fact this chain collapses to the set of Walrasian allocations.

Recall Lemma 1.16 used in Chapter 1 to characterize core allocations geometrically, repeated here for convenience.

Lemma 8.13 *For any exchange economy $\mathcal{E}$, $x \in C(\mathcal{E})$ iff $0 \notin \sum_{i \in S} \Delta_w P_i(x_i)$ for all $S \subset I$.*

The following result turns Lemma 8.13 into a powerful statement about the core.

Lemma 8.14 *If $x \in F(\mathcal{E}, I)$, then the set*

$$\Psi(x) := \{ \sum_{t \in T} \lambda_t \Delta_w P_t(x_t) \;\Big|\; 0 \le \lambda_t \le 1 \quad and \quad \sum_{t \in T} \lambda_t = 1 \}$$

is convex provided that each set $\Delta_w P_t(x_t)$ is convex.

Proof This follows immediately from Rockafellar (1970), Theorem 3.3: if T is a finite index set and $\{ C_t \mid t \in T \}$ a collection of convex sets, then $\{ x \in \sum_{t \in T} \lambda_t C_t \mid 0 \le \lambda_t \le 1 \quad and \quad \sum_{t \in T} \lambda_t = 1 \}$ is convex. $\square$

You can easily anticipate what we want to prove next. The accompanying Figure 8.6 should make the proof much easier to follow.

Lemma 8.15 *If $x \in \overline{C(\mathcal{E}^r)}$ for all $r \geq 1$, then $0 \notin \Psi(x)$.*

Proof Suppose that $x \in \overline{C(\mathcal{E}^r)}$ and $0 \in \Psi(x)$. If $0 \in \Psi(x)$, then $0 \in \sum_{t \in T} \lambda_t \Delta_w P_t(x_t)$ for some choice of scalars $\{\lambda_t \mid t \in T\}$. More specifically, $0 = \sum_{t \in T} \lambda_t \Delta_w z_t$ where $\Delta_w z_t \in \Delta_w P_t(x_t)$ for all $t \in T$. For any r, clearly $0 = \sum_{t \in T} r\lambda_t \Delta_w z_t$. Given a choice of $r > 0$, let β_t^r be the largest integer such that $\beta_t^r \leq r\lambda_t$ for all $t \in T$. Because each $\lambda_t \leq 1$, we have $\beta_t^r \leq r\lambda_t \leq r$. Without loss of generality, we can assume each $\lambda_t > 0$, which means that, provided r is chosen large enough, β_t^r will be a *positive* integer. For r sufficiently large, let

$$\Delta_w z_t^r = \left(\frac{r\lambda_t}{\beta_t^r}\right) \Delta_w z_t \quad \text{for each} \quad t \in T.$$

Since $\sum_{t \in T} r\lambda_t \Delta_w z_t = 0$, we have $\sum_{t \in T} \beta_t^r \Delta_w z_t^r = 0$. Therefore, a coalition which contains β_t^r consumers of each type $t \in T$ can achieve an allocation giving $\Delta_w z_t^r$ to each member of type t. Because β_t^r is the largest integer less than or equal to $r\lambda_t$, as r increases the ratio $r\lambda_t/\beta_t^r$ converges to 1. Therefore, $\Delta_w z_t^r \to \Delta_w z_t$ and so, since $\Delta_w P_t(x_t)$ is open, eventually $\Delta_w z_t^r \in \Delta_w P_t(x_t)$. But this means that $x \notin \overline{C(\mathcal{E}^r)}$, a contradiction. We conclude that $0 \notin \Psi(x)$. $\qquad \square$

Finally, we reach the *pièce de résistance*:

Theorem 8.16 (Debreu-Scarf) *If $x \in \overline{C(\mathcal{E}^r)}$ for all $r \geq 1$, then $x \in$* $\text{WE}^x(\mathcal{E})$.

Proof The preceding lemmas have established that $\Psi(x)$ is convex and $0 \notin \Psi(x)$. By the Separating Hyperplane Theorem, there exists a price functional $p \neq 0$ such that $\Psi(x) \subset H^+(p, 0)$. The definition of $\Psi(x)$ implies that[3] $\Delta_w P_t(x_t) \subset H^+(p, 0)$ for all $t \in T$, which means that (x, p) is a Walrasian quasi-equilibrium for the economy $\mathcal{E}$ with $I^1 = T$. $w_t \gg 0$ implies that $p \cdot w_t > \inf p \cdot X_t$ for all $t \in T$, which, when coupled with the assumption that $X_t = \mathbf{R}_+^{\mathbf{m}}$, guarantees that (x, p) satisfies the cheaper point property and hence that $(x, p) \in \text{WE}(\mathcal{E})$. $\qquad \square$

The Debreu-Scarf Theorem suggests that the right way to view the Edgeworth box is to think of each consumer as representative of a type with each type present in equal measure. As the number of consumers of each type increases, the only allocation which remains in the core is the Walrasian allocation.

---

3 Just take $\lambda_t = 1$ for each t in turn.

8.2.2 Core convergence

While Debreu-Scarf equivalence is a remarkable result, replication seems rather special. The strategy of proof hinges crucially on equal treatment, a property which need not hold if the fractions of consumers of each type are the least bit unequal. Is the Debreu-Scarf Theorem a knife-edge result, crumbling to pieces once we leave the specialized setting of the replication experiment? And does the result hold only in the limit, an artifact of infinite replication? Or, in some sense, does the core converge as the number of consumers increases, giving something close to core equivalence in economies with a large but finite number of consumers?

The seminal contribution of Debreu and Scarf inspired a large body of work addressing, and answering, questions such as these. I will focus on one remarkable result, leaving you to explore the many variations covered in the excellent discussions by Hildenbrand (1982) and Mas-Colell (1985b).

Although the result I am about to give had several antecedents, the sparkling formulation and proof by Anderson (1978) established its place in the literature. We begin by defining a crucial constant and illustrating its computation.

Definition 8.17 *Given an exchange economy* $\mathcal{E} := \{\, X_i, P_i, w_i \mid i \in I \,\}$ *with a finite number of consumers and commodity space* $\mathbf{R^m}$, *the* **Anderson bound** *is given by* $M := \sup\{\, \sum_{i \in S} w_{ij} \mid j \in J,\ \#S = m \,\}$ *where* $J := \{\, 1, \ldots, m \,\}$.

The specification of an exchange economy favored most often in the text and problems of Chapter 1 provides a convenient illustration of how M is computed. In those examples, the commodity space was typically $\mathbf{R}^2$ with endowments $w_1 = (1, 3)$ and $w_2 = (3, 1)$. Since the number of consumers is two, we have no choice but to take $S = I$. Computing the sums gives $\sum_{i \in S} w_{i1} = 1 + 3 = 4$ and $\sum_{i \in S} w_{i2} = 3 + 1 = 4$, yielding as Anderson bound $M = \sup\{\, 4, 4 \,\} = 4$.

What happens if, instead of two consumers, each consumer in the box represents a more numerous type with, say, n_1 of type one and n_2 of type two? Since $m = 2$, we consider sums $\sum_{i \in S} w_{ij}$ over sets S of size two. For either commodity $j \in J$,

- taking one consumer of each type yields $\sum_{i \in S} w_{ij} = 1 + 3 = 4$ as before, while
- taking two consumers of the same type yields $\sum_{i \in S} w_{ij} = 3 + 3 = 6$.

Thus, in this expanded economy the Anderson bound is $M = \sup\{\, 4, 6 \,\} = 6$,

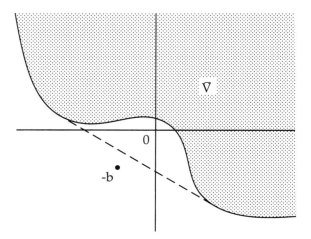

Fig. 8.7. Proof of Theorem 8.18.

which is larger than the bound obtained when there were only two consumers. However, this increase in M really doesn't matter. What is significant is that, no matter how many consumers we add of each type, the bound never gets larger than 6.

Before getting bogged down in the proof of the Anderson Theorem, you might want to look to the subsequent discussion for some motivation.

Theorem 8.18 (Anderson) *Let $\mathcal{E} := \{\, X_i, P_i, w_i \mid i \in I \,\}$ be an exchange economy with a finite number of consumers and commodity space $\mathbf{R}^{\mathbf{m}}$. Assume that for each consumer $i \in I$, the preference relation $\succ_i$ is irreflexive, transitive, and monotonic. For every allocation $x \in C(\mathcal{E})$, there exists a price functional $p \in \Delta$ such that*

(a) $\sum_{i \in I} |p \cdot \Delta_w x_i| \leq 2M$, and
(b) $\sum_{i \in I} |\inf p \cdot \Delta_w P_i(x_i)| \leq 2M$.

Proof Apart from notation, this proof follows Hildenbrand (1982) quite closely. For each consumer $i \in I$ define the set $V_i := \Delta_w P_i(x_i) \cup \{0\}$, and let $\overline{V} := (\sum_{i \in I} V_i)/\#I$ denote the average over I. Since this proof is rather long, I will break it into steps.

Step 1: Show that $\overline{V} \cap \mathbf{R}^{\mathbf{m}}_{-} = \{0\}$.

Suppose not. In that case there exists $v = \sum_{i \in I} \Delta_w y_i$ such that $\Delta_w y_i \in V_i$

for all $i \in I$ and $v < 0$. Form the coalition $S = \{ i \in I \mid \Delta_w y_i \neq 0 \}$ and consider the net trade allocation

$$\Delta_w z_i = \begin{cases} \Delta_w y_i - v/\#S & \text{for } i \in S; \\ 0 & \text{for } i \notin S. \end{cases}$$

This net trade allocation is feasible for S because $\sum_{i \in S} \Delta_w z_i = 0$. Since $\Delta_w y_i \neq 0$ for each $i \in S$, it follows that $\Delta_w y_i \in \Delta_w P_i(x_i)$ and hence $y_i \succ_i x_i$ for all $i \in S$. By construction, $\Delta_w z_i > \Delta_w y_i$ and so $z_i \succ_i y_i$ by monotonicity of preferences. Since $z_i \succ_i y_i$ and $y_i \succ x_i$, transitivity implies that $z_i \succ_i x_i$ for all $i \in S$. We conclude that the coalition S can improve upon x, contradicting the assumption that $x \in C(\mathcal{E})$.

If $\overline{V}$ were convex, we could now claim existence of a hyperplane separating $\overline{V}$ from the negative orthant. However, $\overline{V}$ need not be convex. Replacing $\overline{V}$ by its convex hull only leads to other difficulties since $\mathrm{co}\, \overline{V}$ may intersect $\mathbf{R}_-^m$. However, if we also translate the negative orthant, that does the trick.

Step 2: Show that $\mathrm{co}\, \overline{V} \cap \{ x' \in \mathbf{R}^m \mid x' \ll -b \} = \emptyset$ *for* $b = (M, \dots, M)/\#I$.

Figure 8.7 illustrates the construction using $\#I = 6$ and $M = 6$, the bound which emerged from the discussion preceding this theorem. Suppose the claim is false so that there exists a point $y \in \mathrm{co}\, \overline{V}$ such that $y \ll -b$. We will show that this implies the existence of a vector $z \in \overline{V}$ such that $z \ll 0$, contradicting Step 1. Appealing to the Shapley-Folkman Theorem 7.17, we can write $y = (1/\#I) \sum_{i \in I} \Delta_w z_i$ where $\Delta_w z_i \in \mathrm{co}\, V_i$ for all $i \in I$ and $\#\{ i \in I \mid \Delta_w z_i \notin V_i \} \leq m$. Let $E = \{ i \in I \mid \Delta_w z_i \notin V_i \}$ denote the exceptional set of consumers, and define $z = (1/\#I) \sum_{i \in A \setminus E} \Delta_w z_i$. Since $0 \in V_i$, we have $z \in \overline{V}$. Monotonicity of preferences implies that $V_i \geq -w_i$ and hence $\mathrm{co}\, V_i \geq -w_i$ for all $i \in I$. We conclude that

$$z = y - \frac{1}{\#I} \sum_{i \in E} \Delta_w z_i \leq y + \frac{1}{\#I} \sum_{i \in E} w_i \leq y + b \ll 0.$$

Step 3: Prove part (a).

Because the sets $\mathrm{co}\, \overline{V}$ and $\{ x' \in \mathbf{R}_+^m \mid x' \ll -b \}$ are nonempty, disjoint, and convex, they can be separated by a hyperplane $H(p, -p \cdot b)$ passing through the point $-b$ (Theorem 4.42). The inclusion $\mathrm{co}\, \overline{V} \subset H^+(p, -p \cdot b)$ implies in turn that $\inf p \cdot \overline{V} \geq -p \cdot b = -M/\#I$ where, in the last step, I used the fact that $p \in \Delta$. Since $\inf p \cdot \overline{V} = (1/\#I) \sum_{i \in I} \inf p \cdot V_i$ and $0 \in V_i$, it follows that $-M \leq \sum_{i \in I} \inf p \cdot V_i \leq 0$. Form the coalition of all consumers whose net trades have negative value, $S = \{ i \in I \mid p \cdot \Delta_w x_i < 0 \}$. Because consumers are locally nonsatiated, $\Delta_w x_i \in \operatorname{cl} \Delta_w P_i(x_i)$ and so $p \cdot \Delta_w x_i \geq \inf p \cdot V_i$. The fact that $0 \in V_i$ implies that $\inf p \cdot V_i \leq 0$. Therefore,

$$\sum_{i \in S} |p \cdot \Delta_w x_i| \leq - \sum_{i \in S} \inf p \cdot V_i \leq - \sum_{i \in I} \inf p \cdot V_i \leq M.$$

Because $x \in C(\mathcal{E})$, $\sum_{i \in I} \Delta_w x_i = 0$ and so $\sum_{i \in I} p \cdot \Delta_w x_i = 0$. Consequently, the negative and positive terms in the sum must exactly cancel, implying that

$$\sum_{i \in I} |p \cdot \Delta_w x_i| = 2 \sum_{i \in S} |p \cdot \Delta_w x_i| \leq 2M.$$

Step 4: Prove part (b).

Letting $d_i := \inf p \cdot \Delta_w P_i(x_i)$, it is easy to see that $d_i \leq p \cdot \Delta_w x_i$, $\inf p \cdot V_i \leq d_i$, and $\inf p \cdot V_i \leq 0$. Once again letting $S = \{ i \in I \mid p \cdot \Delta_w x_i < 0 \}$, we conclude that

$$
\begin{aligned}
\sum_{i \in I} |d_i| &= \sum_{i \in I} \max(0, d_i) + \sum_{i \in I} \max(0, -d_i) \\
&\leq \sum_{i \notin S} p \cdot \Delta_w x_i + \sum_{i \in I} (- \inf p \cdot V_i) \\
&\leq M + M.
\end{aligned}
$$

$\square$

Figure 8.8 illustrates the Anderson Theorem for the favorite context of Chapter 1: two-person, two-commodity economies with $w_1 = (1, 3)$, $w_2 = (3, 1)$, and Anderson bound $M = 6$.[4] Because of the symmetry between consumers, in most of these examples the separating price vector is $p = (.5, .5)$. Two **bounding hyperplanes** are drawn, $H(p, -3)$ passing through the point $-b = (-3, -3)$ and $H(p, 3)$ passing through $b = (3, 3)$. For reference, also shown is the hyperplane $H(p, 0)$, which would be the **equilibrium hyperplane** for a Walrasian equilibrium at prices $p = (.5, .5)$.

The net trades $\Delta_w x_1$ and $\Delta_w x_2$ represent a core allocation. Feasibility demands that they lie on a line through the origin, on opposite sides and equidistant from $(0, 0)$.

- Part (a) of Theorem 8.18 says that each of these net trades must lie within the bounding hyperplanes. If $\Delta_w x_1$, for example, touches the lower bounding hyperplane, then its value would be $p \cdot \Delta_w x_1 = -6$. Its opposite twin, $\Delta_w x_2$, would then be touching the upper bounding hyperplane with value $p \cdot \Delta_w x_2 = 6$, and inequality (a) would bind exactly.

---

4 As noted earlier, with just two consumers $M = 4$ will do. However, shortly I will increase the number of consumers of each type.

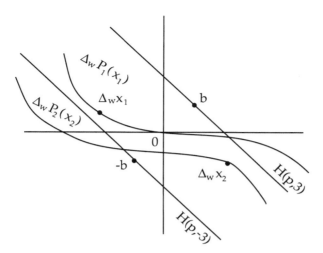

Fig. 8.8. The Anderson bounding hyperplanes.

- Part (b) of Theorem 8.18 restricts the extent to which the net strict preferred sets $\Delta_w P_i(x_i)$ corresponding to a core allocation x can dip below
  the putative equilibrium hyperplane $H(p, 0)$. As Exercise 8.8 asks you to
  demonstrate, at worst the preference set of one of the consumers could
  touch $H(p, -6)$, twice the distance from $H(p, 0)$ as the lower bounding
  hyperplane.

What happens as the number of consumers of each type increases? Since
the bound remains $M = 6$, any core allocation resembles a Walrasian allocation more and more closely in an average sense. Dividing the inequalities
in Theorem 8.18 by $\#I$ gives

$$\frac{1}{\#I} \sum_{i \in I} |p \cdot \Delta_w x_i| \leq \frac{2M}{\#I} \quad \text{and} \quad \frac{1}{\#I} \sum_{i \in I} |\inf p \cdot \Delta_w P_i(x_i)| \leq \frac{2M}{\#I}.$$

As the number of consumers increases, the right hand sides converge to zero,
and so therefore do the average deviations on the left. With a large enough
economy, the average deviation of a net trade core allocation from an equilibrium hyperplane $H(p, 0)$ will be very small, as will be the average protrusion
of preferred net trade sets below the hyperplane. Thus, thickening markets
forces core allocations to resemble quasi-equilibria.

What is remarkable about Anderson's theorem is the weakness of its hypotheses, especially the absence of any assumption concerning convexity. Sharper results can be obtained, but only with much stronger hypotheses. The main objection to Theorem 8.18 is that it only establishes that, in large economies, core and Walrasian allocations have similar market value. Core allocations may be nowhere near what consumers would demand at any market clearing price p. My own view is that Theorem 8.18 is just about perfect. Convexity at the individual level is not a very credible assumption, and theorems which use that hypothesis are suspect. Anderson's theorem helps us understand why it is unnecessary. Competition is an abstraction which makes sense only in the limit.

8.2.3 The integral of a correspondence

Mimicking the proof of Anderson's theorem turns out to be one of the most insightful ways to prove Aumann's theorem, the equivalence of core and Walrasian allocations in economics with a nonatomic measure space of consumers. But if we are to follow this approach we first have to decide what we mean when we replace the average $\overline{V} = (1/\#I) \sum_{i \in I} V_i$ of a finite number of sets $V_i \subset \mathbf{R^m}$ with the integral $\overline{V} = \int_I V(i) \, d\mu(i)$ averaging a continuum of sets $V(i) \subset \mathbf{R^m}$. The object we want to define, $\int_I V := \int_V V(i) \, d\mu(i)$, is called the integral of the correspondence $V: I \to (2^{\mathbf{R^m}})_o$ mapping $i \mapsto V(i)$.

I want to emphasize that for the moment I stands for an arbitrary measure space, not necessarily the interval $[0,1]$. It will facilitate comprehension if you tolerate this modest amount of ambiguity.[5] Recall from Chapter 3 that, given a measure space $(I, \mathcal{C}, \mu)$, the function $f: I \to \mathbf{R^m}$ which maps $i \mapsto (f_1(i), \ldots, f_m(i))$ is **integrable** if each of its coordinate functions f_j is integrable. Assuming that f is integrable, we define $\int_I f := (\int_I f_1, \ldots, \int_I f_m)$. Given a correspondence $F: I \to (2^{\mathbf{R^m}})_o$, define the set $\mathcal{L}_F := \{ f: I \to \mathbf{R^m} \mid f(i) \in F(i), \ f \text{ integrable} \}$ consisting of all the **integrable selections** from F.

Definition 8.19 *The* **integral of the correspondence** $F: I \to (2^{\mathbf{R^m}})_o$ *is the set*

$$\int_I F := \left\{ x \in \mathbf{R^m} \mid x = \int_I f, \ f \in \mathcal{L}_F \right\}.$$

Our goal is to show that, provided $(I, \mathcal{C}, \mu)$ is an atomless measure space, the integral $\int_I F$ is a convex subset of $\mathbf{R^m}$. The key to this result is the much heralded Liapunov Convexity Theorem:

---

5 If you find this intolerable, replace I with Ω as in Chapter 3, or read Hildenbrand (1974), Part I, Section D.II, from which this material is drawn.

Theorem 8.20 (Liapunov) *If $\{\,\mu_i \mid i = 1, \ldots, m\,\}$ is a collection of atomless measures on the measurable space $(I, \mathcal{C})$, then $\{\,(\mu_1(S), \ldots, \mu_m(S)) \in \mathbf{R}^m \mid S \in \mathcal{C}\,\}$ is a compact, convex subset of $\mathbf{R}^m$.*

Proof See Rudin (1973), 114, Theorem 5.5. □

Remark 8.21 *The function on $(I, \mathcal{C})$ defined by $\mu(S) := (\mu_1(S), \ldots, \mu_m(S))$ is often called a **vector measure**. Using this terminology, Liapunov's theorem can be paraphrased: the range of a vector measure on a nonatomic measure space is compact and convex.*

From Liapunov follows the result we are looking for:

Theorem 8.22 *If $F\colon I \to (2^{\mathbf{R}^m})_o$ where $(I, \mathcal{C}, \mu)$ is a nonatomic measure space, then $\int_I F$ is convex.*

Proof Let x and y be any pair of points in $\int_I F$ and α any scalar in $(0, 1)$. By definition of $\int_I F$, there exist integrable selections f and g such that $x = \int_I f$ and $y = \int_I g$. According to Liapunov's theorem, the set $\{\,(\int_S f, \int_S g) \in \mathbf{R}^m \times \mathbf{R}^m \mid S \in \mathcal{C}\,\}$ is convex. Therefore, since both $(0,0)$ and (x, y) belong to this set, so does their convex combination

$$(\alpha x, \alpha y) = (1 - \alpha)(0, 0) + \alpha(x, y),$$

and hence there exists a set $E \in \mathcal{C}$ such that $(\alpha x, \alpha y) = (\int_E f, \int_E g)$. Define a function $h \in \mathcal{L}_F$ by

$$h(i) = \begin{cases} f(i) & \text{if } i \in E; \\ g(i) & \text{if } i \notin E. \end{cases}$$

Then

$$\int_I h = \int_E h + \int_{I \setminus E} h = \int_E f + \int_{I \setminus E} g = \int_E f + \int_I g - \int_E g = \alpha x + (1 - \alpha)y$$

and so $\alpha x + (1 - \alpha)y \in \int_I F$. □

It is worth emphasizing that Theorem 8.22 makes no assumptions about the correspondence F apart from nonatomicity of its domain: the integral of any correspondence from a nonatomic measure space into $\mathbf{R}^m$ is convex-valued.

8.2.4 Aumann's Theorem

The proof of Aumann's core equivalence theorem follows exactly along the lines of the proof of Anderson's theorem, but with the Liapunov Theorem used in place of the Shapley-Folkman Theorem.[6]

Theorem 8.23 (Aumann) *Let $\mathcal{E} := \{X_i, P_i, w_i \mid i \in I\}$ be an exchange economy with $(I, \mathcal{B}(I), \lambda)$ a nonatomic measure space of consumers and λ Lebesgue measure. Assume that for all $i \in I$:*

- *the consumption set $X_i = \mathbf{R}_+^{\mathbf{m}}$;*
- *the strict preference relation $\succ_i$ is irreflexive, transitive, and monotonic with open graph in $X_i \times X_i$; and*
- *$\int_I w \gg 0$.*

Then $\mathrm{WE}^x(\mathcal{E}) = \mathrm{C}(\mathcal{E})$.

Proof The inclusion $\mathrm{WE}^x(\mathcal{E}) \subset \mathrm{C}(\mathcal{E})$ was established in Chapter 3 (Theorem 3.16). To prove the opposite inclusion, define for each $i \in I$ the set $V(i) = \Delta_w P_i(x_i) \cup \{0\}$ just as in the proof of Anderson's theorem. Let $\overline{V} = \int_I V$. By Theorem 8.22, $\int_I V$ is convex. Mimicking Step 1 of the proof of Anderson's theorem, we will now establish that $\overline{V} \cap \mathbf{R}_-^{\mathbf{m}} = \{0\}$. From the definition of $V(i)$, it clear that $0 \in \overline{V}$ and hence that $0 \in \overline{V} \cap \mathbf{R}_-^{\mathbf{m}}$. Suppose that this intersection contains some other point $v = \int_I \Delta_w y$ such that $\Delta_w y_i \in V(i)$ for a.e. $i \in I$ and $v < 0$. Form the coalition $S := \{i \in I \mid \Delta_w y_i \neq 0\}$ and consider the net trade allocation

$$\Delta_w z_i = \begin{cases} \Delta_w y_i - v/\lambda(S) & \text{for } i \in S; \\ 0 & \text{for } i \notin S. \end{cases}$$

This net trade allocation is feasible for S because $\int_S \Delta_w z_i \, di = 0$. Since $\Delta_w y_i \neq 0$ for each $i \in S$, it follows that $y_i \succ_i x_i$ for all $i \in S$. By construction, $\Delta_w z_i > \Delta_w y_i$ and so $z_i \succ_i y_i$ by monotonicity of preferences. Since $z_i \succ_i y_i$ and $y_i \succ x_i$, transitivity implies that $z_i \succ_i x_i$ for all $i \in S$. We conclude that the coalition S can improve upon x, contradicting the assumption that $x \in \mathrm{C}(\mathcal{E})$.

Since $\overline{V}$ and $\mathbf{R}_-^{\mathbf{m}}$ are nonempty, disjoint, and convex, the Separating Hyperplane Theorem 4.42 guarantees existence of a hyperplane $H(p, 0)$ passing through 0 with $\overline{V}$ in its upper halfspace. By definition of $\overline{V}$, this means that $\Delta_w P_i(x_i) \subset H^+(p, 0)$ for a.e. $i \in I$. Since $x \in \mathrm{C}(\mathcal{E})$, we also have $\int_I \Delta_x x_i \, di = 0$. Therefore, (x, p) is a quasi-equilibrium for the economy $\mathcal{E}$.

---

6 For a proof along the lines of Aumann's original proof, see Hildenbrand (1982), 843–845, Theorem 1.

Since $\int_I w \gg 0$, $\succ_i$ is monotonic with open upper contour sets, and $X_i = \mathbf{R}_+^\mathbf{m}$ for all $i \in I$, the quasi-equilibrium (x,p) is a Walrasian equilibrium. $\qquad\square$

The requirement that $\int_I w \gg 0$ is innocuous, asserting simply that a positive per capita amount of every commodity is available for trade. Its role in the proof is simply to guarantee that a nonnegligible fraction of consumers have strictly positive wealth and hence that $p \gg 0$. Just as with Theorem 8.18, Aumann's theorem is remarkable for the weakness of its hypotheses, particularly the absence of convexity requirements on preferences. Although the assumption $X_i = \mathbf{R}_+^\mathbf{m}$ rules out indivisibilities, this assumption was used only to show that the quasi-equilibrium was a Walrasian equilibrium. Indivisibilities can be accommodated provided that at least one commodity is perfectly divisible and universally desired (see Mas-Colell (1977)).

One advantage of proving Aumann's theorem in this way is that the proof also suggests why nonconvexity at the individual level is not an impediment to proving existence of equilibrium. Theorem 8.22 implies that the market demand correspondence in an Aumann exchange economy is convex-valued. Specifically, given a pure exchange economy defined on the nonatomic measure space of consumers $(I, \mathcal{B}(I), \lambda)$ and individual demand correspondences ϕ_i for each $i \in I$, Theorem 8.22 immediately implies that the **per capita market demand correspondence** Φ defined by $\Phi(p) := \int_I \phi_i(p)\,di$ is convex-valued. Coupled with a proof that Φ is upperhemicontinuous (see Aumann (1976)), proving existence of a Walrasian equilibrium follows easily (see Debreu (1982), 725–730, for the details).

8.3 Infinite dimensional commodity spaces

Aumann provides a powerful foundation for competitive theory. In a certain sense, however, his model stacks the deck too heavily in favor of the competitive hypothesis. With an infinite number of consumers and only a finite number of commodities, markets are almost inevitably thick. Aumann is quite right that without a continuum of consumers, price-taking behavior makes no sense. But forcing all of the complexity of the economic world into finite dimensions also makes little sense. Variations in time, location, and state of the world all point to the infinite variability present in the marketplace. Can this manifest complexity be approximated reasonably well by a world of finite periods, regions, and events? Neoclassical economics swept this issue under the rug. Modern economics does not. Finite approximation may work, but we need to know how and why.

This book was written with infinite dimensional economics in mind. Although our focus has been almost exclusively finite dimensional, I have taken pains to talk throughout of the finite dimensional TVS L rather than the Euclidean space $\mathbf{R}^m$ and of the price functional $p \in L'$ rather than the price vector $p \in \mathbf{R}^m$. This approach is about to pay rich dividends. Viewed from a **coordinate-free** perspective, finite dimensional competitive analysis blends naturally into infinite dimensions, requiring only a few new concepts and almost no new notation.

I don't want to overstate the case. Understanding competition in infinite dimensions does require more mathematical sophistication than this book presumes. Nevertheless, I think you will be surprised at how much you can understand without such background. What makes possible such a discussion in a rather small space is the splendid review of the literature by Mas-Colell and Zame (1991). This section is intended as a reader's guide to their article, smoothing the transition from finite to infinite dimensions. You should look to the original for most of the proofs: though easy to follow, there is no reason to repeat them here. But unless you look at the proofs, your understanding of this material will not be very satisfactory.

8.3.1 Vector spaces

The simplest way to think about a vector space in infinite dimensions is as a function space. The set $\mathrm{Map}(X, \mathbf{R})$ of Chapter 1 is a vector space with elements $f \colon X \to \mathbf{R}$ and vector space operations αf (defined by $x \mapsto \alpha f(x)$) and $f + g$ (defined by $x \mapsto f(x) + g(x)$). However, even though it is a vector space, $\mathrm{Map}(X, \mathbf{R})$ does not have enough in common with $\mathbf{R}^m$ to be of much use. In particular, $\mathbf{R}^m$ is not just a vector space but also a locally convex topological vector space (Definition 4.33) and an ordered vector space (Definition 2.12). We require of our infinite dimensional commodity space L the same properties: i.e., that L be

- a locally convex topological vector space (LCTVS); and
- an ordered vector space with a nondegenerate, closed, convex cone $L_+ = \{\, x \in L \mid x \geq 0 \,\}$ serving as nonnegative orthant.

Three classes of function space which fit this bill are particularly useful for economic applications: the ℓ_p-spaces, the L^p-spaces, and the space of measures $M(K)$. We consider each in turn.

I. The vector space ℓ_p: The "little ell p" spaces, as the vector spaces ℓ_p are called, are popular in applications involving a countably infinite sequence of time periods. A period can be anything from a day to a generation.

Assuming for simplicity a single type of commodity available each period, a typical element of the vector space $\ell_p \subset \mathrm{Map}(T, \mathbf{R})$ is a sequence

$$x = (x(0), x(1), \ldots, x(t), \ldots)$$

where $x(t)$ represents quantity consumed in period $t \in T$. For each p such that $1 \leq p \leq \infty$, the ℓ_p-**norm** on ℓ_p is defined by $\|x\|_p := [\sum_{t \in T} |x(t)|^p]^{1/p}$ if $p < \infty$ and $\|x\|_\infty := \sup_{t \in T} |x(t)|$ otherwise.[7]

Definition 8.24 *For $1 \leq p \leq \infty$, the locally convex topological vector space (ℓ_p, τ) is the set $\{ x \in \mathrm{Map}(T, \mathbf{R}) \mid \|x\|_p < \infty \}$ with topology generated by the ℓ_p norm.*

II. The vector space L_p: The L_p spaces find frequent application in models of continuous, rather than discrete, time and in models involving uncertainty:

- In intertemporal models, the time set is a measure space $(T, \mathcal{B}(T), \lambda)$ with T either bounded, $T = [0, \bar{T}]$, or unbounded, $T = [0, \infty]$. $\mathcal{B}(T)$ denotes the sigma-algebra of Borel sets of T and λ Lebesgue measure. A typical element of $L_p(T, \mathcal{B}(T), \lambda) \subset \mathrm{Map}(T, \mathbf{R})$ is a measurable function[8] $x : t \mapsto x(t)$ with $x(t)$ representing consumption at time $t \in T$.

- In models of uncertainty, a probability space (S, Σ, μ) of **states of the world** takes the place of the time set. Σ is a sigma-algebra of subsets of S and μ a measure with $\mu(B)$ interpreted as the probability that the true state s lies in the measurable set $B \in \Sigma$. A typical element of $L_p(S, \Sigma, \mu) \subset \mathrm{Map}(S, \mathbf{R})$ is a measurable function $x : s \mapsto x(s)$ with $x(s)$ representing quantity consumed in state $s \in S$.

To cover both of these cases, we will use the notation $L(\Omega, \mathcal{F}, \mu)$ where $(\Omega, \mathcal{F}, \mu)$ is a σ-finite measure space. For $1 \leq p \leq \infty$, the L_p-norm on L_p is defined by $\|x\|_p := [\int_S |x|^p]^{1/p}$ if $p < \infty$ and $\|x\|_\infty = \inf\{ M \in \mathbf{R} \mid \mu\{ \omega \mid |x(\omega)| > M \} = 0 \}$ otherwise.[9]

Definition 8.25 *For $1 \leq p \leq \infty$, the locally convex topological vector space $(L_p(\Omega, \mathcal{F}, \mu), \tau)$ is the set $\{ x \in \mathrm{Map}(\Omega, \mathbf{R}) \mid \|x\|_p < \infty \}$ with topology generated by the L_p norm.*

---

7 You may recall that we encountered the sup norm $\|\cdot\|_\infty$ in Chapter 3.

8 Technically, the elements of L_p are equivalence classes of functions. Functions equal a.e. belong to the same equivalence class.

9 The norm on $L_\infty(\Omega, \mathcal{F}, \mu)$, called the essential sup, has a simple interpretation: $\|x\|_\infty$ is the supremum of $|x|$ over Ω ignoring sets of measure zero.

III. The space of measures $M(K)$. We encountered the vector space $M(K)$ in Chapter 3 where it was used to model competitive product differentiation (hedonic theory). A typical element of the vector space $M(K) \subset \text{Map}(\mathcal{B}(K), \mathbf{R})$ is a measure $x \colon \mathcal{B}(K) \mapsto \mathbf{R}$ where $(K, \mathcal{B}(K))$ is a measurable space and $x(B)$ is interpreted as the total quantity of commodities in the bundle x whose characteristics lie in the Borel set $B \in \mathcal{B}(K)$. In contrast to the vector spaces just described, the topology of $M(K)$ is not defined by a norm.[10] Instead $M(K)$ is given the **weak* topology**, the weakest topology such that the linear functional

$$p \mapsto p \cdot x := \int_K \pi(k) \, dx(k)$$

is continuous for all $\pi \in C(K)$ where $C(K)$ denotes the set of all continuous functions on K.[11]

Definition 8.26 *Let* $(K, \mathcal{B}(K))$ *be a measurable space with* K *a compact metric space and* $\mathcal{B}(K)$ *its collection of Borel subsets. The locally convex topological vector space* $(M(K), \tau)$ *consists of the set of signed[12] measures on* $(K, \mathcal{B}(K))$ *with* τ *the weak* topology.*

8.3.2 *Linear functionals*

As noted in Chapter 4, one of the most profound differences between finite and infinite dimensions is the need to distinguish between the **algebraic dual space** L' and the **topological dual space** L^*. In finite dimensions, all linear functionals are continuous, $L' = L^*$, but in infinite dimensions L' can be a proper subset of L^*. The dual spaces for each of our candidates for the commodity space L are easily characterized:[13]

---

10 Actually, $M(K)$ can be given a norm topology, generated by the variation norm, but we will not do so here.

11 We could also write this as $\int_K p(k) \, dx(k)$ with the function p doing double duty as a linear functional $p \colon x \mapsto p \cdot x \in R$ on $M(K)$ and as a continuous, but typically nonlinear, functional $p \colon k \mapsto p(k) \in R$ on K. In the present context, however, it seems better to avoid the ambiguity. Convergence under the weak* topology is precisely the notion of convergence exploited in the central limit theorem of probability theory. It characterizes, for example, the sense in which the binomial distribution converges to the normal as sample size increases.

12 I.e., the measure is allowed to take on negative as well as positive values.

13 To avoid confusion with the parameter p used to characterize the spaces ℓ_p or L_p, I use x^* rather than our preferred p to denote a typical linear functional. The notation ℓ_p and L_p is too well established to change! When I say that $\ell_p^* = \ell_q$, $L_p^* = L_q$ or $M(K)^* = C(K)$, equality really means "is isomorphic to." And, as noted earlier, in the case of L_p the elements of the vector space or its dual are really equivalence classes of functions equal a.e. Most of these comments will be meaningful only if you have had a graduate course in real analysis, which is why they have been buried in a footnote!

(IA) If $L = \ell_p$ and $1 \leq p < \infty$, then $L^* = \ell_q$ where $1/p + 1/q = 1$. Thus, $x^* \in L^*$ can be represented in the form

$$x^*: L \to \mathbf{R}, \quad x \mapsto x^* \cdot x := \sum_{i=0}^{\infty} x^*(t)x(t) \tag{$*$}$$

provided that

$$\left[\sum_{i=0}^{\infty} |x^*(t)|^q\right]^{1/q} < \infty. \tag{$\dagger$}$$

A functional x^* on ℓ_p which satisfies $(*)$ but not $(\dagger)$ is linear but not continuous. The dual space ℓ_q with topology generated by the ℓ_q norm is itself an LCTVS.

(IB) If $L = \ell_\infty$, then the dual space is much larger than ℓ_1, a space too large to be of much use.

(IIA) If $L = L_p(\Omega, \mathcal{F}, \mu)$ and $1 \leq p < \infty$, then $L^* = L_q$ where $1/p + 1/q = 1$. Thus, $x^* \in L^*$ can be represented in the form

$$x^*: L \to \mathbf{R}, \quad x \mapsto x^* \cdot x := \int_S x^*(\omega)x(\omega) \, d\mu(\omega) \tag{$*$}$$

provided that

$$\left[\int_S |x^*(\omega)|^q \, d\mu(\omega)\right]^{1/q} < \infty. \tag{$\dagger$}$$

A functional x^* on L_p which satisfies $(*)$ but not $(\dagger)$ is linear but not continuous. The dual space $L_q(\Omega, \mathcal{F}, \mu)$ with topology generated by the L_q norm is itself an LCTVS.

(IIB) If $L = L_\infty(\Omega, \mathcal{F}, \mu)$, then the dual space is much larger than L_1, a space too large to be of much use.

(III) If $L = M(K)$ under the weak* topology, then $L^* = C(K)$ where $C(K)$ represents the set of continuous functions on K. Thus, $x^* \in L^*$ can be represented in the form

$$x^*: L \to \mathbf{R}, \quad x \mapsto x^* \cdot x := \int_K \pi(k) \, dx(k) \tag{$*$}$$

provided that

$$\pi \in C(K). \tag{$\dagger$}$$

A functional x^* on $M(K)$ which satisfies $(*)$ but not $(\dagger)$ is linear but not continuous. The dual space $L^* = C(K)$ with topology generated by the sup norm (i.e., the norm defined by $\|x^*\|_\infty := \sup_{k \in K} |x^*(k)|$) is itself an LCTVS.

The possibility that linear functionals on an infinite dimensional commodity space may be discontinuous manifests itself most seriously with the failure of the Separating Hyperplane Theorem 4.42. Given two nonempty, disjoint, convex subsets A and B in an infinite dimensional LCTVS L, it is possible that

- A and B cannot be separated by any linear functional, continuous or not;
- A and B can be separated by a linear functional, but not by a continuous linear functional.

Separation can be guaranteed if we impose an additional requirement: at least one of the sets has nonempty interior.

Theorem 8.27 *If A and B are nonempty, disjoint, convex subsets of the topological vector space L and if one of the sets has nonempty interior, then A and B can be separated by a hyperplane $H(p, \alpha)$ where $p: L \to \mathbf{R}$ is a nonzero, continuous linear functional.*

Proof See Giles (1982), 66.   □

If A and B are nonempty, disjoint, convex subsets of a TVS L and if one of the sets has a nonempty **linear interior** (see Definition 4.38), then A and B can be separated by a hyperplane $H(p, \alpha)$ but the linear functional p may be discontinuous (see Giles (1982), 32). Under those circumstances, the halfspaces $H^+(p, \alpha)$ and $H^-(p, \alpha)$ will each be dense in L, a very pathological state of affairs! Continuity of the linear functional p seems essential if separation is to make much economic sense.

8.3.3 Dual pairs and dual topologies

We now have three natural candidates for our infinite dimensional commodity space L, and each comes equipped with an easily characterized topological dual space L^*. Now for the bad news. The topologies associated with these pairings of a TVS L with its dual L^* typically do not give us the structure we need to establish existence of Walrasian equilibrium. Fortunately, there is a way out. Infinite dimensional vector spaces give us more flexibility than do those of finite dimension: more than one linear topology can turn these spaces into LCTVS's. The key to exploiting this flexibility is to consider jointly the pairing of L and L^*.

Suppose that we are given a pair of vector spaces $\langle L, M \rangle$ and a **value**

map on $L \times M$ mapping $(x, p) \mapsto p \cdot x$ which is linear and nonsingular[14] in both x and p. The obvious illustration, of course, is the dual pair $\langle L, M \rangle = \langle \mathbf{R}^m, \mathbf{R}^m \rangle$ we have been using all along to value commodities using the map defined by

$$(x, p) \mapsto p \cdot x := \sum_{i=1}^{m} p_i x_i.$$

But the same construction applies to any of our three families of infinite dimensional commodity space:

(IA) $L = \ell_p$ and $M = \ell_q$ with $1/p + 1/q = 1$, $1 \leq p < \infty$, and value map $x^* \cdot x = \sum_{t \in T} x^*(t) x(t)$;

(IIA) $L = L_p(\Omega, \mathcal{F}, \mu)$ and $M = L_q(\Omega, \mathcal{F}, \mu)$ with $1/p + 1/q = 1$, $1 \leq p < \infty$, and value map $x^* \cdot x = \int_\Omega x^*(\omega) x(\omega) \, d\mu(\omega)$; and

(III) $L = M(K)$ and $M = C(K)$ with value map $x^* \cdot x = \int_K \pi(k) \, dx(k)$ where $\pi \in C(K)$.

We seek topologies on L and M, which work well together in the sense that

- the topology on L implies that $L^* = M$ (i.e., the continuous linear functionals on L are given by M); and
- the topology on M implies that $M^* = L$ (i.e., the continuous linear functionals on M are given by L).

Definition 8.28 *Let $\langle L, M \rangle$ be a dual pair.*

- *A locally convex linear topology τ_L on L is a dual-$\langle L, M \rangle$ topology if $L^* = M$.*

- *A locally convex linear topology τ_M on M is a dual-$\langle M, L \rangle$ topology if $M^* = L$.*

The fundamental result which establishes the limits within which we can find useful topologies is the following:

Theorem 8.29 (Mackey-Arens) *Let $\langle L, M \rangle$ be a dual pair.*

- *There exist topologies $\sigma(L, M)$ and $\tau(L, M)$ on L such that a locally convex topology τ_L on L is a dual-(L, M) topology iff*

$$\sigma(L, M) \subset \tau_L \subset \tau(L, M).$$

---

14 I.e., for each $x \in L$ there exists a $p \in M$ such that $p \cdot x \neq 0$, and for each $p \in M$ there exists a $x \in L$ such that $p \cdot x \neq 0$.

- *There exist topologies $\sigma(M, L)$ and $\tau(M, L)$ on M such that a locally convex topology τ_M on M is a dual-(M, L) topology iff*

$$\sigma(M, L) \subset \tau_M \subset \tau(M, L).$$

Proof See Reed and Simon (1972), Chapter V, for a proof of this theorem as well as an exceptionally clear discussion of dual pairs and dual topologies.
□

The topologies $\sigma(L, M)$ and $\sigma(M, L)$, the **weak topologies**, and $\tau(L, M)$ and $\tau(M, L)$, the **Mackey topologies**, are readily characterized:

- $\sigma(L, M)$ is the weakest topology on L such that $x \mapsto p \cdot x$ is continuous for all $p \in M$. Equivalently, a net $x^\alpha \to x$ under the topology $\sigma(L, M)$ iff $p \cdot x^\alpha \to p \cdot x$ for every $p \in M$.
- $\sigma(M, L)$ is the weakest topology on M such that $p \mapsto p \cdot x$ is continuous for all $x \in L$. Equivalently, a net $p^\alpha \to p$ under the topology $\sigma(M, L)$ iff $p^\alpha \cdot x \to p \cdot x$ for every $x \in L$.
- $\tau(L, M)$ is the topology of uniform convergence on $\sigma(M, L)$-compact, convex subsets of M: i.e., a net $x^\alpha \to x$ in the $\tau(L, M)$ topology iff $p \cdot x^\alpha \to p \cdot x$ uniformly for all p in any convex subset of M which is compact in the $\sigma(M, L)$ topology.
- $\tau(M, L)$ is the topology of uniform convergence on $\sigma(L, M)$-compact, convex subsets of L: i.e., a net $p^\alpha \to p$ in the $\tau(M, L)$ topology iff $p^\alpha \cdot x \to p \cdot x$ uniformly for all x in any convex subset of L which is compact in the $\sigma(L, M)$ topology.

The most important application of this framework is to the dual pair $\langle L, L^* \rangle$ consisting of an LCTVS L with topology τ_L and its topological dual L^*. According to the Mackey-Arens Theorem, τ_L lies between $\sigma(L, L^*)$ and $\tau(L, L^*)$. Similarly, any locally convex linear topology on L^* must lie between the weak* topology $\sigma(L^*, L)$ and the Mackey* topology $\tau(L^*, L)$.

8.3.4 The economic significance of topology

Why is all of this "abstract nonsense" about dual topologies of any concern to us? Because in infinite dimensions we have many linear topologies from which to choose, and the choice we make has economic significance. The Mackey-Arens Theorem sets the limits of the choices we can make, establishing the range of topologies for which the commodity space L has continuous dual L^*. When we characterize a consumer's preferences in terms of one of these topologies, we are making a statement about what constitutes a "good substitute" for that consumer. In infinite dimensions, too much complementarity is the enemy of competition. Competition requires that consumers not regard a specific commodity available at a particular place, time, and state of the world as too distinctive, too unique. If competition is to be sustained, the consumer should feel that altering any one of these commodity characteristics a little bit yields an alternative which is a good substitute for the commodity in question.

Recall what it means for a preference relation $\succ_i$ to be continuous: the graph of $\succ_i$ is open (or, equivalently, the graph of $\not\succ_i$ is closed) in $X_i \times X_i$ where the consumption set X_i is given the relative topology it inherits from the commodity space L. Continuity of $\succ_i$ in turn implies that the strict contour sets $P_i(x_i)$ and $P_i^{-1}(x_i)$ are open for all $x_i \in X_i$ or, equivalently, that the contour sets $R_i(x_i)$ and $R_i^{-1}(x_i)$ are closed. Weakening the topology on L, and hence X_i, means that the topology contains fewer open sets and hence fewer closed sets. Requiring consumer preferences to meet any of these continuity requirements under a weaker topology is, therefore, more difficult: fewer preference relations will satisfy the conditions. Mas-Colell and Zame provide three illuminating illustrations of what imposing a more restrictive continuity requirement on preferences means economically:

Example 1: Consider the commodity space $L = \ell_\infty$, a popular setting for models of intertemporal allocation. Recall that when ℓ_∞ is given its norm topology, the topological dual space is not ℓ_1, but rather a space which is much bigger — too large to be economically meaningful. Suppose now that we strengthen our continuity requirement on preferences by requiring that the upper contour sets $R_i(x_i)$ be closed with respect to the weak topology $\sigma(\ell_\infty, \ell_1)$. Preferences which meet this stiffened requirement exhibit a form of myopia in which consumers discount gains in the far distant future. To validate this assertion, for each $s \in \mathbf{Z}_+$ let z^s denote a vector which is zero up to time s and 1 thereafter. For any $y \in L$, I claim that $y^s := y + z^s \to y$ in the weak topology $\sigma(\ell_\infty, \ell_1)$. By definition, $y^s \to y$ weakly requires that $p \cdot y^s \to p \cdot y$ for all $p \in \ell_1$. Any $p \in \ell_1$ can be represented as a functional $x \mapsto \sum_{t \in T} p(t) x(t)$ where $\sum_{t \in T} |p(t)| < \infty$. But $\sum_{t \in T} |p(t)| < \infty$ implies that $\sum_{t=s}^{\infty} |p(t)| \to 0$ as $s \to \infty$. Therefore, $p \cdot z^s = \sum_{t=s}^{\infty} p(t) \to 0$ and so $p \cdot y^s = p \cdot y + p \cdot z^s \to p \cdot y + 0 = p \cdot y$ as claimed. If $R_i(x)$ is closed (or, equivalently, $P_i^{-1}(x)$ is open) with respect to the $\sigma(\ell_\infty, \ell_1)$ topology, then $x \succ_i y$ and $y^s := y + z^s \to y$ implies that $x \succ y^s$ for large enough s: provided that the perturbation z^s occurs far enough in the future, y^s and y are good substitutes. Loosely speaking, the commodity space behaves as though it were finite dimensional. In contrast, if we require only that $R_i(x)$ be closed in the norm topology for ℓ_∞, then it is easy to see that $y + z^s \not\rightarrow y$: continuity with respect to the norm topology does not require this form of myopia, and perturbations in the far distant future can have a nonnegligible impact on decisions made today.

Example 2: Let $L = L_\infty(S, \Sigma, \mu)$ where (S, Σ, μ) is a probabilistic measure space. Under the norm topology, the topological dual of L_∞ is much larger than L_1. Suppose that we strengthen the continuity requirement on preferences by requiring the upper contour sets $R_i(x_i)$ to be closed in the weak topology $\sigma(L_\infty, L_1)$. Let $\langle E^n \rangle$ be a sequence of measurable sets with measure $\mu(E^n)$ converging to zero as $n \rightarrow \infty$, and define $z^n = 1_{E^n}$ where 1_{E^n} is the **characteristic function** of E^n (i.e., 1^{E^n} is the measurable function on S which equals 1 on E^n and 0 otherwise). For any $y \in L$, I claim that $y^n := y + z^n \rightarrow y$ in the weak topology $\sigma(L_\infty, L_1)$. By definition, $y^n \rightarrow y$ weakly iff

$$p \cdot y^n = \int_S (p(\omega)y(\omega) + p(\omega) \cdot 1_{E^n}(\omega))\, d\mu(\omega) \rightarrow p \cdot y$$

or, equivalently, $\int_S p(\omega) \cdot 1_{E^n}(\omega)\, d\mu(\omega) \rightarrow 0$ for all $p \in L_1$. But

$$\int_S p(\omega) 1_{E^n}(\omega)\, d\mu(\omega) = \int_{E^n} p(\omega)\, d\mu(\omega) \rightarrow 0$$

since $p \in L_1$ and $\mu(E^n) \rightarrow 0$. If $R_i(x)$ is closed (or, equivalently, $P_i^{-1}(x)$ is open) with respect to the $\sigma(L_\infty, L_1)$ topology, then $x \succ_i y$ and $y^n := y + z^n \rightarrow y$ implies that $x \succ_i y^n$ for large enough n: if the event $\mu(E^n)$ is not very likely, then $y + 1_{E^n}$ and y are good substitutes. In contrast, y^n does not converge to y under the norm topology: although the probability of the perturbation goes to zero, its impact on preferences does not follow suit.

Example 3: Finally suppose that $L = M(K)$, a popular setting for models of product differentiation. Let δ_{k^n} represent the probability measure which concentrates all of its mass at the point k^n, interpreted as a commodity bundle consisting of one unit of the commodity with characteristics $k^n \in K$ (see Section 3.4). The sequence $\delta_{k^n} \rightarrow \delta_{k^*}$ in the weak topology[15] $\sigma(M(K), C(K))$ provided that $\int_K \pi(k)\, d\delta_{k^n}(k) \rightarrow \int_K \pi(k)\, d\delta_{k^*}(k)$ for all $\pi \in C(K)$. But by definition of the delta function, $\int_K \pi(k)\, d\delta_{k^n}(k) = \pi(k^n)$,

---

15 You are probably wondering why I now call this the weak rather than the weak* topology. The terms weak and weak* are used interchangeably for the topology $\sigma(M(K), C(K))$ on $M(K)$. Historically, the weak* topology arose from consideration of the dual pairing $\langle C(K), M(K) \rangle$ where $C(K)$ is given its sup topology. The weak* topology on $C(K)$'s topological dual $M(K)$ is $\sigma(M(K), C(K))$, which is the same as the weak topology $\sigma(M(K), C(K))$ applied to $M(K)$ in the dual pair $\langle M(K), C(K) \rangle$.

$\int_K \pi(k)\, d\delta_{k^*}(k) = \pi(k^*)$, and so

$$\int_K \pi(k)\, d\delta_{k^n}(k) \to \int_K \pi(k)\, d\delta_{k^*}(k) \quad \text{iff} \quad \pi(k^n) \to \pi(k^*).$$

Since $\pi \in C(K)$ and $k^n \to k^*$ implies that $\pi(k^n) \to \pi(k^*)$ (see Theorem 4.17(d)), we conclude that $\delta_{k^n} \to \delta_{k^*}$ weakly iff $k^n \to k^*$: commodities with similar characteristics are good substitutes.

8.3.5 Walrasian equilibrium

The basic assumptions introduced by Mas-Colell and Zame are similar to those employed earlier in this book.

Definition 8.30 *Let* (L, τ_L) *be an LCTVS ordered by* $\geq$ *with positive orthant* $L_+ := \{\, x \in L \mid x \geq 0 \,\}$ *a nondegenerate, closed, convex cone. An* **exchange economy** $\mathcal{E} := \{\, X_i, \succ_i, w_i \mid i \in I \,\}$ *consists of a finite set of consumers* $I = \{\, 1, \dots, n \,\}$ *characterized by a consumption set* $X_i \subset L_+$, *a strict preference relation* $\succ_i$ *on* X_i, *and an endowment* $w_i \in L_+$. *The following assumptions are adopted for each* $i \in I$:

- X_i *is closed, convex, and satisfies a* **free-disposal** *condition* $X_i + L_+ \subset X_i$;
- $\succ_i$ *is a weak ordering with open graph in* $X_i \times X_i$ *and convex upper sections* $R_i(x_i)$ *for every* $x_i \in X_i$. $\succ_i$ *is also* **monotonic** *in the sense that there exists a* $v_o \in L_+$ *such that* $x_i + \alpha v_o \succ_i x_i$ *for all* $x_i \in X_i$ *and for every* $\alpha > 0$.
- $w_i \in X_i$.

The set of feasible allocations is modified to allow for free disposal:

Definition 8.31 *The set of* **attainable allocations for the economy** $\mathcal{E}$ *is the set*

$$Z := \Big\{ x\colon I \to L_+ \;\Big|\; \sum_{i \in I} x_i \leq \sum_{i \in I} w_i \;\&\; x_i \in X_i \; \forall\, i \in I \Big\}.$$

Let $\overline{w} := \sum_{i \in I} w_i$ denote the aggregate endowment for the economy.

The only change to the definition of Walrasian equilibrium is the requirement that prices be continuous.

Definition 8.32 *A* **Walrasian equilibrium** *for* $\mathcal{E}$ *is a pair* (x, p) *consisting of an attainable allocation* $x \in Z$ *and a continuous linear functional* $p \in L^* \backslash \{0\}$ *such that* $x_i \in \phi_i(p)$ *for all* $i \in I$.

The notion of a quasi-equilibrium is also modified slightly from our earlier definition.

Definition 8.33 *A* **quasi-equilibrium** *for the economy $\mathcal{E}$ is a pair (x, p) consisting of an attainable allocation $x \in Z$ and a continuous linear functional $p \in L^* \backslash \{0\}$ for which $\mathrm{p} \cdot \overline{w} \neq 0$ and $\Delta_w P_i(x_i) \subset H^+(p, 0)$ for all $i \in I$.*

Since the conditions required to pass from a quasi-equilibrium to a true equilibrium are the same in finite and infinite dimensions, Mas-Colell and Zame establish their existence results only for quasi-equilibria. We will follow their lead.

8.3.6 Proving existence

Proving existence of a Walrasian equilibrium is more complicated in infinite than in finite dimensions. The proof presented by Mas-Colell and Zame, a variation on a technique employed in finite dimensions by Negishi (1960) and Arrow and Hahn (1971), incorporates as a basic ingredient the utility possibility set for the economy. The assumptions made about the economy suffice to guarantee existence of a representing utility function u_i for each consumer, normalized so that $u_i(w_i) = 0$. Define the function $u \colon Z \to \mathbf{R^n}$ by $x \mapsto u(x) := (u_1(x_1), \ldots, u_n(x_n))$.

Definition 8.34 *The* **utility possibility set** *for the economy $\mathcal{E}$ is given by*

$$U := \{ v \in \mathbf{R^n} \mid v \leq u(x),\ x \in Z \} = u(Z) - \mathbf{R_+^n}.$$

Note that U is **comprehensive** in the sense that it includes not only the image $u(Z)$ of the set of feasible allocations but also any vector v weakly dominated by a point in $u(Z)$. This is a harmless convention.

Another basic ingredient in their approach is the set of price functionals which can support a given utility vector $u \in U$.

Definition 8.35 *A price vector $p \in L^*$* **supports the utility vector** *$u \in U$ if $\mathrm{p} \cdot \overline{w} \neq 0$ and $p \cdot \sum_{i \in I} \Delta_w x_i' \geq 0$ for all x' such that $u_i(x') \geq u_i$ for all $i \in I$. A price vector $p \in L^*$* **supports the allocation** *$x \in Z$ if it supports $u(x)$. For any $u \in U$, the* **set of supporting prices** *is denoted $P(u)$.*

The following theorem is the central organizing device for the exposition of Mas-Colell and Zame, isolating the two key assumptions which are the main roadblocks to proving existence in infinite dimensions.

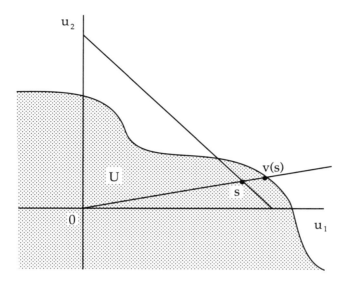

Fig. 8.9. Mapping from simplex to utility frontier.

Theorem 8.36 *Assume, in addition to the assumptions imposed by Definition 8.30, that*

(a) *the utility possibility set U is closed; and*

(b) *every Pareto optimum[16] can be supported by some $p \in K$ where K is a convex, $\sigma(L^*, L)$-compact subset of L^* for which $\mathrm{p} \cdot \overline{\mathrm{w}} \neq 0$ for all $p \in K$.*

The economy $\mathcal{E}$ has a quasi-equilibrium.

Proof As for all of the material in this section, you should look to Mas-Colell and Zame for the details. Here I simply sketch the proof. Figure 8.9 illustrates the key construction. Let Δ denote the $n - 1$ dimensional unit simplex.

- *The mapping v:* For each $s \in \Delta$, let $v(s)$ denote the point in $U \cap \mathbf{R}^{\mathbf{n}}_{+}$ on the ray from 0 to s which is furthest from 0. (Since U is closed and bounded above by $u(\overline{w})$, the point $v(s)$ exists for all $s \in \Delta$.) Thus, the function $v \colon \Delta \to U$ maps the simplex onto the **utility frontier**, that portion of U consisting of utility vectors which are

---

16 Mas-Colell and Zame use weak optimum for what I call an optimum and optimum for what I call a strong optimum.

both Pareto optimal and individually rational. (Remember that we have normalized $u_i(w_i) = 0$ for all $i \in I$.)

- *The correspondence F:* For each $s \in \Delta$, choose an allocation $x(s) \in Z$ such that $u(x(s)) \geq v(s)$ and $\sum_{i \in I} x_i(s) = \overline{w}$. Let $Q(s) = P(v(s)) \cap K$, and let $F: \Delta \to (2^\Delta)_o^F$ be the correspondence defined by

$$s \mapsto \{\, s + q \cdot \Delta_w x(s) \mid q \in Q(s) \,\}.$$

F is an uhc correspondence from the nonempty, compact, and convex set Δ into itself, and F is nonempty-, convex-, and compact-valued. Therefore, by the Kakutani Fixed Point Theorem, F has a fixed point: $s^* \in F(s^*)$ or, equivalently, $s^* = s^* + q^* \cdot \Delta_w x(s^*)$. Letting $x := x(s)$ and $p := q^*$, it follows directly from the definitions of F, $Q(s^*)$, and K that (x, p) is a quasi-equilibrium. $\hfill\square$

In finite dimensions, the two requirements of Theorem 8.36 are automatically satisfied: (a) since Z is compact and utility functions are uppersemicontinuous, U is closed; and (b) every Pareto optimum can be supported by a price functional $p \in \Delta$ (the Second Fundamental Theorem). However, in infinite dimensions both requirements can fail.

8.3.7 Nonempty interior

The most direct way to deal with the possibility that condition (b) of Theorem 8.36 may fail is to require that $\operatorname{int} L_+ \neq \emptyset$. Coupled with the "free disposal" assumption $X_i + L_+ \subset X_i$, this implies that $\operatorname{int} X_i \neq \emptyset$ and finally, since preferences are continuous and strictly monotonic, that the strict upper contour sets $P_i(x_i)$ have nonempty interior. Therefore, according to the Separating Hyperplane Theorem 8.27, the upper contour sets can be supported by a price functional, and the proof of Theorem 8.36 can proceed as planned.

Unfortunately, within the three families of commodity space we have been considering, this tack works only for $L = \ell_\infty$ or $L = L_\infty(\Omega, \mathcal{F}, \mu)$: in every other case, $\operatorname{int} L_+ = \emptyset$. For the remainder of this section, we confine our attention to the L_∞ case.

If $L = L_\infty(\Omega, \mathcal{F}, \mu)$, then we can take for the set K of Theorem 8.36 the set $\{\, p \in L^* \mid p \geq 0 \ \& \ p \cdot \overline{w} = 1 \,\}$. Provided that $\overline{w} \in \operatorname{int} L_+$, the set K will be $\sigma(L^*, L)$-compact. All that remains is to verify that the utility possibility set U is closed. The attainable set Z is not compact under the L_∞ norm. However, if we assume that consumption sets X_i and upper contour sets $R_i(x_i)$ are $\sigma(L_\infty, L_1)$ closed, then Z will be $\sigma(L_\infty, L_1)$-compact and U will be closed.

It seems then that we are done: Theorem 8.36 applies, yielding a quasi-equilibrium with price functional $p \in L_\infty^*$. But, as mentioned earlier, the topological dual L_∞^* is huge, containing linear functionals with no obvious economic interpretation. Prices confined to $L_1 \subset L_\infty^*$ have a much more satisfactory interpretation since $p \in L_1(\Omega, \mathcal{F}, \mu)$ can be viewed as assigning price $p(\omega)$ to a commodity available at time or state $\omega \in \Omega$. Equilibrium prices can be forced into L_1 provided that more stringent hypotheses are imposed.

Theorem 8.37 (Bewley) *Assume, in addition to the assumptions imposed by Definition 8.30, that*

- $X_i = L_\infty(\Omega, \mathcal{F}, \mu)_+$ *for all $i \in I$;*
- $\succ_i$ *is continuous in the Mackey topology $\tau(L_\infty, L_1)$ for all $i \in I$;*
- $\succ_i$ *is strictly monotone for all $i \in I$ in the sense that $x_i + v \succ_i x_i$ for all $x_i \in L_\infty(\Omega, \mathcal{F}, \mu)_+$ and for all $v \in \mathrm{int}\, L_\infty(\Omega, \mathcal{F}, \mu)_+$; and*
- $\overline{w} \in \mathrm{int}\, L_\infty(\Omega, \mathcal{F}, \mu)_+$.

The economy $\mathcal{E}$ has a quasi-equilibrium (x, p) with $p \in L_1(\Omega, \mathcal{F}, \mu)$.

Proof See Mas-Colell and Zame (1991), Theorem 8.2. □

The astute reader might wonder how Bewley can strengthen the topology from weak to Mackey without losing compactness of the set of attainable allocations. However, all dual topologies lying between $\sigma(L, L^*)$ and $\tau(L, L^*)$ agree on which convex sets are closed. Since we have assumed that consumption sets and upper contour sets are convex, if they are closed in the Mackey topology $\tau(L_\infty, L_1)$ then they are closed in the weak topology $\sigma(L_\infty, L_1)$. Thus, the utility possibility set U remains closed under Bewley's hypotheses.

8.3.8 Properness

Apart from ℓ_∞ or L_∞, the commodity spaces we are considering have positive cone L_+ with empty interior. In those spaces supportability must be assumed directly. The key concept is properness.

Definition 8.38 *Suppose that $X_i \subset L_+$ where L is an LCTVS and $L_+ := \{ x \in L \mid x \geq 0 \}$ a nondegenerate, closed, convex cone. A strict preference relation $\succ_i$ on X_i is **proper at x_i with respect to** $v \in L$ if there is an open, convex cone $C(x_i)$ containing v such that*

$$(x_i - C(x_i)) \cap R_i(x_i) = \emptyset.$$

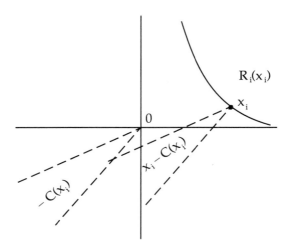

Fig. 8.10. Properness.

$\succ_i$ *is* **uniformly proper** *with respect to v on a subset* $Y \subset X_i$ *if it is proper at every* $y_i \in Y$ *and if the properness cone can be chosen independently of* y_i.

Figure 8.10 illustrates the main idea. Typically the upper contour set $R_i(x_i)$ will have empty interior. To guarantee that $R_i(x_i)$ can nevertheless be supported by a hyperplane $H(p, p \cdot x_i)$ passing through x_i, we posit the existence of an open cone $x_i - C(x_i)$ lying on the other side of the proposed hyperplane: since this cone is open, it will have a nonempty interior. By hypothesis the sets $x_i - C(x_i)$ and $R_i(x_i)$ are disjoint, and $x_i - C(x_i)$ is nonempty and convex with nonempty interior. If $R_i(x_i)$ is nonempty and convex, then by Theorem 8.27 the sets $x_i - C(x_i)$ and $R_i(x_i)$ can be separated by a hyperplane $H(p, \alpha)$ with $p \in L^*$,

$$x_i - C(x_i) \subset H^-(p, p \cdot x_i) \quad \text{and} \quad R_i(x_i) \subset H^+(p, p \cdot x_i).$$

Thus, provided that $\succ_i$ is proper at x_i with respect to v, the upper contour set $R_i(x_i)$ can be **supported** by a continuous price functional p.

While properness is enough to guarantee supportability of the convex upper contour set of an individual consumer, it is not strong enough to guarantee supportability of a Pareto optimal allocation. As Mas-Colell and Zame show by example, supporting an optimum requires more:

• uniform properness, not just properness;

- $X_i = L_+$ for all $i \in I$; and
- L is a topological vector lattice.

Only the last requirement requires comment. Suppose that L is a vector space ordered by $\leq$, and S a subset of L.

- An element $y \in L$ is an **upper bound** for S if $y \geq x$ for all $x \in S$ and a **supremum** for S if $z \geq y$ for all other upper bounds z of S. The supremum of S, if it exists, is denoted $\sup S$.
- An element $w \in L$ is a **lower bound** for S if $x \geq w$ for all $x \in S$ and an **infimum** for S if $w \geq v$ for all other lower bounds v of S. The infimum of S, if it exists, is denoted $\inf S$.

If the set S consists only of a pair of points, say $S = \{x, y\}$, then we usually write

$$\sup\{x, y\} = x \vee y \quad \text{and} \quad \inf\{x, y\} = x \wedge y.$$

The supremum and infimum of a set generalize concepts we have been using in $\mathbf{R}$ to an arbitrary ordered vector space. However, in contrast to $\mathbf{R}$, not every pair of vectors in an arbitrary ordered vector space has an infimum or a supremum.

Definition 8.39 *Let L be an ordered vector space. If $x \vee y$ and $x \wedge y$ exist for all $x, y \in L$, then L is a **vector lattice** (or **Riesz space**). If the lattice operations $(x, y) \mapsto x \vee y$ and $(x, y) \mapsto x \wedge y$ are uniformly continuous, then L is a **topological vector lattice**. If the topological vector lattice L is also a Banach space, then L is called a **Banach lattice**.*

Leading examples of a topological vector lattice (and a Banach lattice) are the L_p spaces for $1 \leq p < \infty$.

Taking advantage of this order structure is exactly what is needed to turn Theorem 8.36 into a result about L_p spaces.

Theorem 8.40 *Assume, in addition to the assumptions imposed by Definition 8.30, that*

- *L is a topological vector lattice;*
- *$X_i = L_+$ for each $i \in I$;*
- *preferences are uniformly proper with respect to $\overline{w}$ on the **order interval** $[0, \overline{w}] := \{x \in L \mid 0 \leq x \leq \overline{w}\}$;*
- *the utility possibility set U is closed.*

Then the economy $\mathcal{E}$ has a quasi-equilibrium.

Proof See Mas-Colell and Zame (1991), Theorem 9.2.   □

If $L = L_p(\Omega, \Sigma, \mu)$ with $1 \leq p < \infty$ and preferences are continuous in the L_p norm topology, then the attainable set is $\sigma(L_p, L_{p'})$ compact (see Mas-Colell and Zame (1991), 1851) and hence the utility possibility set U is closed. Thus, Theorem 8.40 gives us an existence theorem for the L_p spaces (except for L_∞, which we handled earlier).

8.3.9 A lattice structure for prices

The technique employed in the last section does not apply to $L = M(K)$ with the weak* topology because this space, though a vector lattice, is not a topological vector lattice: the lattice operations are not continuous. However, its dual space $L^* = C(K)$ is a topological vector lattice, and this fact suffices to push through an existence result. Actually, less is needed. We require that L be a vector lattice and L^* be closed under the lattice operations: i.e., if $p, q \in L^*$, then $p \vee q \in L^*$ and $p \wedge q \in L^*$.

Theorem 8.41 *Assume, in addition to the assumptions imposed by Definition 8.30, that*

- *L is a vector lattice and L^* is closed under the lattice operations;*
- *$X_i = L_+$ for all $i \in I$;*
- *$\succ_i$ is uniformly proper on $[0, \bar{w}]$ for all $i \in I$;*
- *the utility possibility set U is closed.*

Then the economy $\mathcal{E}$ has a quasi-equilibrium.

Proof See Mas-Colell and Zame (1991) and Mas-Colell and Richard (1991).
                                                                        □

In the case of $M(K)$ with the weak* topology, the attainable set is compact (and hence the utility possibility set closed) provided that consumption sets are weak* closed, a property which holds if $X_i = L_+$ for all $i \in I$ (see Mas-Colell and Zame (1991), 1851). Thus, Theorem 8.41 provides an existence proof for our third, and final, candidate for a commodity space.

8.4 The large square economy

Allowing for an infinitude of commodities brings an important new dimension to competitive theory. Neoclassical analysis blithely assumed what is needed, asserting without proof that commodities can be grouped into a finite number of homogeneous aggregates. In contrast, modern analysis regards the commodity as endogenous. From the modern perspective, homogeneity of physical attributes is not what matters. Goods or services offered for sale are homogeneous enough to serve as good substitutes only if consumers (or firms) view them that way. Existence of equilibrium requires continuity of preferences with respect to a topology coarse enough to guarantee compactness of the set of attainable allocations. Commodities exhibit infinite variability over time, place, and state of the world. If competition is to work, consumers must compress this variability. What continuity with respect to a weak topology means in essence is that, despite the infinite variety which the market has to offer, consumers act as though the marketplace is nearly finite dimensional.

There is one respect, however, in which our discussion is distinctly retrogressive. By focusing on existence, we once again court irrelevancy. We know that in an economy with a finite number of consumers and commodities, Walrasian equilibrium almost never makes sense. Expanding the number of commodities can only make matters worse. If our Walrasian model is to be a proper representation of competition, we need to couple our infinite dimensional commodity space with a continuum of consumers.

Joseph Ostroy (1984b) has suggested the happy phrase **large square economy** for this double infinity of consumers and commodities. The small square economy, with a finite number of consumers and a finite number of commodities, is the world of the Edgeworth box, a world inhospitable to the competitive hypothesis. Aumann's economy is rectangular, piling a continuum of consumers onto a finite number of markets, and almost unavoidably competitive. The large square economy offers a compromise: a world in which competition might make sense (when markets are thick), but where it also might not (because complementarity might run rampant). In this setting core equivalence is a possibility (see, for example, Bewley (1973b), Mas-Colell (1975), Jones (1984)), but not an inevitability (see, for example, Gretsky and Ostroy (1986) or Ostroy and Zame (1988)).

8.5 Summary

This chapter represents both an end and a beginning. The core equivalence and core convergence results presented here fulfill a promise made in Chapter 1, justifying Edgeworth's claim that thick markets are competitive and closing the books on our investigation of competition in finite dimensions. But economic reality fits uncomfortably into such confines. Location, time, and uncertainty all force attention on infinite dimensions. As we have seen, the concepts of finite dimensional competitive theory extend readily to infinite dimensional commodity spaces and a continuum of consumers. But the large square economy is far more complex, and far richer, than its small square analog. It awaits your exploration.

Exercises

8.1   Show that $0 \in \operatorname{cl} \Delta_x P_i(x_i)$ if consumer i is locally nonsatiated at x_i.

8.2   Assuming that the commodity space L is a TVS, explain why:

    (a) $\Delta_x P_i(x_i)$ is open in the relative topology of $\Delta_x X_i$ if and only if $P_i(x_i)$ is open in the relative topology of X_i.

    (b) $\operatorname{cl} P_i(x_i) - x_i = \operatorname{cl} \Delta_x P_i(x_i)$.

8.3   Using an Edgeworth box, illustrate how Theorem 8.5 can fail if strict upper contour sets are convex but $x_i \notin \operatorname{cl} P_i(x_i)$ for some consumer i.

8.4   Verify the claim made in proving Theorem 8.5: if $\Delta_{\tilde{w}} P_i(x_i)$ is open and the cheaper point property is satisfied, then $\Delta_{\tilde{w}} y_i \in \Delta_{\tilde{w}} P_i(x_i)$ implies that there exists a commodity bundle $\Delta_{\tilde{w}} x_i^* \in \Delta_{\tilde{w}} P_i(x_i) \cap H_o^-(p, 0)$.

8.5   Fill in the missing details in the proof of Lemma 8.6.

8.6   Prove Theorem 8.10.

8.7   Show that if $\succ_i$ is strictly convex, then demand ϕ_i is singleton-valued.

8.8   Using a diagram like Figure 8.8, illustrate the possibility of a core allocation where $|\inf p \cdot \Delta_w P_i(x_i)| = 2M = 12$.

8.9   Compute the Anderson bound and sketch a diagram like Figure 8.8 for an economy with commodity space $\mathbf{R}^2$, separating price vector $p = (1/3, 2/3)$, and three consumers with endowments $w_1 = (2, 10)$, $w_2 = (6, 7)$, and $w_3 = (8, 3)$.

8.10   Show that $(T, \mathcal{B}(T), \lambda)$ with $T = [0, \infty]$ and λ Lebesgue measure is σ-finite (i.e., $T = \cup_{i=i}^\infty T_i$ with $\lambda(T_i) < \infty$ for each T_i.)

8.11   Is the probability space $(S, \mathcal{B}(S), \mu)$ σ-finite?

8.12   Which of the following sequences is in ℓ_1? in ℓ_2? in ℓ_∞?

    (a) $x \in \operatorname{Map}(\mathbf{Z}_+, \mathbf{R})$ such that $x(t) = t$ for all $t \in T$;

    (b) $x \in \operatorname{Map}(\mathbf{Z}_+, \mathbf{R})$ such that $x(t) = 1$ for all $t \in T$;

    (c) $x \in \operatorname{Map}(\mathbf{Z}_+, \mathbf{R})$ such that $x(0) = 1$ and $x(t) = 1/t$ for all $t > 0$.

8.13   For which values of r is the function on $T = [0, \infty]$ defined by $f: t \mapsto t^r$ in $L_p(T, \mathcal{B}(T), \lambda)$ where λ is Lebesgue measure?

8.14   What is the topological dual space of ℓ_2? of ℓ_1?

8.15   Show that if $L = \mathbf{R}^{\mathbf{m}}$, then $\sigma(L, M)$ is the weakest topology such that $x \mapsto x_i$ is continuous for all $i = 1, \ldots, m$.

8.16   Prove the First Fundamental Theorem of welfare economics for the economy $\mathcal{E}$ described in Section 8.3.5. Does the proof require the equilibrium price functional p to be continuous?

Bibliography

Aliprantis, C.D. & D.J. Brown (1983). Equilibria in markets with a Riesz space of commodities. *Journal of Mathematical Economics*, **11**, 189–207.

Aliprantis, C.D., D.J. Brown & O. Burkinshaw (1985). Examples of excess demand functions in infinite-dimensional commodity spaces. In *Advances in Equilibrium Theory, Lecture Notes in Economics and Mathematical Systems No. 24*, ed. C.D. Aliprantis, O. Burkinshaw and N. Rothman. New York: Springer-Verlag.

Aliprantis, C.D., D.J. Brown & O. Burkinshaw (1987a). An economy with infinite dimensional commodity space and empty core. *Economic Letters*, **23**, 1–4.

Aliprantis, C.D., D.J. Brown & O. Burkinshaw (1987b). Edgeworth equilibria. *Econometrica*, **55**, 1109–1137.

Aliprantis, C.D., D.J. Brown & O. Burkinshaw (1987c). Edgeworth equilibria in production economies. *Journal of Economic Theory*, **43**, 252–291.

Aliprantis, C.D., D.J. Brown & O. Burkinshaw (1989a). Equilibria in exchange economies with a countable number of agents. *Journal of Mathematical Analysis and Applications*, **142**, 250–299.

Aliprantis, C.D., D.J. Brown & O. Burkinshaw (1989b). *Existence and Optimality of Competitive Equilibria*. New York: Springer-Verlag.

Aliprantis, C.D., D.J. Brown & O. Burkinshaw (1990). Valuation and optimality in the overlapping generations model. *International Economic Review*, **31**, 275–288.

Aliprantis, C.D. & O. Burkinshaw (1988). The fundamental theorems of welfare economics without proper preferences. *Journal of Mathematical Economics*, **17**, 41–54.

Aliprantis, C.D. & O. Burkinshaw (1990). An overlapping generations model core equivalence theorem. *Journal of Economic Theory*, **15**, 362–380.

Aliprantis, C.D. & O. Burkinshaw (1991). When is the core equivalence theorem valid? *Economic Theory*, **1**, 169–182.

Anderson, R.M. (1978). An elementary core equivalence theorem. *Econometrica*, **46**, 1483–1487.

Araujo, A.P. (1985). Lack of equilibria in economies with infinitely many commodities: the need for impatience. *Econometrica*, **53**, 455–462.

Araujo, A.P. (1986). A note on the existence of Pareto optima in topological vector spaces. *Economics Letters*, **23**, 5–7.

Araujo, A.P. (1987). The non-existence of smooth demand in general Banach spaces. *Journal of Mathematical Economics*, **17**, 1–11.

Araujo, A.P. & P.K. Monteiro (1989). Equilibrium without uniform conditions. *Journal of Economic Theory*, **48**, 416–427.

Arrow, K.J. (1951). An extension of the basic theorems of classical welfare economics. In *Proceedings of the Second Berkeley Symposium on Mathematical Statistics and Probability*, ed. J. Neyman. Berkeley and Los Angeles: University of California Press. [Reprinted as Chapter 2 of Arrow(1983).]

Arrow, K.J. (1971a). The firm in general equilibrium theory. In *The Corporate Economy: Growth, Competition, and Innovative Potential*, ed. R. Marris and A. Wood. Cambridge: Harvard University Press. [Reprinted as Chapter 8 in Arrow (1983).]

Arrow, K.J. (1971b). *Selected Readings in Economic Theory from Econometrica*. Cambridge: M.I.T. Press.

Arrow, K.J. (1983). *Collected Papers of Kenneth J. Arrow: Volume 2, General Equilibrium*. Cambridge: Harvard University Press.

Arrow, K.J. & G. Debreu (1954). Existence of an equilibrium for a competitive economy. *Econometrica*, **22**, 265–290. [Reprinted as Chapter 4 in Debreu(1983) and Chapter 4 of Arrow(1983).]

Arrow, K.J. & F.H. Hahn (1971). *General Competitive Analysis*. San Francisco: Holden-Day.

Arrow, K.J. & M.D. Intriligator, eds. (1981). *Handbook of Mathematical Economics, Volume I*. New York: North-Holland.

Arrow, K.J. & M.D. Intriligator, eds. (1982). *Handbook of Mathematical Economics, Volume II*. New York: North-Holland.

Aubin, J.P. & I. Ekelund (1974). A discrete approach to the bang-bang principle. *Mimeo.*

Aumann, R.J. (1964). Markets with a continuum of traders. *Econometrica*, **32**, 39–50. [Reprinted as Chapter 19 in Arrow(1971b) and Chapter 16 in Newman(1968).]

Aumann, R.J. (1965). Integrals of set-valued functions. *Journal of Mathematical Analysis and Applications*, **12**, 1–12.

Aumann, R.J. (1966). Existence of competitive equilibrium in markets with a continuum of traders. *Econometrica*, **34**, 1–17.

Aumann, R.J. (1976). An elementary proof that integration preserves upper-semicontinuity. *Journal of Mathematical Economics*, **3**, 15–18.

Back, K. (1988). Structure of consumption sets and existence of equilibrium in infinite-dimensional spaces. *Journal of Mathematical Economics*, **17**, 89–99.

Becker, G.S. & K.M. Murphy (1988). A Theory of Rational Addiction. *Journal of Political Economy*, **96**, 675–700.

Becker, R.A. (1991). The fundamental theorems of welfare economics in infinite dimensional commodity spaces. In *Equilibrium Theory with Infinitely Many Commodities*, ed. M.A. Khan and N. Yannelis. New York: Springer-Verlag.

Bergstrom, T.C. (1976). How to discard 'free disposability' at no cost. *Journal of Mathematical Economics*, **3**, 131–134.

Bergstrom, T.C., R.P. Parks & T. Rader (1976). Preferences which have open graph. *Journal of Mathematical Economics*, **3**, 265–268.

Bewley, T.F. (1972). Existence of equilibrium in economies with infinitely many commodities. *Journal of Economic Theory*, **4**, 514–540.

Bewley, T.F. (1973a). Edgeworth's conjecture. *Econometrica*, **41**, 425–454.

Bewley, T.F. (1973b). Equality of the core and set of equilibria in economies with infinitely many commodities and a continuum of agents. *International Economic Review*, **14**, 383–394.

Bewley, T.F. (1981). A critique of Tiebout's theory of local public expenditures. *Econometrica*, **49**, 713–740.

Bojan, P. (1974). A generalization of theorems on the existence of competitive economic equilibrium to the case of infinitely many commodities. *Mathematica Balkanica*, **4**, 491–494.

Border, K.C. (1985). *Fixed Point Theorems with Applications to Economics and Game Theory*. Cambridge: Cambridge University Press.

Borglin, A. & H. Keiding (1976). Existence of equilibrium actions and of equilibrium. *Journal of Mathematical Economics*, **3**, 313–316.

Bowen, R. (1968). A new proof of a theorem in utility theory. *International Economic Review*, **9**, 374.

Broome, J. (1972). Approximate equilibria in economies with indivisible commodities. *Journal of Economic Theory*, **5**, 224–249.

Brown, D.J. (1976). Existence of a competitive equilibrium in a non-standard exchange economy. *Econometrica*, **44**, 537–546.

Brown, D.J. & A. Robinson (1972). A limit theorem on the cores of large standard exchange economies. *Proceedings of the National Academy of Sciences of the U.S.A.*, **69**, 1258–1260.

Buchanan, J.M. (1965). An economic theory of clubs. *Economica*, **32**, 1–14.

Buchanan, J.M. (1967). *Public Finance in Democratic Process*. Chapel Hill: University of North Carolina Press.

Choquet, G. (1969). *Lectures on Analysis, Volumes 1–3*. Reading, Mass.: Benjamin.

Cournot, A. (1838). *Recherches sur les Principes Mathématiques de la Théorie des Richesses*. Paris: Hachette. [Translated as: *Researches into the Mathematical Principles of the Theory of Wealth*. New York: Kelley (1960).]

Debreu, G. (1952). A social equilibrium existence theorem. *Proceedings of the National Academy of Sciences of the U.S.A.*, **38**, 886–893. [Reprinted as Chapter 2 in Debreu(1983).]

Debreu, G. (1956). Market equilibrium. *Proceedings of the National Academy of Sciences of the U.S.A.*, **42**, 876–878. [Reprinted as Chapter 7 in Debreu(1983).]

Debreu, G. (1959). *Theory of Value*. New York: Wiley.

Debreu, G. (1962). New concepts and techniques for equilibrium analysis. *International Economic Review*, **3**, 257–273. [Reprinted as Chapter 10 in Debreu(1983).]

Debreu, G. (1963). On a theorem of Scarf. *Review of Economic Studies*, **30**, 177–180.

Debreu, G. (1974a). Excess demand functions. *Journal of Mathematical Economics*, **1**, 15–23. [Reprinted as Chapter 16 in Debreu(1983).]

Debreu, G. (1974b). Four aspects of the mathematical theory of economic equilibrium. *Proceedings of the International Congress of Mathematicians, Vancouver*, **I**, 65–77. [Reprinted as Chapter 18 in Debreu(1983).]

Debreu, G. (1982). Existence of competitive equilibrium. In *Handbook of Mathematical Economics, Volume II*, ed. K.J. Arrow and M.D. Intriligator. New York: North-Holland.

Debreu, B. (1983). *Mathematical Economics: Twenty Papers of Gerard Debreu.*

Cambridge: Cambridge University Press.

Debreu, G. & H. Scarf (1963). A limit theorem on the core of an economy. *International Economic Review*, **4**, 235–246. [Reprinted as Chapter 11 in Debreu(1983).]

Debreu, G. & H. Scarf (1972). The limit of the core of an economy. In *Decision and Organization*, ed. C.B. McGuire and R. Radner. New York: North-Holland.

Demsetz, H. (1970). The private production of public goods. *Journal of Law and Economics*, **13**, 293–306.

Dierker, E. (1971). Equilibrium analysis of exchange economies with indivisible commodities. *Econometrica*, **39**, 997–1008.

Dierker, E. (1974). *Topological Methods in Walrasian Economies*. New York: Springer-Verlag.

Duffie, D. (1986). Competitive equilibria in general choice spaces. *Journal of Mathematical Economics*, **15**, 1–25.

Duffie, D. (1988). *Security Markets: Stochastic Models*. New York: Academic Press.

Dugundji, J. (1966). *Topology*. Boston: Allyn and Bacon.

Edgeworth, F.Y. (1881). *Mathematical psychics*. London: Paul Kegan.

Ellickson, B. (1973). A generalization of the pure theory of public goods. *American Economic Review*, **63**, 417–432.

Ellickson, B. (1978). Public goods and joint supply. *Journal of Public Economics*, **9**, 373–382.

Ellickson, B. (1979). Competitive equilibrium with local public goods. *Journal of Economic Theory*, **21**, 46–61.

Ellickson, B. (1983a). Indivisibility, housing markets and public goods. In *Research in Urban Economics, Volume 3*, ed. J.V. Henderson. London: JAI Press.

Ellickson, B. (1983b). Is a local public good different from any other? In *The Urban Economy and Housing*, ed. R.E. Greison. Lexington: D.C. Heath.

Farrell, M.J. (1959). The convexity assumption in the theory of competitive markets. *Journal of Political Economy*, **67**, 377–391.

Florenzano, M. (1982). The Gale-Nikaido-Debreu lemma and the existence of transitive equilibria with and without the free-disposal assumption. *Journal of Mathematical Economics*, **14**, 113–134.

Florenzano, M. (1983). On the existence of equilibria in economies with an infinite dimensional commodity space. *Journal of Mathematical Economics*, **12**, 207–219.

Foley, D.K. (1967). Resource allocation and the public sector. *Yale Economic Essays*, **7**, 42–98.

Foley, D.K. (1970). Lindahl's solution and the core of an economy with public goods. *Econometrica*, **38**, 66–72.

Franklin, J. (1980). *Methods of Mathematical Economics*. New York: Springer-Verlag.

Frank, C.R. & R.E. Quandt (1963). On the existence of Cournot equilibrium. *International Economic Review*, **4**, 92–96.

Friedman, J.W. (1976). Reaction functions as Nash equilibria. *Review of Economic Studies*, **43**, 83–90.

Friedman, J.W. (1977). *Oligopoly and the Theory of Games*. New York: North-Holland.

Gale, D. (1955). The law of supply and demand. *Mathematical Scandinavica,* **3,** 155–169. [Reprinted as Chapter 10 in Newman(1968).]

Gale, D. & A. Mas-Colell (1975). An equilibrium existence theorem for a general model without ordered preferences. *Journal of Mathematical Economics,* **2,** 9–15.

Gale, D. & A. Mas-Colell (1979). Corrections to an equilibrium existence theorem for a general model without ordered preferences. *Journal of Mathematical Economics,* **6,** 297–298.

Geanakoplos, J.D. (1987). Overlapping generations model of general equilibrium. In *The New Palgrave: A Dictionary of Economics,* ed. J. Eatwell, M. Milgate and P. Newman. New York: Macmillan.

Geanakoplos, J.D. & H.M. Polemarchakis (1991). Overlapping Generations. In *Handbook of Mathematical Economics, Volume IV,* ed. W. Hildenbrand and H. Sonnenschein. New York: North-Holland.

Giles, J.R. (1982). *Convex Analysis with Application in Differentiation of Convex Functions.* Boston: Pitman.

Green, J.R. (1972). On the inequitable nature of core allocations. *Journal of Economic Theory,* **4,** 132–143.

Green, J. & W.P. Heller (1981). Mathematical analysis and convexity with applications to economics. In *Handbook of Mathematical Economics, Volume I,* ed. K.J. Arrow and M.D. Intriligator. New York: North-Holland.

Greenberg, J. (1977a). Quasi-equilibrium in abstract economies without ordered preferences. *Journal of Mathematical Economics,* **4,** 163–165.

Greenberg, J. (1977b). Existence of an equilibrium with arbitrary tax schemes for financing local public goods. *Journal of Economic Theory,* **16,** 137–150.

Greenberg, J., B. Shitovitz & A. Wieczorek (1979). Existence of equilibrium in atomless production economies with price dependent preferences. *Journal of Mathematical Economics,* **6,** 31–41.

Gretsky, N.E. & J.M. Ostroy (1986). Thick and thin market nonatomic exchange economies. In *Advances in Equilibrium Theory,* ed. A. Aliprantis, O. Burkinshaw and N. Rothman. New York: Springer-Verlag.

Halmos, P.R. (1958). *Finite-Dimensional Vector Spaces.* New York: Van Nostrand Reinhold.

Hansen, T. (1968). *On the approximation of a competitive equilibrium.* Ph.D. thesis, Yale University.

Hart, O.D. & H.W. Kuhn (1975). A proof of the existence of equilibrium without the free disposal assumption. *Journal of Mathematical Economics,* **2,** 335–343.

Hart, S., W. Hildenbrand & E. Kohlberg (1974). On equilibrium allocations as distributions on the commodity space. *Journal of Mathematical Economics,* **1,** 159–166.

Hart, S. & E. Kohlberg (1974). Equally distributed correspondences. *Journal of Mathematical Economics,* **1,** 167–174.

Hildenbrand, W. (1970). Existence of equilibria for economies with production and a measure space of consumers. *Econometrica,* **38,** 608–623.

Hildenbrand, W. (1971). Random preferences and equilibrium analysis. *Journal of Economic Theory,* **3,** 414–429.

Hildenbrand, W. (1972). Metric measure spaces of economic agents. In *Proceedings of the Sixth Berkeley Symposium on Mathematical Statistics and Probability, Volume II,* ed. L. LeCam et al. Berkeley: University of California Press.

Hildenbrand, W. (1974). *Core and Equilibria of a Large Economy.* Princeton: Princeton University Press.

Hildenbrand, W. (1975). Distributions of agents' characteristics. *Journal of Mathematical Economics,* **2**, 129–138.

Hildenbrand, W. (1977). Limit theorems on the core of an economy. In *Frontiers of Quantitative Economics, Volume IIIA,* ed. M.D. Intriligator. New York: North-Holland.

Hildenbrand, W. (1982). Core of an economy. In *Handbook of Mathematical Economics, Volume II,* ed. K.J. Arrow and M.D. Intriligator. New York: North-Holland.

Hildenbrand, W. (1983). On the "law of demand." *Econometrica,* **51**, 997–1019.

Hildenbrand, W. & A.P. Kirman (1976). *Introduction to equilibrium analysis.* New York: North-Holland.

Hildenbrand, W. & A.P. Kirman (1988). *Equilibrium analysis.* New York: North-Holland.

Hildenbrand, W., D. Schmeidler & S. Zamir (1973). Existence of approximate equilibria and cores. *Econometrica,* **41**, 1159–1166.

Hildenbrand, W. & H. Sonnenschein, eds. (1991). *Handbook of Mathematical Economics, Volume IV.* New York: North-Holland.

Holmes, R.B. (1975). *Geometric Functional Analysis.* New York: Springer-Verlag.

Ichiishi, T. (1983). *Game Theory for Economic Analysis.* New York: Academic Press.

Jones, L. (1983a). Existence of equilibrium with infinitely many consumers and infinitely many commodities: a theorem based on models of commodity differentiation. *Journal of Mathematical Economics,* **12**, 119–138.

Jones, L. (1983b). Special problems arising in the study of economies with infinitely many commodities. In *Models of Economic Dynamics,* ed. H. Sonnenschein. New York: Springer-Verlag.

Jones, L. (1984). A competitive model of commodity differentiation. *Econometrica,* **52**, 507–530.

Jones, L. (1987). Existence of equilibrium with infinitely many commodities: Banach lattices revisited. *Journal of Mathematical Economics,* **16**, 89–104.

Jones, L. (1990). Equilibrium in competitive, infinite dimensional settings. In *Advances in Economic Theory (forthcoming),* ed. J.J. Laffont. Cambridge: Cambridge University Press.

Kakutani, S. (1941). A generalization of Brouwer's fixed point theorem. *Duke Mathematical Journal,* **8**, 457–459. [Reprinted as Chapter 4 in Newman(1968).]

Kannai, Y. (1970). Continuity properties of the core of a market. *Econometrica,* **38**, 791–815.

Karlin, S. (1959). *Mathematical Methods and Theory in Games, Programming, and Economics, Volume 1.* Reading, Mass.: Addison-Wesley.

Kelley, J.L. (1955). *General Topology.* New York: Van Nostrand Reinhold.

Kehoe, T.J. (1991). Computation and multiplicity of equilibria. In *Handbook of Mathematical Economics, Volume IV,* ed. W. Hildenbrand and H. Sonnenschein. New York: North-Holland.

Khan, M.A. (1984). A remark on the existence of equilibria in markets without ordered preferences and with a Riesz space of commodities. *Journal of Mathematical Economics,* **13**, 165–169.

Khan, M.A. (1986). Equilibrium points of non-atomic games over a Banach space. *Transactions of the American Mathematical Society*, **293**, 737–749.

Khan, M.A. & R. Vohra (1984). Equilibrium in abstract economies without ordered preferences and with a measure space of agents. *Journal of Mathematical Economics*, **13**, 133–142.

Khan, M.A. & R. Vohra (1985). On the existence of Lindahl equilibria in economies with a measure space of non-transitive preferences. *Journal of Economic Theory*, **36**, 319–332.

Khan, M.A. & N.C. Yannelis, eds. (1991a). *Equilibrium Theory with Infinitely Many Commodities*. New York: Springer-Verlag.

Khan, M.A. & N.C. Yannelis (1991b). Existence of a competitive equilibrium in markets with a continuum of agents and commodities. In *Equilibrium Theory with Infinitely Many Commodities*, ed. M.A. Khan and N.C. Yannelis. New York: Springer-Verlag.

Klein, E. & A.C. Thompson (1984). *Theory of Correspondences*. New York: John Wiley.

Koopmans, T.C. (1957). *Three Essays on the State of Economic Science*. New York: McGraw-Hill.

Kreps, D.M. (1990). *A Course in Microeconomic Theory*. Princeton: Princeton University Press.

Kuenne, R.E. (1963). *The Theory of General Economic Equilibrium*. Princeton: Princeton University Press.

Kuhn, H.W. (1956). A note on 'The law of supply and demand.' *Mathematica Scandinavica*, **4**, 143–146. [Reprinted as Chapter 11 in Newman(1968).]

Kuratowski, K. (1966). *Topology, Volume I*. New York: Academic Press.

Kuratowski, K. (1968). *Topology, Volume II*. New York: Academic Press.

Lemke, C.E. (1965). Bimatrix equilibrium points and mathematical programming. *Management Sciences*, **11**, 681–689.

Lemke, C.E. & J.T. Howson, Jr. (1964). Equilibrium points of bimatrix games. *SIAM Journal of Applied Mathematics*, **12**, 413–423.

McKenzie, L.W. (1954). On equilibrium in Graham's model of world trade and other competitive systems. *Econometrica*, **22**, 147–161.

McKenzie, L.W. (1955). Competitive equilibrium with dependent consumer preferences. In *Proceedings of the Second Symposium in Linear Programming*, ed. H.A. Antosiewicz. Washington, DC: USAF. [Reprinted as Chapter 15 in Newman(1968).]

McKenzie, L.W. (1959). On the existence of general equilibrium for a competitive market. *Econometrica*, **27**, 54–71. [Reprinted as Chapter 17 in Arrow(1971b).]

McKenzie, L.W. (1961). On the existence of general equilibrium: some corrections. *Econometrica*, **29**, 247–248. [Reprinted as Chapter 17 in Arrow(1971b).]

Makowski, L. (1979). Value theory with personalized trading. *Journal of Economic Theory*, **20**, 194–212.

Mantel, R. (1968). Toward a constructive proof of the existence of equilibrium in a competitive economy. *Yale Economic Essays*, **8**, 155–196.

Mantel, R. (1974). On the characterization of aggregate excess demand. *Journal of Economic Theory*, **7**, 348–353.

Mantel, R. (1977). Implications of microeconomic theory for community excess demand functions. In *Frontiers of Quantitative Economics, Vol. IIIA*, ed. M.D. Intriligator. New York: North-Holland.

Mantel, R. (1979). Homothetic preferences and community excess demand functions. *Journal of Economic Theory*, **12**, 197–201.

Mas-Colell, A. (1974). An equilibrium existence theorem without complete or transitive preferences. *Journal of Mathematical Economics*, **1**, 237–246.

Mas-Colell, A. (1975). A model of equilibrium with differentiated commodities. *Journal of Mathematical Economics*, **2**, 263–295.

Mas-Colell, A. (1977). Indivisible commodities and general equilibrium theory. *Journal of Economic Theory*, **16**, 443–456.

Mas-Colell, A. (1978). A note on the core equivalence theorem: how many blocking coalitions are there? *Journal of Mathematical Economics*, **5**, 207–215.

Mas-Colell, A. (1985a). Pareto optima and equilibria: the infinite dimensional case. In *Advances in Equilibrium Theory*, ed. C. Aliprantis, O. Burkinshaw and N. Rothman. New York: Springer-Verlag.

Mas-Colell, A. (1985b). *The Theory of General Economic Equilibrium: A Differentiable Approach*. Cambridge: Cambridge University Press.

Mas-Colell, A. (1986a). The price equilibrium existence problem in topological vector lattices. *Econometrica*, **54**, 1039–1054.

Mas-Colell, A. (1986b). Valuation equilibrium and Pareto optimum revisited. In *Contributions to Mathematical Economics*, ed. W. Hildenbrand and A. Mas-Colell. New York: North-Holland.

Mas-Colell, A. & S. Richard (1991). A new approach to the existence of equilibria in vector lattices. *Journal of Economic Theory*, **53**, 1–11.

Mas-Colell, A. & W.R. Zame (1991). Equilibrium theory in infinite dimensional spaces. In *Handbook of Mathematical Economics, Volume IV*, ed. W. Hildenbrand and H. Sonnenschein. New York: North-Holland.

Meade, J. (1952). External economies and diseconomies in a competitive situation. *Economic Journal*, **62**, 54–67.

Merrill, O.H. (1972). *Applications and extensions of an algorithm that computes fixed points of certain upper semi-continuous point to set mappings*. Ph.D. dissertation, Department of Industrial Engineering, University of Michigan.

Milleron, J.C. (1972). Theory of value with public goods: a survey article. *Journal of Economic Theory*, **5**, 419–477.

Muench, T.J. (1972). The core and the Lindahl equilibrium of an economy with public goods: an example. *Journal of Economic Theory*, **4**, 241–255.

Munkres, J.R. (1975). *Topology: A First Course*. New York: Prentice-Hall.

Nash, J.F. (1950). Equilibrium points in n-person games. *Proceedings of the National Academy of Sciences of the U.S.A.*, **36**, 48–49.

Negishi, T. (1960). Welfare economics and existence of an equilibrium for a competitive economy. *Metroeconomica*, **12**, 92–97.

Newman, P. (1968). *Readings in Mathematical Economics, Volume 1*. Baltimore: Johns Hopkins Press.

Nikaido, H. (1956a). On the classical multilateral exchange problem. *Metroeconomica*, **8**, 135–145. [Reprinted as Chapter 13 in Newman(1968).]

Nikaido, H. (1956b). A supplementary note to 'On the classical multilateral exchange problem'. *Metroeconomica*, **9**, 209–210. [Reprinted as Chapter 14 in Newman(1968).]

Nikaido, H. (1968). *Convex structures and economic theory*. New York: Academic Press.

Ostroy, J.M. (1980). The no-surplus condition as a characterization of perfectly competitive equilibrium. *Journal of Economic Theory*, **22**, 183–207.

Ostroy, J.M. (1981). Differentiability as convergence to perfectly competitive equilibrium. *Journal of Mathematical Economics*, **8**, 59–73.

Ostroy, J.M. (1984a). A reformulation of the marginal productivity theory of distribution. *Econometrica*, **52**, 599–630.

Ostroy, J.M. (1984b). On the existence of Walrasian equilibrium in large-square economies. *Journal of Mathematical Economics*, **13**, 143-164.

Ostroy, J. & W.R. Zame (1988). Non-atomic economies and the boundaries of perfect competition. *Econometrica*, forthcoming.

Pareto, V. (1906). *Manuel d'Économie Politique*. Paris: Marcel Giard.

Rader, T. (1964). Edgeworth exchange and general economic equilibrium. *Yale Economic Essays*, **4**, 133–180.

Rader, T. (1972). *Theory of General Economic Equilibrium*. New York: Academic Press.

Reed, M. & B. Simon (1972). *Methods of Modern Mathematical Physics, I: Functional Analysis*. New York: Academic Press.

Richard, S.F. (1989). A new approach to production equilibria in vector lattices. *Journal of Mathematical Economics*, **18**, 41–56.

Richard, S.F. & S. Srivastava (1988). Equilibrium in economies with infinitely many consumers and infinitely many commodities. *Journal of Mathematical Economics*, **17**, 9–22.

Richard, S.F. & W. Zame (1986). Proper preferences and quasi-concave utility functions. *Journal of Mathematical Economics*, **15**, 231–248.

Richter, D.K. (1975). Existence of general equilibrium in multi-regional economies with public goods. *International Economic Review*, **16**, 201–221.

Richter, D.K. (1978). Existence and computation of a Tiebout general equilibrium. *Econometrica*, **46**, 779–805.

Roberts, D.J. (1973). Existence of Lindahl equilibrium with a measure space of consumers. *Journal of Economic Theory*, **6**, 355–381.

Rockafellar, R.T. (1970). *Convex Analysis*. Princeton: Princeton University Press.

Rosen, S. (1974). Hedonic prices and implicit markets: product differentiation in pure competition. *Journal of Political Economy*, **82**, 34–55.

Rothenberg, J. (1960). Non-convexity, aggregation, and Pareto optimality. *Journal of Political Economy*, **68**, 435–468.

Royden, H.L. (1968). *Real Analysis*. Toronto: Macmillan.

Rudin, W. (1973). *Functional Analysis*. New York: McGraw-Hill.

Rudin, W. (1974). *Real and Complex Analysis, Second Edition*. New York: McGraw-Hill.

Rustichini, A. & N.C. Yannelis (1991). The core-Walras equivalence in economies with a continuum of agents and commodities. In *Equilibrium Theory with Infinitely Many Commodities*, ed. M.A. Khan and N.C. Yannelis. New York: Springer-Verlag.

Samuelson, P.A. (1954). The pure theory of public expenditure. *Review of Economics and Statistics*, **36**, 387–389.

Samuelson, P.A. (1969a). Contrast between welfare conditions for joint supply and for public goods. *Review of Economics and Statistics*, **51**, 26–30.

Samuelson, P.A. (1969b). Pure theory of public expenditure and taxation. In *Public Economics: An Analysis of Public Production and Consumption and Their Relations to the Private Sectors: Proceedings of a Conference Held by the International Economic Association*, ed. J. Margolis and H. Guitton. London: Macmillan.

Scarf, H.E. (1962). An analysis of markets with a large number of participants. *Recent Advances in Game Theory (The Princeton University Conference)*.

Scarf, H.E. (1967a). On the computation of equilibrium prices. In *Ten Economic Essays in the Tradition of Irving Fisher*, ed. W.J. Fellner. New York: Wiley.

Scarf, H.E. (1967b). The approximation of fixed points of a continuous mapping. *SIAM Journal of Applied Mathematics*, **15**, 1328–1343.

Scarf, H.E. (1967c). The core of an n-person game. *Econometrica*, **35**, 50–69.

Scarf, H.E. (with the collaboration of T. Hansen) (1973). *The Computation of Economic Equilibrium*. New Haven: Yale University Press.

Scarf, H.E. (1982). The computation of equilibrium prices: an exposition. In *Handbook of Mathematical Economics, Volume II*, ed. K.J. Arrow and M.D. Intriligator. New York: North-Holland.

Schmeidler, D. (1969). Competitive equilibria in markets with a continuum of traders and incomplete preferences. *Econometrica*, **37**, 578–585.

Shafer, W.J. (1976). Equilibrium in economies without ordered preferences or free disposal. *Journal of Mathematical Economics*, **3**, 135–137.

Shafer, W.J. & H.F. Sonnenschein (1975a). Some theorems on the existence of competitive equilibrium. *Journal of Economic Theory*, **11**, 83–93.

Shafer, W.J. & H.F. Sonnenschein (1975b). Equilibrium in abstract economies without ordered preferences. *Journal of Mathematical Economics*, **2**, 345–348.

Shafer, W.J. & H.F. Sonnenschein (1976). Equilibrium with externalities, commodity taxation, and lump sum transfers. *International Economic Review*, **17**, 601–611.

Shafer, W.J. & H.F. Sonnenschein (1982). Market demand and excess demand functions. In *Handbook of Mathematical Economics, Volume II*, ed. K.J. Arrow and M.D. Intriligator. New York: North-Holland.

Shaked, A. (1976). Absolute approximations to equilibrium in markets with non-convex preferences. *Journal of Mathematical Economics*, **3**, 185–196.

Shoven, J.B. (1974). A proof of the existence of a general equilibrium with ad valorem commodity taxes. *Journal of Economic Theory*, **8**, 1–25.

Shoven, J.B. & J. Whalley (1974). General equilibrium with taxes: a computational procedure and an existence proof. *Review of Economic Studies*, **40**, 475–489.

Shubik, M. (1959). Edgeworth market games. In *Contributions to the Theory of Games, IV, Annals of Mathematical Studies, Volume 40*, ed. R.D. Luce and A.W. Tucker. Princeton: Princeton University Press.

Smale, S. (1982). Global analysis and economics. In *Handbook of Mathematical Economics, Volume II*, ed. K.J. Arrow and M.D. Intriligator. New York: North-Holland.

Sondermann, D. (1974). Economies of scale and equilibria in coalition production economies. *Journal of Economic Theory*, **8**, 259–291.

Sonnenschein, H.F. (1971). Demand theory without transitive preferences, with applications to the theory of competitive equilibrium. In *Preferences, Utility, and Demand*, ed. J. Chipman, L. Hurwicz, M.K. Richter and H.F. Sonnenschein. New York: Harcourt-Brace-Jovanovich.

Sonnenschein, H.F. (1973a). Do Walras' identity and continuity characterize the class of community excess demand functions? *Journal of Economic Theory*, **6**, 345–354.

Sonnenschein, H.F. (1973b). The utility hypothesis and market demand theory. *Western Economic Journal*, **11**, 404–410.

Sonnenschein, H.F. (1974). Market excess demand functions. *Econometrica*, **40**, 549–563.

Starr, R.M. (1969). Quasi-equilibria in markets with non-convex preferences. *Econometrica*, **37**, 25–38.

Thom, R. (1975). *Structural Stability and Morphogenesis*. Reading, Mass.: W.A. Benjamin.

Tiebout, C. (1956). A pure theory of local expenditures. *Journal of Political Economy*, **64**, 416–424.

Tompkins, C.B. (1964). Sperner's lemma and some extensions. In *Applied Combinatorial Mathematics*, ed. E.F. Beckenbach. New York: Wiley.

Toussaint, S. (1985). On the existence of equilibria in economies with infinitely many commodities. *Journal of Economic Theory*, **13**, 98–115.

Uzawa, H. (1956). Note on the existence of an equilibrium for a competitive economy. Department of Economics, Stanford University.

Uzawa, H. (1962a). Aggregative convexity and the existence of competitive equilibrium. *Economic Studies Quarterly*, **12**, 52–58.

Uzawa, H. (1962b). Walras' existence theorem and Brouwer's fixed point theorem. *Economic Studies Quarterly*, **13**, 59–62.

van Tiel, J. (1984). *Convex Analysis: An Introductory Text*. New York: Wiley.

Varian, H.R. (1992). *Microeconomic Analysis (Third Edition)*. New York: Norton.

Vind, K. (1964). Edgeworth-allocations in an exchange economy with many traders. *International Economic Review*, **5**, 165–177.

Vind, K. (1965). A theorem on the core of an economy. *The Review of Economic Studies*, **5**, 165–177.

Wald, A. (1936). Über einige Gleichungssysteme der mathematischen Ökonomie. *Zeitschrift für Nationalökonomie*, **7**, 637–670. [Translated as: "On some systems of equations of mathematical economics," *Econometrica* **19** (1951): 368–403.]

Walras, L. (1874–7). *Elèments d'économie politique pure*. Lausanne: Corbaz. [Translated as: *Elements of Pure Economics*. Chicago: Irwin (1954).]

Yamazaki, A. (1978). An equilibrium existence theorem without convexity assumptions. *Econometrica*, **46**, 541–555.

Yannelis, N.C. (1985). On a market equilibrium theorem with an infinite number of commodities. *Journal of Mathematical Analysis and Applications*, **108**, 595–599.

Yannelis, N.C. (1987). Equilibria in non-cooperative models of competition. *Journal of Economic Theory*, **41**, 96–111.

Yannelis, N.C. (1991). The core of an economy without ordered preferences. In *Equilibrium Theory with Infinitely Many Commodities*, ed. M.A. Khan and N.C. Yannelis. New York: Springer-Verlag.

Yannelis, N.C. & N.D. Prabhakar (1983). Existence of maximal elements and equilibria in linear topological spaces. *Journal of Mathematical Economics*, **12**, 233–245.

Yannelis, N.C. & W.R. Zame (1986). Equilibria in Banach lattices without ordered preferences. *Journal of Mathematical Economics*, **15**, 75–110.

Yosida, K. (1971). *Functional Analysis*. New York: Springer-Verlag.

Zame, W.R. (1987). Competitive equilibrium in production economies with an infinite-dimensional commodity space. *Econometrica*, **55**, 1075–1108.

Zangwill, W.I. & C.B. Garcia (1981). *Pathways to Solutions, Fixed Points, and Equilibria.* Englewood Cliffs, NJ: Prentice-Hall.

Zeeman, E.C. (1977). *Catastrophe Theory: Selected Papers, 1972–1977.* Reading, Mass.: Addison-Wesley.

Index